CITIZEN RAUH

CITIZEN RAUH

AN AMERICAN LIBERAL'S
LIFE IN LAW AND POLITICS

MICHAEL E. PARRISH

The University of Michigan Press   *Ann Arbor*

Copyright © by the University of Michigan 2010
All rights reserved
Published in the United States of America by
The University of Michigan Press
Manufactured in the United States of America
⊗ Printed on acid-free paper

2013   2012   2011   2010   4   3   2   1

A CIP catalog record for this book is available from the British Library.

Library of Congress Cataloging-in-Publication Data

Parrish, Michael E.
    Citizen Rauh : an American liberal's life in law and politics / Michael E. Parrish.
        p.   cm.
    Includes bibliographical references and index.
    ISBN 978-0-472-11737-6 (cloth : alk. paper)
    ISBN 978-0-472-02415-5 (e-book)
    1. Rauh, Joseph L., 1911–   2. Lawyers—United States—Biography.   3. Labor
lawyers—United States—Biography.   4. Civil rights workers—United States—
Biography.   5. Liberals—United States—Biography.   I. Title.
KF373.R38P37   2010
340.092—dc22
[B]   2010004476

For all the Rauhs, but especially
Olie, Michael, & Carl.

ACKNOWLEDGMENTS

This book would not have been possible without the encouragement and patience of many people and institutions to which I am forever grateful. My biggest debt is to Joe and Olie Rauh, who often hosted me at their home in Washington, D.C., during the early stages of my research. In addition to enduring many hours of taped interviews, Joe opened his legal files and personal correspondence to me prior to their journey to the Library of Congress. He unlocked many doors to other interviews with both admirers and critics, such as the late Katharine Graham and Max Kampelman. Someone who made large contributions to American public life over half a century, Joe seldom failed to credit others, to candidly admit his own mistakes, and to understate his own achievements. I deeply regret that Olie, a woman of remarkable energy and intelligence, did not live to see this book published. For their encouragement in the face of my own tardiness I thank Michael and Carl Rauh and Michael's son, Terry, keeper of the family photos.

A number of historians commented on various sections and drafts of the evolving manuscript over a decade or more. I am especially grateful to the late Arthur M. Schlesinger Jr., who shared with me his personal memories of Joe Rauh as well as his unsurpassed knowledge of the history of Americans for Democratic Action and the Kennedy administration. For their advice and criticism I thank Melvin Urofsky, Nelson Lichtenstein, and the anonymous reviewers for the University of Michigan Press. Melody Herr, acquisitions editor at the press, saw the significance of Joe Rauh's life from the beginning of our correspondence and coaxed from me revisions that sharpened the book's thematic focus. Scott Griffith kept me on schedule and banished numerous infelicities from the final version.

For financial support I thank the Committee on Research at the University of California, San Diego. And, finally, I could not have completed this project without the sustained enthusiasm, love, and timely prodding of my wife, Peggy.

Michael E. Parrish
LA JOLLA, CALIFORNIA

CONTENTS

PROLOGUE

This guy [Rauh] has got to take one star out of one eye.
He can leave one star in the other eye, but you can't have
stars in both eyes, boy, when you're in the practice of law.
— THOMAS G. CORCORAN

Washington, D.C., 2009

At the traditional Capitol Hill luncheon following his swearing in on January 20, 2009, President Barack Obama was approached by eleven-term Georgia congressman John Lewis, a former Freedom Rider and the last living speaker from the 1963 March on Washington, where Dr. Martin Luther King Jr. made his "I Have a Dream" speech. Lewis asked the president to sign a commemorative photograph of the historic inauguration they had just witnessed. "Because of you, John," wrote the forty-fourth president of the United States.[1]

Lewis knew, of course, that many Americans, both black and white, had made January 20, 2009, possible. In a historic photograph of the March on Washington taken at the Lincoln Memorial in 1963, a youthful, rather lanky John Lewis stands near a very tall man who wears glasses and a bow tie. The man was Joseph L. Rauh Jr., who would shortly join Lewis in Mississippi as the lawyer for the infant Freedom Party, a coalition of blacks and whites eager to challenge the regular, all-white state delegation to the 1964 Democratic National Convention in Atlantic City. "On the surface he was an outsider in every way," Lewis recalled of Rauh in his autobiography, "with his lawyer-like bow tie and eyeglasses, his Northern accent and, of course, his white skin. But he was a serious, skillful, brilliant attorney, very polite and very passionate about basic human rights."[2] This is a study of that "serious, skillful, brilliant attorney" who was "very passionate about basic human rights" and who helped, like John Lewis, to make January 20, 2009, a reality.

Washington, D.C., 1946

In the winter of 1946, a bitter strike raged in the nation's automobile industry, between the United Automobile Workers Union and the major companies. Joe Rauh, then a thirty-five-year-old lawyer just beginning his postwar practice in Washington, D.C., contributed money and time to the striking UAW members. Rauh's efforts irritated his old boss from New Deal days, Thomas G. "Tommy the Cork" Corcoran, one of the city's most influential attorneys and lobbyists, whose clients included many powerful corporations. Corcoran had sometimes sent legal business over to his former protégé, but now he poured out his frustrations to their mutual friend, Ben Cohen, another former New Dealer: "This guy has got to take one star out of one eye," Corcoran said. "He can leave one star in the other eye, but you can't have stars in both eyes, boy, when you're in the practice of law."[3]

For Corcoran, lawyers once associated with the New Deal should move on to less radical and more lucrative pursuits. For Joe Rauh, however, the New Deal, with its agenda dedicated to social and economic justice, remained a continuing enterprise to be defended and extended into the postwar world. The New Deal had sealed the transformation of American liberalism from its largely antigovernmental roots into a robust commitment to an active state that sought to restrain corporate economic power, impose greater discipline on private markets, and reduce the inequalities generated by capitalism. Between 1933 and 1941, New Deal liberalism brought sizable benefits to groups such as commercial farmers, industrial workers, and the disabled and the elderly, but generally paid less attention to issues of racial injustice and civil liberties. Those areas constituted the core of liberalism's unfinished agenda, and Joe Rauh became their passionate advocate. In the post–New Deal world he found himself both in alliance with and often opposed to others who once carried the New Deal banner, including Corcoran, but most notably Lyndon B. Johnson and the southern wing of the Democratic Party.

As a young lawyer, freshly minted by Felix Frankfurter at Harvard Law School, Rauh had learned how to practice law while working for Corcoran and Cohen in the early days of the New Deal. He had absorbed much from these two mentors and harnessed it to the essentials of the new liberalism. He had learned from Cohen the importance of legal craftsmanship, attention to procedure, legal technicalities, and thorough preparation. From Corcoran he learned that law could seldom be divorced from bare-knuckle politics. A successful lawyer, however superb his technical skills, needed to know how to move the levers of political power and public opinion on behalf of a client, whether he happened to be the president of the United States or a single victim of racial discrimination. When shaping legislation or a legal brief, Corcoran taught, always push the boundaries of what might be achievable. Don't compromise too early. "Tommy the Cork," who had largely abandoned his New Deal liberalism by the late 1940s, left his imprint on Rauh's pugnacious style of legal combat. Cohen, on the other hand, became Joe Rauh's ideal of the lawyer devoted to public service and the public interest.

Not long after the auto strike, Rauh and his partner, Irv Levy, became Walter Reuther's top lawyers at the UAW, where they benefited from a substantial retainer that permitted their firm to take other, less remunerative clients, many of them victims of racial injustice and political persecution. The American labor movement had always been at the center of struggles over civil liberties in the years of the New Deal, when union efforts at organizing workers, picketing, and work stoppages raised important legal questions of freedom of association, assembly, and speech. But except in rare cases, the unions manifested little concern and often hostility to the claims of African-Americans and other racial minorities.

Now, at the conclusion of World War II, with a guarantee of collective bargaining, limitations on union busting by corporations, and a racially mixed labor force, the most progressive union leaders such as Reuther could invest more deeply in the causes of civil liberties and civil rights. Rauh became a major beneficiary of this expanded labor liberalism and one of its major practitioners. Fortunately for the labor movement, civil liberties, civil rights, and the progressive wing of the Democratic Party, Joe Rauh did not take Corcoran's advice on sharpening his eyesight. Over the next fifty years, until his death in 1992, he kept a few stars in his eyes, defended and advanced the legacy of the New Deal, and made a living in the practice of law.

"A Knee-Jerk Liberal"

His critics often called Joe Rauh "a knee-jerk liberal," because on most issues touching law and politics his position seemed predictable, always and emphatically on the left of the country's political spectrum. They said, too, that Joe Rauh staked out extreme positions, abhorred compromises, and preferred a defeat on principles to a victory of expediency. He took such criticism in stride and never shunned the liberal label, even as other jettisoned it when the political and legal winds shifted. He tended, often alone, the dying embers of the redistributive liberalism the New Deal had begun, especially when large sectors of the Democratic Party turned against it.

With equal passion, he spoke out for half a century on behalf of the legacy of judicial liberalism, first articulated by the Supreme Court under Charles Evans Hughes in the 1930s and driven forward by Earl Warren's Court in the 1950s and 1960s. He wore the label "knee-jerk liberal" as a badge of honor. It fit someone who believed that the wealthy should pay more income taxes, who believed in a vibrant, democratic labor movement, and who preferred the freedoms of the Bill of Rights, smaller defense budgets, a woman's right to choose an abortion, and affirmative action programs for women and racial minorities.

Joe Rauh was a big man in his physical size, his sense of humor, and his passion for justice. Before federal courts where he argued many cases, his six-foot, two-inch frame and vibrant baritone commanded attention if not always victory. Even when they turned off his microphone, he could be heard before the credentials committees or on the floor of virtually every Democratic National Convention from 1948 through the 1980s. He wore a signature bow tie beneath what his client Lillian Hellman described as a "nice, unbeautiful, rugged, crinkly face that gives one confidence about the mind above it."[4]

Joe Rauh could be tough-minded, unsentimental, often unyielding when values he cherished were at stake. "He fought for his country in wartime," his good friend Arthur M. Schlesinger Jr., recalled, "and he fought for it in peacetime. He enjoyed a good fight and much preferred winning to losing."[5] But Joe Rauh also exhibited a gentleness and generosity often hidden from those who battled him across a courtroom, on a convention floor, or in the corridors of Congress. Jim Turner, one of his last partners, considered him the softest touch on earth when it came to taking on impecunious clients who needed his help.

"Shrewdness seldom goes with an open nature," Hellman noted when she first met him, "but in this case, it does."[6] Joe Rauh had his share of famous and celebrated clients—Hellman, Arthur Miller, Walter Reuther, Jock Yablonski—but most of the men and women who found their way to his unadorned office in downtown Washington arrived with little more than their tales of legal troubles and modest pocketbooks. If he could not take their case because he already had too many other clients, he usually found a lawyer who would. He combined passionate commitments with a robust sense of humor, especially when recounting his own foibles and mistakes. "Do your best," he often told aspiring young lawyers, "and don't take yourself too seriously." In a town where most attorneys kept an eye on the bottom line, Joe Rauh kept an eye on the bottom principle. "Others made all the money," he liked to say, "but we had all the fun." The "we" paid tribute to able partners and associates: Levy, John Silard, Dan Pollitt, Elliott Lichtman, Mary Levy, and Turner.

On the tennis courts and softball diamonds of the District of Columbia, until his hip betrayed him, Joe Rauh wielded a powerful serve and an aggressive bat. He liked nothing better than a good, vigorous debate against a conservative opponent and a dinner of dry martinis, lamb chops, and large bowls of ice cream, but he reserved his biggest love for his wife, Olie, his two sons, Michael and Carl, and a growing band of grandchildren. They were the private center and anchor of his extraordinary public life.

September 13, 1987

The "knee-jerk liberal" seldom hesitated to tell you where he stood, except when two principles or people he valued came into conflict. On the opening day of the regular National Football League season in 1987, for example, he went as usual to RFK Stadium, where the Washington Redskins played one of their archrivals, the Philadelphia Eagles. A rookie, Randall Cunningham, only the second African-American to call signals in the NFL, opened at quarterback for the Eagles. "I'm not sure who I should be rooting for," the seventy-six-year-old civil rights lawyer told his companions as they downed turkey sandwiches and fuzzy navels at a tailgate party before the kickoff.

Since the late 1930s no resident of the District of Columbia had been a more loyal or fanatical Redskins fan than Joe Rauh, even during the lily-white era of owner George Preston Marshall, when Washington lagged behind other NFL teams in the recruitment of black players. Cunningham's debut with the Eagles that bright September afternoon therefore tested a fundamental Joe Rauh loyalty. Early in the first quarter, Cunningham's completed passes and elusive runs evoked more cheers from Rauh than anything done on the field by his beloved but hapless Redskins.

But fortunately for Rauh's dissonant loyalties, the Redskins' starting quarterback, Jay Schroeder, an erratic passer, went down with a shoulder injury four minutes into the game. Onto the field replacing Schroeder came Doug Williams, a recent acquisition from the Tampa Bay Buccaneers, where he had broken the NFL's color barrier as their starting quarterback. Joe Rauh could root again for the Redskins that day and for the rest of the season, even against the Eagles and Randall Cunningham. With Williams at the controls,

passing for 272 yards and two touchdowns, Washington defeated Philadelphia, 34-24, rolled to the NFL championship over the remainder of the season, and won the Super Bowl.[7]

September 3, 1992

On the evening of September 3, 1992, Joe Rauh faced another choice of values. Tired after a long afternoon of standing in a reception line for new students at the District of Columbia School of Law, Rauh sat in the den of his
Washington home, eating a favorite meal of lamb chops and corn on the cob.
That day he had received an invitation from a local Jewish organization to introduce retired Supreme Court Justice Brennan at a dinner honoring the jurist's contribution to civil liberties. Brennan had no more fervent admirer
than Joe Rauh, but the dinner presented a hard choice. It would be held at a
Washington hotel where his daughter-in-law, Maggie, had once claimed sex
discrimination. He had vowed never to set foot in the place again.

Seeking family guidance, Rauh retired to the upstairs bedroom and asked
Olie to place a call to his daughter-in-law. He explained to Maggie his
dilemma and she told him to go to the dinner, with one condition. He and the
justice should avoid any photographs with the hotel's owner. "Don't worry,"
Rauh assured her, "if that son-of-a-bitch comes near us with a camera we'll
give him the finger."

He hung up the phone and prepared for bed. Minutes later, Joe Rauh fell
to the floor, victim of a fatal heart attack. The lion of American liberalism,
one of the last New Dealers, died at the age of eighty-one.[8]

"Mostly he pitched for democracy," the *New York Times* editorialized
later. "His deep, craggy voice resonated through the halls and chambers of
Congress. He demanded to be heard and he got his hearing through lean and
fat years for his cause. Those who knew him will miss his attentiveness, and
his pressure on others to be attentive to human rights. Many who never knew
him are the beneficiaries of that pressure and passion."[9]

In his eighty-one years, Joe Rauh never did anything indifferently or at
half speed, whether playing tennis, defending a client, managing a political
campaign, lobbying a congressman, writing a law review article, or bouncing
a grandson. He had a thousand best friends who loved and worshiped him as
a tireless champion of social justice. He had more than his share of opponents who regarded him as a stubborn, unyielding idealist for lost, liberal
causes.

From his years as a young lawyer in the Wage and Hour Division of the
Roosevelt administration until his death, Joe Rauh embodied the triumphs

and travails of post–New Deal liberalism. He played a pivotal role in many arenas that reshaped the landscape of American law and public policy after World War II: the struggle for racial justice and efforts to extend and protect the social-economic reforms of the New Deal, to revitalize democracy inside America's labor unions, and to defend individual rights against the abuses of public and private power.

In the days after World War I, Justice Louis Brandeis once referred to Felix Frankfurter as "the most useful lawyer in America." In the post–World War II era, Joe Rauh, a Frankfurter protégé, earned that same accolade from Ben Cohen. "For you there has been no generation gap," his New Deal mentor once told him, "because you have never been beguiled by the belief that fundamental freedoms must yield to progress or that true progress requires the surrender of fundamental freedoms. You have ever been a champion and staunch defender of good causes before they became popular causes."[10]

CHAPTER ONE

THE EDUCATION OF JOE RAUH: RACE

He lived up to every hope I ever had for good white people.
—ROY WILKINS, 1992

Coalition of Outsiders

Franklin Roosevelt's New Deal may have been, as Peter Irons once wrote, "a lawyer's deal," but it was also "an outsider's deal" that extended recognition and power to many Americans who had been marginalized by their ethnicity, race, religion, social class, or region. New Deal labor legislation, for example, gave a place at the economic table to union leaders, many of whom, like Walter Reuther and his brothers, traced their roots to Russia and eastern Europe. FDR tapped the first Irish Catholic to become solicitor general of the United States and the first to be named ambassador to England. Westerners like William O. Douglas, chairman of the Securities and Exchange Commission, Texas congressman Lyndon Johnson, and Marriner Eccles, a Utah Mormon who became governor of the Federal Reserve Board, formed essential parts of Roosevelt's new coalition.

Among the largest beneficiaries of the Roosevelt revolution were American Jews, many of them young lawyers from the best schools, who faced both declining employment opportunities in private practice and blatant anti-Semitism at law firms in the major cities of the East and Midwest. By 1935, however, Jewish lawyers provided the brains and idealism that infused the burgeoning New Deal legal bureaucracy, from the Agricultural Adjustment Administration (AAA) to the Tennessee Valley Authority (TVA).

African-Americans, victimized as sharecroppers and often excluded from public works projects, became the last to join FDR's coalition of minorities and the last to enjoy its fruits, often handed out at the back door. While the president's wife, Eleanor, and his secretary of the interior, Harold Ickes, spoke out publicly against racial segregation, FDR never did so, but met quietly and unofficially with a few African-American leaders such as Walter White of the National Association for the Advancement of Colored People. When lawyers in the AAA attempted to protect the eviction of sharecroppers, the president banished them to other agencies. The New Deal's Department of Justice did not create a civil rights division until the end of the decade. Nonetheless, by 1936 African-Americans for the first time abandoned the Republican Party and joined the New Deal coalition.

By the end of World War II, blue-collar industrial workers in the North, white Southerners, Jews, and African-Americans constituted the core of the Roosevelt coalition and the Democratic Party, but the coalition had begun to unravel as a result of the migration of blacks into northern cities and their systematic challenges to segregation and disfranchisement in the South. Joseph L. Rauh Jr., a lawyer and a Jew, emerged from the New Deal with a foot planted in these multiple worlds that remained essential to the life of the liberal project after Roosevelt. Contributing to these worlds and navigating among them became the central theme of his public life.

Los Angeles, 1985

More than 3,000 men and women packed the ballroom of the Beverly Wilshire Hotel in Los Angeles on a November afternoon in 1985 to honor Joe Rauh, as the recipient of the Maurice N. Eisendrath Bearer of Light Award, the highest honor for public service given by the Union of American Hebrew Congregations, the leading voice of Reform Judaism in the United States. A standing ovation greeted the seventy-four-year-old civil rights and civil liberties lawyer as he made his way slowly to the podium, leaning on a cane, hobbled by an aching hip. He began his remarks by reminding his audience of the historic contributions to racial justice made by American Jews, from the founding of the NAACP to the civil rights workers Michael Schwerner and Andrew Goodman, who had been brutally murdered in Mississippi a decade earlier.

Then the tone and substance of his remarks changed. The Jewish community's "greatest mistake during my lifetime," he said, had been its "unwillingness to support the preferential aspects of affirmative action for qualified minorities and women." When their own self-interest in education and employment had been threatened, many Jews abandoned civil rights, "preferring self-interest to principle." Next he launched into a criticism of those who proclaimed the sanctity of a "color-blind" Constitution. "The Constitution wasn't color blind in slavery and it wasn't color blind in Jim Crow," he noted. "The color blind argument today is nothing more than a cover for the denial of any recompense for past discrimination based on color."[1]

Many in the Los Angeles audience recalled that their honored speaker had been in the vanguard of lawyers defending affirmative action programs against arguments that they constituted unconstitutional reverse discrimination against whites. Some perhaps recalled his words to the Milwaukee Jewish Council in 1973, when he scolded his audience for opposing affirmative action goals and timetables: "The descendants of the Jewish ghettos of Europe, upon whom American democracy has shone so brightly, must not be found wanting when the rights of the less fortunate are at stake."[2]

And some in his audience probably recalled that in 1974 Rauh and Marian Edelman of the Children's Defense Fund had filed a friend-of-the-court brief supporting the University of Washington's efforts to promote minority representation in its law school and that their efforts had been supported by the National Council of Jewish Women and the Social Action Commission of the same Union of American Hebrew Congregations.[3] Three years later, in the case of Allan Bakke's lawsuit against the University of California, Rauh filed a similar brief defending the university's program that reserved sixteen out of one hundred seats in its entering medical school class for "disadvantaged" minorities, defined as African-Americans, Asians, and Hispanics. But by then no Jewish organization signed on with him, despite his pleas.

"Many white people will suffer," he told reporters at the time of the *Bakke* case, "but the problem is comparing [Bakke's] rights against those who have been so long discriminated against. Who has the higher right?"[4] Those words had rankled the leadership of the Union of Hebrew Congregations in 1977, and his words in Los Angeles irritated them eight years later. Only polite, tepid applause greeted the end of his remarks. That evening in his hotel room, nursing a gin and tonic, Rauh reflected on the response of the audience. He had felt like "a skunk at a garden party," he said, or like Adlai Stevenson, Rauh imagined, when he criticized Joe McCarthy at a convention of the American Legion. But, he concluded, he would say the same thing again to the same audience.[5]

New York, 1979

Five years earlier, on the morning of August 22, 1979, Rauh sat alone in an office at the Manhattan headquarters of the National Association for the Advancement of Colored People. A week earlier, Andrew Young, the highest-ranking African-American in the Carter administration and U.S. ambassador to the United Nations, had resigned his post in the wake of news reports that he had met in his New York apartment with a representative of the Palestine Liberation Front. Although Young had informed Israel's U.N. representative about the meeting and although it did not violate American policy, various Jewish leaders accused the ambassador of conducting secret negotiations with a terrorist organization. Angry African-American leaders came to Young's defense and blamed Jewish groups for destroying the ambassador's career.

One of three white members on the NAACP board, Rauh had been summoned to New York for an emergency meeting in a telegram signed by some of the most important African-American leaders in the country, including Ben Hooks, Coretta Scott King, Kenneth Clark, and Vernon Jordan. The purpose of the meeting, they said, would be to assess the impact of Young's resignation "on our role in shaping American foreign policy, black-Jewish relations and black-administration relations." From this session, they hoped, "a consensus will be reached . . . including the possibility of a subsequent conference with principal Jewish leaders."[6]

When he arrived at the organization's offices, however, Rauh discovered that the other white board members had declined to appear and that the members of the board seemed reluctant to begin the meeting. Hooks, the chairman of the NAACP board, and Clark, the distinguished psychologist, drew Rauh aside and explained that several people who were not board members had turned up to join the session. Hooks also suggested that Rauh's presence might inflame the discussion. Clark became angry at that suggestion and said he would boycott the meeting unless Rauh could attend. In an attempt to calm the waters, Rauh said he would sit in a nearby office, where they could keep him informed about the discussions.[7]

For several hours, the former lawyer for A. Philip Randolph's union of sleeping car porters and the Mississippi Freedom Democratic Party in 1964 found himself excluded from a meeting likely to have a major impact on the future of black-Jewish relations. In the adjoining conference room, the organization's board members held heated discussions, with Clark popping in and out to keep Rauh informed. Clark feared the group would draft a resolution linking Young's demise to the mounting tensions over affirmative action. In an attempt to counter that impression, Rauh pleaded for a clear statement that "there is no evidence of Jewish pressure . . . and the President should make clear that his decision was based rather on the State Department's insistence."[8]

Rauh knew that Young had been forced out, not by Jewish pressure, but by his enemies at State, including secretary of state Cyrus Vance. The ambassador had not endeared himself to the secretary by comparing dissidents in the Soviet Union to American civil rights protestors or by alleging that the United States had "hundred, perhaps thousands of political prisoners."[9] But Rauh's effort to shift responsibility to the State Department never made it into the NAACP's final announcement, which simply urged Carter "to give a full and clear explanation of the reasons for the acceptance of that [Young's] resignation."[10]

Hooks soon escalated the Young controversy in a separate pamphlet noting that the white American ambassador to Austria had not been fired when he met with PLO representatives, that Jews employed an "Orwellian perversion of language" when they equated affirmative action programs with quotas, and that Israel engaged in military traffic with "the illegitimate and oppressive racist regimes in South Africa and Southern Rhodesia."[11]

Many Jewish leaders, led by Rabbi Alexander Schindler of the Union of American Hebrew Congregations, immediately rebuked the NAACP for fomenting "a needless and hurtful confrontation between Blacks and Jews." Once reports of Rauh's banishment from the board meeting hit the newspapers, he received messages of condolence from some Jews, while others expressed delight in what they regarded as a humiliation that confirmed their belief in the unbridgeable political gap now separating blacks and Jews.[12]

Cincinnati, 1921

The journey that took Joe Rauh to the Union of Hebrew Congregations meeting in Los Angeles in 1985 and to the NAACP board meeting in 1979 began decades earlier, in his hometown of Cincinnati. *New York Post* columnist Jimmy Wechsler, his longtime friend, used to quip that Rauh gained his sympathy for the underdog when he played center for the Harvard University basketball team in the late 1920s. In truth, Rauh learned his first lesson about underdogs and race at the age of ten from his family's black chauffeur and handyman, Eugene Smith. As part of the bargain for a third child, Sarah Rauh had secured from her husband Joseph Sr. the promise of a new automobile and a chauffeur to drive it. In the spacious yard of their comfortable home on Marion Avenue in the predominantly Jewish section of Cincinnati known as Avondale, young Joe frequently lured Eugene into a game of catch and plagued the older man with endless questions about baseball.

"Who's the best pitcher in baseball?" young Joe asked Smith one afternoon.

"Satchel Paige," Smith replied, not missing a beat. And then he added, "all the great players are colored."

"That can't be," Joe said. "I've never seen a colored player on the Reds."

"That's because they aren't allowed to play in the major leagues," Smith told him.[13]

His father's flourishing business manufacturing men's sports shirts meant that Joe Jr. enjoyed a world of security and comfort unknown to most Americans in the years before World War I. The senior Rauh and other Jews owned and operated three-quarters of the Queen City's thriving ready-made clothing industry, and they played major roles in the dry goods business, the liquor trade, real estate developments, banking, and insurance. By the time of young Joe's fifteenth birthday, Jews in Cincinnati had been elected as mayors and district attorneys, in addition to holding positions on the court of common pleas, the police commission, the city council, and the school board. No less an authority on power in his city than President Taft had remarked that "none of the great charities, none of the theatres, none of the societies of art . . . or music, could live [in Cincinnati] if it were not for the support of the Jews."[14]

While not ranking financially among Cincinnati's Jewish elite—the Fleischmanns, Freibergs, and Krohns—the senior Rauh's success permitted vacations on lakes in upstate Michigan, summer camp in Maine for young Joe and his brother Carl, and a Wellesley College education for their precocious older sister, Louise, who soon went on to medical school. Sarah Rauh and her husband could afford a nurse to tend Joe Jr., and saw to it that all the children entered the University School, an institution funded in large part by German Jews who had experienced discrimination at the city's elite private schools. For the Rauh family, Cincinnati, despite its lingering anti-Semitism, remained, as one earlier historian observed, "a sort of paradise for the Hebrews."[15] But Eugene Smith had given young Joe his first significant hint that another world, riddled with discrimination and injustice, existed side by side with his own sheltered one. Joe absorbed a second lesson when he followed his older brother to Harvard College in 1928.

Cambridge, 1930

In 1930, the Harvard basketball team sent on the court one Jew, center Joe Rauh, and one African-American, William (Bill) Baskerville, a short, wiry guard who could dribble circles around opponents and possessed a devastating outside shot as well. When the team traveled, the Jew and the African-

American roomed together, an arrangement as significant as the storied columns at Widener Library.

These were the twilight years at the Harvard of President Abbott Lawrence Lowell, whose family had played an active role in the school's destiny since the American Revolution. A sometime defender of academic freedom for his professors, Lowell's tolerance did not extend to matters of race, religion, and ethnicity. As national vice president of the Immigration Restriction League, he expressed alarm at the increase in Jewish enrollment at Harvard, which had risen from 7 percent in 1900 to slightly over 21 percent by 1922.

President Lowell believed that many German Jews, who behaved like Yankees, could be, like the Irish, absorbed by Harvard, but he reserved a special animus for Jews from eastern Europe and Russia, whom he blamed for the increase in general campus rowdiness and disciplinary problems. His was not the only voice of bigotry at Harvard. English professor Barrett Wendell made it clear that his annual dinner for scholars in the college would have to be dropped "if a Jew ever turn[ed] up among them."[16]

The Harvard faculty rejected Lowell's suggestion in 1922 that freshmen applicants who "belong to the Hebrew race . . . be rejected except in unusual and special cases." By 1927, despite objections from the Board of Overseers, the president had achieved his objective through piecemeal revisions of admissions criteria that capped total freshmen numbers, denied automatic entrance to high school graduates in the top seventh of their class, and favored applicants from the South, Midwest, and Far West. This last provision helped open Harvard's doors to two young Jews from Cincinnati, Carl Rauh, a math whiz, and his younger brother, Joe.

Money, political influence, academic achievement, and athletic prowess could soften the edges of hard ethnic and religious boundaries at Lowell's Harvard, but not for African-Americans. Small in numbers, they suffered the worst discrimination. When it opened new halls for freshmen in 1914, Harvard told its black students to find lodgings elsewhere. Roscoe Conkling Bruce, a black Phi Beta Kappa graduate in the class of 1902, attempted to break this racial barrier for his son in 1922, but Lowell personally vetoed the idea: "We owe to the colored man the same opportunities for education that we do to the white man; but we do not owe to him to force him and the white man into social relations that are not, or may not be, mutually congenial."[17]

Harvard's color line followed its basketball players to New York City when the team arrived at the Vanderbilt Hotel for scheduled games against Columbia and the City College of New York. As Joe Rauh entered the lobby, he watched his roommate turn, grim-faced, from the reservations desk, pick up his suitcase, and head for the door.

"Hey, Bill," he asked, "where are you going in such a hurry?"

"They won't let me stay here, Joe. They don't accept Negroes."

Baskerville quickly explained to his stunned roommate and the other Harvard players that white Southerners owned the Vanderbilt and did not want their patrons forced to mingle with African-Americans. The Harvard team huddled for a moment, then marched as a group to the front desk, canceled their reservations, and left the Vanderbilt.[18] They were ahead of their time. The Harvard Corporation would not take a stand against racial discrimination in sports until 1941, when another group of athletes protested a decision by the school's athletic director, who had bowed to pressure from the United States Naval Academy and benched a black lacrosse player scheduled to play against Annapolis.[19]

Rauh's Harvard contemporary, the journalist Theodore White, divided the undergraduates of the time into three sociological groups—white men, gray men, and meatballs. The white men arrived in Cambridge with grand names, great wealth, or both—Saltonstalls, Morgans, Roosevelts, Harrimans. They drove fancy automobiles, belonged to social clubs, wore fine clothes, escorted debutantes to lavish parties, and could afford out-of-town football games in New Haven or New York. White proudly placed himself among the meatballs. They often arrived as day students on scholarships. Children of immigrants—Irish Catholics, Jews, Italians—they ate their lunches from paper bags, owned one suit of clothes, and endlessly debated the virtues of socialism or communism on Dudley Hall's ground floor, set aside for them.

In contrast, White's gray men came from public schools or second-tier private schools. "Neither aristocracy nor of the deserving poor," resolutely middle class, they staffed the *Crimson* and the *Harvard Advocate,* dominated the athletic teams, earned good grades, and ran the school's student government.[20] With his Buick automobile, sporty clothes, spending money, and supply of bathtub gin, undergraduate Rauh could have been mistaken for a white, but he remained a gray, someone capable of navigating up and down Harvard's social ladder, cultivating friendships across the class divide. Barred from prominent social clubs such as Porcelain, Rauh and other grays studied harder than whites and earned better grades, while their enthusiasm for sports and politics brought them into alliance often with meatballs.

Driven by competition with his two bright roommates, Joe Keller, a wizard at engineering, and Bernard Meyer, destined for a distinguished career in psychiatry, Rauh completed his major in economics, earned a Phi Beta

Kappa key, and graduated magna cum laude. He might have garnered hon-
ors as Harvard's best athlete, too, had it not been for Barry Wood, a future
physician, who earned straight A's, lettered in four sports, and quarterbacked
the Crimson football team.[21]

He also experienced little overt anti-Semitism as a Harvard undergraduate, despite the Lowells, the Wendells, and others on the faculty and among
the student body who probably shared their prejudice. The episode at the
Vanderbilt stirred his growing sense of kinship with the Bill Baskervilles of
America; so, too, did his visit to Berlin in 1932.

Berlin, 1932

On the eve of the stock market crash in 1929, Rauh and two friends from
Cincinnati went to western Europe. Typical college-age tourists, they ate,
drank, and visited the great sites, but did not engage a single European in
discussions about the swirling economic and political forces about to plunge
the continent and the world into disaster. By 1932, unemployment spawned
by the Great Depression rocked democratic regimes across Europe, especially in Germany, where Adolf Hitler's National Socialist Party had become
the single largest voting bloc in the Reichstag on a platform that stressed military rearmament, revision of the Versailles Treaty, full employment, and
anti-Semitism.

Rauh arrived in Berlin that year under false pretenses as part of a jazz
band organized by his Harvard classmate, Jim Plaut, a gifted piano player
and the future director of the Boston Museum of Contemporary Arts. Although Rauh could not read music or keep time, Plaut described him as a
backup drummer for the group, a ruse that apparently fooled officials who
approved the trip. All illusions vanished, however, when the band went to
Berlin's vast Wannsee Stadium on the night of a huge rally hosted by Hitler's
Nazi Party. Perhaps 100,000 Germans marched into the stadium in military
fashion, many wearing the uniforms of their particular occupation, trade, or
profession, and they carried aloft the party's red-and-black swastika banners.

When the last marcher had settled into a seat, doors opened only twenty
feet from where Rauh stood, and a car slowly emerged bearing Hitler and
other party leaders, who waved to the crowd as the vehicle made several pas-
sages around the stadium. On each pass of the car, Hitler came so close that
Rauh could have knocked off his hat with a long stick. Minutes later, the Nazi
leader launched into one of his hate-filled diatribes against Versailles, the
craven leaders of the Weimar Republic, and Jews. "Niedrig mit den Juden,"
he shouted. "Down with the Jews. Down with the Jews." The crowd, now

worked into a fury, picked up his chant and hurled it back: "Niedrig mit den Juden! Niedrig mit den Juden!" Joe Rauh had never heard anything like it.[22]

Several weeks later, as the jazz band prepared to sail home to America, Hitler's party suffered a temporary setback in Reichstag elections. On the eve of entering Harvard Law School, Rauh told curious friends in Cincinnati that the Nazi Party's influence in Germany had probably dissipated. But in January 1933, President Hindenberg proved that prediction utterly wrong. He elevated Hitler to the chancellorship.

CHAPTER TWO

THE EDUCATION OF JOE RAUH:
LAW AND POLITICS

You learn no law in Public U
That is its fascination
But Felix gives a point of view
And pleasant conversation.

— FRANCIS PLIMPTON, *Reunion Runes*

December 1924

As patriarch of the Rauh household, Joseph Sr. voted the straight Republican
Party ticket in national, state, and local elections. He marched for William
McKinley against William Jennings Bryan and backed Senator Henry Cabot
Lodge against President Wilson in the debate over the Versailles Treaty and
the League of Nations. He shared the prejudice of many German Jews at the
time who regarded Zionists as misguided fanatics who espoused a pipe
dream of building a Jewish homeland in Palestine.

The elder Rauh endured his wife's support for an insurgent Republican
candidate, Murray Seasongood, against the party machine in the city elections of 1924, but his daughter's political rebellion proved too much. Louise
came home from Wellesley College for the holidays and promptly announced that she had voted for the old Progressive Robert M. La Follette,
the presidential candidate supported by the remnants of Eugene Debs's Socialist Party. Later she triggered a bigger explosion by declaring her support
for two Italian anarchists, Nicola Sacco and Bartolomeo Vanzetti, then under
sentence of death in Massachusetts following their conviction for a double
homicide and robbery. Louise, who had studied the case carefully, said they

had been tried in an atmosphere of anti-Italian, antiradical hysteria, convicted on dubious evidence, and condemned by a bigoted judge. As young Joe Jr. watched, his father, Louise, and Carl shouted at one another until the older brother, enraged, slapped his sister. It was young Joe's first experience with the passions aroused by the intersection of law and politics.[1]

Camp Kennebec, Maine, and Boston, 1927

From his Cincinnati home to the Maine woods, the case of Sacco and Vanzetti shadowed sixteen-year-old Joe in the summer of 1927. On a humid August evening after a long canoe trip, a Camp Kennebec counselor suggested that the boys paddle over to a nearby town where they could listen to music on the radio. When Joe and the other campers arrived, they discovered that someone had rigged up loudspeakers to broadcast the executions of Sacco and Vanzetti in Massachusetts's electric chair. The announcer reported on crowds of demonstrators who marched in London, Paris, New York, and Boston to demand clemency. He noted that Supreme Court justice Oliver Wendell Holmes Jr. had refused to stay the executions. Finally, he announced that the two men had been put to death.[2]

In Boston that same evening, Harvard Law School professor Felix Frankfurter, who had denounced the trial of the two Italians in the *Atlantic Monthly,* heard the same radio broadcast. His wife Marion, who would later coedit the death house letters of the two Italians, collapsed after hearing the news. Young Joe returned to Cincinnati that summer and began to read voraciously about Sacco and Vanzetti. He did not know it at the time, but he had already forged an emotional bond with a man who would shape profoundly his adult life and work.

Olie

In early September 1932, Joe Rauh came back to Cambridge from Cincinnati to do what generations of young men had done since 1817 when they gathered for Asahel Stearns's first class at Harvard Law School. Those who had made the same pilgrimage before him included legendary figures of the American bench and bar—Benjamin Robbins Curtis, who dissented in the Dred Scott case; Horace Gray, the youngest man ever appointed to the Massachusetts Supreme Judicial Court; Oliver Wendell Holmes Jr., whose father had cautioned him that "a lawyer can't be a great man"; and Louis Dembitz Brandeis, who graduated in 1877 with the highest marks in the school's history.

Boston that September, like other American communities in the third and bleakest year of the Great Depression, presented an eerie mixture of despair and hope. Across the nation, nearly a quarter of the nation's workers could not find jobs. Outside the Boston train station, Rauh saw middle-aged men attempt to earn a living by selling apples for a nickel. Further down the block, a long line of men, women, and children stood outside a church waiting for a distribution of food and clothing. James Michael Curley, the commonwealth's most colorful political figure, the former mayor of Boston and now governor, arrived on the same train with Rauh and proceeded to tell a large crowd of reporters that salvation would arrive in November when Franklin Roosevelt, governor of New York, defeated President Herbert Hoover. "I went out west to tell them that the president was a son-of-a-bitch," Curley said, "but they knew it before I got there."[3]

When Rauh registered for classes at storied Langdell Hall, he did not know he was about to enter an institution and meet a man both of whom would soon play pivotal roles in Roosevelt's efforts to bring a New Deal to America. He would soon meet Professor Frankfurter, the first and only Jew on the law school faculty, perhaps the most famous (critics said infamous) law professor in America. The bête noire of Boston conservatives, Frankfurter had become a legal icon among intellectuals and liberal reformers who regarded him as the model of the lawyer who put public service above private gain. He counted among his close friends the future president and three Supreme Court justices—Holmes, Brandeis, and Benjamin Cardozo. Each year he sent them his brightest students, who served as their secretaries, the title *law clerk* yet to be coined.

As he had done to other young men who had arrived at Harvard Law since before the war, Professor Frankfurter soon cast his spell on Joe Rauh as mentor, cheerleader, career manager, and surrogate father. In return, he demanded intellectual rigor, physical stamina, devotion to the law, a commitment to public service, and unquestioned acceptance of his plans for their future legal careers. Most of his students regarded Frankfurter as the most vital, nurturing influence in their lives; not a few, however, chafed at his demands and paternalism. Rauh would soon count himself among the former, but he had earlier met a person of far greater influence on his life during his final year as an undergraduate.

As a favor to Jimmy Plaut, he had agreed to pick up two young women at the Boston train station on a Friday afternoon in the fall of 1931. One, Mary Eisfelder, he had met before; the other he knew only as one of Mary's classmates at Marot, a junior college in Connecticut, someone named Olie Westheimer. She was to be a blind date that weekend for one of Mary's friends.

Arriving in his blue Buick convertible, Joe Rauh could not take his eyes off Eisfelder's lovely eighteen-year-old companion from St. Louis.

Olie Westheimer, honey-haired and high spirited, was the granddaughter of a German Jewish immigrant who arrived in the United States at the age of thirteen and soon made a living selling dry goods from a horse and buggy in and around St. Joseph, Missouri. Entering the wholesale liquor trade with his brother, he made a tidy fortune that he passed on to seven children before national Prohibition put their firm out of business. Olie's father, one of the seven, scorned the high-flying stock trading of the Coolidge-Hoover era and turned another profit on his share of the inheritance before the market crashed. He moved his family often—to Pasadena, California; Kansas City; and finally, Switzerland, where Olie attended school for two years—before the Westheimers settled finally in St. Louis.

Joe Rauh left the train station already enamored, but the future Mrs. Rauh had serious doubts about the young man in the shiny convertible. Handsome, but not very smart for a Harvard man, she thought. Mr. Rauh appeared to murder the English language by lapsing into the use of *ain't* and other uncouth constructions. Only later did she realize that he employed such expressions in order to hide his intellectual gifts, ones not valued highly by many of his peers, who prized athletic prowess, hard drinking, and rowdy behavior. Among Joe's circle of close friends at Harvard, brain power often ranked below partygoing and having a good time. With some hesitation, Olie Westheimer agreed to their first date at the Harvard-Princeton football game a few weeks later.

She soon discovered a young man unlike others she had known. Even after a long night in a Boston speakeasy, Joe's hook shots still found the basket. Who else, to settle a bet, dared to take off his pants at the fifty-yard line of the Yale Bowl? Or throw a box of pucks onto the ice in the middle of a varsity hockey game? Who could perform these outrageous stunts yet still graduate near the top of his Harvard College class and enter its prestigious law school?[4]

Olie Westheimer's own streak of rebellion had found a kindred spirit. Officials at Marot dismissed her and three companions during their first year for sneaking out of the dormitory past curfew. She returned to Marot, but only when her father agreed to pay a full year's tuition in advance, a proposition that so infuriated her that she left the school and enrolled at Washington University in St. Louis. During that year, she saw Joe only during holidays, but it became enough to convince her that she wanted to be with him in Cambridge. In Joe's second year at the law school, Olie entered Wheelock, a teachers' college in Boston. They had become inseparable, as she often waited in his convertible on freezing evenings outside Langdell Hall. After his class ended, they usually ate dinner at St. Clair's in Harvard Square, where Joe indulged in Cambridge's largest hot fudge sundaes. Finally, with his law degree almost in hand, he proposed marriage.[5]

A majority of his law school classmates, sheltered from the economic storm, voted for Herbert Hoover in 1932. Joe cast his ballot for Roosevelt, less from profound faith in the candidate's murky campaign promises than from disgust at the Republican incumbent. Nor had he entered law school with the goal of transforming the world, but for simple, pragmatic reasons: the shrinking revenues at the Rauh Shirt Company could not support another son in the business. Carl Rauh had abandoned his dreams of teaching mathematics and returned to Cincinnati to manage the business, now plagued by labor troubles in addition to falling revenues. Their father believed it made good business sense to have a lawyer in the family. His youngest son reluctantly agreed to law school, but promised only a single year, a limited commitment his father refused to accept.

Dean Pound's Faculty

The Harvard Law School faculty, led by Dean Roscoe Pound, prized its collective learning, wit, and arrogance. The dean, trained in botany and the law, had been recruited from the University of Nebraska in 1910 and assumed leadership of the law school five years later. He possessed a relentless, encyclopedic mind for the common law and legal history, which inspired a parody by Francis Plimpton, who graduated in 1925:

> In Jurisprudence you should hear
> Him talk in manner quizzic
> Of Pufendorf, DeGrolof, Beaussire,
> All jurists metaphysic.

> He knows the laws from nuts to soups,
> And classifies decisions
> In eighteen heads, and forty groups,
> With ninety subdivisions.[6]

Pound presided over a faculty that included Samuel Williston, author of prodigious legal treatises such as *The Restatement of Contracts,* who introduced students to the mysteries of offer and acceptance and the statute of frauds. Francis P. Sayre, son-in-law of the former president Woodrow Wil-

son, initiated students into the criminal law. Calvert Magruder, soon to become one of the New Deal's top lawyers and a distinguished federal judge,
taught torts, while another critic of the Sacco-Vanzetti case, Edmund Morgan, offered courses on evidence. Zechariah Chafee, who had written a landmark book on freedom of speech, taught perhaps the school's dullest course,
Bills and Notes. In the demonology of conservative Bostonians, however, he
ranked next to Frankfurter as the school's most poisonous influence on young
minds.

At the law school in the depths of the Depression, folklore said that those
students who made A's would become law professors, the B students would
join the ranks of the judiciary, and the C students would make all the money
practicing corporate law in New York or Boston. Two of Joe's classmates,
Nelson Adams and Fairfax Leary, later taught law, while another, J. Willard
Hurst, revolutionized the field of American legal history from his post at the
University of Wisconsin. Max Rabb went on to become ambassador to Italy.
A small but talented band of Jewish students—David Ginsburg, Milton and
Harold Cohen, and Arnold Levy—joined Joe in New Deal Washington after
graduation. But the vast majority, whether A or C students, followed the path
of Paul Reardon, who began his career at the Wall Street firm of Davis, Polk,
where he soon became a leading tax attorney.

Joe had the good luck to room with David B. Stern Jr., son of a Chicago
investment banker, who brought a well-developed social conscience to the
law school. While Joe had a vivid recollection of Sacco and Vanzetti, a memory reinforced by his sister's strong opinions and his own reading, he discovered that Stern had mastered everything written about the case, including
the trial record and the appellate briefs. Stern told him the two defendants
had been victims of antiradical hysteria and a flawed judicial system. He also
burned Joe's ears with examples of the legal outrages inflicted on Negroes,
especially their inability to vote below the Mason-Dixon Line, the epidemic
of lynching, and the near impossibility of receiving a fair trial in southern
state courts. In Frankfurter's seminar they teamed up to write their papers
on the expanding role of federal courts in protecting the constitutional rights
of persons tried and convicted in state courts.

While Stern educated Joe about the political dimensions of the legal system and the social consequences of its rules, most of his professors drained
such material from their courses. They required students only to dissect the
opinions of appellate courts in common-law litigation, and preached their vision of law as the continuing refinement of human reason and morality.
Sooner or later, they affirmed, thanks to brilliant judges, enlightened legal
rules would triumph over archaic ones. Public law, constitutional or adminis-

trative, remained an orphan of the curriculum, and questions of legal ethics merited no discussion. Dean Pound summarized the institution's inherent conservatism when he delivered an address entitled "What Is the Common Law?" during Harvard's 300th anniversary celebration in 1936. The dean attributed all of the scientific, social, and economic progress "since the chaos of the earlier Middle Ages" to the benefactions of the common law, "by which the fundamentally unrational has been tamed to reason and law and order."[7]

Blessed with a trenchant memory and an aptitude for mathematics and logic, Joe navigated easily through his first two years, led his class academically, and gained a coveted position on the *Harvard Law Review*. The first year of law school resembled the ordeal of a Roman galley slave, while the second year exhausted one with boredom. Aside from Morgan's course on evidence, the conventional menu of agency, sales, trusts, and wills went down week after week like a stale glass of beer. He finally reaped intellectual rewards in his final year of law school under the influence of Erwin Griswold, Thomas Reed Powell, and Frankfurter. Griswold brought a reformer's zeal to his teaching. With a surgeon's precision, he demonstrated how the Harding and Coolidge administrations, influenced by Treasury secretary Andrew Mellon, had secured numerous legislative provisions and bureaucratic rulings to relieve the wealthy of their federal taxes and how these gaping loopholes might be closed by the Roosevelt administration.

A notorious skeptic who skewered both liberals and conservatives without mercy, Powell delighted in deflating the myth of judicial infallibility by quoting directly from the official reports of the Supreme Court. He took special pleasure in mocking conservative justices such as James McReynolds, George Sutherland, and Pierce Butler, opponents of government regulation and ardent defenders of property rights. Powell became especially fond of reciting Holmes's famous passage in *Buck v. Bell,* where the Court permitted the sterilization of a mentally retarded young woman institutionalized in Virginia. "Three generations of imbeciles are enough," Holmes wrote. Then Powell noted, dryly, "Mr. Justice Butler dissenting."[8]

The Frankfurter Method

Finally, the ebullient Professor Frankfurter bounded into Joe's life. Occasionally during his first year, he caught a fleeting glimpse of this diminutive, nattily attired man who rushed through the halls of Langdell, usually with a large band of students in tow, all engaged in high-spirited, acrimonious debate. He saw even less of Frankfurter during the 1933–34 academic term, when Oxford University invited Harvard's celebrated law professor to hold the Eastman Chair, a post that appealed to Frankfurter's unabashed Anglophilia. In Joe's final year, however, Frankfurter offered to advanced students a course on public utilities and another on federal jurisdiction. Joe enrolled in the second, although the official course descriptions did not convey the content of either one. Whatever the subject matter, a Frankfurter course remained a dazzling arena of bare-knuckled intellectual combat that mixed tedious case analysis with long discussions on federal procedure, endless historical anecdotes, and frequent digressions into current political and judicial events. As one student later recalled,

You learn no law in Public U
That is its fascination
But Felix gives a point of view
And pleasant conversation.[9]

Joe discovered on the first afternoon of class that Frankfurter had unorthodox teaching methods. The professor, resembling a quick, easily irritated sparrow, rushed into the room, sat on the desk, and held up a thick volume. "This," he announced, "is Frankfurter and Landis, *A History of the Federal Courts.* Read all of it. There will be an examination in two weeks. I will see you again in class thereafter." He then left the room as swiftly as he had entered, an exit that left Rauh and the others sitting in stunned silence.[10]

The hefty volume, produced by Frankfurter and his student, James Landis, a future law school dean, promoted more sleep than enthusiasm, but Joe excelled on the exam, impressing the professor, who seemed intrigued by his new student's Cincinnati roots and by his family's strong anti-Zionist views. Frankfurter's estimation of his new student took another leap forward when Joe mastered the voluminous record in the landmark *Muskrat* decision[11] and gave the class a cogent account of its significance for the jurisdiction of the federal courts. But Joe committed a major gaffe when the class focused on the case of Tom Mooney, a militant labor leader convicted in California prior to World War I and originally sentenced to death for setting off a bomb during a Preparedness Day parade in San Francisco. Unknown to Joe, Mooney's fate had preoccupied Frankfurter for decades.

Each Friday when the class met, Frankfurter distributed advance sheets of recent Supreme Court decisions and expected the students to discuss them the following week. In December 1934 he passed out, among others, *Mooney v. Holohan,*[12] where the Hughes Court ruled that prosecutors in San Francisco had knowingly used perjured testimony during the defendant's trial. That misconduct, the Court declared, violated the due process guarantee of the Fourteenth Amendment. Joe had barely skimmed the opinion before class and did not know that Frankfurter had been assigned by President Wilson to investigate the Mooney affair in 1916 and that he had also written a detailed report demolishing the prosecution's evidence. Frankfurter's report and Wilson's intervention probably spared Mooney from the gallows, but the labor organizer had continued to languish in a California prison cell.

When Frankfurter called on him to discuss the case, Joe threw up a smoke screen he soon regretted. To understand the significance of the *Mooney* decision, he began, "You had to know what things were like in California around the time of the trial." Frankfurter exploded. "Mr. Rauh," he said, leaping off his desk, "do you have any idea where I was then? Well, let me tell you." There followed a thirty-minute historical lecture on labor-management conflicts during World War I, the president's Mediation Commission, and Frankfurter's pivotal role as its legal counsel during the Mooney case.[13]

Their relationship survived Tom Mooney and flourished. Joe soon ate lunch regularly with Frankfurter at the law school and received a coveted invitation to the professor's afternoon teas at his Brattle Street home. There Marion Frankfurter, the attractive but neurotic daughter of a Congregational minister, presided regally over an ever-shifting retinue of students, faculty, politicians, and journalists. Although he had not been to Washington, Joe now felt a part of the New Deal, as Frankfurter regularly took the Federal Express to Washington, where he advised Roosevelt and touched base with many of his former students, now known as "Felix's happy hot dogs," who worked in various government agencies.

Frankfurter assumed that he had found another eager, talented recruit for FDR's New Deal. He therefore expressed surprise and annoyance when Joe announced in the spring of 1935 that he planned to take a job with Paxton & Seasongood, the largest Jewish law firm in Cincinnati, one headed by Murray Seasongood, the city's legendary municipal reformer. The firm had trained its sights on Rauh once he made law review and offered him the princely salary of one hundred dollars a week.

Frankfurter scotched that idea. "Oh, we can't go there," he said, peering over his eyeglasses with only the trace of a smile. Rauh now discovered that once Felix took you under his protective wing, he expected you to fly his course. "He loved his proteges," Mrs. Mark Howe later recalled, "but he also owned them. . . . There was a sweet side to Felix's paternalism, but he didn't care whether what he wanted was good for them."[14] As he did with others—

Howe, Louis Jaffe, Tom Corcoran, Ben Cohen, David Lilienthal, Archibald MacLeish—Frankfurter took charge of Rauh's initial legal career.

He tried to place his newest protégé with Cardozo, but the justice had assured the deans at Yale and Columbia law schools that unlike Holmes and Brandeis, he would not give Frankfurter a monopoly over his secretaries. According to the rotation, Yale stood next in line, not Harvard. Rauh would have to wait for Cardozo. Undaunted, Frankfurter arranged for Joe to meet John Burns, another law school graduate and now chief counsel at the newly created Securities and Exchange Commission, the New Deal agency charged with policing the nation's stock exchanges and securities industry. After a brief interview, Joe got the job with Burns.

Burns told him to show up for work on September 3, which pleased Frankfurter, but gave Olie a taste of what life would soon be like married to a man perpetually in motion. Their wedding had been scheduled for the evening of September 1 in St. Louis. Joe had also agreed to play softball for a Cincinnati country club against a St. Louis team on the morning of the ceremony. With the St. Louis players still groggy from a heavy bout of drinking the night before and with Joe on the mound, the Cincinnati team won. Several hours later, at 6:30 in the evening, Rabbi James Heller from Temple Isaac Wise in Cincinnati married Joe Rauh and Olie Westheimer. The groom, according to one witness, had "an ethereal look" on his face when the bride came down the aisle.

Recalling the pranks he had played on other bridegrooms, Joe took out a five-dollar bill, tore it in half, and gave it to the porter as they boarded a train that night to Washington. "If you don't tell anyone where our stateroom is," he said, "the other half is yours when the train pulls out." The porter earned his tip. The newlyweds reached the nation's capital early the next day, in time to rent an apartment and join the New Deal on schedule.[15]

CHAPTER THREE

NEW DEALER

They all claimed to be friends of somebody . . .
and mostly of Felix Frankfurter.

— GEORGE PEEK

Lawyer's Deal

George Peek, the crusty first chief of the New Deal's Agricultural Adjustment Administration, called them "a plague of young lawyers . . . young men
with their hair ablaze," who descended upon Washington, D.C., in the 1930s.
"They floated airily into offices, took desks, asked for papers and found no
end of things to be busy about," he complained. "I never found out why they
came, what they did or why they left."[1]

Peek's plague of young lawyers included Joe Rauh, who, except for
wartime service, would not leave Washington for fifty-eight years. He arrived
with several platoons of other newly minted attorneys, many, but not all, sent
by Felix Frankfurter—Nathan Witt, Abe Feller, Nathan Nathanson, Milton
and Harold Cohen, Nathan Marigold, and Paul Freund. Others soon followed—Telford Taylor, Ed Prichard Jr., Phil Graham, James Rowe Jr., and
Adrian "Butch" Fisher. They came to Washington to serve under an older
generation of lawyers recruited in the first years of the New Deal—Ben Cohen, Tom Corcoran, Jerome Frank, John Burns, James Landis, Robert Jackson, and Thomas Emerson. And they came to save Roosevelt's New Deal
from the machinations of other lawyers.

FDR and his administration stood at a critical crossroads the summer
Rauh arrived in the nation's capital. August 1935 climaxed a year of stunning
legislative victories for the president. In the space of a few months, during
what admirers soon called "the second Hundred Days," Congress had passed

and Roosevelt had signed into law a major restructuring of the Federal Reserve banking system; a revenue measure that closed income tax loopholes and placed a heavier burden on the wealthy; an emergency relief and public works appropriation of $4.8 billion; the National Labor Relations Act that guaranteed collective bargaining for industrial workers; a Social Security package that included old-age pensions and unemployment insurance; and the Public Utility Holding Company Act, which brought the nation's most powerful gas and electric companies under federal regulation and threatened to dissolve the largest ones within a decade.

But whether the gains of this second New Deal could be preserved and its momentum sustained remained an open question in September 1935. Those who lost in the titanic legislative battles of 1935, especially bankers, antilabor manufacturers, and taxpayers in the highest bracket, redoubled their attacks on the president and his administration as destroyers of the nation's economic system and the Constitution of the United States. They opened their wallets to organizations such as the Liberty League, a DuPont–Wall Street financed effort, dedicated to limited government, free enterprise, and the defense of property rights. They awaited eagerly the 1936 elections when, they anticipated, the American people would come to their senses and vote Roosevelt out of office. Above all, they placed their faith in the federal judiciary, the one branch of government that had not, in the judgment of the anti-Roosevelt faction, succumbed to the New Deal's reckless experiments.

Judicial Vetoes

By the summer of 1935, federal judges, most appointed by Republican presidents between 1921 and 1933, had issued hundreds of injunctions against New Deal measures, with more anticipated in the wake of the 1935 legislative session. The nation's highest court, presided over by Chief Justice Charles Evans Hughes, had exhibited a degree of toleration for initial New Deal reforms. By the narrowest of margins, five to four, the justices had sustained the authority of Congress to regulate the nation's monetary system, including its abrogation of provisions in private and public contracts that specified payment in gold.[2] In dissent, Justice James McReynolds labeled the congressional action confiscation and declared, "This is Nero at his worst. . . . The Constitution as we know it is gone."[3]

Within days, however, the Supreme Court rediscovered constitutional limits. Ignoring almost fifty years of precedent, five justices voted to overturn Congress's attempt to provide a mandatory retirement program for interstate railroad workers.[4] Then on May 27, soon branded "Black Monday" by New Dealers, the justices put the constitutional ax to three other New Deal measures. Without dissent, Hughes and company struck down the Frazier-Lemke Act, designed to provide mortgage relief to debt-ridden farmers.[5] They overturned unanimously the president's attempt to oust a reactionary member of the Federal Trade Commission.[6] Finally, the justices unanimously toppled the National Recovery Act, the keystone of Roosevelt's program to restore business prosperity. Congress, they ruled, had improperly delegated legislative authority to the president, and in its attempt to reform wages and hours in New York's live poultry industry the NRA exceeded federal authority to regulate as provided for in the commerce clause.[7]

At a press conference, Roosevelt complained bitterly that the railroad retirement decision and the NRA ruling had relegated the nation "to the horse-and-buggy definition of interstate commerce." The Court, he said, had crippled the government's ability to find national solutions to a national economic crisis. Even justices known to be sympathetic to the New Deal—Cardozo, Brandeis, and Harlan Stone—had voted against the administration on Black Monday. More recent New Deal reforms, including Social Security, the National Labor Relations Act, and the Tennessee Valley Authority, now appeared destined for the constitutional graveyard when the Supreme Court reconvened in October 1935.

Joe Rauh had become a part of Frankfurter's strategy to rescue the New Deal from further judicial mutilation. While the president heaped abuse on the justices for his predicament, others, including Frankfurter, placed much of the blame squarely on the lack of first-rate lawyers to draft and defend early New Deal statutes. From the first days of the New Deal, Frankfurter sought to raise the quality of legal talent in the administration, but having declined Roosevelt's invitation to become solicitor general in 1933, he shared responsibility for the low level of competence in the Department of Justice during the early years of the New Deal. Frankfurter recouped his fortunes with FDR by taking a major hand in writing the Securities Act of 1933 and later the Public Utility Holding Company Act. He also opened a channel of private dialogue between the president and Justice Brandeis, and he encouraged many of his former students to join the federal government.[8]

Although critics usually exaggerated their numbers, the influence of these Harvard-trained lawyers rose sharply in dozens of New Deal programs by 1935, due to a combination of the professor's tireless recruitment efforts and the lack of opportunities elsewhere, especially on Wall Street, where anti-Semitism closed many doors. Fired from one New Deal agency when they stepped on too many political toes, they usually landed on their feet in another. Peek and other government bureaucrats ridiculed them as legal busybodies, "who all claimed to be friends of somebody . . . and mostly of Felix Frankfurter."[9] Like a general commanding his troops, Frankfurter made frequent appearances in Washington, usually staying at the White House, to check on the morale and stamina of his forces. On a daily basis, however, the soldiers took their marching orders from Frankfurter's chief lieutenants, Cohen, Corcoran, and Landis.

Ben and Tom

By 1935, Landis, a Presbyterian missionary's son who had studied with Frankfurter and clerked for Brandeis, played an important role in drafting the Securities Act, and had been named chairman of the Securities and Exchange Commission following the resignation of Joseph P. Kennedy. Officially, Rauh answered to Landis and his general counsel, John Burns, but he soon found himself working for the team of Cohen and Corcoran, who did not occupy exalted positions, but whose legal skills and political savvy made them indispensable to the success of the New Deal.

Painfully shy, reclusive, and given to bouts of depression and volcanic anger, the forty-two-year-old Cohen inspired awe and reverence among the younger Frankfurter disciples, most of whom considered him the most astute legal mind in the government. A native of Muncie, Indiana, the "Middletown" made famous by Robert and Helen Lynd, and the youngest son of Polish immigrants, Cohen sped through the University of Chicago in three years, graduated cum laude from its law school in 1915, and then studied under Frankfurter at Harvard. On Frankfurter's recommendation, he clerked briefly for federal circuit court judge Julian Mack, twice failed his army physical because of bad vision, and spent the war years working for the United States Shipping Board.

Following the Armistice, Cohen labored in the Zionist vineyards with Frankfurter, Mack, and Brandeis until their bid to run the international movement generated fierce opposition from Chaim Weizmann and European Jews. During the boom years on Wall Street, Cohen specialized in corporate reorganizations, mastered many forms of financial chicanery, made a tidy profit, and worked for Florence Kelley and the National Consumers League on minimum wage legislation.[10] Passed over for the most prestigious legal posts in the administration, Cohen frequently threatened to quit the New Deal, but remained on duty because of loyalty to Frankfurter and the cause of social reform. "Felix is trying to shanghai me into the power situation and hold me in Washington," he complained at one point. "I don't want to stay, but he puts it on personal [grounds]. . . . I am afraid I will have to do it anyway."[11]

In 1935 Cohen drew his government paycheck as general counsel to the National Power Policy Committee, little more than a desk inside Harold Ickes' Interior Department. In fact, he had become general counsel to everybody in the administration who had important legislation to write or defend in the courts. He turned up at meetings wearing clothes that had been slept in for days, seldom missed a new motion picture (although he usually dozed off before the credits), and, despite a reputation for gentleness, could become quite wrathful when drawn into legal combat. In a high-pitched, whining voice he usually referred to his opponents as "yellowbellies" or, more forcefully, as "yellow-bellied sons-of-bitches."[12]

A meticulous legal craftsman, Cohen insisted on absolute perfection when it came to writing briefs and preparing litigation. He taught his young staff members how to be lawyers, often working Rauh, Nathanson, David Ginsburg, and the other attorneys far past midnight and never hesitating to criticize and reject their efforts. Ginsburg recalled that Cohen would read their product at the end of the day, throw entire drafts into the wastebasket, and start over himself. "I think this was one of Joe's early comeuppances," Ginsburg recalled, "to see Ben discard the best work that we could produce."[13]

Cohen lived with six other bachelors, including Corcoran, in a redbrick house on R Street in Georgetown that Republican congressmen soon christened "the little Red House on R Street" in honor of the alleged radicals who inhabited it. On the surface, the Jew from Muncie and Corcoran, the Irish Catholic from Pawtucket, Rhode Island, seemed worlds apart. Tommy the Cork dominated any party he attended, always ready with sea chanties at the piano or accordion. Justice Holmes, who employed him as a secretary in 1926, found him "quite adequate and quite noisy." In college, Cohen earned all A's, except in public speaking. Corcoran, on the contrary, had relished debate and drama at Brown University. Their admirers regarded Cohen as the legal brains of the partnership, the intellectual strategist and political idealist, while Corcoran possessed the keener political instincts and a certain ruthlessness that carried their plans to fruition.

Beneath Corcoran's charm and gaiety there moved deeper intellectual currents. Valedictorian at Brown in 1921, he remained in Providence another year to earn a master's degree with special emphasis on Greek and Latin. At Harvard Law School he became notes editor of the law review, won the coveted Sears Prize in his final year, worked as Frankfurter's research assistant, and coauthored with him "Petty Offenses and the Constitutional

Guaranty of Trial by Jury," an article that appeared in the *Harvard Law Review* and earned Corcoran a doctorate in law. After a year with Holmes, Corcoran joined the Wall Street firm of Cotton Franklin, where he became, in his own words, "expert devisor of schemes to cheat the cheater." This knowledge served him well when called upon to draft new laws regulating the securities industry and the stock exchanges.

Joe Rauh had the shortest tenure of any attorney in the history of the SEC—about one week—before Burns dispatched him to the National Power Policy Committee to help Cohen and Corcoran fend off the escalating legal attacks on the Public Utility Holding Company Act. It was a lucky break. At the SEC he had been assigned the mind-numbing task of codifying all the agency's decisions, work unlikely to captivate a young attorney inspired by visions of social reform. At the National Power Policy Committee, however, he found himself shaping legal briefs and carrying out strategy for Cohen and Corcoran, the brightest legal stars in the New Deal firmament, then locked in combat with the highest-paid Wall Street lawyers.

Fresh from law school, Rauh found his new job heady stuff. As he geared up for legal warfare with Ben and Tom, he received a pep talk from the pugnacious Harold Ickes, Cohen's boss at Interior, the quintessential New Dealer, a public servant always ready for verbal fisticuffs with the administration's foes. Frankfurter also bounced in occasionally to be briefed on developments by those he called the "the boys," who now included Rauh. Corcoran's flamboyant activities made a deep impression. The Cork seemed to have offices and secretaries scattered everywhere throughout the government and spent endless hours on the telephone. He acquired a special attachment to the one in the office Joe shared with Nathanson. From that remote outpost Corcoran regularly cajoled congressmen, senators, and various members of the burgeoning federal bureaucracy.

"Hello, Congressman?" he would boom. "This is Tom Corcoran, calling from the White House. The President is very anxious for you to . . ."[14]

Battling the Holding Companies

Corcoran's bravado could not, however, solve the challenge posed by lawyers for the public utility holding companies. Faced with legislation that subjected them to SEC regulation and possible dismemberment, the companies and their attorneys, led by John W. Davis, a former presidential candidate, devised a simple strategy: block enforcement of the law and have it declared unconstitutional quickly. They also plotted to limit the participation of government attorneys by engineering a friendly lawsuit that would frame the legal issues in favor of the companies. Cohen and Corcoran sought to avoid a multiplicity of suits, hoped to delay an immediate constitutional battle over the statute, and wished to focus on the narrow question of registration requirements in a test case against the largest company, Electric Bond and Share.

The initial legal skirmish took place in Baltimore before federal district judge William Coleman, a known opponent of the New Deal, where the trustees of a bankrupt holding company had petitioned for instructions about complying with the new law. Davis, whose firm represented the Edison Electric Institute, had located a willing bondholder, one Ferdinand Lautenbach, an obscure dentist, whom he persuaded to file suit against the trustees on the grounds that compliance with the statute threatened his financial interests as a creditor.

Davis and his colleagues had carefully manufactured the suit. Neither the trustees nor Lautenbach wished to comply with the law. Davis hoped this friendly suit would afford Judge Coleman the opportunity to rule on the constitutionality of the Public Utility Holding Company Act and to do so without confronting a real adversary: the government of the United States. Often federal courts had refused to hear such friendly contests because they failed to meet the "case or controversy" requirement of the Constitution,[15] but the fate of similar litigation testing New Deal measures remained in doubt in 1935.[16]

Fresh from Frankfurter's seminar on the federal courts, Rauh helped with the jurisdictional arguments in the government's brief, but Cohen gave him the chief assignment of finding Mr. Lautenbach, serving him with a subpoena, and forcing him to testify. Interrogated on the witness stand by John Burns, the dentist confessed ignorance about his own attorney and his relationship to the lawsuit.

"Did you sign these papers?"

"Yes."

"Who's your lawyer?

"I think some guy named Davis, but I'm not really sure."[17]

This evidence of a legal charade did not impress Judge Coleman, however, who refused to rule on the issue of collusion, requested briefs on the constitutional issues, and permitted the United States to participate in the case only as *amicus curiae!* Coleman appeared to share Davis's disdain for the government's counsel. Reaching new oratorical heights, he glared at the assembled government lawyers, including Rauh, and declared: "If these be the representatives of the United States, God help America!"[18]

Cohen, outraged, cursed Coleman under his breath as a "yellowbelly" and threatened to prepare a memo telling the court in the bluntest terms why the government would not discuss the merits of the case. Rauh and others talked him out of that reckless strategy, and instead they all began to work on a brief that addressed the constitutional issues in what became known as the *Burco* case. They also prepared to fight injunctions against the statute pending in other courts and took the initiative against the utilities by filing their own suit in New York against Bond and Share for failure to register with the SEC. Rauh worked many hours on these combined cases, long after the offices of the Interior Department shut down. Olie, pregnant with their first son, Michael, settled down with a book on her husband's office couch each evening to await the end of strategy sessions that continued long past midnight.[19]

As expected, Judge Coleman ruled against the government on every point by holding the law unconstitutional on three grounds: Congress had exceeded its authority under both the commerce clause and the postal power; and the government had denied the company due process guaranteed by the Fifth Amendment. American States Electric Company could not be compelled to register with the SEC.[20] In his first trial experience, Joe Rauh found himself on the losing side. Cohen and company had no better luck the following February before the Fourth Circuit Court of Appeals. That three-judge panel brushed aside the government's argument on collusion and affirmed a critical part of Coleman's decree that blocked the registration requirements. The judges refused, however, to affirm that portion of Colman's decision which had held the entire law unconstitutional.[21]

Victory at the Supreme Court

Elated by the circuit court ruling, the utilities counted on a decisive victory before the Supreme Court, where they hoped the justices would strike down the whole measure. To the astonishment of his exhausted and dispirited crew, Cohen announced that they would ask the Supreme Court to refuse to hear the case by declining to grant certiorari. On Cohen's staff, those eager for another round with the companies thought his strategy too timid; others, given the mood of the justices, believed it to be doomed. But Cohen reasoned that if the justices denied certiorari, the lower-court rulings would stand, and the ultimate decision about the law's constitutionality would be put off, perhaps until the government's own Bond and Share case reached the High Court later.

Rauh came to regard Cohen's strategy and his eloquent brief opposing certiorari in the *Burco* case as one of the most memorable legal achievements of the New Deal years. It didn't hurt, of course, that Cohen had the assistance of Rauh, Nathanson, Henry Herman, and Freund from the Solicitor General's Office. And it helped Cohen's cause that Brandeis's powerful concurrence in *Ashwander v. Tennessee Valley Authority*, which admonished the Court not to decide constitutional issues in similar cases, had appeared a month earlier.[22] On March 30, 1936, to everyone's surprise but Cohen's, the Hughes Court refused to hear *Burco v. Whitworth et al.*[23] The New Deal had some real lawyers now.

Cohen's team still faced another fierce battle: convincing federal judges to stay injunctions against the law until the question of registration had been settled in the Bond and Share case. Attorney general Homer Cummings had announced that no company would be prosecuted for failing to register with the SEC until the Supreme Court had ruled on the statute, but over fifty firms had filed suits in federal courts seeking injunctive relief, most with the hope of securing a constitutional decision against the New Deal. The leading case had been initiated by the North American Company in the Supreme Court of the District of Columbia against the SEC chairman, Landis.

While he helped Cohen polish the briefs in *Burco,* Rauh spent many hours with Corcoran preparing arguments for Cummings to use in his attempt to stay the injunctions in the D.C. court. Well primed, the attorney general made a powerful presentation against a dazzling group of Wall Street opponents to win the stay, although a divided court of appeals overturned that ruling a few months later.[24] By the time the Supreme Court decided *Landis v. North American Co.* in the winter of 1936, Rauh had again switched employers. He left the battlefields of litigation under Cohen and Corcoran for the ethereal judicial chambers of Justice Cardozo.

Cardozo

At the Supreme Court, Rauh had the satisfaction of watching Cohen and Corcoran argue the North American case on behalf of the United States and later reading Cardozo's opinion, which reversed the court of appeals and sent the suit back to the lower court with directions for a limited stay. That order clearly favored the SEC and vindicated Cohen's clever strategy of defending the holding company act.[25] The ultimate triumph for the New Dealers came two years later, when a reconstituted Supreme Court upheld the registration provisions against Bond and Share.[26]

In New Deal Washington, Rauh often found himself in the right place at the right time. By joining Cardozo in the late summer of 1936, he secured more than a front row seat for the holding company litigation. He found himself at the center of the greatest constitutional crisis since the Civil War, when Roosevelt proposed to reorganize the federal courts, including the addition of new justices of the Supreme Court. In the spring of 1936, usually by a vote of five to four, the justices had issued decisions that toppled the New Deal's program to restore agricultural prices, as well as the Guffey Coal Act, designed to stabilize the nation's bituminous coal industry.[27] These economic activities, according to the majority, were essentially local and therefore lay beyond the authority of Congress to regulate interstate commerce. For good measure, the justices also reaffirmed their constitutional objections to state minimum wage laws.[28] Cardozo, Brandeis, and Stone dissented in all three cases. Even the Republican Party criticized the minimum wage decision in its 1936 national platform.

Roosevelt did not make the Court's vetoes a central feature of his reelection campaign, but after his overwhelming victory in November he stunned the country, many of his closest advisers, and congressional leaders with a reorganization bill that called for adding additional judges to the federal bench when sitting jurists reached the age of seventy and did not retire within six months. The measure also included some desirable procedural reforms, including one that required federal judges to hear arguments from government lawyers before issuing injunctions against federal laws. But at its core, the bill would permit the president to enlarge the Supreme Court from nine to a maximum of fifteen members. Critics in the president's own party soon labeled his scheme the "Court-packing plan." The battle had been joined.

Rauh's new employer believed his brethren on the Supreme Court had been badly mistaken on the law when they struck down several New Deal measures. Cardozo admired Roosevelt, a fellow New Yorker, and sympathized deeply with the administration's reforms, a position that distinguished him from other justices, including his fellow dissenters, Brandeis and Stone. Compared to the austere and moralistic Brandeis, Cardozo conveyed patience, serenity, and courteousness, even when faced with the boorish behavior of Justice McReynolds or when assigned pedestrian cases by the chief justice, who usually kept the choice ones for himself. Frankfurter, hearing that Cardozo had been given another routine tax or patent opinion, privately denounced the chief justice as "a swine," but Cardozo took such disappointment in stride. "You know, Mr. Rauh," he would say, "some people might think this is not a very interesting case, but I think you and I can find some interest in it." It took a year before the fastidious Cardozo began to call Rauh by his first name, and that informality seemed to unsettle the justice's sense of decorum.[29]

Rauh recalled only three occasions when Cardozo's unflappable exterior cracked. The justice thought Hughes and Brandeis had acted outrageously in sending to the Senate's Judiciary Committee, without consulting the other members of the Court, a joint letter opposing Roosevelt's "Court packing" legislation. No sitting judge could favor Roosevelt's plan, he told his clerk, but the Hughes-Brandeis correspondence threatened the Court's independence by dragging it into the middle of the political fight between the president and Congress. He also directed regular criticism at Justice Butler, a former railroad attorney, who always voted to review federal employer liability cases that threatened the carriers' profits. And Cardozo became highly agitated on the evening of King Edward VIII's abdication speech, when his chauffeur's cautious driving threatened to prevent him from hearing the king's address live over the radio. With Cardozo urging his driver on, they made it to his apartment just in time for the broadcast.[30]

David Ginsburg believed that Rauh's years with Cardozo had a transforming effect upon the young attorney. You could not be around Cardozo, Ginsburg recalled, "without moving into an almost mystical, often somewhat emotional mode." After Frankfurter's basic training, Cohen's postgraduate boot camp, and Corcoran's floating political seminar, Rauh had moved into a more deliberative and contemplative arena. It provided, Ginsburg thought, "a very . . . very humanizing influence." Law school and New Deal litigation produced intellectual toughness and stamina, "but Cardozo represented poetry in life."[31]

Rauh quickly discovered that his judicial employer needed assistance from a law clerk about as much as Lou Gehrig benefited from a batting coach. After the Court's regular Saturday conference, where the justices voted on cases previously argued, he and Cardozo waited for assignments from Hughes, with the package usually delivered by messenger around six o'clock in the evening. Rauh then went home for the weekend to help Olie care for young Michael, to whom they had given the middle name Benjamin. The justice, meanwhile, wrote out his initial opinions on long yellow legal pads. On Monday morning, Cardozo presented them to his clerk with the usual caveat:

"Mr. Rauh, I have noted the relevant federal New York cases, but you should check the citations and correct my errors. You may wish to add a few cases from other jurisdictions as well, because we don't wish to appear to be too parochial." Cardozo, his clerk soon discovered, had an encyclopedic memory of the cases and their exact citation, a talent that made checking for errors redundant.[32]

In addition to the routine work of checking citations, Cardozo gave Rauh the more challenging task of preparing advisory memoranda on the hundreds of petitions for certiorari that reached the High Court each year. Cardozo wanted each memo to offer a recommendation that he either vote to hear the case or reject it. When briefs arrived prior to oral argument, Rauh often wrote a memo to Cardozo that set forth his views on the merits. One of his initial efforts in this area proved less than a triumph.

Three American citizens, charged with crimes in France, had fled back to the United States. The New York police who arrested them turned the suspects over to federal immigration officials pending extradition under a 1909 treaty between the United States and France. That pact declared that the two countries "mutually agree to deliver up persons who, having been charged with or convicted of any of the crimes specified . . . shall seek an asylum or be found within the territories of the other." But another provision stated that "neither of the contracting Parties shall be bound to deliver up its own citizens or subjects under . . . this convention."

Immigration officials argued that these provisions gave them (and by implication the president) sufficient authority to send the accused back to France. A federal district judge had agreed with the government that the statute vested discretion in the president with respect to the extradition of American citizens. He declined to issue the writ of habeas corpus for the accused. A federal appeals court, however, had reversed the district court and ruled that the treaty did not give the president such discretion.

Rauh wrote a memo vigorously supporting the district court and presidential discretion, based on his reading of similar treaty provisions and past practices. However, when he asked Cardozo about the case following the Saturday conference where a vote had been taken, the justice replied: "That was a brilliant piece of writing you did, Mr. Rauh, but unfortunately the Court did not agree with your interpretation of the treaty." When the published opinion came down a few weeks later, he discovered that not a single member of the Court, including Cardozo, had supported his interpretation.[33]

Except as it revealed the Hughes Court's abiding distrust of presidential power, the obscure *Valentine* extradition case did not raise profound constitutional issues. As Cardozo's clerk, sounding board, and surrogate son, however, Rauh observed closely the Court's internal conflicts and its final constitutional showdown with the New Deal. In past years, Cardozo had met regularly with Brandeis and Stone on Friday evenings to plot their strategy for the Saturday conference against the Court's conservatives. When Brandeis endorsed Hughes's letter to the Judiciary Committee, however, it chilled that relationship. Cardozo also expressed dismay when Hughes and Justice Owen Roberts suddenly adopted a new perspective on the commerce clause that began to diffuse the court's confrontation with the New Deal.

Affirming the New Deal

The turning point came shortly after Roosevelt's stunning reelection triumph, when Roberts voted to sustain a minimum wage law from Washington State. Then in April, to everyone's surprise, including Cardozo and Rauh, the justices upheld the National Labor Relations Act by a five-to-four vote, with Roberts and Hughes voting with the majority and endorsing a broad conception of the commerce power and regulation of labor relations that the majority had appeared to reject six months earlier in the *Carter Coal* case. "You know, Mr. Rauh," Cardozo said wistfully, as they journeyed home that evening from the Saturday conference, "they didn't even mention *Carter Coal* or give it a decent burial."[34]

Hughes and company helped the Senate bury Roosevelt's judicial reorganization bill in May, however, when the justices voted five to four to sustain the landmark Social Security Act and Justice Van Devanter announced his retirement, a decision that opened the way for Roosevelt to nominate his first justice. As was his habit, Hughes had kept the minimum wage and *Labor Board* cases for himself, but he now assigned the Social Security opinion to Cardozo. With Rauh's assistance, that opinion became one Cardozo's finest, a constitutional landmark with respect to Congress's powers of taxation and spending.

In the summer of 1937, as Joe, Olie, and Michael vacationed on Lake Michigan, he received a packet of certiorari petitions from Cardozo along with a note that celebrated "our grand and glorious victory." The justice meant not only the Social Security decision, but the defeat of FDR's judicial reorganization plan, which the Senate had rejected in early July. The reforms of the New Deal that Cardozo admired survived. And so did the Court and the principle of judicial independence. But the justice would not serve another term.

In December 1937, soon after writing his opinion in *Palko v. Connecticut*,[35] Cardozo was struck by a devastating case of herpes zoster, or shingles, an affliction that quickly spread to his heart. In the absence of immediate family (except for numerous cousins who appeared infrequently), his physician, Worth Daniels; a close friend, Irving Lehman; and Joe Rauh became the justice's caregivers, all forced to watch the slow, painful physical disintegration of a man they loved. "I remember . . . seeing Joe as he [Cardozo] shrank near death," Ginsburg recalled. "This was bound to sear him [Rauh] in ways that, I think, still hold."[36]

Rauh now functioned as law clerk, secretary, nurse, and even on one occasion as surrogate justice of the Supreme Court. On the day his illness struck, Cardozo had written an opinion in one of several appeals from the Court of Claims that again challenged the authority of Congress to pay government bondholders in legal tender rather than gold. Before the opinion came down, however, Stone wrote a concurrence that Rauh believed weakened Cardozo's central holding. He knew Cardozo could respond to Stone's position, but Dr. Worth refused to allow him to see the ailing justice that day. Rauh therefore wrote what he believed would have been Cardozo's answer, wove it into the original opinion, and took his effort to the chief justice. Hughes, ever anxious to expedite the Court's business, did not blink an eye at this bit of nonjudicial intervention. Decades later, Rauh could not identify his own separate contribution to the opinion, so seamlessly had he woven it into Cardozo's original.[37]

Taking the Justice Home

In an effort to stave off what others thought inevitable, Lehman insisted in the spring of 1938 that Cardozo be taken to his estate in Westchester, New York. On a stretcher, Cardozo, enduring much pain, was lifted by railroad employees through the windows of a train for the journey north from Washington. When the train stopped in Grand Central Station, he asked if they had arrived yet in New York. Assured by Lehman and Rauh that he was now back in his home state, Cardozo seemed momentarily to gain vitality from the news, but soon suffered another relapse.

The three Rauhs now moved in with Cardozo's relatives, who lived nearby, while Joe resumed his limited duties at the Lehman estate, where the justice lay dying. Not one to abandon hope, Lehman prevailed upon Albert Einstein to visit for several days in the belief he might rekindle Cardozo's enthusiasm and save his life. But not even the world's most renowned scientist could rescue America's greatest jurist, who died quietly on July 9, 1939.

Not long after the funeral, Lehman told Rauh he could take any item he wished from the justice's apartment. Joe chose a letter from Holmes to Cardozo, written in 1928, which the justice had framed and kept in his office. Rauh noticed that Cardozo often glanced at the letter when he entered the room. Holmes had written in response to an earlier letter from Cardozo that said: "I believe in all sincerity that you are the greatest Judge that ever lived, though of course, it may be that in the Stone Age or beyond there was juridical genius or achievement beyond our ken today."

Holmes had soon replied: "The only ground that warrants a man for thinking that he is not living in a fool's paradise, if he ventures such a hope, is the voice of a few masters, among whom you hold a conspicuous place."[38]

In later life, Rauh acquired the original Cardozo letter and, along with Holmes's response, it became one of his most treasured possessions. He donated both letters to Harvard Law School in the 1980s. The constitutional crisis of the New Deal passed away in the summer of 1938, but so had one of the Constitution's ablest defenders. His last law clerk needed a new assignment.

CHAPTER FOUR

"YOUNG WHIPPERSNAPPER"

What we need is somebody with a little realism and less idealism. . . .
a man of his age, brilliant though he may be, does not have that
mature judgment that comes only with age.

— CONGRESSMAN ALBERT J. ENGLE OF MICHIGAN

Fair Labor Standards

Cardozo's slow, painful death in 1937–38 mirrored the fate of the New Deal
and Roosevelt's wounded presidency. Except for a few procedural reforms,
the Senate killed FDR's judicial reorganization bill. The House of Representatives held hostage the administration's proposal for federal wages and
hours legislation. In March 1938, the House also gutted the president's
sweeping plan to reorganize the executive branch. And finally, the president's
own decision to reduce federal expenditures for relief and public works, coupled with a hike in interest rates by the Federal Reserve Board, plunged the
nation into what critics soon called "the Roosevelt recession." In terms of unemployment, business failures, and falling prices, the winter of 1937–38 recalled for many Americans the bitter years of 1932–33.

FDR fought back and rallied his troops in the spring and summer of 1938
for what proved to be one last burst of domestic reform before events in Europe created other priorities. Lubricated by White House patronage and
persuasion, the House finally passed the Fair Labor Standards Act and Roosevelt signed it into law a month before Cardozo died. He nominated Frankfurter to fill Cardozo's seat on the Court. Joe Rauh soon found himself
drafted to advance FDR's new agenda and two causes that remained central
to his legal career. First deployed to implement the new Fair Labor Standards Act, he pursued economic justice for the African-American redcap

porters in his hometown of Cincinnati. Later, sent to the struggling Federal Communications Commission (FCC), he waged a guerrilla war on behalf of civil liberties by opposing FDR's effort to expand federal wiretapping.

The first assignment came from Cohen and Frankfurter soon after FDR signed the FLSA. Rauh's former professor, Calvert Magruder, general counsel of the newly created Wage and Hour Division, needed good lawyers immediately who could fashion the agency's rules and regulations and draft bulletins that detailed the scope of the new statute. Rauh seemed a perfect choice because Cohen had given him the job of reviewing several drafts of the FLSA legislation during its long journey through Congress.[1]

The new law mandated an initial minimum wage of twenty-five cents an hour for workers in interstate commerce, limited hours to forty-four in a week, and banned child labor. It represented Cohen's final, monumental contribution to the New Deal. Southern legislators, fearing the loss of their region's low-wage advantage in industries such as textiles, nearly killed the measure in Congress. It also drew muted opposition from key union leaders such as John L. Lewis of the mine workers, who resented any government intrusion into wage negotiations. Secretary of labor Frances Perkins, a major proponent of the legislation, also chafed over its final form, which placed implementation in a Wage and Hour Division housed in her department, but under an independent administrator.[2]

The Ordeal of Enforcement

The FLSA's labored birth, Rauh soon discovered, would be exceeded by the daunting problems of its enforcement. Congressmen had taken exquisite care to exempt large categories of workers from any coverage, especially domestic employees, agricultural workers, and those classified as executives, administrators, professionals, and outside salespersons, but the precise boundaries of these legislative exemptions remained unclear. When Magruder placed him in charge of drafting Wage and Hour legal opinions, Rauh had to develop quick answers to a long list of thorny questions.

Were cannery workers who labored near a farm, for example, "within the area of production" and therefore exempt? What about night watchmen and elevator operators employed by large companies? Were they employees "engaged in commerce" or "in the production of goods for commerce," as the statute required? Could the statute regulate or abolish "homework," manufacturing inside a household, which utilized many children between the ages of eight and ten?

Did Congress intend to exclude tips from the calculation of the minimum wage? What role should trade associations play in adjusting the wage upward to a forty-cent minimum by 1945? Did the FLSA give federal regulators any jurisdiction over company stores?

As Cohen and Frankfurter had hoped, Rauh pushed for the broadest possible coverage. Even at twenty-five cents an hour the measure would help the poorest workers, especially in the South, where politicians like "Cotton Ed" Smith had once declared, "It takes only 50 cents a day to live reasonably and comfortably."[3] He could count on the support of Irv Levy, his associate in the Opinion Section and his future law partner, and he soon found another staunch ally in Carroll Daugherty, chief of the FLSA's economics division, who shared his concern to boost the income of workers at the bottom of the wage pile. "The survival of democracy," Rauh wrote in the spring of 1939, "is dependent upon its ability to satisfy the just demands of its people for food and shelter and for the dignity of honest work. It is my belief that only a more social and economic democracy than ours today will be able to solve these fundamental problems." Unless America solved its economic problems, he noted, "Our Bill of Rights will be submerged under the morass of false promises. The freedom to go hungry and ill-clad are but sad birthrights, rights for which men will not struggle."[4]

When Magruder left the General Counsel's Office, however, Rauh found himself in conflict with his successor, George McNulty and with Secretary Perkins, both of whom feared a backlash in Congress if the division moved too quickly on the wage front. And he received little encouragement from the parade of Wage and Hour administrators, beginning with Elmer Andrews and Colonel Philip Fleming, who spent most of their time fighting bureaucratic turf wars with Perkins.

The breadth of Rauh's opinions soon incurred the wrath of farmers, assorted business interests, mine workers, and members of Congress. Congress intended the law to cover even the employees of farmer-owned warehouses where growers stored their potatoes and beans, Rauh opined, unless the business employed fewer than seven workers. They would not be exempt under the law's "area of production" clause relating to processing plants. He also ruled that while the statute exempted certain retail occupations, it did not exempt the warehouse or delivery workers of national chain retailers, such as Schrafft's Ice Cream. On behalf of the outraged growers, Congressman Albert Engle of Michigan attacked the Wage and Hour Division for sponsoring what he called "a children's hour" when it gave decision-making authority to a twenty-nine-year-old lawyer four years out of law school. "What we need,"

Engle told the House of Representatives, "is somebody with a little realism and less idealism. . . . I submit that a man of his age, brilliant though he may be, does not have that mature judgment that comes only with age."[5]

Even stalwart New Dealers denounced Rauh and his legal staff. Normally a reliable liberal and a rising power on the House Judiciary Committee, Emanuel Celler of New York counted Schrafft's Ice Cream among his private clients. He steamed into Rauh's office brandishing a letter to the ice cream company informing it that it was in violation of the law.

"Are you Joseph L. Rauh Jr.?" Celler demanded.

"Yes, sir."

"How dare you browbeat these people," he began, and then launched into a tirade against the Opinion Section and what he called its draconian enforcement of the Fair Labor Standards Act.

Several years later, when Congress debated and passed the Administrative Procedure Act, a conservative effort to curb the rule-making power of many New Deal agencies, Celler defended the new order of administrative law, but he could not resist taking another jibe at what he called those "young whippersnappers," like Joseph L. Rauh Jr., who ran the Wage and Hour Division.[6]

In order to circumvent the law, many employers attempted to reclassify their workers into a variety of exempt categories. Rauh proposed to counter this stratagem with a regulation denying classification as an executive, professional, or administrator to any employee who earned less than thirty dollars a week. Anticipating an outcry from businessmen, Magruder urged his deputy to hold an informal hearing before issuing a bulletin on the problem. With the exception of Cyrus Ching, head of United States Rubber, who said the requirement seemed reasonable, the assembled corporate leaders denounced the regulation. Rauh issued it anyway.[7]

Opposition to Rauh's rulings came from other than corporate executives. Several days after he released a bulletin that placed all company-owned stores operated by coal operators on a nonprofit basis when employers continued to deduct such purchases from wages, he received an urgent summons to Andrews's office. The chief of the Wage and Hour Division meekly introduced him to an angry man identified only as Mr. Lewis, who represented the United Mine Workers Union. Assuming this to be *the great* John L. Lewis, czar of the UMW, founder of the CIO, Rauh endured a tongue-lashing over his company-store regulation.

"Young man," Mr. Lewis said, "you have just wrecked all of our existing union contracts. We always negotiate with the coal operators about prices in their stores and we don't want any goddamned federal bureaucrat telling us what to do!"

Having made his point, Lewis stormed out. Rauh assumed his regulation would not survive, until Andrews referred to their visitor as Danny Lewis, the great John L.'s little brother. Less intimidated by the encounter, Rauh spoke up in defense of his proposal. Lewis and the United Mine Workers, he argued, had taken care of their own members by negotiating sweetheart deals with major coal operators to set store prices, but these agreements did little to protect the nonunion miners in places like Alabama and Kentucky. Rauh's company-store regulations, requiring employers to open up their books and justify their prices, remained in force.[8]

Launching the Fair Labor Standards Act in 1938–39 presented Rauh and other New Deal lawyers with their most daunting task since reopening the banks or initiating the National Recovery Act in 1933. Olie sometimes did not see her husband except at a hurried breakfast. Asked in nursery school what his father did for a living, Michael Rauh replied, "He comes home at four in the morning." Joe Rauh's day suddenly grew even longer when rumors began to circulate that Roosevelt might nominate Frankfurter to the Cardozo vacancy on the Supreme Court. After leaving the Wage and Hour Division each evening, Rauh rushed to Cohen's office, where Ben and Corcoran directed the efforts of a small but loyal army of Frankfurter protégés, all devoted to his nomination.

Felix's Barbershop

Despite Frankfurter's faithful service to the New Deal and long friendship with the president dating back to World War I, his nomination presented FDR with several problems. Democratic leaders in the Midwest and West clamored for a justice from their part of the country. With Brandeis still sitting, Frankfurter would become the second justice from Massachusetts and the second Jew, a prospect that alarmed rabid anti-Semites and also disturbed a number of influential Jews, led by Arthur Hays Sulzberger of the influential *New York Times*. Sulzberger and others argued that a Frankfurter appointment would further inflame ethnic and religious prejudice. Over lunch at Hyde Park, the president even informed Frankfurter that the appointment would likely go to "someone west of the Mississippi."[9]

The professor and his supporters refused to surrender. With the aid of Rauh and other acolytes, Cohen and Corcoran launched a two-front campaign. Whenever rumors of other candidates surfaced, they researched the man's judicial or political record and fed negative information to allies in the Senate or the White House. Rauh took special pleasure in combing through the opinions of Judge Harold M. Stephens on the D.C. Circuit Court, a favorite with some western senators, but a jurist who had usually sided with the holding companies against the SEC. Rauh's research deflated Stephens's balloon.

While shooting down other candidates, Frankfurter's supporters bombarded the president with glowing accounts of their candidate's many virtues. Harold Ickes and others told Roosevelt that Frankfurter's appointment would permit the New Dealers to dominate the Supreme Court for a generation. Robert Jackson informed the president that only Frankfurter had the legal firepower to stand up to Chief Justice Hughes. Everywhere he went, FDR later told Frankfurter, "People said I should nominate you," to which Cohen later quipped: "Of course they did. That's what Tommy and I told them to say."[10] And when he later recounted the story to friends and wrote his memoirs, Frankfurter claimed that Roosevelt's phone call offering him the nomination in December came as a complete surprise. When he heard that version of events, Cohen whined, "How can Felix say such a thing? We were on the phone to him every night in Cambridge reporting our activities."[11]

Rauh knew that Frankfurter would join the Court in midterm and need an experienced law clerk who required little tutoring in the institution's arcane routines. He suspected Felix would turn to him, but he hated to leave the Wage and Hour Division, where his influence had grown and where major policy conflicts loomed. For a lawyer who relished a good fight, writing certiorari memos again did not compare with squaring off against disgruntled congressmen, the mine workers, or the textile companies.

Despite the objections of a few right-wing cranks who branded Frankfurter as a central figure in the Bolsheviks' plot to destroy America, his nomination breezed through the Senate. The anticipated phone call came and Rauh took a leave from Wage and Hour to join the new justice. He soon found himself plowing through stacks of certiorari petitions while Katherine Hiss, wife of Frankfurter's former student Donald Hiss, answered the piles of congratulatory letters and telegrams that arrived at the office each day. Olie Rauh took care of the Frankfurters' immediate household needs. She found them a spacious home to rent on Prospect Street in Georgetown, one with a sweeping view of the Potomac River that satisfied the claustrophobic Marion. She also hired a housekeeper and cook who remained with the couple for decades.

Rauh quickly discovered that clerking for the voluble, irrepressible Frankfurter bore little resemblance to his time with the ascetic Cardozo.

People soon dubbed their suite of offices at the new Supreme Court building "Felix's barbershop," where a steady clientele of journalists, federal bureaucrats, young lawyers, and politicians came seeking advice, influence, and the latest gossip, domestic and foreign. Cardozo had loathed most social occasions and seldom ventured out after dark. Frankfurter rarely declined an invitation. "He's living the life of Riley," reported his former colleague Thomas Reed Powell. At the Court and at home the justice remained tethered to the telephone. Her husband, Marion remarked, had one thousand best friends. A reporter remarked that being Felix Frankfurter "is in itself a violent form of exercise."[12]

Rauh carried a heavy workload during his short tenure as a result of the justice's extensive off-the-bench activities, which included frequent visits to the White House. Fortunately, the Court's docket in early 1939 did not present cases of pressing constitutional significance. In his first two opinions for the Court, Frankfurter, the apostle of judicial restraint and the ardent New Dealer, declared a Florida statute unconstitutional and ruled against the Roosevelt administration by holding that Congress had not granted the Reconstruction Finance Corporation immunity from tort liability.[13] "Ain't it funny," he wrote to Reed Powell, "that in the first opinion which it fell to me to deliver, I declared a statute unconstitutional, and that in the next one I was agin the government!"[14]

By the time he joined Frankfurter, Rauh had worked at four different jobs in three years. He had become one of the New Deal's emergency firemen, someone who changed offices and assignments as often as he changed clothes. But the excitement of working for Cohen, Corcoran, Cardozo, and Frankfurter did not always quench the desire for a more sustained focus and sense of achievement. Grateful for Rauh's temporary help, Frankfurter also sensed his former student's restiveness. Brandeis's illness and retirement in early 1939 presented the justice with the opportunity to reshuffle law clerks and restore Rauh to his unfinished work at the Wage and Hour Division.

"Marion and I think you're not happy here," Frankfurter told him one morning. "We think you'd be happier with Magruder. If I took Butch Fisher [Brandeis's last clerk, Adrian S. Fisher], would you go back to Wage and Hour?" Rauh jumped at the offer.[15]

Fighting for the Redcaps

The bureaucratic squabbles between the Labor Department and its satellite had not abated when Rauh returned as assistant general counsel at the Wage and Hour Division in the spring of 1939. He found himself again supporting important litigation that tested the scope of the division's powers as well as its capacity to resist political pressure from influential congressmen.

Because it was so widespread and decentralized, home manufacturing that utilized subcontractors presented Rauh and his staff with vexing enforcement problems. These employers routinely flouted the law's provisions. The Bull Durham Company, for example, hired children as young as eight to hand stitch its tobacco pouches through a putting-out system, but the company kept no employment records. Rauh pushed for the abolition of such practices when he and Levy focused initially on the knitwear industry and brought indictments against its major employers, all of whom were Jews. Not wishing to stoke the fires of anti-Semitism, they asked Cohen for advice. Indict them, Cohen said, "but make certain the newspapers report that those prosecuting them are Irving Levy and Joseph L. Rauh."[16]

Many employers had fought against the statute and its enforcement, but northern textile producers supported efforts to fix an industry-wide wage that would reduce the competitive edge of southern mills. When the administrator accepted recommendations of an industry advisory committee and set a new minimum wage for textile workers at 32.5 cents an hour beginning in 1940, Opp Cotton Mills, a small Alabama company backed by the powerful Southern Cotton Manufacturers Association, launched the first constitutional assault against the Fair Labor Standards Act. The suit challenged the use of such committees and the adoption of industry-wide standards.

Rauh and Levy devoted long hours to the *Opp Cotton Mills* brief in the summer of 1939 and savored the administration's complete victory a year later, when both the Fifth Circuit Court of Appeals and the Supreme Court sustained the statute, the use of industry advisory panels, and the administrator's wage decision for the textile industry. *Opp Cotton Mills* represented a major constitutional triumph for the New Deal and economic gains for some of America's poorest, most exploited workers.[17]

During Rauh's tenure in the Opinion Section, the Wage and Hour Division compiled an impressive string of legal victories that extended the benefits of the FLSA to millions of workers, but he suffered a notable defeat in his hometown of Cincinnati when he battled the Union Terminal Company on behalf of railway porters. The combined interests of labor and African-Americans made this case a high priority for Rauh.

Prior to 1938, companies such as the Union Terminal kept African-American porters stranded in an economic twilight zone. Union Terminal furnished the red caps with uniforms and permitted porters to handle passengers' baggage, but refused to recognize them as employees or pay them compensation. From the perspective of the companies, redcaps functioned as independent contractors who lived off their tips. Shortly before the Fair Labor Standards Act took effect, however, the Interstate Commerce Commission ruled that the redcaps were employees under the Railway Labor Act, which automatically entitled them to both collective bargaining privileges and the federal minimum wage.

Faced with the ICC ruling, Union Terminal and other companies quickly adopted a new policy under which all tips received by the redcaps would be treated as wages—and as income to the employee—with the porters required to keep records and the companies making up any difference between the tips and the federal minimum wage. Rauh and his colleagues believed this ploy violated the clear intent of the Fair Labor Standards Act and filed suit in Cincinnati to stop it. The redcaps also sued Union Terminal and other companies to recover what they alleged were back wages owed to them under the FLSA, exclusive of tips, which they regarded as gratuities.

Rauh traveled to Cincinnati to argue the government's case before federal district judge John H. Druffel, who displayed little sympathy for the redcaps and hostility to the young lawyer representing the United States. Druffel refused to enjoin Union Terminal, reprimanded Rauh for putting his hands in his pockets during oral argument, and threatened him with contempt when he turned away from the bench to retrieve a few legal papers. "Don't you dare turn your back on me," snapped the judge.[18]

If Rauh had any doubt that race played a major role in the struggle between the Cincinnati redcaps and their local employers, he received a quick reminder during the court's lunchtime recess when he and Frank McKnight, an African-American employed by the Wage and Hour Division, ordered sandwiches at a nearby diner. Rauh's roast beef came on a plate, but McKnight's was served in a paper bag. Surrounded by other patrons with sullen expressions, Rauh picked up the plate and the bag and invited McKnight to sit down at an empty table. They hastily downed their sandwiches, with Rauh expecting the owner to call the police any minute.[19]

The redcaps and Rauh fared little better before other district judges or the Fifth Circuit Court of Appeals, which sustained the employers' policy of treating tips as wages. In 1942, long after Rauh had left the Wage and Hour Division, a divided Supreme Court affirmed these rulings as well. In dissent, Justice Hugo Black denounced the employers' policy as a "deception" through which the companies evaded a statutory duty under the Fair Labor Standards Act and placed the responsibility for paying wages on railroad passengers. Rauh could not have expressed it better.[20]

By the fall of 1939, however, events in Europe absorbed more and more of Rauh's attention. Like other Jews in the administration, he had watched with rising anger and frustration the unfolding disaster in Germany and Europe since 1933: the systematic repression of Jews, trade unions, and liberals; Hitler's reoccupation of the Rhineland in 1936; the formation of the Rome-Berlin Axis; the annexation of Austria; and the extinction of Czechoslovakia following the Munich Conference in 1938. Then, on September 1, 1939, German panzers rolled across the Polish border while the Luftwaffe rained bombs on Warsaw. Two days later, England and France declared war on Germany. From that day forward, Rauh attempted to join the real fight against Hitler as soon as possible. But his growing frustration with McNulty in the General Counsel's Office and sudden vacancies at the Federal Communications Commission put those battle plans on hold.

Fly's FCC

Corcoran, now the New Deal's chief legal recruiter, remained more concerned with legal problems at the FCC and elsewhere in the government than with Adolf Hitler. At that agency, he complained to Rauh, "We've got [Lawrence] Fly and six idiots. . . .You and Tel[ford] Taylor are going over to help shape it up." Rauh cleaned out his desk at Wage and Hour, penned a note of explanation to his old allies, and took up a fresh assignment as legal counsel to James Lawrence "Larry" Fly. FDR's new man on the FCC, Fly had launched an epic battle to strengthen federal regulation of the radio, telegraph, and cable industries.

Like Corcoran, his classmate at Harvard Law School, Fly had joined the federal government during the Hoover years as a special assistant to the attorney general. A devout liberal, he easily made the transition to the New Deal and became one of its star litigators in cases representing the Agricultural Adjustment Administration, the National Labor Board, and the Tennessee Valley Authority.[21] Roosevelt appointed Fly as chairman of the FCC with the hope he might inject some spark into an agency that had stalled on the New Deal's reform agenda. Fly had recruited one able assistant in Nathan David, and with the addition of Rauh and Taylor, he had the legal firepower to move forward on his program for the agency.

Fly and his young legal team gave American consumers an important victory early in Rauh's tenure, when they took on the infant television-manufacturing industry, which hoped to saturate the market with primitive receiver sets that would pressure the government to accept the industry's technological standards and limit future innovations. Fly made it clear that the FCC would promote a variety of different systems, an announcement that sent sales plummeting and outraged companies like General Electric.[22]

In harmony with FDR's newfound love for antitrust laws, Fly and his staff also launched an investigation into the monopolistic practices of the major radio networks and broadcast stations. The FCC's Chain Broadcasting Report, written by Rauh and Taylor, sent a tremor through the industry by recommending the breakup of NBC's Red and Blue networks, the creation of a new competitor (ABC), a cap on the number of stations owned by a single network, and a limit on the broadcast range of major stations. Although they stood to gain from the breakup of NBC, William Paley and the leaders of CBS fought the plan because they feared it would weaken their grip on local CBS affiliates.[23]

The Rauh-Taylor report, later adopted by the FCC, almost died before it reached the mimeograph machine. As they polished the document in Fly's office, a call came from the White House. Someone in the FCC had leaked a draft of the report to Mark Ethridge, the publisher of the *Louisville Courier Journal,* a strong supporter of FDR, whose holdings included the largest radio station in Louisville. Ethridge had complained bitterly to Roosevelt. "Mark tells me there's a lot of bad stuff in that report," Roosevelt told Fly, and he suggested that the document be sent over to the White House for further study.

Fearful that FDR's political advisers would water down their recommendations, Rauh and Taylor shook their heads and slipped Fly a note: "Tell him [Roosevelt] the report is already set in type." Without skipping the beat, Fly lied to the president about the report's status. Rauh and Taylor rushed the document to completion a few hours later, and the FCC quickly approved it, including provisions that gave local stations more choice over programs and eliminated exclusive broadcast rights to events such as the World Series.[24]

A few scattered advertisements for television sets in 1940 and a visit to Dumont Laboratories alerted Rauh to the coming revolution in broadcasting and the potential threat of monopoly presented by joint control of radio, newspaper, and television enterprises in a single city. As early as 1937, one member of Congress, Otha Wearin of Iowa, had introduced legislation to prohibit newspaper ownership or control of radio broadcasting stations. At the urging of Rauh and Taylor, Fly persuaded the other FCC commissioners to hold hearings on the subject, but in the wake of the chain broadcasting controversy, the full commission declined to take action.[25] The commissioners also shied away from another proposal generated by Fly's staff that would have required television development on the abundant UHF frequencies rather than the limited and prized VHF.[26]

Resisting the President

Rauh worked vigorously under Corcoran's direction for Roosevelt's reelection in 1940, including extensive research on Wendell Willkie's career that gave the White House important ammunition against the Republican candidate. Rauh worshiped FDR, but this reverence had its limits when it clashed with civil liberties. Roosevelt crossed that line in 1940–41, when he attempted to push through Congress new legislation to authorize wiretapping by the Department of Justice. The Federal Communications Act of 1934 prohibited any person "not authorized by the sender" from intercepting "any communication" and divulging its contents. In 1937 and again in 1939, the Supreme Court ruled that this ban applied to federal law enforcement officials and required the exclusion from federal courts of evidence obtained by wiretaps. Frankfurter, perhaps the most zealous defender of the Fourth Amendment on the Court, had authored the second opinion. But faced with a war in Europe and concerned about foreign espionage, Roosevelt made it clear he wanted Congress to overrule the Court.[27]

With equal passion, civil libertarians vowed to defeat the president's bill, scheduled for hearings before Congressman Hatton Summers's House Judiciary Committee. They counted in their ranks Max Lowenthal, an old ally of Frankfurter and Brandeis, whose wide-ranging legal activities and liberal views had earned him the enmity of Wall Street bankers and the Federal Bureau of Investigation. Soon after the Judiciary Committee began hearings, Lowenthal turned up one morning at Rauh's office.

"You've got to help kill this thing," he said. "You've got to get Fly to testify against the bill. I know he has great confidence in your judgment." When Rauh raised the obvious problem of Fly, an administration appointee, testifying against the president's own bill, Lowenthal assured him that FDR had gone on a fishing trip in the Caribbean and would never find out. Besides, Lowenthal added, Fly could always testify behind closed doors in executive session![28]

With heavy arm-twisting by Rauh and others on the FCC staff, Fly agreed to testify against the wiretapping bill, but only in a closed executive session, as Lowenthal had promised. Rauh briefed his boss on the fine points of the Supreme Court decisions and accompanied him to the hearing, where Fly's presentation made a powerful impression on the committee. The FCC conspirators, however, failed to count on Roosevelt's own intelligence network. A few days later, Fly called Rauh into his office and handed him a telegram from the president, then cruising somewhere in the Caribbean. Roosevelt demanded a copy of Fly's remarks before the House committee. A member of the Judiciary Committee had leaked Fly's testimony to the Department of Justice, where someone had forwarded a radio message to FDR's fishing companion, attorney general Robert Jackson, an ardent supporter of the wiretapping bill.

For the next forty-eight hours, Rauh and Fly attempted to draft a memorandum to the president explaining, as he later put it, "how you can commit treason without fault." Their many versions ran the gamut from open defiance to abject apology, but finally concluded somewhere in the middle. Rauh dutifully delivered the document to the White House and kept his fingers crossed. Fly, of course, had been confirmed by the Senate, and could not be touched, but other heads, including Rauh's, might roll. He breathed easier when his boss came back from his next scheduled meeting with the president. Fly assured him that Roosevelt had been annoyed, but not furious about their rebellion.[29]

The president responded mildly because he prevailed on the wiretapping issue, but not through new legislation. Congress refused to pass the proposed measure, but FDR, encouraged by FBI director J. Edgar Hoover, ordered the Department of Justice to begin wiretapping individuals and groups on national security grounds without the statute. That secret order served as the legal justification for electronic surveillance by the executive branch for the next thirty years.[30]

The fall of France in the summer of 1940 and the beginning of the Battle of Britain brought America a step closer to the war when Roosevelt proposed to transfer aged American destroyers to England. FDR drafted Cohen for legal advice, and Cohen turned to Rauh as his research assistant. The National Defense Appropriations Act signed by FDR in 1940 permitted only the transfer of military equipment that had been certified as not essential for national defense, a provision that seemed to prohibit what FDR wished to do: to transfer ships of World War I vintage to the British. On the other hand, an exchange of these aging destroyers for valuable British naval bases in Newfoundland, Bermuda, and the British West Indies could be defended as boosting American national security in the hemisphere. Despite a contrary opinion from the attorney general, stiff resistance in Congress, and a blizzard of hostile editorials, Cohen's brief, which justified the destroyers-for-bases deal, carried the day with Roosevelt. The exchange, soon endorsed by candidate Willkie, symbolized the sunset of American isolation.[31]

Following the election, Roosevelt announced a bolder strategy for assisting the British and, he asserted, one designed to keep America out of the war. Instead of the cash-and-carry requirements of the existing neutrality laws, he proposed legislation to permit England to lease war materials from the United States. His Lend-Lease program, FDR told the country, would "eliminate the dollar sign" and turn America into "the great arsenal of democracy." With the support of most southern Democrats, Willkie, and other moderate Republicans, the $7 billion Lend-Lease bill went through Congress on March 11, 1941, over the opposition of diehard isolationists.

"This decision," the president said, "is the end of any attempt at appeasement . . . the end of compromise with tyranny and the forces of oppression." Like others who had long advocated more vigorous efforts against Hitler, Rauh cheered Roosevelt's fighting words and Lend-Lease. A few weeks later, Oscar Cox, known around the administration as Harry Hopkins's lawyer and the new general counsel at the Lend-Lease Administration, invited him to become his deputy. The New Dealer would go to war at last.[32]

CHAPTER FIVE

JOE, PRICH, AND PHIL

And put something in the order for the Poles, too.
The President is getting a lot of heat from the Poles,
who are not being hired in Buffalo.
— WAYNE COY TO JOE RAUH, JUNE 1941

Three Musketeers

Joe Rauh, twenty-nine in 1940, married with a young son, was the old man of
the trio. Edward Prichard Jr., five years younger, tipped the scales at a hefty
250 pounds. A native of Kentucky, he had been an academic whiz at Princeton and then impressed the faculty at Harvard Law School with his sharp
mind. During World War II he would write and implement some of the
country's pivotal economic policies. Many of his friends believed Prich would
one day be a United States senator, but in the late 1940s he went to prison for
stuffing a ballot box in an inconsequential Kentucky election. The third
young man, Philip Leslie Graham, also twenty-five, tall, lean, and handsome,
had been born in South Dakota and raised in Florida. He once flunked out
of the University of Florida, but graduated like the others from Harvard Law
School. He married the daughter of a former governor of the Federal Reserve Board and became the publisher of the *Washington Post*. Phil Graham
also seemed destined for high political office, perhaps president. Instead,
suffering from manic-depression, he blew his brains out with a shotgun in
1963.

   Despite their varied social roots, Rauh, Prichard, and Graham shared
many things in common on the eve of the nation's involvement in World War
II: acolytes of Felix Frankfurter, they loved liberal, Democratic politics, admired FDR, and hated fascism. They were the three musketeers of the late

New Deal as it transitioned to war, and they became as important to that moment as Cohen, Corcoran, and Landis had been earlier.

In signing on with Cox and the new Lend-Lease Administration, Rauh joined an extraordinary legal team poised to help a president who had become Dr. Win the War rather than Dr. New Deal. As general counsel, the indefatigable Cox, a graduate of Yale Law School, functioned both as the top lawyer in the Office of Emergency Management, which had been created to coordinate war production, and as assistant solicitor general of the United States with the responsibility of giving legal advice to the president. A Jew from Maine who wore his faith so lightly that his own son did not know his beliefs until he died, Cox labored tirelessly to reverse the administration's lamentable policies with regard to Jewish refugees. His past employment with Henry Morgenthau Jr. at Treasury and with Harry Hopkins also gave Cox unchallenged access to the White House.[1]

As Cox's assistant, Rauh soon learned that he wore a second hat as deputy general counsel to Wayne Coy, a free-wheeling Indiana native whom Roosevelt had placed in charge of something called the Office of Emergency Management. A protégé of former Indiana governor Paul McNutt, Coy also carried the official title of special assistant to the president. He shared Cox's hatred of the Nazis and had an unusual knack for breaking up bureaucratic logjams, a talent that appealed to FDR, who relied on Coy to get things done despite the tangled lines of authority that the president himself had created in the sprawling war production effort. Cox had recruited into Lend-Lease a phalanx of able young lawyers in addition to Rauh: Abe Feller, a future general counsel to the United Nations, Lloyd Cutler, legal adviser to several presidents, George Ball, a future undersecretary of state, and Prichard and Graham, who became Rauh's closest friends and allies in the bureaucratic wars to speed military aid to Britain and the Soviet Union and prepare America for war.

Prichard arrived at Harvard Law School several years after Rauh with an affected southern drawl and a gift for friendship, practical jokes, mimicry, and penetrating legal analysis. Unlike many Frankfurter students, the whimsical Kentuckian displayed considerable irreverence toward his mentor and seldom felt the need to flaunt his brilliance as a lawyer. These qualities, combined with his zest for political intrigue, charmed Frankfurter, who brought him to the Supreme Court as his third law clerk following Rauh and Butch Fisher.[2]

In Cambridge and Washington, Frankfurter sponsored, encouraged, and promoted the careers of many Jews, but he always had a place in his large, floating entourage for talented non-Jews, including Dean Acheson, Corcoran, the Hiss brothers, Alger and Donald, and Prichard. Some of his Jewish students complained that Frankfurter worked them harder because he knew they would face more social discrimination. But Jew or non-Jew, they all had to be brainy, sophisticated, filled with promise, and devoted to him. Phil Graham fit those requirements. He did everything effortlessly. He dazzled in the classroom, ranked tenth in a law school class of four hundred, and soon ran the *Harvard Law Review* as a combination intellectual salon and all-night fraternity party.

Frankfurter brought Graham to Washington first as Justice Stanley Reed's clerk in 1939–40, with the promise of moving him to his own chambers the following year. Nothing appeared beyond Graham's abilities or vaulting ambition. At Hockley House, where Graham lived with Prichard and others, he first met and wooed Katharine Meyer, the tall, shy daughter of Eugene Meyer, publisher of the then-struggling *Washington Post.* He married her a year later, with Frankfurter's blessing that included allowing Graham to continue as his law clerk, a violation of his general rule against such marital entanglement that he had only broken out of necessity for Joe and Olie.[3]

Self-Inflicted Wound

On serious issues related to the Supreme Court and the Constitution the trio of Rauh, Prich, and Graham learned they had little influence on their justice. Frankfurter relished goading them into vigorous arguments, but he also hated to lose these debates. And once he made up his mind, he seldom changed course and usually became intolerant of dissent. Soon after the Graham-Meyer wedding, Rauh and the other clerks failed to prevent Frankfurter's self-inflicted wound in the first flag-salute case, an opinion that undermined his influence on the Court and destroyed his reputation among liberals. With newspapers reporting German troops on the outskirts of Paris, Prich rang the doorbell at the Rauh home on Courtland Place late at night, distraught and out of breath.

"Read this," he said, slumping into a chair and handing Rauh a draft of Frankfurter's proposed opinion for the Court in *Minersville School District v. Gobitis.*[4]

Frankfurter proposed to sustain the school board's policy of expelling the children of Jehovah's Witnesses who refused on religious grounds to salute the American flag each morning. That secular, patriotic ritual, Frankfurter argued, did not restrict the free exercise of their religion any more than it burdened the faith of Catholics, Baptists, or Jews. Construing the free exercise clause narrowly, he argued that the school board had not attempted to

inculcate any sectarian religious views or prevent the Witnesses from practicing their religion. With war on the horizon, the school board sought to promote unity among its diverse ethnic population, a legitimate and noble effort
that did not offend the Constitution. Chief Justice Hughes as well as Hugo
Black and William O. Douglas endorsed the opinion. Only Justice Harlan F.
Stone would dissent. Prichard, shocked by Frankfurter's insensitivity to the
religious issues and by his florid, patriotic rhetoric, had tried without success
to change the justice's mind. After reading the draft opinion, Rauh shared his
dismay.

"You've got to do something to stop this disaster," Prich pleaded. "He
won't listen to me and he won't listen to Phil [Graham] either. If this opinion
comes down it will destroy him."

Rauh agreed the opinion would produce two casualties: the Bill of Rights
and the justice's reputation. Frankfurter had written, he recalled years later,
"about the worst pile of crap I had ever read." At the same time, he saw no
path of intervention without compromising the sacred rules of confidential-
ity that governed relations between law clerks and justices.

"Well, Prich," he said, "what do I say when he asks me how I know about
his opinion? Do I tell him that you showed it to me? Do I tell him that a little bird brought it over?"

"Oh, God, no," Prich said. "You can't tell him that. He'd kill me and
Phil."[5]

On that note, the campaign to save Justice Frankfurter from himself collapsed. Over a powerful dissent by Stone, the Court marched off to Frankfurter's drumbeat in *Gobitis,* a result that generated vigilantism against the
Witnesses when superpatriots read the decision as an invitation to brutalize
religious dissenters who refused to salute the flag. Two years later, partly in
response to such violence, the Court, speaking through Justice Robert Jackson, overruled *Gobitis* by a vote of six to three, but not without Frankfurter
writing a belligerent, self-serving dissent that eroded further his standing
with New Deal liberals.[6] By the time the Court repudiated Frankfurter's
views in *Gobitis,* he had pulled up the drawbridge and stopped discussing
cases with former clerks.

Breaking Bottlenecks

Even during the distractions of Supreme Court decisions, the three young
lawyers never lost sight of their most important objective: defeat Hitler by
boosting vital war production for England and the Soviet Union. At their
Lend-Lease post Rauh and Graham had access to top secret military pro-

curement figures from the War Department. The data shocked them: in August 1941 only a single, four-engine bomber had been delivered to the air force, while Roosevelt continued to fill his speeches with allusions to "clouds of bombers" that would be sent to the British and the Russians. Armed with the Rauh-Graham intelligence, Coy fired off a memo to the White House informing the president about this production bottleneck. He received back a blunt note from Hopkins, who questioned Coy's figures and said that the president should not be annoyed with such flawed reports.

Convinced their figures were correct, Rauh and Graham went to see Bob Nathan, an economist and statistical wizard in the Office of Production Management, who turned ashen after reviewing his own data. "You gave Coy the wrong information," Nathan said. Their hearts sank, until he added: "There were *no* four-engine bombers delivered in August. Not one. Zero!"[7] During a late-afternoon session in Cox's office, Feller added to their statistical arsenal by noting that when you compared the War Department figures with reports in *Time* magazine from the Russian front, the Soviets had lost in the first week of fighting more equipment than the United States then had on order with American factories.

Rauh and Graham also parlayed this information into a meeting between Dean Acheson and Walter Reuther, the young, charismatic leader of the United Auto Workers and a zealous antifascist, who had put forward a bold plan to immediately convert the nation's automobile plants to the full-time production of airplanes. With Acheson's sponsorship, Reuther made a dramatic speech to the Washington Press Club in which he outlined his proposal and predicted that through it the United States could turn out 500 planes per day. "England's battles, it used to be said, were won on the playing fields of Eton," Reuther told a radio audience. "America's can be won on the assembly lines of Detroit."[8]

Reuther denounced the auto companies, which waited for the government to finance the construction of new factories and continued to make profits on the sale of new cars and home appliances. But his attacks could not budge the aircraft manufacturers, the Army Air Corps, or William S. Knudsen, president of General Motors and an old nemesis. "Mr. Knudsen and I met previously, on opposite sides of the table," Reuther said. "I thought on this matter of national defense we might sit on the same side. I was mistaken." Roosevelt also hesitated to clamp down on auto production and adopt Reuther's policies—until Pearl Harbor.[9]

Although the young lawyers in Lend-Lease seldom lacked access to those in higher authority through Frankfurter, they often took matters into their own hands without going up the chain of command. Rauh and fellow staffer

William Stix Wasserman improvised that strategy. On leave from Wall Street, Bill Wasserman loathed Hitler and did not tolerate behavior that interfered with fighting Nazis. When Rauh showed him a Lend-Lease requisition for gold-mining equipment bound for the government in South Africa, Wasserman hit the roof. That same equipment, he said, could be put to far better use digging copper and other vital war metals. They lodged a protest with Cox, who said he could do little about the deal and reminded them that Jan Smuts, the South African prime minister, had powerful friends in Washington, including the president and Justice Frankfurter.

Undaunted, Wasserman shoved Rauh into a cab and ordered the driver to take them across town to the South African embassy. After informing startled secretaries that they came on official government business from Lend-Lease, the two men were given a speedy appointment with the ambassador, who greeted them warmly until Wasserman pulled the requisition for gold-mining equipment from his pocket and launched into a speech.

"I'm here on behalf of the general war effort," he barked, "and in that capacity I ask you to withdraw this request!"

Neither amused nor impressed, the South African official ordered them out of his office with a stream of profanity. By the time Rauh and Wasserman returned to their office at Lend-Lease, secretary of state Cordell Hull had already called their boss, Edward Stettinius, to express his anger at two obscure government employees harassing the South African ambassador. Cox softened the blow by telling them that Stettinius could not stop laughing when he recounted Hull's indignation. But as Cox had predicted, Jan Smuts got his gold-mining equipment.[10]

Opposition on the Left

Even when they fully engaged their own resources and mobilized allies in the government, Rauh and his band of war hawks faced formidable obstacles to the mobilization effort, none more so than the American Communist Party, which exercised important influence in the labor movement. Until Hitler invaded the Soviet Union in June 1941, American Communists, following a script from Moscow, denounced Roosevelt as a warmonger, heaped abuse on Great Britain, made alliance with the right-wing leaders of America First, and encouraged workers in various industries to strike, notably at North American Aviation near Los Angeles. Rauh knew several CP members in the Wage and Hour Division and at the National Labor Relations Board, where its secretary, Nathan Witt, actively recruited for the party. Their indifference to Hitler shocked him. So, too, did their opposition to FDR's reelection in 1940 and their support for Wall Street's candidate, Willkie.

The party's antiwar stance before the summer of 1941 left ideological scars on Rauh that were deepened when Roosevelt asked Coy to begin preparing legislation that would give him authority to commandeer vital war necessities, including machine tools, private airplanes, and boats. Coy gave the drafting assignment to Cox and Rauh and told them to secure support from labor, especially the CIO president, Philip Murray. When Rauh read their proposed legislation over the phone to the CIO's general counsel, Lee Pressman, this member of the CP denounced the idea. "As far as I'm concerned," Pressman fumed, "British imperialism is every bit as great a threat to the world as Hitler." Pressman added that he would discuss the matter with Murray, "but I can give you his answer now—no!"[11]

"Mr. Randolph Says It Isn't Strong Enough"

In early June 1941 Coy's secretary told Rauh to meet their boss in the executive office building next to the White House. There he found Coy and Bernard Gladieux, a lawyer from the Bureau of the Budget. Coy immediately asked Rauh, "Can you write an executive order?" When Rauh replied that it wouldn't be too difficult once he knew something about the subject matter, Coy told him that FDR wanted an executive order to prohibit racial discrimination by companies that received federal defense contracts.

"Some guy named Randolph is complaining about discrimination against Negroes at defense plants," Coy continued, "and he's threatening a big protest march here unless we do something about it. The Budget Bureau is waiting for the order. We need it right now." As he turned to go, Coy added: "And put something in the order for the Poles, too. The President is getting a lot of heat from the Poles, who are not being hired in Buffalo."[12]

Gladieux and Rauh set to work writing the executive order that would ban discrimination in defense industries and government contracting on grounds of "race, creed, or color." Following Coy's orders to "do something for the Poles in Buffalo," Rauh added the words "national origins" as well. He made history with the first appearance of that concept in America's public law.

At the time, Rauh knew very little about Asa Philip Randolph, the soft-spoken, tenacious African-American who had forged the Brotherhood of Sleeping Car Porters into an effective labor union and who had calmly told FDR a few days earlier that he would march 100,000 people down Pennsylvania Avenue unless the president broke the color barrier in federal procurement. Nor did Rauh know immediately that the president had given his wife, Eleanor, and New York congressman Fiorello LaGuardia the task of brokering a deal with Randolph to call off the march, in exchange for the executive order.

Rauh and Gladieux labored all night to produce a draft of the executive order and presented it to Coy next morning. He approved it, but told them to await further instructions. A few hours later, Coy called on the telephone with disappointing news.

"Mr. Randolph says it isn't strong enough," Coy reported. "You better try again."

The two lawyers went back to work, modifying a phrase here and there and inserting some new language. Coy picked up the new draft, rushed out, and called them back a second time.

"Randolph says it's still not strong enough," he repeated.

By now exhausted and impatient, Rauh exploded: "Who the hell is this fellow Randolph you're all so scared of? Is he a lawyer?"

When Coy explained Randolph's role and that Mrs. Roosevelt and LaGuardia functioned as intermediaries, Rauh hit upon a solution.

"Tell them to ask Mr. Randolph how he would like us to strengthen the order," he proposed.

Only a few minutes passed before Coy called back. As Rauh had guessed, Randolph knew that if he kept asking for more changes, the lawyers would strengthen the language for him.

"Mr. Randolph," Coy reported, "says it's exactly right." Roosevelt quickly signed the historic document and created a Fair Employment Practices Committee to enforce its provisions. Randolph, much to the chagrin of some supporters, called off the march on Washington. For the first time since Lincoln, the White House had acted through law to advance the civil rights of African-Americans. And Mr. Randolph and Mr. Rauh, total strangers, had begun a long and important relationship at arm's length.[13]

"Action Truly Necessary for the National Safety"

With their executive order, Rauh and Gladieux helped to advance the long march toward racial justice in America. By failing to stop another executive order shortly after Pearl Harbor, Rauh shared responsibility for the worst civil liberties disaster in the nation's history—the forced evacuation and internment of Japanese-American citizens on the West Coast.

Despite the absence of evidence suggesting disloyalty among resident

Japanese, influential Californians led by Governor Culbert Olson, Attorney General Earl Warren, and major newspapers such as the *Los Angeles Times* demanded their removal from the West Coast on grounds of both national security and domestic peace. Japanese-Americans, according to these leaders of opinion, constituted a dangerous fifth column and could not be protected from angry white vigilantes. John L. DeWitt, commanding general of the Western Defense Command who believed "a Jap is a Jap," endorsed evacuation with enthusiasm, as did the provost marshall general, Allen W. Gullion.

At the highest levels of the Roosevelt administration, conflict and indecision about restrictions prevailed for several months. Secretary of War Henry Stimson and his chief deputy John McCloy, ultimately convinced by DeWitt and the Californians of the necessity for removal, hesitated at first to take that drastic step, especially with regard to native-born Japanese. "We cannot discriminate among our citizens on the ground of racial origin," Stimson initially confided to his diary.[14] Attorney general Francis Biddle and his assistant, Jim Rowe, backed by FBI director Hoover, argued that the government should not succumb to white hysteria by trampling on the rights of Japanese-Americans.

When Biddle looked for support beyond his own department, he solicited advice from Cohen and Cox, who in turn enlisted Rauh's help in preparing a memorandum for the attorney general. The Cohen-Cox-Rauh team regarded removal and internment of the Japanese as a legal and political disaster that would weaken the nation's war effort by sparking protest and confirming the country's disunity. But they also feared that, given the pressure from West Coast politicians, DeWitt's position would prevail unless some compromise could be found between the call for removal and the dithering in Biddle's department. California congressmen, Cohen said, were spreading fantastic lies, including allegations that white citizens had "had their throats cut by Japanese traitors."[15]

The Cohen-Cox-Rauh memorandum found some constitutional sanction for restrictions on American citizens in the event of genuine military necessity. "Action truly necessary for the national safety," they wrote, "cannot lightly be assumed to be barred [by] constitutional constructions which would make our Constitution in time of war either unworkable or non-existent."[16] Those were dangerous words, and the three lawyers soon regretted writing them. Their memo concluded by offering what they believed to be less drastic remedies: a dawn-to-dusk curfew, exclusion from certain limited geographic areas, and "special reservations . . . at safe distances from the West Coast . . . where American citizens of Japanese extraction could go voluntarily and where they could be usefully employed and live under special restrictions."[17]

Disaster followed. Despite its intentions, the Cohen-Cox-Rauh memo weakened Biddle's resolve and undermined lawyers in the Department of Justice who vigorously opposed removal and internment of the Japanese. It gave sanction to the selective curfew regulations soon promulgated under Roosevelt's Executive Order 9066, which gave military commanders broad authority to impose them against a single group of American citizens. The proposal for "limited geographic areas" and "special reservations" where citizens of Japanese extraction could "go voluntarily" soon became the forced exclusion and relocation of those who refused to leave their homes, farms, universities, and fishing boats.

McCloy, a principal architect of the removal, attempted to justify the decision to Frankfurter. "In many respects I think it is a real protection to the Japanese to do this. . . . Innocent lives are of course uprooted, and it is a most painful thing to bear and to administer, but since when has war distinguished between the innocent and the guilty?" At the same time, McCloy revealed the racist dimensions of the removal by noting that with respect to Italian and German aliens in the United States "some kind of board will be set up so that such refugees and perhaps others can be exempted from the evacuation orders."[18]

In defense of Cohen, Cox, and Rauh it can be argued that their entire discussion rested on claims by the military of necessity, claims they might have questioned, but which neither they nor later courts had the will or means to challenge in 1941. Military necessity on the West Coast did not in fact exist, except in the fevered imaginations of certain officials in the War Department and politicians in California. Despite contrary advice from the FBI, those voices continued to manufacture a Japanese-American threat throughout the litigation before the Supreme Court.[19] In retrospect, Rauh believed that their efforts had been too weak and inadequate, that Biddle had probably been right, and that their memo helped fuel exclusion and removal. Several days after the forced evacuation of 120,000 Japanese-American citizens got under way, Cohen showed Rauh a newspaper photo of a small Japanese boy leaning out of a train window waving an American flag. Cohen had tears in his eyes.[20]

CHAPTER SIX

NEW DEALER AT WAR

Joe Rauh came in today in a uniform and looked as
pleased as punch.

—JOHN MCCLOY TO FELIX FRANKFURTER

Pearl Harbor

On Sunday afternoon, December 7, 1941, Joe Rauh and Phil Graham stood
on the corner of Virginia Avenue and Twenty-second Street waiting for a
traffic light to change. Back in their Lend-Lease offices, an unfinished report
to Congress awaited revisions. They had labored over the document with Oscar Cox all morning, but the conclusion seemed inescapable and grim. Since
the passage of Lend-Lease in March, only a trickle of military equipment had
reached England and the Soviet Union. The ammunition in Roosevelt's "arsenal of democracy" remained sparse, and projections for future factory de-
liveries did not inspire more confidence.

Neither man had much enthusiasm for finishing the report, until Larry
Fly's car came roaring through the intersection with its radio blaring. Spot-
ting Rauh and Graham, he slammed on the brakes, threw the car into reverse, and shouted to them:

"The Japanese have bombed Pearl Harbor."

"Thank God!" Rauh yelled in a voice that could be heard above the whine
of Fly's engine.

"Jesus, Joe, shut up!" Graham snapped. Even on the nearly deserted
street, he feared the remark would be interpreted as enthusiasm for war at a
time when Americans had surely died in Hawaii.[1]

As Fly sped off, Rauh and Graham, now revitalized to complete their report, raced back to Lend-Lease. The hard statistics that documented a
lethargic past could not be altered, but after huddling with Cox, they rewrote

the introduction to suggest a future of boundless war production and inevitable victory. Before noon on December 7 their report told a tale of pessimism that suggested the United States could not move a sailboat into Thailand. By four in the afternoon, when the document went to the printer, Rauh and Graham had rhetorically painted the skies of the Pacific full of American aircraft.

Rauh and Graham wanted to fight Hitler with more than Lend-Lease documents, but when they attempted to enlist, their efforts generated only amusement from recruiting officers in the air force, who pointed out that they were both too old, married with children, and plagued by poor eyesight. Rauh then appealed to Frankfurter to use his influence with Henry Stimson, Harry Hopkins, or even FDR to find him an active duty position in the real war. When Frankfurter failed to produce immediate results, Rauh's impatience generated a caustic response from the justice, who told his former clerk, "Hold your horses . . . after all, your parents endowed you with sense in order that you may use it." He would approach Hopkins, the justice said, but only at the right moment. "I understand your restlessness," Frankfurter concluded. "Some of the rest of us are restless too because we spend a good deal of time on matters further removed from the war than is true of your work. So, I say, hold your horses."[2]

Rauh returned the volley. After nine weeks of waiting, he did not need what he called an "outrageous" lecture on patience. Frankfurter had promised to see Hopkins immediately and now seemed prepared "to stall the whole matter further." Rauh even threatened to take his case to Corcoran, saying, "I refuse to enter another period of agonizing pain watching others fight the war for me."[3] Frankfurter returned Rauh's letter with a blunt, handwritten note: "Dear Joe—I'm sure you will want to tear this up yourself & not have me do it. Ever yours, FF."[4]

In early spring, however, armed with letters from Stimson and Frankfurter, Rauh finally secured a commission on General Douglas MacArthur's staff in Australia. "Joe Rauh came in today in a uniform and looked as pleased as punch," McCloy reported to Frankfurter. "I am delighted that this worked out so well."[5] Before sailing for the South Pacific as a first lieutenant, however, he waged one final, unsuccessful battle at Lend-Lease and had his first encounter with J. Edgar Hoover's Federal Bureau of Investigation.

"Alleged to Be Affiliated with Subversive Organizations"

At a Lend-Lease staff meeting in early February 1942, Rauh learned that England had secured approval from the agency to reexport mining equip-

ment to Spain, where it would be used by the huge Rio Tinto copper company, a British-owned and operated enterprise and one of the major industrial interests that supported General Francisco Franco's fascist dictatorship.
Britain's attempt to curry favor with Franco, who had crushed the Spanish
Republic, infuriated Rauh, and he suspected that little copper from Rio
Tinto would ever reach the Allies. His vocal opposition did not impress others in the meeting, who noted the deal had been approved at the highest levels in the White House. Why offend the British, they said.[6]

Blocked in official channels, Rauh took a page from Ed Prichard's book
on the art of influencing policy through friendly journalists. He leaked the
Rio Tinto debate, including portions of Lend-Lease documents, to I. F.
Stone at the left-leaning *P.M.*, a New York daily. Stone had acquired a reputation as one of the country's best investigative reporters, but also as a journalist with friends and contacts in the American Communist Party. When
Stone's story entitled "British Tory Scheme for Helping Franco" hit the
newsstands, officials at the British Embassy became furious and protested
loudly to the State Department. State demanded an explanation from Lend-
Lease, and Stettinius called in the FBI to track down the source of the leak.[7]

Stettinius had no sooner sat down with Special Agent McKee to explore
the problem than Cox interrupted their meeting to announce that "the presence of representatives of the FBI in the building had become known to the
guilty party, and that he had confessed his full participation in the disclosure
of the confidential information to I. J. [*sic*] Stone."[8] After Cox identified
Rauh as "the guilty party," Stettinius telephoned Hoover to ask that the investigation cease. He assured the FBI's director that Lend-Lease would handle the affair internally. Further, he asked Hoover to keep Rauh's identity
confidential, because "he did not wish to ruin the career of this young man in
Washington."[9] A few days later, however, McKee reported to Hoover that
Stettinius "did not know what disposition would be made as to RAUH but
did say that he would probably be transferred to another unit."[10]

Unfortunately for Rauh, his confession sparked renewed interest by the
FBI in an investigation that dated back to January 1941. The Bureau had
then learned that his name appeared on a membership list of the Washington Committee for Democratic Action, a group branded as a "subversive organization" by the House Special Committee on Un-American Activities,
chaired by Red-baiting congressman Martin Dies Jr. of Texas.[11]

Dies detested the New Deal, labor unions, and immigrants. Dangerous
radicals ran the administration, he believed, and Congress should pass new
laws barring Communists from government employment and should outlaw
the party.[12] In the fall of 1941, Dies had turned over to the Department of

Justice and the FBI a list of sixty-six individuals employed by the federal government that he and his committee "alleged to be affiliated with subversive
organizations." Rauh's name appeared on that list. By the time the Rio Tinto
inquiry began, therefore, Hoover's sleuths had already gathered information
on Rauh for four months and wanted to interview him. At the same time,
Robert Stripling, secretary to the House committee, had recently told the
FBI that the committee's original information was incorrect—Rauh's name
did not appear on the membership list of the Washington Committee for
Democratic Action. But Olie Rauh had been listed as a member.[13]

The new FBI's investigation, based on the old Dies committee list,
turned up one "confidential informant" who branded Rauh as "communistically inclined." Another reported him to be "extremely antagonistic toward
the present social system." And a third advised the Bureau that one of Rauh's
friends "openly championed" the cause of the Soviet Union in its war against
Finland because the Finns were "capitalistic and should be liquidated."
Some of Rauh's associates and friends, the Bureau also noted, could be found
on the membership lists of suspect organizations such as the American Peace
Mobilization and the National Federation for Constitutional Liberties.[14]

The "confidential informant" who believed Rauh to be "communistically
inclined" also reported that the target of the inquiry subscribed to periodi-
cals that "seemed to advocate socialistic and Communistic doctrines," although the informant could not recall their names. As final proof of Rauh's
radical tendencies, the informant noted that the couple violated the rules of
their apartment building when they "advised their negro maid . . . to enter
the front door when coming to work" and that Mrs. Rauh had complained to
the management that "negro maids and other help should be given the same
consideration as white tenants." This "equality of race" behavior led the informant to conclude that Rauh adhered "to some extent [to the] principles of
the Communist Party."[15]

After salting its file with damaging accusations against Rauh, the FBI synopsis of its investigation noted that other "confidential informants" described
the young lawyer as "capable, energetic, thoroughly loyal to the United
States and not associated in any way with individuals or organizations seeking
to overthrow the present form of Government." One person interviewed
thought it "an outrage to talk about such a good American or to question his
loyalty," while another described Rauh as "belligerently patriotic."[16]

Interviewed by the FBI on March 12, 1942, Rauh admitted membership
in the Automobile Club, but denied that he had ever been affiliated with the
Washington Committee for Democratic Action or any other organization
listed by the Dies committee. With specific reference to the American Peace

Mobilization, he told the agent, "I opposed everything they stood for." All the "peace groups" he added, "were a pain in the neck to me and if any are around now, they still would be."[17]

When Hoover sent a copy of the FBI's report to Coy it brought an immediate, angry response. Any accusation that Rauh belonged to or had been associated with organizations bent on the overthrow of the government, Coy told Hoover, "is absurd and fantastic." Since he had been the source of the observation about Rauh's "belligerent patriotism," Coy concluded that his young associate had been "completely exonerated of the charges as made against him by the Dies Committee."[18]

Told of Coy's complaints, Hoover admitted that the synopsis in Rauh's case had been "unfortunately phrased and not as complete as it should have been." He pledged to eliminate such summaries in the future and to have the entire reports read and evaluated "in accordance with [their] true worth," a promise the director never kept. Hoover soon closed the Dies investigation on Rauh by noting that "no administrative action is being taken against the subject." From that day forward, however, the Rio Tinto leak and the Dies accusations served as introductions to every subsequent FBI probe into Rauh's activities and beliefs.[19]

Across the Pacific

Despite pleas from Coy and Dave Ginsburg, who feared for his safety and needed his legal skills in Washington, Rauh remained determined to join the war in the South Pacific. Coy wanted him full time at the Office of Emergency Management and the White House. Ginsburg held out the enticing offer of a post with the Office of Price Administration, where he would supervise a thousand lawyers, a job that finally went to Tom Emerson.

Eager for active duty, Rauh turned down both jobs and boarded a ship for Australia in May, saying good-bye to Olie and his two sons, Michael, six, and Carl, two. Via Hawaii, Fiji, Auckland, New Zealand, and Tasmania, the voyage to Melbourne took thirty days through rough water in the Tasman Sea. For at least half of the trip they lacked convoy protection. Directly north of Rauh's route, one of the decisive naval battles of the war raged in the Coral Sea, where the United States Navy inflicted heavy losses on a Japanese armada and secured Australia's supply lines to America.[20]

When they docked in Auckland, Rauh discovered to his chagrin that all the local bars had been cleaned out by British sailors whose ship had been torpedoed a few days earlier. The disappointment grew when he reported for duty at General MacArthur's general headquarters in Sidney. General Dicky

Marshall, the deputy chief of staff, took one look at his resume and sent him to Colonel Joseph Stevenson, who managed the Lend-Lease operation between the United States and Australia, the same administrative job he had fled in Washington. Eager for real combat, Rauh found himself anchored to another desk. Now he expedited shipments that brought American sewing machines to Australia, where women turned out uniforms for the army.

His luck took a turn for the better one evening in Sidney near the end of 1942, when he met a fellow officer who described a clandestine military operation based at Port Moresby on the southern tip of Papua New Guinea. There, he was told, small boats ran supplies to the Allied troops leapfrogging their way up the 1,500-mile New Guinea coast en route to the Philippines, MacArthur's ultimate destination. With General Marshall's reluctant assent and a quick promotion, Captain Rauh went to the front at Port Moresby.[21]

He dodged only a few stray bullets while loading boats and supplying troops from Port Moresby, but at last he felt a part of the real war. The Japanese cut short his limited combat role, however, when they shot down Colonel Stevenson's plane over the Solomon Islands, leaving no survivors. General Marshall had little choice but to order Captain Rauh back to Australia to manage the Lend-Lease program. For the remainder of the Pacific War, he never again got close to the front, but the return to Sidney soon presented a different challenge—the opportunity to try his first criminal case.

Rauh for the Defense

After a few days back behind a desk, Rauh looked up one morning to see a sergeant whose crisp salute did not hide a stricken demeanor. The sergeant pleaded with him to come to the stockade. There he found the former chief of the motor pool, who had killed an Australian citizen while driving intoxicated on the wrong side of the road in a jeep taken without permission. The jailed chief now faced a court martial charge for second-degree murder, and he begged Rauh to take his case.

"I've never tried a criminal case, let alone one before a military court," Joe demurred.

"But they told me you were a law clerk to two Supreme Court justices," came the response.

"That's right," Rauh admitted, "but neither of those guys could save you. I think you're going up for about ten years."

Against his better judgment, Rauh agreed to defend the sergeant. He tracked down witnesses to the accident, insisted that the court visit the scene, called on officers from MacArthur's headquarters to testify about the defendant's exemplary record, and made certain his client wore all his medals to trial. Much to Rauh's astonishment, the court acquitted the sergeant on both the murder and manslaughter counts and returned a guilty verdict only for taking a military vehicle without authorization! The court imposed a lenient six-month sentence, which ignited bitter criticism in the local press and a formal complaint from the Australian government.

Given the seriousness of the offenses and the modest sentence, Rauh did not expect further relief when he filed a petition for rehearing, but he prepared one anyway. He showed the petition to Jim Davis, chief of the civil affairs desk at the War Department, then on tour of MacArthur's headquarters. Davis, a partner in the Cleveland firm of Squires, Sanders and Dempsey, rewrote significant portions of Rauh's petition and sharpened others. Instead of granting the motion, however, the appeals court reduced the sentence on the remaining charge of unauthorized use of a military vehicle. As news of the final decision circulated through the officer's mess that evening, Abner Rosenthal, one of Rauh's friends, proposed a toast to the new king of criminal defense in the Pacific theater: "If Joe keeps appealing this," Rosenthal quipped, "Pretty soon the guy will get a silver star."[22]

Civil Affairs

Soon reassignment to the civil affairs side of MacArthur's operations compounded Rauh's frustrations. Far from the front, he faced the daunting task of training Filipino units to govern the islands following the planned American invasion. He came under the command of General Bonner Fellers, a MacArthur acolyte, whose own political views made MacArthur's seem liberal by comparison. Fellers took an instant dislike to Rauh and briefly exiled him to Sixth Army headquarters. Fortunately, Courtney Whitney, another favorite of MacArthur's, soon replaced Fellers as civil affairs chief, and he proved to be the perfect boss. Usually absorbed in the task of writing MacArthur's speeches, Whitney had little time to supervise junior officers and left them alone to run their piece of administrative turf.

Rauh also had the good luck to be teamed with Edgar G. Crossman, a senior partner at Davis, Polk in New York, who had once served on Stimson's staff in the Philippines in the 1920s. On the eve of an interview with Major General John Hildring, the War Department's chief of civil affairs, Crossman worried that he might be asked how he planned to get supplies to the Philippines, a question to which he did not have an answer. But a lieutenant colonel, Frederick Davis, told Crossman where to go: "Ask Joe Rauh," he said. Crossman took the advice and soon discovered that "in Australia, New

Guinea and the Philippines . . . Davis had the right man."[23] Joe Rauh moved supplies.

By virtue of his experience in the Philippines, Crossman convinced MacArthur to send him back to the United States to recruit skilled Filipinos and Americans who could train them. While Crossman secured new talent, Rauh received further sage advice from Ray Cramer, another civil affairs officer, who had become famous on Wall Street before the war when his Postal Telegraph Company successfully challenged Western Union's monopoly. After Rauh complained about his lack of experience for the job, Cramer pulled out a well-thumbed copy of John Hersey's *A Bell for Adano*, a first-hand account of the early days of the American invasion and occupation of Italy.

"Here, read this," Cramer said. "It's the bible of civil affairs. All you need to know is right in there."

Rauh fell asleep that night reading Hersey and thanking Cramer. From rebuilding roads and airfields to fighting disease, combating the black market, and organizing a temporary government, Hersey's volume offered a crisp introduction to civil affairs, and it read far better than War Department manuals. Italy wasn't the Philippines, but the problems that arose in Cebu or Manila in the wake of their liberation proved to be not unlike those in Taranto or Rome. "I've always said," Rauh told an interviewer many years later, "I helped write the battle plan on civil affairs for the Leyte invasion out of John Hersey's *A Bell for Adano*."[24]

The Mayor of Manila

In late October 1944, eight all-Filipino civil affairs units, trained by Rauh and Crossman, prepared to go ashore on Leyte with the Sixth Army while Admiral Chester Nimitz's armada attacked the remnants of Japan's air and sea forces in the gulf. Prior to the invasion, Carlos Romulo, the distinguished Filipino journalist and later president of the United Nations' General Assembly, delivered one of the most moving speeches Rauh had ever heard when he proclaimed that white and brown soldiers, fighting side by side, would soon restore self-government and democracy in his homeland.[25]

For six days, Rauh, Crossman, and their Filipino civil affairs unit rode in their LST from Hollandia to Leyte. They shared the ordeal with Dick Bolling, MacArthur's adjutant general, a future Missouri congressman and House majority leader. Once they hit the beach at Leyte, Rauh and Bolling lost track of each other and did not meet again for three years, until an organizational meeting in Chicago for Americans for Democratic Action.[26] The civil affairs units organized by Crossman and Rauh made a decisive contribution at the battle at Leyte when they recruited a local labor force that enlarged local airfields sufficiently for American P-38s to land on the island. With that construction, the Allies soon gained crucial air superiority over Leyte, much to the relief of both infantrymen and Nimitz's naval units. On October 23, with flashbulbs popping, MacArthur and his entourage, which included Romulo and President Sergio Osmena, waded ashore at Red Beach, Palo, Leyte.[27]

Rauh quickly discovered that reading John Hersey did not prepare him for living the experience on Leyte. While combat raged, even the most skilled and dedicated civil affairs workers remained ornaments in a larger and more chaotic military picture. Attempts to immediately introduce a new currency on Leyte quickly failed with nothing to purchase. The invasion and the Japanese retreat disrupted the local economy, and military provisions took priority over civilian needs. Fearing that American soldiers in the First Cavalry Division might rape Filipino women in Tacloban, the commanding officer ordered his troops withdrawn, including military police. To Rauh's frustration, rampaging gangs of civilians proceeded to loot the city's buildings, including two bank branches, and carted away large stores of Japanese rice and other food.[28]

Leyte, however, proved to be a simple task of reconstruction and administration compared to Manila, a city of over one million, now ravaged by both the invading Allies and the retreating Japanese. Informally designated "the mayor of Manila," Rauh arrived with his civil affairs teams in January 1945 to find bombed-out streets littered with rotting corpses, a city without water or electricity, and a population on the verge of starvation. A much-needed portable hospital unit, unloaded hastily by the navy, wound up scattered along the beach, but its cargo of alcohol had mysteriously vanished.[29]

As a substitute for rice, the dietary staple of Filipinos, the military shipped in large quantities of cracked corn to feed the population, but weevils reached the sacks first. The corn couldn't be given away. Tomas Confesor, a fearless guerrilla fighter known as "The Stormy Petrel of Congress" from his days in the Philippine legislature before the war, told Rauh that riots would soon erupt throughout Manila unless food reached the masses quickly.[30] After a survey of recent reports from army quartermasters, Rauh discovered that most of them had on hand more than the ninety-day supply of flour mandated by War Department regulations. The total oversupply topped nearly a million pounds. Mixed with coconut oil, he reasoned, the surplus flour could be turned into tortillas and temporarily solve the city's food crisis. To hasten the quartermasters' cooperation, Rauh reinterpreted the regulations to be a ceiling on flour and told them their warehouses would soon be subjected to an official investigation, with dire consequences likely to follow because of their surplus. Only one quartermaster questioned this hijacking when Rauh and his crew pulled their trucks up to his loading dock.

"Who's going to sign for all this flour, Colonel?" he asked.

"I am," said Rauh, not skipping a beat. He scribbled out an IOU and signed it Lt. Col. Joseph L. Rauh Jr. The "mayor of Manila" turned army flour into tortillas and prevented a social disaster. Decades later, Rauh still feared that one day an officer from the Pentagon would turn up on his front steps with his IOU and demand payment.[31]

As the chief civil affairs officer, Rauh constantly found himself in the middle of local political and ethnic conflicts involving rival Filipino factions or between Filipinos and Chinese, who had maintained a major presence in the economy. On the night of his arrival, Rauh received an invitation to dine with one of the leaders of the city's Chinese community. A week later a delegation of Chinese businessmen turned up at his headquarters to show him an edict signed by Tomas Confesor, which banned them from selling goods in the main Manila market.

When Rauh reminded Confesor that the Chinese had fought against Japan, the guerrilla leader launched into a tirade. The Chinese, he said, monopolized trade, defrauded his people, and impoverished others. He vowed to keep the ban in place. Rauh spent the next week persuading General Whitney and, through him, MacArthur that the anti-Chinese edict would only compound the city's economic and political woes. Responding to this plea, MacArthur invalidated it.

Manila's other businessmen, many of whom had known MacArthur or Whitney before the war, exploited that relationship by demanding that Rauh meet their immediate needs for trucks and gasoline. When the mayor failed to meet their demands, they went directly to Whitney, who took out his frustrations on the chief of civil affairs. "Goddamn it, Colonel," Whitney said to Rauh. "Get that thing settled. I don't want to be bothered by these guys. I'm writing speeches for the General!"[32]

As early as the Normandy invasion in June 1944, the War Department had established a point system for sending service personnel home. With over two years of active duty and two small children, Rauh easily qualified by January 1945. He filled out the forms and prepared to pack his bags. At 6:00 a.m. on April 12, 1945, five months before his tour of duty finally ended, someone in Rauh's barracks switched on the usual Voice of America program, which always began with three minutes of music followed by war news. On this morning, however, the station played a funeral dirge.

"Roosevelt's dead," Rauh said to the captain in the next bunk, a prediction confirmed by the broadcast that followed. In depression and war, FDR had been, as a young soldier soon expressed it for *Yank, the Army Weekly,* "the Commander-in-Chief, not only of the armed forces, but of our generation." For Rauh and others, an era ended on April 12.[33]

Another era began a few days before Rauh boarded a ship to return to the United States. On the morning of August 6, an American bomber dropped an atomic bomb on Hiroshima, a blast that incinerated four square miles of the city and killed instantly more than sixty thousand people. Over drinks in a Manila bar that evening, Rauh and Graham, then an intelligence officer on the staff of MacArthur's air chief, General George Kenney, absorbed what they both agreed was terrible news and speculated darkly on the consequences of letting the atomic genie out of the bottle.

Several days later, despite a freeze on all military travel as a result of the second atomic bombing at Nagasaki, Rauh headed home with a special priority pass arranged by MacArthur. He reached Washington on September 1, his and Olie's tenth wedding anniversary. The war in the Pacific officially ended a day later on the decks of the battleship *Missouri* in Tokyo Bay. But a new war, foreign and domestic, had already begun.

CHAPTER SEVEN

LIBERAL ANTICOMMUNIST

This . . . is military control in its worst form, under the
cloak of a civilian commission.

—JOE RAUH

The Bomb

Lt. Colonel Joe Rauh came home from the Pacific War with a chest full of
medals, but without a clear plan for his future. His uncertainty mirrored
America's transition from war to peace. Harry S Truman, an obscure United
States senator from Missouri until tapped by FDR to be his vice president a
year before, now sat in the White House, an enigma. Truman's tendency to
elevate many of his cronies to positions of influence dismayed the old New
Dealers, who regarded most of them as incompetent, corrupt, or both. Over
the next year, Truman forced the resignations of or simply fired a parade of
old New Dealers—Henry Morgenthau Jr., Francis Biddle, Frances Perkins,
Harold Ickes, Chester Bowles, and James Landis. "It's more important to
have a connection with Battery D, 129th Field Artillery [Truman's World
War I unit], than with Felix Frankfurter," quipped one observer.[1]

Many of Rauh's closest friends struggled with the same dilemma about
their immediate future. Phil Graham, offered leadership of the *Washington
Post,* hesitated because he loved to practice law and hoped to run for public
office in Florida. It required arm-twisting by Rauh, Cox, and others to persuade Graham that he could turn the paper into a leader of national opinion.[2]
Many of the New Deal's best young lawyers, once the nemesis of big business, now followed the example of Tommy Corcoran and opened firms that
specialized in helping business clients navigate through the many government agencies the same lawyers had helped to create. David Ginsburg and

Harold Leventhal launched one such venture, as did Frank Shea and Bill Gardner. Rauh took a different path, one that forecast his future in law and politics. He rejected both a large firm and corporate practice. He would have preferred to follow Ben Cohen and remain in government service, but with no such post on the horizon, he opened his own office on Jefferson Place. Several clients and their liberal causes soon knocked.

At the urging of *Post* editor Al Friendly and Edward Levy, a future president of the University of Chicago, Rauh agreed to become general counsel for an organization called the National Committee for Civilian Control of Atomic Energy, a broad coalition of scientists, academics, liberal politicians, and a few public utility leaders who feared that the U.S. military establishment would dominate all research and development connected with atomic energy. Absolute military control, they believed, would subject scientists to a regime of complete secrecy, prevent the open exchange of scientific research, and thwart efforts at the international control of atomic energy through the United Nations.

The scientists' worst fears had been realized in the fall of 1945, when Senator Edwin Johnson and Congressman Andrew May introduced a bill written largely by lawyers in the War Department. Backed by General Leslie Groves, the head of the Manhattan Project, and Robert Patterson, the new secretary of war, the Johnson-May bill vested control over all nuclear materials and facilities in an Atomic Energy Commission composed of four military and five civilians who would be appointed by the president, but serve for indefinite terms. Most alarming, the military appointees would exercise a veto over all decisions by the proposed commission.

While some atomic scientists, notably Robert Oppenheimer and Enrico Fermi, endorsed the Johnson-May bill, the proposal drew opposition from other giants of science such as Harold Urey and Leo Szilard, who spearheaded the National Committee for Civilian Control. With Rauh as its new general counsel, the National Committee for Civilian Control threw its support behind an alternative measure produced by a new Senate Committee on Atomic Energy chaired by Brian McMahon of Connecticut. McMahon's initial bill vested control over the critical fissionable materials in a nine-person commission composed entirely of civilians. It also stressed the peaceful uses of atomic energy, international controls, and the sharing of information, all ideals supported by scientists such as Szilard and Urey.

Szilard, the brilliant, iconoclastic Hungarian refugee whose overtures to Albert Einstein and Alexander Sachs initiated the American atom bomb project in 1939, became the driving intellectual force on the committee. His brother, John, would later become Rauh's law partner. Leo converted Rauh's office into a bivouac for the scientists and other activists who descended on Washington to support McMahon's bill.

The Szilard-Rauh forces counted among their allies Army Chief of Staff Dwight D. Eisenhower, who endorsed the McMahon bill, but in early February 1946, Americans awoke to news reports that Alan Nunn May, a British scientist attached to the Manhattan Project, had been a key figure in a Soviet spy ring that operated in Canada with the intention of acquiring samples of enriched uranium as well as other classified information about the atom bomb. Soon news leaks, later traced to General Groves, hinted that a similar spy ring had penetrated America's bomb project.[3]

As the clouds of the Cold War thickened, Truman threw the original McMahon bill overboard and endorsed changes that favored greater military influence and secrecy. Over the objections of its own chairman, McMahon's committee approved an amendment by Senator Arthur Vandenberg that created a military liaison board to the civilian Atomic Energy Commission with the power to appeal AEC decisions directly to the president.

Rauh attacked the Vandenberg amendment immediately. "This . . . is military control in its worst form, under the cloak of a civilian commission," he noted in a memorandum drafted to oppose the proposal. "Putting atomic energy in the hands of the military is an announcement to the rest of the world that we have chosen to use this force primarily and almost exclusively as a weapon of war."[4] The final Senate bill modified the Vandenberg proviso by vesting appeals of AEC decisions in two civilians, the secretaries of war and the navy, but the army retained control of fissionable materials and remained in charge of collecting and assessing intelligence on the development of atomic weapons elsewhere.[5] In short, the military retained a decisive veto.

Rauh accepted defeat. The final legislation was not ideal, he noted, but "there are no easy solutions to as hard a problem as this." At least it would be a civilian commission, not one dominated totally by the military. But many of Szilard's disillusioned followers thought the final version about as bad as the original Johnson-May bill.[6]

Renewed Attention from Mr. Hoover

While the battle raged in Congress over the control of atomic energy, Rauh took on two additional assignments, one out of friendship with Walter Reuther and his striking autoworkers, the other to keep his law practice afloat. Both efforts caught the attention of the FBI, which already had Rauh and members of Szilard's committee under regular surveillance. FBI scrutiny increased dramatically in the fall of 1946 when Rauh voiced criticism of the atomic bombing of Japan and Truman's strident anti-Soviet rhetoric.

Midway through the 113-day auto strike, his treasury empty, Reuther organized a national Committee to Aid the Families of GM Strikers, which solicited funds to pay the rent and purchase food for those who walked picket lines. Joe and Olie ran the Washington office, raised money for the strikers, publicized the union's bargaining position, and distributed hundreds of buttons that proclaimed: "We fight for a better tomorrow. I gave to win higher wages—no price increases." The Rauhs' allies included Eleanor Roosevelt and Oregon's liberal senator Wayne Morse, in addition to such Republican stalwarts as Harold Stassen and Henry Luce, the editor of *Time* magazine.[7]

Rauh also undertook a short-term engagement at Covington and Burling, a firm then representing the Polish Supply Mission, which sought credits from the Export-Import Bank and economic aid for refugees through the United Nations. Rauh's new Polish client soon attracted renewed attention of the FBI, which had earlier opened a file on him in response to false accusations by the Dies committee and the Rio Tinto leak at Lend-Lease. In 1946, old-line Polish diplomats such as Ludwig Reighman still represented the Supply Mission in Washington, but FBI director Hoover and his agency assumed that any nation within the new Soviet sphere of influence also promoted Joseph Stalin's plan of world conquest. The FBI's interest in Rauh peaked when it learned through "a highly confidential source" that his co-counsel at Covington and Burling was Donald Hiss, whose brother Alger, still in the State Department, had been on the Bureau's list of suspected Soviet agents since 1939.

The FBI's "highly confidential source" appears to have been an extensive wiretap on Tommy Corcoran, authorized by President Truman, who regarded Corcoran as the central figure in a wide-ranging plot by old New Dealers to "dump" him from the Democratic ticket in 1948 in favor of Supreme Court justice William O. Douglas. From the Corcoran wiretaps the FBI learned not only the financial details of the Rauh-Hiss retainer ($10,000 down and $1,500 monthly), but that Corcoran had second thoughts about his sponsorship of Rauh at Covington and Burling.

Joe Rauh's biggest fault, Corcoran told Cohen, remained his penchant for "fighting the revolution." Law firms could tolerate at least one left-winger, Corcoran said, but their old protégé appeared "entirely undisciplined" because "it is one thing to luxuriate in a Government position with such ideals, and another thing to try to carry on that way in the law business." Rauh should have avoided any role in the GM strike, Corcoran added, because the firm "will not put up with this sort of activity." After digesting this wiretapped information about Rauh's activities, Hoover scrawled at the bottom of his agent's report: "Rauh is another example of perfect 'boring from within,'" a phrase that in FBI jargon usually meant a secret Communist agent who had infiltrated elite institutions.[8]

Hoover made certain that Rauh had complied with the Foreign Agents Registration Act, and he assigned agents to watch this lawyer who worked with Alger Hiss's brother and represented the Polish Supply Mission and the Committee for Civilian Control of Atomic Energy. That combination of associates suggested to Hoover the possibility of subversive activities.[9] On the evening of October 23, 1946, at La Salle du Bois restaurant on M Street, the FBI agent tailing Rauh struck what Hoover regarded as a rich vein of treason when he overheard a spirited conversation between Rauh and two others concerning the atomic bomb, President Truman, and U.S.-Soviet relations.

According to the agent's summary, Rauh, whose "conversation was louder than that of the other two," declared that the dropping of the bomb on Japan had been "contrary to American principles of Justice." The weapon had been used too soon, he added, should not have been dropped "for destructive purposes, but . . . should have been released in such a manner as to prove its effect without the civilian destruction." Rauh attributed much of his information to Phil Graham and added that many military leaders at the time had not endorsed the unannounced use of the weapon.[10]

The agent claimed that Rauh also criticized the Truman administration's diplomatic posture vis-à-vis the Soviet Union and Eastern Europe. On the one hand, according to the agent's report, Rauh declared the United States had "double crossed Poland, and . . . should be sued for breaching the promises which we gave." On the other hand, Rauh commented, "I am very sympathetic towards the Communists. I am in complete disagreement with the American policy of pretending we want peace and at the same time preparing for war."[11]

Rauh, the report added, also criticized secretary of state James Byrnes for negotiating with the Soviets in Paris while American factories "were working night and day turning out bombs." And he praised Henry Wallace, the former vice president who had been fired by Truman in September when he suggested a softer line toward the Russians. Rauh, according to the report, said he could have written a better speech than the one Wallace gave, "but nevertheless . . . WALLACE was right."[12]

Mail Cover, Wiretaps, and "Confidential Informants"

Hoover regarded the La Salle du Bois report as confirmation of his suspicions concerning Rauh's loyalty to the United States. Three days after receiving the summary, he ordered a full-scale FBI investigation to determine "the extent of his sympathies toward the Communists and the Soviet Union . . . as well as the disposition which he might make of such information to the detriment of the United States."[13] On December 31, Special Agent Hottel received permission from Hoover to place a mail cover on Rauh.[14] For the next eight months, employing a mail cover, wiretaps, and interviews with assorted "confidential informants," Hoover's sleuths added many new pages to Rauh's official FBI file.

The Bureau discovered, for example, that the Rauhs maintained a checking account at the Hamilton National Bank on Pennsylvania Avenue. As of April 1946, their balance was $889.65. Olie Rauh had recently written checks to the United Negro College Fund, the National Child Labor Committee, the National Committee to Aid Families of GM Strikers, *The Nation* magazine, and the *New Republic*.[15] The FBI also discovered that from his law office on Jefferson Place, Rauh had spoken by telephone with, among others, David Niles, special assistant to Truman, Chester Bowles, the former chief of OPA, Richard Salant, "reported to be a member of the National Lawyers Guild as of January, 1939," and Gardner Jackson, "known to have Communist sympathies and . . . reported to have been a member of the Communist Party at one time."[16]

The FBI's Washington office called upon special agents in New York, Boston, Los Angeles, Dallas, Philadelphia, Houston, Louisville, Cincinnati, and Chicago to provide information about Rauh's mail correspondents and telephone contacts, who included Judge Irving Lehman's widow, singer Frank Sinatra's former booking agent, Alfred Levy, and Harry S. Dube, publisher of *Circus Magazine,* the official publication of Ringling Brothers, Barnum and Bailey Circus. But this fishing expedition, like the others, failed to turn up a single Soviet agent or subversive organization. Finally, in early September 1947, the Bureau had to confess that "inasmuch as this investigation has failed to reflect any actual connection between subject [Rauh] and the Communist Party and has failed to indicate any activity in Russian matters this case is being closed."[17] The case might be closed, but not Rauh's file.

Americans for Democratic Action

The winter of 1946–47 brought Rauh and other exiled New Deal liberals to a crossroads. They felt abandoned by Truman, who cashiered their friends, lacked a coherent domestic agenda, and whose foreign policy played only anti-Soviet chords. Shortly after Christmas, the first challenge to Truman took shape in New York City with the formation of the Progressive Citizens of America (PCA), a merger of the National Citizens Political Action Committee (NCPAC) and the Independent Citizens Committee of Artists, Scientists, and Professionals (ICCASP). These two antifascist organizations had embraced liberals, socialists, and Communists during the struggle against Hitler and fascism. By the time of the merger, however, the Communists and their allies held the balance of power in both NCPAC and ICCASP. While denouncing right-wing dictatorships in Spain and Argentina, neither NCPAC, ICCASP, nor the new platform of Progressive Citizens of America condemned abuses of civil liberties in the Soviet Union or Soviet conduct in Eastern Europe.[18]

PCA vowed to accept all members from the left, whether liberal, socialist, or Communist, and stressed the dangers of fascism, monopoly capital, and American imperialism. Within a short period of time, the Communists and the die-hard Wallace supporters dominated PCA. Many stalwart New Dealers and liberals, including Harold Ickes and Morris Cooke, refused to follow Wallace. They had abandoned NCPAC and ICCASP even before the merger, disillusioned by the influence of the Communists.[19]

Among other American liberals, James Loeb and Reinhold Niebuhr doubted the possibility of a progressive coalition with an American Communist Party that always danced to Stalin's tune. In 1941, Loeb, a former socialist, translator of Alexandrian poetry, and future publisher of the *Adirondack Enterprise*, and Niebuhr, the country's most formative theologian of human limitations, organized the Union for Democratic Action (UDA), which combined an antifascist foreign policy with a progressive domestic agenda and vigorous opposition to Communism.

Loeb and Niebuhr knew they walked a fine line and risked accusations of "Red-baiting" when they decided their new, expanded organization—soon named Americans for Democratic Action (ADA)—would be unequivocally noncommunist, but not stridently anticommunist. "We reject any association with Communists or sympathizers with communism in the United States as completely as we reject any association with Fascists or their sympathizers," the ADA's founding document stressed. Loeb, a future ambassador to Peru, rejected what he called "the stifling and paralyzing influence of the Communists and their apologists in America." Further, he wrote, "No movement that maintains a double standard on the issue of human liberty can lay claim to the American liberal tradition."[20]

Beginning in 1946, Loeb and Niebuhr recruited, one by one, a talented group of like-minded, anti-Stalinist liberals: James Wechsler, an influential journalist, who had quit *PM* and joined the *New York Post* because of what he regarded as *PM*'s dogmatic pro-Soviet editorial position; Arthur M. Schlesinger Jr., the brightest new star in the historical profession, whose book *The Age of Jackson* had recently won the Pulitzer Prize and who had equated Communist dictatorship with fascism in a widely read *Life* magazine article.[21] Eager to counter the influence of the Communist Party in organized labor, Loeb also brought into this planning group Boris Shiskin from the American Federation of Labor and George Weaver of the CIO.

Loeb recruited Rauh into the ADA, and the latter's Washington home soon became a regular meeting place for the budding ADA organization in the fall and winter of 1946. Rauh deplored the growing influence of the American Communist Party in other liberal organizations. He watched the party's cadres inside the American Veterans Committee (AVC) shift the organization's efforts away from pressing domestic issues to a preoccupation with foreign policy, where its views parroted those of the Soviet foreign minister. Charles Bolte, chairman of the AVC, became an ADA founder. Rauh also feared the tactics of the Communist faction in the National Lawyer's Guild, who drove that organization in the same general pro-Soviet direction. Finally, he had become close to Reuther, then waging a fierce battle to wrest control of the United Auto Workers from its powerful Communist contingent.[22]

On January 4, 1947, two weeks after Wallace and his supporters launched the Progressive Citizens of America, Loeb and his troops unveiled Americans for Democratic Action at the Willard Hotel in Washington. Elmer Davis, the former radio commentator and head of the Office of War Information, presided over the morning session, and Rauh ran the afternoon meeting. Davis greeted the hundred or so ADA founders with an appropriate salutation as "fellow members of the government-in-exile."

The Willard gathering resembled a reunion of the New Deal with Mrs. Roosevelt, Franklin Roosevelt Jr., Leon Henderson, John Kenneth Galbraith, Loeb, Wilson Wyatt, and Rauh in attendance along with Reuther, David Dubinsky, from the International Ladies' Garment Workers, and Jim Carey, secretary of the CIO. Wyatt's former boss, Barry Bingham, the publisher of the *Louisville Courier-Journal,* handed out the ADA's first press releases.

At the ADA's first annual convention two months later, the delegates elected Wyatt chairman, Henderson chief of the executive committee, and Rauh secretary of the board. The *Washington Post,* now directed by Phil Graham, heralded the organization's birth with the headline: "Liberals without Reds." In *PM,* however, Max Lerner lamented the divisions on the left, as did Freda Kirchwey in the *Nation,* who denounced what she regarded as the ADA's excessive anticommunism. The *New Republic,* with Wallace serving as editor, commenced a drumbeat of criticism of its rival.[23]

For the next year and a half, ADA founders fanned out across the country to recruit new members and raise money in preparation for the 1948 elections. Rauh worked the vineyards of California and the Midwest. In Hollywood, he signed up actor Melvyn Douglas, whose wife, Helen, the congresswoman, a close friend of Eleanor Roosevelt, remained neutral between the ADA and the PCA.[24] Rauh drew in several rising political stars as well, notably the young mayor of Minneapolis, Hubert H. Humphrey, and George Edwards, the charismatic president of the Detroit City Council, destined for Michigan's Supreme Court and the Sixth Circuit Court of Appeals.[25]

As the crucial 1948 presidential season opened, Rauh and other ADA leaders, who saw themselves as the true keepers of the New Deal flame, fought over political strategy as they attempted to wrest the mantle of liberalism from Wallace's third party and from President Truman, both of whom also claimed to embody the legacy of FDR. "The entire problem of creating a non-Communist left organization must be handled with the greatest of delicacy lest we give the reactionaries additional comfort," Rauh told Willard Hurst, a former Brandeis clerk and law professor at the University of Wisconsin. "But the difficulty must not prevent its happening or we will some day find ourselves in the middle of the street having to take cover with the reactionaries of the right on the one side, or the reactionaries of the left on the other."[26] That day arrived sooner than Rauh had planned.

When classified government documents turned up in the pages of a left-wing New York journal, *Amerasia,* whose editor Louis Jaffe had ties to the Communist Party of America, Truman issued an executive order that established an unprecedented federal program intended to eliminate from the executive branch all persons who might be disloyal to the United States or endanger its national security. Rauh had endorsed the recently announced Marshall Plan of broad economic aid to Europe and even military aid to Greece and Turkey, but he promptly denounced the new loyalty-security program, especially its procedures that relied upon so-called confidential FBI informants. Wechsler also blasted the president for fomenting an "artificial uproar" to dramatize his anticommunist credentials, and the *Nation* predicted (accurately as it turned out) that the program would become a repressive vehicle for "malicious gossip, character assassination, and the settlement of private grudges."[27]

Courting Ike

From Rauh's perspective, Truman had burned too many liberal bridges by early 1948 to merit support. But few real alternatives presented themselves when the ADA insurgents gathered in Philadelphia that February for their first convention. Wallace, his fortunes now tied to his Communist patrons, inspired no confidence. Like others, Rauh hoped that General Eisenhower would declare his allegiance to the Democrats, but the supreme commander sat sphinx-like in New York as president of Columbia University. A third faction pushed the candidacy of Justice Douglas, whose ambitions were exceeded only by his indecision.

In the months following the convention, discontent mounted among those within the ADA who wanted a clear declaration of war against Truman. In an effort to resolve this impasse, the leadership called for an "expanded board meeting" in Pittsburgh where members could vent anti-Truman sentiment and support other candidates, perhaps Eisenhower or Douglas. The "expanded board" finally approved a resolution endorsing Eisenhower and Douglas, a solution that left the question of a vice presidential candidate undecided and was the subject of much ridicule.

Armed with this curious ADA endorsement, Rauh and Henderson journeyed to New York to persuade the general. Eisenhower, however, deflated the ADA balloon by expressing no interest in challenging Truman for the nomination. But when Rauh and Henderson, still optimistic, approached the general's brother, Milton, a few weeks later, they received an extraordinary proposal.

"You fellows want to know how to work this thing out?" the brother inquired. "I think it would be best if my brother were nominated by both parties." After recovering his poise, Rauh informed Milton that his scheme would never work. Ike had great stature, but he was not George Washington in 1789. Rauh could not decide if the bizarre proposal had originated with Milton or sprang from Ike's own considerable ego.[28]

With the collapse of the Eisenhower boom, the Douglas candidacy also began to deflate. The justice stirred most enthusiasm when harnessed to an Eisenhower ticket. Alone, he had neither the money nor organization to threaten Truman. Lacking a candidate, Rauh and other ADA insurgents began to focus their attention on the party platform, determined that Truman should run on their principles, especially in the area of civil rights, the long-neglected agenda of the Democratic Party and the New Deal. Their success in Philadelphia would depend on winning a battle inside the party, not outside.

The Sunshine of Human Rights

In Philadelphia, Rauh and the other ADA rebels ate some humble pie and endorsed Truman for reelection. When Justice Douglas dropped out of the vice presidential race, the ADA liberals were left with only two issues: the racist, lily-white Mississippi delegation and the national platform. Fearing

Wallace on his left, Truman now hoped to keep as many Democrats inside the tent as possible, including white Southerners. The president wanted to avoid a nasty fight over issues of race, although his own Committee on Civil Rights had recommended actions by the federal government to abolish the poll tax, desegregate the armed forces, and make lynching a federal crime.

Truman gave the task of drafting a civil rights platform acceptable to both Mississippi and the ADA to Senator Francis Myers of Pennsylvania, a former House member with strong ties to the southern wing of the party. With the president's active support, Myers and the platform committee rammed through a mild statement on civil rights that resembled the 1944 platform statement. It affirmed the party's commitment to equal opportunity, the right of minorities "to live . . . to work . . . to vote," and vowed the support of the federal government "to the limit of its constitutional authority."[29]

Rauh and the ADA delegates regarded this statement as a complete surrender to the segregationists. It failed to endorse a single goal of Truman's own civil rights committee. Three ADA members on the platform committee—Humphrey, Andy Biemiller from the CIO, and Senator Hugh Mitchell of Washington—wanted tougher language that would commit the Democrats to abolition of the poll tax, desegregation of the armed forces, a permanent fair employment practices commission, and federal prosecution of lynching. The platform committee voted down all those amendments, with Illinois senator Scott Lucas accusing the ADA members of conspiring to destroy the party.

Eager for a fight on the floor, Rauh put the final touches on the minority report. Biemiller sponsored it on behalf of the committee dissenters, but Humphrey, their big oratorical weapon, had developed sudden caution on the eve of the great convention debate. He had fought bravely in the platform committee, but he also wanted to be Minnesota's next United States senator, and he coveted financial support from the White House.

Truman's top advisers, party chairman Howard McGrath and David Niles, showered Humphrey with threats and promises. The minority plank would rupture the party, weaken Truman in the fall, and threaten Humphrey's race in Minnesota. The mayor of Minneapolis hesitated, torn between his friends in the ADA and the White House. Eugenie Anderson, his longtime confidant in the Farmer-Labor Party, came to the rescue. Looking over Rauh's draft of the minority report, she inserted a key sentence: "We commend President Truman for the report of his commission on civil rights." That sentence seemed to put Truman squarely behind the minority report and the report behind the president. Appeased, Humphrey agreed to speak on behalf of the minority, although Arthur Schlesinger recalled that "he did not, at the end, want to give the speech and had to be shamed into it, and physically transported to the convention hall, by Joe Rauh."[30]

But speak he did. Humphrey offered some of the most memorable words ever delivered at a national convention, words written by ADA staff member Milton Stewart: "I say the time has come to walk out of the shadow of states' rights and into the sunshine of human rights." Supporters of the minority platform roared their approval as Rauh and the other ADA delegates worked the convention floor in search of votes, especially among the large delegations from northern cities.

Truman's advisers, sensing the momentum shifting against them, made a last-ditch effort to derail the minority report. David Niles grabbed Rauh on the floor as the roll call began. He predicted disaster for the ADA, Humphrey, the liberal cause, and the party. "You're ruining the greatest talent we have," Niles shouted. "You won't get 50 votes here, and Hubert will lose Minnesota, too."[31] Instead of 50, the minority platform got 651.5 votes to 582.5 for the regulars. ADA liberals and urban bosses carried the day. David Lawrence, the mayor of Pittsburgh, delivered Pennsylvania against his own United States senator.

Joe Rauh, Hubert Humphrey, and their ADA allies had changed the face of the Democratic Party on the issue of race in America. The path ahead would be steep, twisting, and filled with detours, but the 1948 platform helped to fuel a revolution in civil rights. The Democrats had now become the party of racial justice, with consequences then unforeseen by Rauh and others. When Truman confounded his critics and pundits by defeating both Dewey and Wallace, despite the bolt by Strom Thurmond and the Dixiecrats, he owed his victory in part to Rauh and the liberals who had forced him to accept their vision of America's racial future. The president lost four southern states to Thurmond, but running on a platform that echoed an ADA position paper, he carried Illinois, Ohio, California, and Massachusetts along with Minnesota, which also sent Humphrey to Washington a United States senator.

As he listened to the election returns that November evening, Rauh found himself already engaged in another battle with the very administration he had helped return to power. He put the finishing touches on a brief appealing the firing of William Remington from his job in the Commerce Department. Anticommunism, propelled in part by Truman and by the ADA's assault on Wallace, had now entered new and more ominous territory, where Rauh found himself in the heart of America's new political darkness.

SYMPATHETIC ASSOCIATIONS

Reasonable grounds exist for belief that . . . the person
is disloyal to the Government of the United States.
— EXECUTIVE ORDER 9835

The Cold War Comes to America

James Kutcher lost both legs at San Pietro, Italy, fighting for his country. After the war, he earned $42 a week as a clerk in the Newark office of the Veterans Administration, in addition to a $329-a-month disability pension. Kutcher made speeches, too, on behalf of the Socialist Workers Party. Officials in the government of the United States did not like his combination of activities.

Bill Remington's past set off alarm bells, too. A former employee of the War Production Board, he had socialized with known Communists while working for the Tennessee Valley Authority and met during the war with a woman he believed to be a journalist, Helen Johnson. Helen turned out to be Elizabeth Bentley, a spy for the Soviet Union. James Kutcher and Bill Remington lived worlds apart and never met, but they and hundreds of other citizens became part of Joe Rauh's life when the Cold War came to America through the federal government's loyalty and security program.

With their economy vibrant and their political institutions intact, and enjoying a monopoly on the atomic bomb, Americans had every reason to believe in 1945 that the shattered postwar world could be repaired in accordance with their values and desires. But neither economic pressure nor the atomic bomb seemed capable of bending the Soviet Union to America's will when it came to the reconstruction of Europe. Reneging on promises made to Roosevelt at the Yalta Conference, Stalin refused to hold free elections in Poland. Behind the Red Army, Communist parties from Poland to Rumania tightened their grip on state power and displayed less and less toleration for opposition parties, especially in Czechoslovakia, where the Stalinists overturned a coalition government and murdered one of its leaders, Eduard Benes.

The Czech coup followed hard in the wake of a stalemate over the future of Germany, where Soviet and American visions of postwar society remained incompatible. When the United States, Britain, and France agreed upon a common economic policy for their zones of occupation, the Russians responded and banned all land traffic into Berlin, a blockade that lasted 321 days until broken by a heroic allied airlift into the city. Lowering an iron curtain across Eastern Europe, the Soviet Union also entered the atomic age in September 1949. Three months later, Mao Tse-tung's forces proclaimed the creation of the People's Democratic Republic of China. The red flag of Communism now flew over the most populous country on earth.

The Truman administration, fearing that the same fate would soon befall the French empire in Indochina, began pumping military aid into the struggle against Communist insurgents in Vietnam led by Ho Chi Minh. Finally, on June 25, 1950, ending years of border skirmishes on both sides, North Korean troops swept into South Korea intent upon unifying that country by force. Within months the United States, acting through the United Nations, had committed thousands of troops to the defense of South Korea in the first hot confrontation of the Cold War that would ultimately claim 33,629 American battle deaths, making Korea the fifth bloodiest war in American history.

On the home front, the publication of classified government documents in left-wing magazines such as *Amerasia* and the arrest of Canadian and British citizens, including physicists Alan Nunn May and Klaus Fuchs, who confessed to atomic espionage, stoked fears of a vast Soviet spy apparatus operating throughout the society. The arrest of Americans Harry Gold, David Greenglass, and Julius and Ethel Rosenberg on similar charges of atomic espionage offered further proof of domestic betrayal. The deepening sense of international crisis encouraged many Republican leaders to believe that the road back to national power could be paved successfully with a heavy application of anticommunism that stressed the Soviet menace, domestic subversion, and the failure of the Democrats to eradicate both. Truman's surprising reelection, the Soviet bomb, Mao's victory, Alger Hiss's conviction for perjury, the arrest of the Rosenbergs, and the North Korean attack gave new momentum to this strategy.

Executive Order 9835

Never one to be outflanked by his political adversaries, Truman declined to cede the Republicans a monopoly on anticommunism. Unable to intimidate the Soviets abroad, he could harass their past and present followers at home, paint Henry Wallace and his party in the reddest possible hues, and secure the indictment of the party's top leaders for violating the Smith Act. Finally, his loyalty-security program, initiated in March 1947 by Executive Order 9835, subjected all present and prospective federal employees in the executive branch to potential investigation by the FBI to determine whether "reasonable grounds exist for belief that the person . . . is disloyal to the Government of the United States."

Truman's edict, covering 2,200,000 jobs, set out six possible grounds for a finding of disloyalty, including evidence of sabotage, espionage, treason, or the unauthorized disclosure "to any person" of "documents or information of a confidential or non-public character." But in addition to these patent examples of illegal and criminal conduct, an employee could be found disloyal and dismissed for "membership in, affiliation with or sympathetic association with" any organization, movement, or group of persons designated by the attorney general as "totalitarian, Fascist, Communist, or subversive."[1] Beginning with attorney general Tom Clark, the Department of Justice compiled lists of banned organizations largely on the basis of information provided by the Federal Bureau of Investigation, but without initially affording the groups a hearing.

The Truman program did give employees suspected of disloyalty a formal hearing before their agency's loyalty board and a right to appeal an adverse decision to a loyalty review board, but those accused never learned the identity of persons who made accusations, and employees had no right to subpoena FBI investigative records. In short, an employee had no right to confront his or her accusers or to cross-examine them.[2] Rauh regarded the nondisclosure and nonconfrontation aspects of the regulations as deadly threats to civil liberties. Protecting American security, he believed, should not be achieved by trashing the Constitution.

As the FBI's investigative machinery ground on, ultimately processing four million files by 1952, thousands of federal employees found themselves charged with disloyalty and threatened with the loss of employment and reputations. Many of these victims found their way to Rauh's offices in a little green house on K Street, where their tales confirmed his worst fears. The small Rauh firm now included, in addition to Irv Levy, his wartime colleague, a soft-spoken, young civil libertarian from North Carolina, Daniel Pollitt, a recent graduate of Cornell Law School. Rauh, Levy, and Pollitt enjoyed a steady but modest income from various unions, including the UAW, the shoe workers, and the timber cutters, as well as some work for the ADA, and a small biochemical firm, Syntex, whose founders had invented an inexpensive synthetic substitute for progesterone.

These regular accounts permitted the Rauh firm to accept hundreds of loyalty cases in situations where the government employee had little or no ability to pay. Since the District of Columbia did not have a chapter of the American Civil Liberties Union in 1947, Rauh's firm became its surrogate. "I wasn't supposed to ask them for any money," Pollitt recalled, "if it would embarrass them."[3] Other Washington attorneys feasted on the loyalty crusade by squeezing every nickel out of poor, frightened government workers. Overburdened with cases at one point, Pollitt referred a client to another lawyer. A few days later, Rauh received a $500 forwarding fee from that attorney, who intended to charge the new client $1,500.[4] He returned the fee.

Machinery of Repression

Beginning in 1947, Rauh and his firm experienced the grim results of the loyalty crusade. During the first six years of the program under Truman, 12,568 employees endured charges of disloyalty and formal hearings that resulted in 519 dismissals. The government cashiered these victims solely on the grounds of their "sympathetic association" with other persons or organizations and usually on the basis of information supplied by confidential informants whose identity remained buried in FBI files. Rauh's first client, for example, faced dismissal because he had been a member of the Washington Book Shop, an organization listed as a Communist front by the attorney general. Like hundreds of others, he had patronized that establishment not out of sympathy for Communism, but because the bookstore sold books cheaper than other retail outlets. He received a clean bill of patriotic health from the loyalty review board, but only after Rauh demonstrated that none of the books purchased had been subversive and produced witnesses who testified to his client's vigorous anticommunist opinions.[5]

Other federal workers faced accusations of disloyalty for purchasing a car from an employee at the Czechoslovakian embassy; donating English translations of the Moscow purge trials to the Library of Congress; providing milk to the children of sit-down strikers of the Workers Alliance; and giving five dollars to the Joint Anti-Fascist Refugee Committee years before it appeared on the attorney general's list.[6] Landlords accused former tenants of receiving regular shipments of "communist literature," which could mean any publication that mentioned Marx, Lenin, or Stalin. An employee who attempted to switch agencies against the wishes of his supervisor found himself accused of disloyalty by this same supervisor and hauled before a hearing board. Finally exonerated, he could not find another department willing to employ him for fear that his presence would inspire new investigations by Congress.[7]

"We Make Up the Rules as We Go Along"

The ordeal of wheelchair-bound James Kutcher personified the loyalty program at its most ludicrous. The thirty-five-year-old veteran, when not on duty at the VA, often spoke for the Socialist Workers Party, a Trotskyite organization violently anti-Stalinist, but listed as subversive by the attorney general. In his speeches Kutcher sounded like the most rabid anti-Soviet member of Congress. These nice ideological distinctions eluded officials in the Veterans Administration who fired him in September 1948 after a hearing board in Philadelphia found him to be disloyal. Seth Richardson's loyalty review board sustained that decision seven months later. "Two years ago, when I learned to use my artificial limbs the Government gave me a job," Kutcher told reporters. "Now it has taken my job away—not because of any fault in my work, but because of my political views."[8]

Kutcher's problems did not end with the loyalty probe. The Newark Housing Authority attempted to evict him and his father from their apartment when the elder Kutcher refused to sign an affidavit that no one in the unit belonged to an organization on the attorney general's list. The Veterans Administration also sought to strip Kutcher of his monthly $329 disability pension. For the next seven years, despite pleas from friends that he defend more appealing clients, Rauh and his firm battled to save Kutcher's job and pension by attacking the loyalty program in several rounds of administrative hearings and judicial proceedings.[9]

Three years after Kutcher's initial dismissal had been upheld by district judge Edward Curran, the federal Circuit Court for the District of Columbia, responding to Rauh's arguments, ordered a new loyalty hearing on the grounds that the VA administrator who fired him had not complied with Truman's executive order, having failed to weigh the totality of evidence and basing his decision solely on the attorney general's list.[10] When a second round of hearings also went against Kutcher and Judge Curran again upheld his termination, Rauh took another appeal to the circuit court. By a two-to-one vote, the appeals court now ruled that Kutcher had been improperly dismissed under general civil service regulations because the charges of disloy-

alty (i.e., membership in the Socialist Workers Party) bore only a vague relationship to the actual findings of the hearing board.

In the summer of 1956, the VA finally reinstated Kutcher in the Newark
office "with full seniority," but not with back pay.[11] Rauh next moved to reverse
the VA's decision to cut off Kutcher's disability benefits, and this task proved
easier, thanks in part to the ineptness of the VA and the assistance of Herblock,
cartoonist for Graham's *Washington Post*. Rauh insisted on a public hearing
before the Committee on Waivers and Forfeitures of the Veterans Administration. Kutcher and the Trotskyites notified the press, which turned out in full
force, and Rauh made certain that Kutcher hobbled into the hearing room
with two canes, festooned with all his battle ribbons and a Purple Heart.

The chairman of the committee, Peyton H. Moss, opened the proceedings by announcing firmly that Kutcher was not on trial for a crime. But, he
added, the VA had been given the authority by Congress to deny benefits to
anyone "shown by evidence satisfactory to the Administrator of Veterans Affairs to be guilty of mutiny, treason, sabotage, or rendering assistance to any
enemy of the United States." Kutcher had been charged specifically, Moss
continued, with giving aid to the nation's enemies by making certain statements. For example, he "liked the Red system of government," while the
government of the United States was composed of "cheaters and crooks who
oppress the working people."

After the charges had been read, Rauh began his defense by asking Moss
for a copy of the rules "under which the committee will be proceeding today." That caught Moss and the committee off guard because they had never
conducted a similar hearing.

"I guess I'll make them up as we go along," Moss replied, which provoked
laughter from the audience.

Rauh's request for the rules and chairman's inept responses doomed the VA
case against Kutcher. The morning edition of the *Post* carried Herblock's car-
toon comparing Moss's conduct to the Mad Hatter's Tea Party in *Alice in Won-
derland*. It bore the caption: "How the Government Intends to Handle the
Kutcher Case: We Make Up the Rules as We Go Along." On January 8, 1956,
Moss's committee announced that Kutcher would keep his benefits because
the government lacked sufficient evidence "beyond a reasonable doubt" that
he had "knowingly and intentionally" given aid to America's enemies.[12]

Miss Bentley Accuses

James Kutcher nearly lost his job, his apartment, and his disability pension
courtesy of the loyalty program. Bill Remington, although vindicated by the

loyalty program, ultimately lost his life. Blessed with brains, good looks, and a resume that included government service on the War Production Board, the Office of War Mobilization, and the President's Council of Economic Advisers, William Walter Remington presented Rauh with a challenging set of circumstances that flowed from his tangled web of personal and ideological associations.

In her confessions to the FBI during November 1945, Bentley, now branded in the press as "the Blonde Spy Queen," named Remington as one among more than 150 persons who, she claimed, had engaged in Communist Party activities or espionage for the Soviet Union during the war years. Remington, she said, had been both a member and a willing spy.[13] A federal grand jury in New York, after grilling Remington in the spring of 1948, declined to indict him on the basis of this testimony. By then, however, Remington himself had become an informant for the FBI, "eager as you," he told agents, "to help rid this country of communists and their sympathizers." Now anxious to assist Hoover's men in their antisubversive campaign, he insisted that he had never been a member of the Communist Party or given Bentley other than public information to which anyone claiming to be a reporter would have been entitled.[14]

In July 1948 before a Senate committee chaired by Homer Ferguson of Michigan, however, Bentley repeated her charges against Remington: from 1941 to 1943 she had passed his reports and others on to her lover, Soviet spymaster Jacob Golos, who had died of a heart attack in 1943. Responding to Bentley's public charges, Remington denied membership in the party or giving Bentley "one single scrap of confidential information." He gave her money as payment for newspapers, he said, not for party dues. He admitted knowing and meeting with Bentley during the war years when she called herself Helen Johnson, a journalist. He had been introduced to Bentley/Johnson and Golos by his mother-in-law, Elizabeth Moos, an active member of the Communist Party, and her lover, Joe North, editor of the Communist weekly *New Masses.*

Remington admitted giving Bentley/Johnson routine reports from the War Production Board similar to those he provided to other journalists. That had been part of his job at the agency. He denied knowing that Bentley/Johnson or Golos had Communist ties. He concluded his rebuttal by pointing to his strong anti-Soviet views, including recent support for the Truman Doctrine and the Marshall Plan. He praised Bentley for coming forward to expose subversion and also Ferguson's committee for supporting such efforts.[15]

Loyalty Board: Round One

Bentley's new accusations, however, triggered a hearing before the Fourth Region Loyalty Board. In addition to the Ferguson hearings, this board also had access to Remington's extensive FBI file, which documented an unusual network of friendships and associations reaching back to Remington's college days at Dartmouth. Classmates and administrators offered a confusing portrait of Remington's ideological leanings. They recalled, for example, that he had denounced leaders of the Communist-dominated American Student Union as "hysterical and irresponsible," but he continued to attend their meetings and those of the Young Communist League, where he "defended his views of Communism with zeal and deep conviction."

Taking a leave from Dartmouth at the start of his junior year in 1936, Remington worked as a messenger at the Tennessee Valley Authority in Knoxville. There he joined the Workers Education Committee and socialized with Howard Bridgman, Muriel Speare, and Kit Buckles, all active in the local Communist Party organization. Bridgman and the others considered him a party member, and a few of them recalled Remington's own recruitment efforts.[16]

In 1938, Remington married Ann Moos, a graduate of Bennington, whom he first met at a conference of the United Student Peace Committee. Ann knew party leaders through her mother, whose Croton-on-Hudson estate had become a gathering place for CP activists and assorted radicals. Ann later claimed that Remington had vowed to remain faithful to the party as a condition of the marriage. They contributed money to the *New Masses* and spent most weekends at Croton, where they met North and other party leaders, who in turn introduced them to Bentley.[17]

Other FBI informants recalled that Remington had defended the Soviet invasion of Finland in 1939–40 and denounced American aid to England prior to the German invasion of the Soviet Union. In the wake of Germany's defeat, Remington's foreign policy views took on a decidedly anti-Soviet cast. He supported the Truman Doctrine and the Marshall Plan as well as efforts to restrict American exports to the Russians. Thomas Blaisdell, his boss at the Commerce Department, claimed that Remington's harsh anti-Soviet views drew criticism from State Department officials.[18]

Truman's executive order instructed hearing boards to determine the present loyalty of federal employees, but Remington's inquisitors discounted the testimony of people like Blaisdell and based their conclusions upon past activities, especially the relationship to Bentley during the war. This, they concluded, involved "imparting non-public information to a person closely identified with communists." Remington soon received an official notification that he had been found disloyal, followed by termination of his employment. The board gave him twenty days to appeal.

More than thirty years after he agreed to represent Remington, Rauh wrote that "the big story is not what Remington did (that will always be shrouded in the gray area of uncertainty) but what a hysterical society did to Remington for, at worst, stupid and show-off activities."[19] At the time, he concluded that his newest client was "a strange combination of integrity and egotism, of reserve and brashness, of brilliance and gullibility."[20] Rauh might have added that Remington had been a victim of his own desire to please everyone who came into his life—professors, classmates, a wife, a mother-in-law, Communists, FBI agents.

In 1948 and later, Rauh doubted he would ever know the whole truth about Remington's life because "hysteria made it impossible for anybody to tell the truth in those days. . . . They were all scared green by the public reaction . . . whipped up by the slightest admission of communist leanings or associates."[21] Rauh took Remington's appeal in 1948 because he believed him to be "a decent boy," someone entitled "to make a mistake, even a bad mistake, without being crucified as disloyal."[22]

Faced with his most challenging loyalty case, Rauh sought the aid of other attorneys with impeccable conservative credentials. He received a positive response from Bethuel M. Webster, who had served in the Department of Justice under Coolidge and Hoover. After reviewing the transcript of the original hearing, Rauh and Webster asked the loyalty review board to invite Bentley to testify. Encouraged by Rauh, Remington also filed a libel suit against the "Spy Queen" in New York after she repeated her accusations against him on the NBC radio program *Meet the Press*. But despite Seth Richardson's intensive efforts, Bentley, who had recently converted to Catholicism, refused to appear at the hearing.

Bentley's unwillingness to come forward, combined with affidavits from prominent government figures that vouched for Remington's loyalty, proved decisive. Richardson and his two colleagues on the board, one of whom had been a national commander of the American Legion, focused largely on Remington's record since the war and placed little weight on events at Dartmouth or the Tennessee Valley Authority. They discounted Bentley's tale of espionage by noting that Russia had been America's ally during the war, that the United States had made every effort to keep the Soviets alive in the struggle against Hitler, and that "giving the Russians information with respect to the progress of our war effort wouldn't necessarily spell disloyalty."[23]

In early February 1949, the Richardson board ordered Remington reinstated in the Commerce Department with back pay amounting to $5,813.72. His vindication received sympathetic treatment from Daniel Lang at the end of May in a long *New Yorker* essay that also cast more doubt on Bentley's credibility. Six months later, federal judge Edward Conger ruled that Remington's libel suit against Bentley, NBC, and radio sponsor General Foods could go to trial. That ruling quickly resulted in an out-of-court settlement for $9,000. Remington's superiors at Commerce demoted him, but he refused to quit, fortified by these victories over the loyalty machinery and Bentley. That choice became his death warrant.[24]

Perjury: Round Two

In the wake of the loyalty board's decision and Remington's symbolic victory in the libel suit, Bentley had a desperate need to rebuild her reputation. She had been fired from a teaching position in Chicago for alleged "moral laxity" and failed to find a publisher for her memoirs. Other persons and organizations had also staked their careers in the anticommunist crusade upon her tales of Soviet espionage, including one John Gilland Brunini, director of the Catholic Poetry Society. He had become Bentley's literary collaborator and, by coincidence, foreman of the federal grand jury in New York charged with investigating Soviet espionage.

At the end of April 1950, Congressman John S. Wood, chairman of the House Un-American Activities Committee, announced that Remington would be called before his body to respond to testimony from former residents of Knoxville who knew him to be a member of the Communist Party there in 1936–37. Wood also urged the loyalty review board to reopen its inquiry in light of this new evidence. Two months later, after calling Bentley, Remington, and Remington's now ex-wife, Ann, to testify, the grand jury dominated by Brunini returned an indictment charging Remington with perjury—specifically, that he had lied about past membership in the Communist Party.

Rauh punched large holes in the testimony of HUAC's "new witnesses" from Remington's days at TVA.[25] But defending his client against the perjury charge proved more difficult. Webster, pleading obligations to his law firm, declined to continue. Rauh kept the defense afloat with a grant of $20,000 from the James Marshall Civil Liberties Trust and attracted another establishment attorney to replace Webster: William C. Chanler, a partner in Henry Stimson's old law firm and a former corporation counsel for New York City.[26]

Remington and his legal team now faced a more formidable accuser than Bentley—Ann Moos Remington, angry and vengeful because her former spouse blamed her and her mother for his legal difficulties. Under intense pressure in the grand jury room, Ann testified for the prosecution that her former husband had been a member of the Communist Party. Her incriminating statements before the grand jury came, however, only after hours of relentless interrogation by Brunini and federal prosecutor Thomas Donegan, a grilling that appeals court judge Learned Hand later described as bordering upon torture.

Donegan declared that he believed Remington had been a Communist when meeting Bentley, but Ann initially fought back: "Well, I am sure he wasn't." She added firmly, "I am convinced that he is not [a Communist] and has not been . . . but he is a devious sort." Later, when denied food, told that she could not invoke either the Fifth Amendment or her marital privilege, and threatened by Donegan with a perjury indictment, Ann altered her story to the grand jury—her husband, she said, had given money to the Communist Party.

At trial, Ann Moos became more confident and incriminating. Her husband had been a Communist at Dartmouth when they met, she said; he contributed financially to the party, recruited for the party, and gave government secrets to Bentley. But under careful cross-examination by Chanler, she also maintained that "we were not orthodox Communists. . . . We were Communists as much as we wanted to be." Ann's conflicting statements, when combined with testimony from Bentley, former classmates in Hanover, and TVA employees who placed Remington at party meetings, helped convict Remington of perjury on February 7, 1951.[27]

Round Three: Appeals

Throughout the trial, Rauh and Chanler tangled regularly with Judge Gregory Noonan, who rejected their motions and imposed the maximum sentence on Remington of five years in prison and a fine of $2,000. The judge even denied an extension of bail pending an appeal. Rauh and Chanler believed they had grounds for appeal because Noonan had given improper instructions on the issue of "membership" in the Communist Party, an error that allowed the jury to roam unchecked and to equate harmless social engagements with active participation in the party.[28]

Rauh also believed Noonan had erred when he rejected a defense motion for a new trial on grounds of foreman Brunini's misconduct during the grand jury proceedings. On the eve of the trial, Remington's lawyers had been told that Brunini had signed a contract in 1950 that gave him a share of profits from Bentley's planned book about her life in the Communist underground. The jury foreman had a pecuniary stake in securing Remington's conviction and vindicating Bentley. Finally, Ann Moos's coerced grand jury testimony remained a potent weapon on appeal.

Chief prosecutor Irving Saypol attacked the credibility of defense witnesses who testified about Brunini's book contract, and he assured Judge Noonan that no irregularities had taken place in the grand jury room. Noonan quickly rejected the defense's motion to throw out the indictment and refused to give Rauh and Chanler access to the grand jury transcripts. Whatever the truth about Brunini and Bentley, Noonan ruled, twelve jurors voted to indict Remington, not one. Rauh wanted to make the grand jury the centerpiece of their appeal in the hope of quashing the original indictment. Chanler opposed that strategy and wanted to place their emphasis instead upon Noonan's instructions about party membership.[29]

The Federal Court of Appeals for the Second Circuit, headed by Judges Tom Swan, Learned Hand, and Augustus Hand, stunned the prosecution when it agreed unanimously with Chanler's core argument that Noonan's instructions on membership had been "too vague and indefinite to constitute any definition at all of what facts the jury must find in order to convict the defendant." The trio also criticized Saypol for constantly invoking the attorney general's list, ordered a new trial for Remington, and further ruled that his lawyers should be granted access to the grand jury proceedings to determine if coercion had taken place in securing the indictment.[30]

Like the prior loyalty review board ruling, the decision by the court of appeals seriously damaged the government's case against Remington. Rauh hoped to bury it with a daring legal maneuver and gamble. Despite their partial victory in the court of appeals, he argued, they should petition the Supreme Court for review, stress the coercion issue, and attempt to have the original indictment thrown out. Chanler, content with a new trial ordered by the appeals court, thought Rauh's strategy would fail, but he reluctantly went along with a petition to the Supreme Court.

Perjury Again

Rauh's bold move provoked an equally unprecedented response from the prosecutors, who a week later procured a new indictment against Remington. They now charged him with five counts of perjury for statements made while testifying at his trial! They also petitioned the Supreme Court to throw out the first indictment. This devious strategy came from the fertile brain of

Saypol's chief assistant, Roy Cohn, the pudgy son of a former New York jurist, whom Chanler referred to as the prosecution's "ever-active genie." Cohen, who counted J. Edgar Hoover among his closest friends, soon played a
major role in the Rosenbergs' espionage trial and later joined Senator Mc-
Carthy's staff. He and Saypol wanted to block further judicial inquiry into
Brunini's relationship to Bentley and the tactics used against Ann Moos before the grand jury.[31]

Rauh led a chorus of legal criticism against the government's new indictment and Cohn's attempt to quash the first one, a tactic designed to avoid the
issue of double jeopardy and to cover up the prosecution's own misconduct.
The Supreme Court rejected a part of Cohn's strategy when it refused to discard the first indictment, but on March 24, 1952, the justices also declined to
hear Rauh's appeal of the grand jury issue. Remington now faced a second
trial for perjury, but he would undergo that ordeal without Rauh, worn down
by the first trial and now at odds over trial strategy with Chanler and with
Chanler's replacement, a seasoned criminal lawyer, John Minton.

In their extraordinary move, the government now claimed that Remington had lied during the first trial about attendance at Communist Party meetings, about giving information to Bentley, about paying party dues, and about
knowledge of the Young Communist League at Dartmouth. Rauh believed
they would never be able to persuade a new jury to acquit Remington on all
of those vague charges in the middle of the Korean War, given the testimony
of Ann Moos and Bentley. The only hope for Remington, he argued, rested
at the court of appeals and the Supreme Court with a frontal attack on the
original perjury indictment.[32]

Chanler and Minton, whose nephew had been killed in Korea, rejected
Rauh's strategy and pushed ahead with the trial. So did Remington, who had
become persuaded that the government would never rest until he had been
acquitted or convicted. Discouraged about their decision, Rauh withdrew
from the trial, but not before telling Chanler that he believed their "path of
least resistance . . . is the road to defeat." He hoped they would prove him
wrong.[33]

But after a trial that lasted ten days in January 1953, the jury found Remington guilty on two of the five counts of perjury: giving Bentley information
to which she was not entitled and knowledge of the YCL at Dartmouth. The
judge sentenced him to three years. Minton's only grounds for appeal focused narrowly on the sufficiency and admissibility of certain evidence.
Rauh, still smarting from the rejection of his strategy, but convinced the case
raised an important constitutional question, urged Remington to appeal on
his grounds of the flawed grand jury indictment. After an emotional dinner

reunion in New York where he further probed Remington's innocence, Rauh agreed to write that brief with the assistance of attorney Richard Green and Dan Pollitt, and to argue their case before the circuit court.[34]

Death Sentence

With Remington already in the Lewisburg Penitentiary, Rauh made a simple and eloquent argument before Judge Swan and the two Hands on October 15, 1953. The United States, he claimed, had procured Remington's indictment and first trial by coerced and corrupt means. It could not therefore indict him a second time for what he said while on the witness stand. The original grand jury transcripts proved that Brunini and Donegan, one a literary collaborator with Bentley and the other her former attorney, coerced testimony from Ann Moos and deceived her concerning her legal rights. Prosecutors had further hidden this misconduct from the defense.

In a recent decision, *United States v. Williams*, Rauh knew, the Supreme Court had ruled that a legally defective indictment did not nullify a conviction for perjury committed while on trial under the indictment. But in *Williams* the indictment had been technically flawed (charging the defendant with the wrong offense), not the result of gross misconduct by a grand jury foreman and prosecutors.[35] Remington's case, Rauh argued, more closely resembled those arising under illegal searches and seizures or wiretapping, where the Supreme Court had ruled that the government could not profit from its own wrongdoing or the use of tainted evidence, the "fruit of the poisonous tree." These decisions, moreover, had been authored by Holmes and Frankfurter, two jurists likely to impress the circuit court.[36]

Rauh asked the circuit court to make a modest intellectual leap from *Silverthorne* and *Nardone* to the facts present in the case of Bill Remington. Judge Learned Hand agreed with Rauh's argument and wrote a blistering critique of the prosecution's conduct before the grand jury. But by a vote of two to one the appeals court affirmed Remington's conviction.[37]

Three months later, after receiving Rauh's petition for certiorari, the Supreme Court again declined to hear Remington's appeal, a decision that led Hand privately to express to Justice Frankfurter his profound sadness about the outcome. Rauh's brief and Hand's impassioned dissent had encouraged at least three justices—Frankfurter, Black, and Douglas—to support review, but they could not secure the vote of Justice Jackson. Rauh learned later that personal rancor and ideological conflict between Black and Jackson played a major role in the Court's refusal to hear the case. Black expressed the view that the Remington case should become the vehicle to overrule *Williams*. Frankfurter, who had also dissented in *Williams*, believed the two cases could be distinguished and blamed Black's intransigence for alienating Jackson.[38]

No macabre twist in Remington's case, however, prepared Rauh for the final horror. In November 1954, eight months before his scheduled release from Lewisburg, other inmates attacked Remington in his dormitory and beat him to death with a brick wrapped in a sock. The prosecutors and prison officials insisted that Remington's killers had been motivated solely by robbery. Roy Cohn claimed until his own death from AIDS in 1986 that Remington had been a victim of "a turgid sexually-motivated murder." But the three men convicted of his murder—George McCoy, Lewis Cagle Jr., and Robert Parker—nursed intense anticommunist sentiments, and their attack had been politically motivated. The Bureau of Prisons kept a lid on those facts for three decades, perpetrating the last government outrage in the Remington case.[39]

Vindication

All of his legal skills could not save Bill Remington from the anticommunist hysteria that spread its venom even inside a federal prison, but his client's death heightened Rauh's resolve to destroy the basic evil at the heart of the loyalty-security program: nonconfrontation. That issue became even more crucial after 1953, when the Eisenhower administration tightened the regulations to include dismissal for "any . . . infamous, dishonest, immoral, or notoriously disgraceful conduct . . . [or] any fact which furnishes reason to believe that the individual may be subjected to coercion, influence, or pressure which may cause him to act contrary to the best interests of the national security."[40]

In 1955, Rauh filed an *amicus curiae* brief on behalf of John Peters, a distinguished faculty member of Yale Medical School who had been dismissed as a special consultant to the surgeon general. The loyalty review board, overruling a lower tribunal, found reasonable doubt about Peters's loyalty. Rauh and others hoped the justices would address the constitutional question and perhaps overturn the decision of *Bailey v. Richardson* (1951), in which a majority of the justices placed administrative hearing outside the protections of the Fifth and Sixth Amendments.[41] But to the dismay of Rauh and other attorneys, a majority of the justices, led by Frankfurter, chose to avoid the constitutional question. They reversed the loyalty review board in Peters's case, but only on the statutory grounds that the board lacked authority to overrule a lower board's decision in favor of an employee.[42]

Two years later, Rauh finally had a case he believed would at last defeat the government on nonconfrontation. He represented Charles Allen Taylor, a member of the United Auto Workers, who had been fired from his job at Bell Aircraft after the Pentagon's loyalty board twice ruled that his access to classified defense information was "not clearly consistent with the interests of national security." At both hearings, the Defense Department board refused to divulge the identity of those who had made statements against Taylor, a ruling upheld by the district court, but which Rauh appealed on the grounds that Taylor had been denied due process.

Rauh had found the perfect case, but not one at the front of the litigation queue. The Warren Court had earlier agreed to hear the appeal of William L. Greene, a businessman who had been banned, like Taylor, from further access to defense "secrets," a few of which he had developed for the navy at his own electronics company. Like Taylor, Greene had been unable to confront his accusers. The justices agreed finally to hear Taylor's case without intermediate review by the court of appeals and docketed it for argument at the same time as Greene's appeal. Fearful that Rauh had a winning case, the Pentagon and Department of Justice capitulated four months before oral argument to avoid a Supreme Court decision. The government announced that "the granting of clearance to Mr. Charles Allen Taylor for access to Secret defense information is in the national interest." Two weeks later, the government's lawyers asked the Supreme Court to dismiss Taylor's suit on grounds that it had become moot. Warren's Court, however, refused to rule on that point until after full argument on the merits.

Over two days in late March and early April 1959, Rauh, representing Taylor, and Carl W. Beruefly, who argued for Greene, asked the justices to rule that their clients had been denied a fundamental right to confront their accusers. A majority of the Court agreed in part, with only Clark in dissent, but the justices again avoided the constitutional question when they ruled that neither executive orders nor congressional legislation authorized the Defense Department to operate its Industrial Security Program without the guarantees of confrontation and cross-examination. Led by Warren, however, five members of the majority made it clear that any loyalty procedures without such guarantees would also violate the constitutional guarantee of due process.[43]

Rauh, who led the fight against nonconfrontation from the beginning of the loyalty program, lost the legal race to Beruefly. The justices ruled Taylor's suit moot on the same day they held for Greene. Although his case did not stand for a towering constitutional principle, Charles Taylor reaped immediate benefits. The government gave an ironclad guarantee that it would restore Taylor's clearance and expunge all evidence in his file that had been used against him. These concessions, Rauh observed, "made Taylor's clearance probably the most rock-ribbed and unassailable in the history of the security programs."[44]

Rauh's decade-long war against the scandal of nonconfrontation in loyalty-security cases displayed all of his considerable virtue as a man and a lawyer—extraordinary stamina, creative legal thinking, and a willingness to make huge personal and financial sacrifices on behalf of important principles of fairness and justice. He mourned that Bill Remington, who had beaten the system even without the protection of due process, had not lived to enjoy that victory.

CHAPTER NINE

NAMING NAMES

Are you now, or have you ever been . . .

—HOUSE COMMITTEE ON UN-AMERICAN ACTIVITIES

HUAC

Lillian Hellman refused to talk about other people's politics or activities. But the thought of going to jail terrified her. Dashiell Hammett, her longtime companion and lover, had barely survived a prison term. She also hated taking the Fifth Amendment against self-incrimination and enduring the label of "Fifth Amendment Communist." Arthur Miller had no fear of congressional investigators, but he wanted to protect his fiancée from swarms of reporters in Washington. John Watkins never wrote an acclaimed drama or won the Pulitzer Prize. But as a veteran of the depression-era labor wars at International Harvester, he became a brave man when faced with inquisitors on the House Committee on Un-American Activities who liked to ask witnesses: "Are you now, or have you ever been, a member of the Communist Party?"

As their lawyer, Joe Rauh quickly discovered that the defense of civil liberties in the fetid climate of the Cold War required more than attacking anonymous character assassins, the loyalty-security apparatus, or the oppressive behavior of grand juries. One had to confront the Federal Bureau of Investigation and its director, J. Edgar Hoover, as well as Congress, its investigative machinery, and powerful politicians such as Joseph McCarthy and Pat McCarran. Few attorneys in Washington had the courage or stamina for confrontations of that magnitude in the heat of the domestic Red Scare.

Chief among the congressional investigative committees stood Martin Dies's old entity, now rechristened the House Committee on Un-American Activities (HUAC). In 1945 it became a standing committee endowed with broad subpoena powers and the only permanent investigative body in that chamber charged with uncovering "the extent, character and object of un-American propaganda activities in the United States." Armed with the threat of sending witnesses to prison for contempt, HUAC's long-running probe into domestic Communism brought Rauh two of his most famous clients—Hellman and Miller—and one of his greatest triumphs in the Supreme Court when he represented Watkins. He also suffered through the ordeal of a close friend, Jimmy Wechsler, the *New York Post* columnist, whose hatred for Senator McCarthy's methods led him into a disastrous confrontation with the junior senator from Wisconsin.

Near the end of February 1952, the House Un-American Activities Committee served a subpoena on Hellman, the distinguished dramatist and screenwriter whose works included *The Children's Hour, The Little Foxes,* and *Watch on the Rhine,* the latter among the most powerful antifascist plays produced during World War II. With Hellman and others in the witness chair, HUAC hoped to launch the second wave of its assault on Communist influence in the nation's entertainment industry, specifically Hollywood. The first round in 1947 brought the committee into sharp conflict with some of the motion picture industry's leading Communist Party members and fellow travelers. The so-called Hollywood Ten, including John Howard Lawson, Dalton Trumbo, and Ring Lardner Jr., defied the committee, refused to answer questions on grounds of the First Amendment, and went to prison for contempt when courts rejected their constitutional claims of privilege.

During and after the Hollywood Ten hearings and trials, many actors, directors, and screenwriters bowed to HUAC's interrogations and agreed to "name names" by identifying friends, colleagues, and acquaintances who had either supported the party or become active members. Others found safety in the Fifth Amendment and refused to answer such questions on grounds of self-incrimination. They quickly earned the label "Fifth Amendment Communists." The major studio executives at first declared they would not be "swamped by hysteria or intimidated from any source," but they soon fired the Hollywood Ten, affirmed their opposition to hiring Reds, and promulgated a new morals clause in all contracts that permitted them to fire any employee whose behavior, including political conduct, embarrassed the studios.[1]

Hellman, outspoken and defiantly left-wing, presented a tempting target for the Red-hunters on HUAC. Since the 1930s she had been to Spain in support of the republic, traveled to the Soviet Union during the war, sponsored the Waldorf Conference for World Peace, interviewed Yugoslavia leader Tito in Belgrade, contributed to the Moscow Art Theater, and campaigned in 1948 for Henry Wallace. Throughout these times, she had lived with Hammett, author of *The Maltese Falcon* and *The Thin Man*, who went to jail in 1951 for refusing to divulge the names of contributors to the bail bond fund of the Civil Rights Congress, a Communist front for which he served as trustee. Hollywood screenwriter Martin Berkeley told HUAC that Hellman attended the founding meeting of the Hollywood section of the party in 1937 along with Hammett, Dorothy Parker, Allen Campbell, V. J. Jerome, and others.[2]

Writing about Hellman in the 1970s, Arthur M. Schlesinger Jr., one of Rauh's closest friends and an ADA ally, found her to be "a woman of quality and charm, sharp, elegant, amusing and great fun," but also "an unreconstructed Stalinist . . . [whose] Stalinoid leanings derive . . . from her long association with Dashiell Hammett and an unthinking contempt for the party members who repented and turned state's evidence."[3]

Lillian's Conditions

After consulting Abe Fortas, whose firm represented others pursued by the congressional hounds, Hellman took her subpoena and problem to Rauh, a man she had met briefly at a dinner party a year before. She presented him with a challenging set of conditions for her appearance before the House committee. She did not wish to plead the Fifth Amendment. She would tell HUAC her own story, but she would not inform on other people. And, finally, her conversations with Hammett had convinced her that she could not survive jail if found in contempt of the committee.

Given Hellman's refusal to name other people, Rauh believed she had to invoke the Fifth Amendment before the committee, but do so with an unprecedented twist: they would immediately issue a statement to the press in which she would discuss candidly her own past affiliations and explain that she had taken the Fifth not to hide from this past, but to refrain from hurting other people who, as she put it, "committed no wrong except that they held unpopular political opinions."[4] He urged Hellman to sit down and write such a statement. The draft Hellman sent to Rauh in late March or early April 1952 contradicted what she wrote twenty-four years later about her relationship to the Communist Party. "I am fairly sure that Hammett joined the Communist Party in 1937 or 1938," she declared in *Scoundrel Time*. "I did not join the Party, although mild overtures were made by Earl Browder and the Party theorist, V. J. Jerome."[5] In the spring of 1952 she offered a rather different account:

My own story is simple. I joined the Communist Party in 1938 and left it sometime in 1940. I was a most inactive member. For a short period I was part of a study group and I saw and heard nothing more than people discussing the history of Marxism and the literary and political events of the day. But, in time, I discovered that my own maverick nature was no more suited to the political left than it had been to the conservative background from which I came. I realized that I had grown up in a liberal democracy and that no other system of government, no other concept of living, would be proper for me or for our country. And so I left the Communist Party and never returned. No pressures were ever brought on me, and no suggestion was ever made that I return to the Party.[6]

In a second, later statement for Rauh, Hellman made a few cosmetic changes. "I was a most inactive member" became "I was a most casual member." And she added, "I drifted away from the Communist Party because I seemed to be in the wrong place." In both drafts she asserted her attachment to "an old fashioned American tradition" that included freedom to think, speak, and write as one pleased; to tell the truth; to be loyal to friends and country; and "not to destroy my neighbor." These traditions, she concluded, were now under attack "to fit the convenience of men who do not truly love their country, and who hold it in disrespect." Nobody deserved credit for refusing to harm innocent people, but "those who have done it, and those who have urged them to do it, owe their God and their country a life time of prayers."[7]

Not entirely happy with Hellman's two drafts, Rauh tried his own hand at another version. To her admission that she had joined the Communist Party in 1938, he now added "with little thought as to the serious step I was taking." Moreover, that decision had been made "while lacking any real information about the nature of the Party." Rauh's draft also took a harsher tone when it came to the party: "I was wrong about the Communist Party and I have no hesitancy in acknowledging that error publicly. Yet I have no bitterness towards the misguided lady who asked me to join or towards the misguided people with whom I associated in my two years as a member of the Party." Finally, since no one in the organizations to which she belonged had ever planned or engaged in acts of sabotage, espionage, force, or violence, she declined to answer HUAC's questions. "They wanted me to inform on persons who long ago held the same political opinions that I then held. On this issue of principle I take my stand."[8]

"A Forthright Declaration"

Two weeks later, Rauh shifted their strategy. After reviewing the legal precedents, he and Pollitt feared that claiming the Fifth Amendment privilege before the committee and later issuing a statement to the press would not be
legally unassailable. And he was especially concerned "whether it is wise
from a legal standpoint to include the 1940 date on leaving the Party." That
piece of information might infuriate the members of the committee and lead
to a contempt citation.[9] Rauh now advised two additional tactics: first, Hellman should write to HUAC in advance of the hearings, state her willingness
to talk about herself, but affirm her refusal to inform on others. Second, she
must revise comments about the Communist Party because her version "is so
little critical of the Communist movement in America that it will be generally considered an acceptance of it." Rauh wanted a stronger denunciation of
the Communists. "The statement almost seems to equate membership in the
Communist Party with membership in the ladies' literary society or 'good
works' club. This may have been your experience, but few will accept it."[10]

Rauh also objected to Hellman's oblique explanation for leaving the party
because she "seemed to be in the wrong place." That comment struck him as
having "a certain air of getting into Schubert's [theater] when you wanted to
be at the Majestic." He told her that "a forthright declaration that you had
been wrong in joining the Communist Party, including reasons, is . . . the only
road to follow here."[11]

By early May, with her appearance before HUAC three weeks away, they
dropped the idea of a posthearing press statement. Legal considerations dictated this choice, no doubt, but so did Hellman's reluctance to incorporate
into her statement the sharp condemnations of the Communist Party and the
mea culpa that Rauh had been urging for weeks. Instead, they now sent a letter to HUAC chairman John S. Wood. She offered to tell everything about
herself and to waive the Fifth Amendment privilege, but with the condition
that the committee not question her about others.

While Rauh framed the outline of the letter to Wood, Hellman provided
the rhetorical flourishes for which the document is justly famous: "I am not
willing, now or in the future, to bring bad trouble to people who, in my past
association with them, were completely innocent of any talk or any action
that was disloyal or subversive. . . . To hurt innocent people whom I knew
many years ago in order to save myself is, to me, inhuman and indecent and
dishonorable. I cannot and will not cut my conscience to fit this year's fashions."[12] Significantly, the letter to Wood did not mention either joining the

party or leaving it. A day later, as Rauh fully expected, HUAC rejected her offer. "The Committee," Wood told her, "cannot permit witnesses to set forth the terms under which they will testify."[13]

Shortly after 11:00 a.m. on May 21, Hellman, Rauh, and Pollitt faced the committee in a hearing room of the Old House Office Building packed with reporters and spectators. Their morale had received a blow earlier that morning, when Rauh had taken a call from Fortas's partner, Thurman Arnold, who upbraided him for sending the letter to Congressman Wood. Because the letter stressed her reluctance to testify about others, Arnold fumed, Hellman had possibly waived her Fifth Amendment privilege. Rauh had likely increased the prospect of a contempt citation and jail.[14]

Arnold's concerns had been echoed by the ACLU's Arthur Garfield Hays. But Rauh and Pollitt remained confident that legal precedent supported invoking the privilege where the admission of a relationship might form a link in "the chain of evidence to establish the commission of a crime by the witness." Furthermore, the letter had been sent, and they had to take their chances. Hellman, despite the conflict among lawyers, wanted to get through the ordeal and rejected a change of course.[15]

"Thank God Somebody Had the Guts to Do It"

HUAC's chief counsel, Frank Tavenner Jr., led Hellman through his initial questions without protest, but when he asked her about Martin Berkeley, she invoked the Fifth Amendment and informed the committee that she would have to stand on the statement made in her letter of May 19. At that point, Chairman Wood and Tavenner made a strategic blunder of major proportions. They asked that Hellman's letter be put into the official hearing record. Rauh and Pollitt jumped to their feet instantly and began passing out mimeographed copies of the letter to the reporters, while Wood, stunned by their move, banged his gavel and demanded order in the hearing room. After a few more questions that Hellman declined to answer, Wood and the committee called it a morning and excused the witness. Rauh told Pollitt to get their client out of the building immediately without talking to reporters.

Rauh's improvised decision to hand out the May 19 letter caught even Hellman by surprise, but it proved to be a master stroke that decisively shifted the momentum of the hearing. As reporters scanned the letter, a voice could be heard loud and clear from the press gallery at the rear of the hearing room: "Thank God somebody finally had the guts to do it."[16]

The letter confirmed that the witness had been prepared to tell all about herself, but had been prevented by the committee and the technical rules of the Fifth Amendment. "I had your letter . . . mimeographed ahead of time," Rauh told Hellman later, "because I had decided to give it out to the press whatever Tavenner did about it. I was determined that your plea of self-incrimination was not going to stand naked and ugly while your motivations were so honorable."[17]

Rauh believed they could measure their success or failure of his gambit by two yardsticks: would the committee move legally against Hellman because of the letter? How would the *New York Times* and other major newspaper treat the story of her appearance? Would they emphasize the letter or the fact that she invoked the the Fifth Amendment?

HUAC chose not to pursue Hellman further. And she had not named names. In view of the letter, they could not attack her as "a Fifth Amendment Communist" either. Rauh had been right about the law. The possibility of finding her in contempt seemed remote.

The answer to the second question came with the morning edition of the *Times,* where the headline read: "Lillian Hellman Balks House Unit." The first and second paragraphs stressed the content of her offer to HUAC, especially the statement that she could not "cut my conscience to fit this year's fashions." Not until the fourth paragraph did the newspaper actually note that she had invoked the Fifth Amendment. When Murray Kempton's laudatory *New York Post* article, "Portrait of a Lady," appeared that same day, they knew they had won a major public relations victory.[18]

"The reaction here has been just too good to believe," Hellman told Rauh a few days later. She remarked that even Edna Ferber, "a very harsh lady, and none too liberal," had told a friend that "she had disliked me as long as she had known me, but that I had finally done a very good thing."[19]

Under Rauh's prodding and direction, Hellman had done a very good thing in 1952, although her later reluctance to admit membership in the Communist Party remains a mystery for someone who wrote eloquently about the morality of telling the truth. Unlike Clifford Odets, Elia Kazan, and Bud Schulberg, she did not inform on others. Although her recantation of Communism never met Rauh's standards, she paid a price for her stand in lost income and creative opportunities. The barons of Hollywood put her on their blacklist along with others who put conscience above conformity.

Arthur Miller's Crucible

Arthur Miller, an equally famous target for HUAC, gave Rauh an easy script when subpoenaed by the committee. Miller said he would, like Hellman, tell the congressmen about himself, but he would not invoke the

Fifth Amendment, and under no circumstances would he name others. In short, Miller said, he would rather go to jail than follow the examples of Odets and Kazan, who had cooperated with HUAC, even though the latter had directed two of his plays, *All My Sons* (1947) and *Death of a Salesman* (1949).

Miller also offered a tempting target to HUAC, which since the Hollywood Ten and the Alger Hiss hearings had been largely pushed off the front pages by the more brazen inquiries conducted by McCarthy and McCarran. Miller had endorsed a number of antifascist causes supported by the Communists, and criticized the Smith Act and the prosecution of Communist Party leaders. He had signed newspaper advertisements such as one in the *Washington Post* that affirmed, "Rob Communists of Their Rights—Then Yours Go Out the Window, Too." Along with Millard Lampell and the Veterans Against Discrimination of the Civil Rights Congress, he had urged the abolition of HUAC.

In 1954, the State Department refused to renew Miller's passport when he sought to travel to Brussels for the European opening of *The Crucible,* and that issue remained pending before the department in 1956. This became the justification for his subpoena when HUAC turned its attention to the unauthorized use of passports, especially foreign travel by citizens who had dared to criticize the government of the United States. In 1956 Miller became engaged as well to Hollywood's reigning sex goddess, Marilyn Monroe, a romantic liaison likely to stimulate an even greater barrage of press coverage for the House committee.

On June 21, 1956, Miller and Rauh appeared before the committee, now chaired by Francis E. Walter of Pennsylvania and managed by staff director Richard Arens, who served as grand inquisitor. It was quickly evident that the committee had very little interest in passports or Miller's conflict with the State Department. Arens turned the hearing quickly to the question of whether Miller had in his passport application and before the Youth Board of New York City denied "supporting the Communist cause or contributing to it" or being "under its discipline or domination."[20] Miller admitted that he had joined and supported various causes and organizations, some supported by Communists. "As for contributing to causes, front groups and so forth, I won't deny that," he told the committee. "I am here to tell you the truth and I wouldn't deny it."[21]

Miller denied membership in the party, but Arens attempted to link him to Moscow through his associations with known Communists, including those who admired his plays. Did Miller realize, Arens asked, that his dramatic works were produced in countries behind the Iron Curtain? "I take no more responsibility for who plays my plays than General Motors can take for who rides in their Chevrolets," Miller retorted.[22] In the space of two and a half hours, Miller answered over a hundred questions fired by Arens, Walter, and other committee members. He admitted joining a Marxist study group in Brooklyn in 1940 and attending "five or six" meetings in 1947 "of Communist Party writers," but he declined to identify those at such gatherings. He specifically refused to tell the committee whether the playwright Arnaud d'Usseau, author of *Deep Are the Roots*, served as chairman at one of the 1947 meetings.[23]

In response to a question from Congressman Gordon Scherer, Miller eloquently defended the constitutional right of writers to advocate unpopular, even revolutionary ideas, but in refusing to answer questions about d'Usseau or others at the 1947 meeting, he declined to invoke either the First or the Fifth Amendments. Taking Rauh's advice, he did challenge the relevance of those questions to the committee's declared intention of investigating the unauthorized use of passports. "All I can say, sir, is that my conscience will not permit me to use the name of another person. And that my counsel advises me that there is no relevance between this question of whether I should have a passport or there should be passport legislation in 1956."[24]

The committee gave Miller ten days to reply to its questions about d'Usseau and provide the names of those who had attended the meeting of Communist Party writers in 1947. Congressman Doyle added the final patriotic flourish: "Why," he asked the dramatist, "do you not direct some of that magnificent ability you have to fighting against well-known Communist subversive activities in our country and in the world?"[25] On the eve of the committee's deadline, with Miller remaining silent, Rauh issued a statement on behalf of his client citing precedents against the contempt penalty. "If that's his [Miller's] answer to the opportunity offered by the committee to avoid contempt," Chairman Walter told reporters, "then it seems to me he is inviting it."[26]

When the full House neared a vote on the contempt citation at the end of July, several congressmen called Rauh with pledges of support. The cause seemed hopeless in the House, Rauh advised. They would fight the next round in the courts. He cautioned these congressmen against making a futile gesture that might threaten their own reelections in the fall. Most took Rauh's advice and joined the 373 House members who voted to cite Miller for contempt, but nine representatives, all in safe districts, stood by Miller and registered opposition to HUAC. Seven months later, bowing to the wishes of prosecutors from the Department of Justice, a federal grand jury indicted the dramatist on two counts of contempt of Congress.[27]

Mrs. Arthur Miller

By the time his trial for contempt opened on May 14, 1957, before federal district judge Charles McLaughlin in the District of Columbia, Miller had married Monroe, whose fame far exceeded his own. On the eve of trial, Miller called Rauh in a panic. His wife insisted on coming to Washington, but he feared reporters and photographers would harass her at any hotel. Rauh offered them a sofa bed in his den. That evening he tossed car keys to his son Carl and gave him the opportunity to fulfill any teenage boy's fantasy: next morning he would drive to Union Station and pick up Marilyn Monroe, who would be disguised. Carl was admonished not to tell anyone about this clandestine assignment or that the actress would be staying at their house. "How will I recognize her?" Carl asked. His father explained that she would be wearing a dark wig, a head scarf, and sunglasses.[28]

Carl carried out his task and brought their famous houseguest back to the Rauhs' Appleton Street home in time for breakfast. When Marilyn asked for a glass of water, both Rauhs sprang into action immediately and nearly knocked one another over on the way to the kitchen sink. Olie Rauh observed that neither her husband nor son had ever moved so quickly from the table. Once they finished eating, but before Rauh and Miller set out for McLaughlin's court, Marilyn insisted on ironing her husband's shirt. And each evening she eagerly read the trial transcripts. "They used to teach us in sixth grade about free speech," Marilyn said to Rauh on one occasion as she tossed the transcript to the floor of the den. "I don't get it."[29]

When the press finally discovered Marilyn's hideout, Carl held an impromptu news conference in the Rauhs' front yard, where reporters asked him what it was like having such a celebrated houseguest. "Well, it's not exactly like sleeping with your brother," he told them. Neither the trial nor the Millers' personal life went well over the next two weeks when they stayed with the Rauhs. Marilyn, then pregnant, became suddenly ill under the emotional strain and miscarried soon after they returned to New York City, an event that probably changed the course of their marriage and perhaps her own life. Meeting Marilyn for the first time in 1962 at President John Kennedy's birthday party, Arthur Schlesinger noted that the only moment she seemed moved was when "I mentioned that I was a friend of Joe Rauh. This produced a warm and spontaneous burst of affection—but then she receded into her own glittering mist."[30]

Judge McLaughlin, who refused to delay the trial pending the outcome of a potentially relevant Supreme Court decision, rejected Rauh's principal argument that HUAC had failed to demonstrate the relevance of its questions in Miller's case to the investigation of unauthorized passports. Instead, McLaughlin permitted the prosecutors to argue successfully that the questions about who attended the writers' meeting and the role of d'Usseau had been pertinent to establishing Miller's veracity and whether or not he had been under the discipline of the Communist Party. The committee, of course, had never probed those issues. McLaughlin also turned back Rauh's additional arguments that the committee had failed to direct Miller to answer in conformity with past judicial rulings and that its inquiry violated the First Amendment. Finally, he ruled that Miller had failed to object in a timely manner to the relevance of the committee's question concerning attendance at the 1947 meeting. On June 28, 1957, McLaughlin gave Miller a suspended one-month prison term and fined him $500.[31]

John Watkins versus HUAC

Rauh had focused much of his artillery at the procedural errors committed by HUAC, but he hoped that with such a celebrated client it might be possible to reopen First Amendment claims that the courts had previously spurned. A victory on those grounds might finally erect a major obstacle to the committee's further inquisitions. That strategy failed. Miller's conviction would be overturned eventually and HUAC restrained not by the case of the famous dramatist, but by that of another client, union organizer John T. Watkins.

A former member of the radical Farm Equipment Workers International Union and a veteran of the labor wars against International Harvester, Watkins had brought the East Moline, Illinois, Harvester plant into the fold of the United Auto Workers in 1954. Watkins told Rauh he had never formally joined the CP, but he had been so close to it that the distinction seemed pointless. As he later told HUAC, he made contributions to party causes, signed their petitions, "and participated in Communist activities to such a degree that some persons may honestly believe that I was a member of the party."[32]

Reuther, a strong anticommunist, had won control of the UAW in 1947 by ousting the Communist faction from the union's executive board and curbing its influence in the locals, but for him these were matters of internal UAW politics. Even in the case of party members who fought him to the end, Reuther did not relish seeing them beaten down by HUAC. He opened the union's coffers to defend UAW members like Watkins who were subpoenaed to appear before the Red hunters in Congress, but he also imposed one condition: the union member could not invoke the Fifth Amendment.

Rauh, who had defended Hellman on those grounds, argued vigorously against Reuther's policy, but could not change the UAW leader's mind even when he shamed him by pointing out that the union behaved like the Hollywood moguls who had blacklisted employees on similar grounds. The issue mattered little to Watkins, however, who said he would tell the committee willingly about himself, would identify persons whom he knew to be current members of the Communist Party, but not others with whom he associated in the past. And he would not invoke the protections of the Fifth.

Watkins refused to discuss the past conduct of six specific persons or confirm the Communist ties of those on a longer list of twenty-five. Reading from a statement Rauh had prepared, the UAW organizer told the committee: "I do not believe that such questions are relevant to the work of this committee nor do I believe that this committee has the right to undertake the public exposure of persons because of their past activities. I may be wrong, but until and unless a court of law so holds and directs me to answer, I most firmly refuse to discuss the political activities of my past associates."[33] Despite the eloquence of Rauh and his client, the committee held Watkins in contempt. He was soon tried and convicted on a seven-count indictment, fined $100, and placed on a year's probation.

In his appeal of Watkins's conviction before the Court of Appeals for the District of Columbia, Rauh stressed two points: HUAC's demand that Watkins discuss the past political conduct of thirty-one people did not manifest a legitimate legislative purpose, but only a desire to expose and humiliate people, a motive outside the scope of Congress's authority. In addition, HUAC had not explained to Watkins why it needed those names or what consequences might follow if he refused to answer. By a vote of two to one, the court of appeals overturned Watkins's conviction, a result that sent HUAC chairman Walters into fits of rage on the House floor and inspired the Department of Justice to request a rehearing *en banc* before the appeals court. Over the dissent of the original majority, the full appeals court reaffirmed Watkins's conviction, thereby setting the stage for Rauh's historic petition to the Supreme Court.[34]

John Watkins versus the United States

In a thirty-page appendix to their Supreme Court brief in *Watkins v. United States,* Rauh and his associates documented the number of times Walters and his colleagues on HUAC had admitted that their request for names arose from a desire "to focus the spotlight of publicity upon their activities" or "to expose people and organizations attempting to destroy this country." On one occasion, the chairman declared that HUAC probed "subversion and subversive propaganda," a topic that chief justice Earl Warren later described as "at least as broad and indefinite as the authorizing resolution of the Committee, if not more so."[35]

On June 17, 1957, while Miller remained on trial before Judge McLaughlin, Warren and five other members of the Supreme Court reversed John Watkins's contempt conviction, a decision that for the first time since HUAC's creation in 1938 placed some restraints upon its investigative methods. The chief justice and the majority overturned Watkins's conviction on narrow due process grounds: the committee had neglected to inform him "with undisputable clarity" of the subject under inquiry and the pertinence of specific questions once he had objected to them. The committee had not, Warren ruled, given Watkins "a fair opportunity to determine whether he was within his rights in refusing to answer." At the same time, Warren laced his opinion with copious references to the rights of privacy, association, and freedom of speech, and he admonished Congress that its broad powers of investigation did not compass exposure for the mere sake of exposure. "Protected freedoms should not be placed in danger," the chief justice wrote, "in the absence of a clear determination by the House . . . that a particular inquiry is justified by a specific legislative need."[36]

The Watkins decision indicated that a majority of the justices on the Supreme Court endorsed some restraints, however limited, upon the worst governmental abuses of the Red Scare. That message did not immediately penetrate the consciousness of Judge McLaughlin, who had tossed out the first count of Miller's conviction on grounds of relevance and timely warning, but refused even in the wake of the *Watkins* decision to overturn the second verdict. He insisted that Miller and Rauh had been obliged to raise a separate objection concerning relevance to each question during the hearing![37]

Fortunately for Miller, the nine judges on the Court of Appeals for the District of Columbia adopted the spirit if not the letter of *Watkins*. On June 11, 1958, Rauh argued Miller's appeal. "Joe made a magnificent oral argument and seemed to have the majority of the Court with him on some point or other," Dan Pollitt reported. "It would be my guess that Judge Burger will write the opinion for a unanimous court reversing the conviction on grounds that Miller was never directed to answer the question."[38] Pollitt's prediction proved accurate. A year after McLaughlin imposed sentence, the court of appeals overturned Miller's conviction on the remaining count in a short *per curiam* opinion. Without reliance on the relevancy requirement of *Watkins*, the judges nonetheless ruled that Miller's conviction could not stand because HUAC interrogators had failed explicitly to direct him to answer the question.[39]

"It is true that the Court of Appeals took the easy way out," Rauh observed, "but this was probably the only ground on which a unanimous decision could have been obtained. I rather look at it this way—Arthur Miller refused to inform on others and he won his case. If a few more people do this and are successful, regardless of the ground of success, we will have shown the courts' displeasure towards forced informing even though they may be unwilling to carve out a legal principle preventing it."[40]

Miller, of course, was overjoyed. "Marilyn swore she'd write you a letter of thanks," he told his attorney. "She keeps asking why you can't run for President. I told her you could if she'd run for Vice President. As for me, all I want is the Treasury."[41]

Miller and Rauh had been fortunate that the court of appeals disposed of their case before a majority of the justices on the Supreme Court retreated significantly from the language in *Watkins*. A year after Miller's conviction had been overturned, in *Barenblatt v. United States* they sustained the contempt conviction of a college instructor who declined to answer questions before HUAC concerning present and past membership in the Communist Party.[42]

"It did not escape me that by a stroke of genius we did press to have my case separated from the others which seem now to be in the doomed department," Miller told Rauh a few days after the Supreme Court decided *Barenblatt*. Rauh reported back that he had recently encountered Chief Judge Henry Edgerton of the court of appeals at a wedding, where the jurist had remarked: "Pretty smart, Joe, getting the *Miller* case speeded up and decided while our Court was under the shadow of *Watkins*, not *Barenblatt*."[43]

By the summer of 1957 a series of events had converged to signal a turning point in the domestic Red Scare that had poisoned the nation's politics and warped its legal system for more than a decade. A month before Rauh won the *Watkins* case in the Supreme Court, one of the main instigators of national hysteria, Senator McCarthy, condemned by the Senate, his spirit broken and his body destroyed by alcohol, died of liver failure. The fires of repression that he and others had stoked, partly cooled by a series of judicial rulings, flickered out in the next decade, in part because of Lillian Hellman, Arthur Miller, John Watkins, and their attorney.

CHAPTER TEN

REUTHER AND RANDOLPH

[Rauh] is just about the loudest, most determined, most
aggressive and least easily silenced battler for civil liberties,
civil rights and union rights practicing law in the capital.
— NEW YORK TIMES REPORTER, 1958

"The Most Dangerous Man in Detroit"

Walter Reuther's enemies branded him "the most dangerous man in Detroit"
and "a more dangerous menace than Sputnik or anything Soviet Russia
might do to America."[1] He was Joe Rauh's kind of labor leader—a pragmatic
idealist, smart, eloquent, fearless. So was Asa Philip Randolph, known as
"Chief" to the members of his union of sleeping car porters. One white, one
African-American, Reuther and Randolph championed working people and
civil rights in post–New Deal America. Rauh enlisted in their struggles, and
they became a formidable trio.

Unlike Harvard-educated Joe Rauh, Reuther had dropped out of high
school in Wheeling, West Virginia. He learned about politics from his Socialist father, Valentine, who in 1919 took Walter and his younger brother, Victor, to visit Eugene V. Debs at the Moundsville Penitentiary, where the
party's beloved leader served time for obstructing the draft in World War I.
Walter soon learned about industrial relations on the shop floor as a tool-and-
die worker at the Wheeling Corrugated Company (later Wheeling Steel),
where he lost a big toe as the result of an industrial accident.

Walter and Victor traveled to Europe and the Soviet Union in the early
1930s, joining thousands of skilled foreign workers disillusioned with Western capitalism and drawn to participate, however briefly, in what many believed would be a new regime of progressive industrial relations under
Stalin's Five-Year Plan. At the Gorky automotive works, Walter and Vic

trained raw peasants in the use of machine tools and waxed enthusiastic about what Victor called "genuine proletarian democracy" in a society "that will forever end the exploitation of man by man." Those naive sentiments would later be used by their opponents inside and outside the UAW to brand them as hard-core Communists.[2]

The brothers returned to the Untied States in 1935 at a critical moment in the history of the American labor movement. The New Deal's National Recovery Act inspired workers in the great mass production industries, such as steel, autos, and textiles, to seek union recognition and collective bargaining. The craft-oriented American Federation of Labor (AFL), long indifferent to the fate of these mostly unskilled workers, created the United Auto Workers (UAW) to skim off the craft workers and channel the rising discontent along the assembly lines at General Motors, Ford, and Chrysler. But when John L. Lewis led his coal miners and other workers out of the AFL to form the Committee on Industrial Organization (CIO), the Reuthers followed him.

Working with veteran organizers, many of them members of the Communist Party later purged from the union, Walter, Vic, and their younger brother, Roy, built the UAW into a disciplined fighting machine. The fledgling union defeated General Motors during the famous sit-down strikes at Flint in 1937 and gained recognition that spring as the official bargaining representative for GM workers. That triumph, combined with union recognition in the steel industry and a Supreme Court ruling sustaining the National Labor Relations Act, brought industry-wide collective bargaining to the heart of industrial America.

While most union leaders in both the AFL and the new CIO stressed the importance of labor's autonomy and focused narrowly on bread-and-butter issues of collective bargaining, craft jurisdictions, wages, and hours, Reuther often articulated a broader vision. The federal government, he believed, should play an active role in maintaining high levels of employment through its fiscal and monetary controls and also guarantee basic levels of economic decency with minimum wages, old-age pensions, and workmen's compensation. Rauh and Reuther shared important values and commitments—to economic justice, racial equality, and civil liberties—that made them natural allies, although different perspectives about how to achieve these goals sometimes brought them into conflict.

Anticommunists

Rauh and Reuther shared an abiding dislike for the American Communist Party, an attitude rooted in their efforts to stimulate greater defense production during the period of the Soviet-Nazi Pact, when the party's leaders and rank-and-file union members often displayed greater devotion to the foreign policy of Stalin than to the goals of the War Department. After the war, a bitter struggle to control the UAW, where his most relentless opponents marched under the Communist banner, reinforced Reuther's hostility. When he finally won the UAW presidency in 1946, the new leader of the autoworkers ran on a platform that denounced his Communist opponents as tools of a sinister institution that sought to undermine the union's autonomy. Joining other CIO and AFL leaders, Reuther condemned virtually all provisions of the Taft-Hartley Act, but at the same time he found the new law's anticommunist affidavit provisions useful in curbing the influence of several UAW rivals who refused to sign the required statements disclaiming adherence to the Communist Party.

Along with other union leaders who rose to power through the New Deal, Reuther linked the UAW's fortunes and his own to the Democratic Party. Beginning in 1947 he also found a comfortable home in the ADA, which included many of his wartime allies from the Union for Democratic Action. With encouragement from Rauh, the UAW soon became the principal financial supporter of the ADA's liberal anticommunism and a major contributor as well to the National Association for the Advancement of Colored People (NAACP) and the Leadership Conference on Civil Rights, a budding coalition of groups dedicated to the advancement of racial justice.

Maurice Sugar, the UAW's general counsel and a former candidate for governor of Michigan on the Communist Party ticket, became one of the first victims of Reuther's anticommunist purge, and Rauh's firm became the immediate beneficiary of the purge when he raised money for the union during the GM strike and secured a favorable ruling from the Internal Revenue Service that contributions to the strike relief fund could be regarded as tax-deductible charitable contributions. When Reuther offered him the union's top legal post, Rauh declined to move to Detroit and hesitated to become tied down with routine union business. Reuther did the next best thing and hired Rauh's partner, Irving Levy.

After Levy's tragic suicide in 1951, Reuther again offered the general counsel post to Rauh, but encountered the same unwillingness to take up full-time duties in Detroit. The UAW chief thus made official what had been unofficial since 1947—Joe Rauh became the UAW's very special Washington counsel. From that agreement until the late 1960s, Reuther and the UAW became the Rauh firm's most important client. The UAW account offered important work in labor law and civil liberties and a steady stream of income that permitted the firm to take up other causes *pro bono*. It also provided identification with one of the most powerful leaders of organized labor, a voice to be taken seriously inside the Democratic Party.

Reuther cashiered his Communist rivals in the UAW hierarchy, aggressively enforced the anticommunist provisions of the Taft-Hartley Act, and even opposed UAW members taking refuge in the Fifth Amendment when called before congressional committees. That position put him at odds with Rauh, who believed the policy morally and legally indefensible, a clear violation of an individual's constitutional rights. Reuther stood firm, however, rejected Rauh's advice, and beat down all opposition to his Fifth Amendment ban.

Defending UAW Members

Despite his stand on the Fifth Amendment, Reuther stood behind Rauh's efforts to defend Allen Taylor, John Watkins, and other UAW members who had been members of the party or very close to it, a decision that kept Rauh and his firm in the forefront of opposition to the government's security program. Reuther's and Rauh's anticommunism did not spare the UAW from the full brunt of the loyalty-security ordeal. The Pentagon's program had become a travesty, Rauh told the Senate Judiciary Committee's subcommittee on constitutional rights, because "the laudable objective of protecting real security information has been so expanded that [it] . . . today applies to all sorts of people who have nothing to do with security information."[3] The UAW's chief counsel, Harold Cranefield, echoed these views when he told Reuther, "The security system has operated . . . to nullify protective provisions of our collective bargaining agreements, especially in the matter of processing of grievances."[4]

UAW members in the aircraft plants faced draconian procedures that gave employers an important tool for blacklisting troublesome workers. Employers held the upper hand because they defined the type of work requiring a security clearance and also initiated requests for screening individuals. This power was often used to rid plants of outspoken union members caught in the machinery of the loyalty-security program. Among the more outrageous cases that Rauh confronted concerned a foundry worker in a nonsecret section of a factory whose employer requested a clearance for him on the grounds that in the future he might be reassigned to a top-secret task. The company never reassigned the employee, who remained in the foundry, but fired him anyway when the Defense Department declared him a security risk![5]

Companies could declare their entire plants top secret, request clearance for all workers, and banish even those in nonsensitive areas of production who failed to pass government scrutiny. Douglas Aircraft, for example, terminated employees from sensitive positions who were found to be security risks and refused to reemploy them elsewhere in nonsecret activities. Once branded by the government as a security risk, moreover, an individual employee found himself unemployable by all companies that held government contracts, top secret or not.

Until Rauh fought his case through the Department of Defense bureaucracy, UAW member James Schuetz lost his security clearance for violating an injunction on a picket line. Faced with criticism for what appeared to be antiunion behavior, the Pentagon reluctantly revised its security guidelines to provide that "legitimate labor activities shall not be considered in determining whether clearance should be granted," but the word "legitimate" still left broad discretion in the hands of the department's loyalty board.[6] Fighting the security program for the UAW on a case-by-case basis proved frustrating and often fruitless. The Supreme Court slapped the Pentagon over the wrist in the *Greene* case, but Rauh did not anticipate immediate reforms. He expected that the Eisenhower administration would issue a new executive order reapplying the old rules, the Supreme Court would sustain them five years later, and "this whole thing means further years of dreary litigation."[7]

Trouble in Sheboygan

As the economic and political clout of Reuther and the UAW rose, so did the intensity of counterattacks by those who regarded the autoworkers' president as a threat to corporate hegemony. In addition to an unending stream of industrial security cases, Rauh found himself defending the UAW against one of the most implacable antiunion employers in the history of labor-management relations—the Kohler Company of Sheboygan, Wisconsin, a major manufacturer of bathroom fixtures in America.

In the spring of 1954, Reuther and the UAW leadership authorized a strike for union recognition against the company, whose president, Herbert Kohler, waved a club against pickets while declaring, "I am the law." In Sheboygan, where the company had crushed earlier strikes in the 1890s, 1930s, and 1950s, this was not an idle boast. Kohler's own nephew, Walter, occupied the governor's chair in Madison. The company's payroll, the largest in the city, earned it broad support from the clergy, the bar, local merchants, and elected officials, most of them Republicans who regarded unions as harbingers of revolution.

Displaying considerable fortitude, Sheboygan's county sheriff, Theodore

Mosch, adopted a neutral stance and refused to use force to break the picket line, a decision that cost him support from the local Republican leadership. But violence flared often between the strikers and Kohler employees who continued to operate the factory after Governor Kohler rejected Mosch's request for National Guard troops to maintain order. Provoked by a company that fired union members summarily, evicted them from company housing, and spied on their meetings, UAW members sometimes responded with violence of their own. UAW pickets surrounded the homes of nonstrikers and doused their automobiles with paint and sulphuric acid. William Vinson, chief union steward at a UAW local in Detroit, attacked a nonstriker in a Sheboygan bar, broke several of his ribs, and punctured his lung. Arrested, tried, and convicted of assault, Vinson served thirteen months in jail. Another UAW picket, John Gunaca, fled the state to avoid prosecution after he and others pummeled a nonstriker, William Bersch, and broke his neck. Bersch died three months later of a heart attack, which critics predictably blamed on the union's mayhem.[8]

Support from the Kennedy Brothers

The Kohler strike dragged on for five years as the company secured an antipicketing order from the Wisconsin Employment Relations Board and the union filed unfair labor practices charges with the NLRB. The frequent episodes of violence in Sheboygan provided a fresh opportunity for Reuther's political enemies in Congress to attack the UAW. Tales of union corruption and the influence of organized crime spurred the Senate to create a Select Committee on Improper Activities in the Labor-Management Field, soon known as the Rackets Committee, chaired by conservative Arkansas Democrat John McClellan. Three Republicans on the committee—Carl Curtis of Nebraska, Karl Mundt of South Dakota, and Barry Goldwater of Arizona—used the hearings as a forum for attacking Reuther and the UAW. Democrats, led by Pat McNamara of Michigan and John F. Kennedy of Massachusetts, whose younger brother, Robert, served as the committee's chief counsel, attempted to keep the spotlight on Jimmy Hoffa and the Teamsters, a union expelled from the AFL-CIO for its corrupt practices.

The McClellan committee's inquiries ultimately produced a new piece of legislation, the Landrum-Griffin Act of 1959, which most union leaders denounced as a dagger aimed at their organizations. Rauh worked with Senator Kennedy to soften portions of the law, and he would ultimately use its provisions in the 1970s and 1980s to vindicate the rights of rank-and-file union members. Touted by its sponsors as a bill of rights for labor, the new law imposed sharp limits on disciplinary proceedings inside unions, required detailed financial reports, mandated secret-ballot elections for union offices, banned secondary boycotts, and barred from office anyone who had belonged to the Communist Party within five years. The Supreme Court soon struck down that last provision as a bill of attainder. Before the committee reported the bill, however, its six-week investigation of the Kohler strike generated little but rancorous exchanges between the Republicans and Rauh and Reuther, who represented the UAW.

The hearings became Rauh's first extended collaboration with Senator Kennedy. Throughout the hearings, behind-the-scenes cooperation flourished among Rauh, Dan Pollitt, and the Kennedy brothers, whose staff members—Kenny O'Donnell and Pierre Salinger—kept the UAW lawyers informed about the subcommittee's general strategy. JFK's staff provided Rauh with drafts of the subcommittee's final report and encouraged his comments on revisions. Kennedy himself made strategic appearances during counterattacks made on Rauh and Reuther by the Republicans. "Whenever there was trouble," Rauh recalled later, "I would look over at one of our guys, and I'd say, 'Where is he? And soon [Kennedy] would walk down the aisle. It was a very well known joke among our crowd that . . . Kennedy would always show up when we were in trouble.'"[9]

Goldwater, eager to link the union to Communist subversion, noted that several UAW organizers had belonged to the Trotskyite Socialist Workers Party and that Communists used violence, "just as it is the cornerstone of the UAW's activities." Kennedy rose to the union's defense. "My brother's name was Joe and Stalin's name was Joe," he retorted, "but this should scarcely support an argument that they had anything else in common."[10] When the UAW's Emil Mazey criticized the leadership of the Catholic Church in Sheboygan for its alleged antiunion bias, the Republicans and McClellan attacked him as a religious bigot, but Robert Kennedy took the gaffe in stride. When a downcast Rauh came to the chief counsel's office at the end of the day after Mazey's performance, Kennedy quipped, "Don't feel so bad, Joe, the Pope hasn't called in yet."[11]

On several occasions when Rauh interrupted and challenged Mundt and Curtis, the chairman threatened to throw him out of the hearing room for attempting to "out talk the committee." A reporter for the *New York Times*, noting that Rauh pronounced his name "row," in the sense of noisy disturbance, thought it very appropriate. The UAW's lawyer, he observed, "is just about the loudest, most determined, most aggressive and least easily silenced battler for civil liberties, civil rights and union rights practicing law in the capital."[12]

Winning at the NLRB

Rauh and the UAW had more success when the issues at Kohler moved from McClellan's committee to the National Labor Relations Board and the federal courts. Six years after the strike began, the NLRB ruled that the company had been guilty of numerous unfair labor practices and ordered remedial steps, but it refused to order the reinstatement of seventy-seven union members who, it argued, had engaged in unprotected, illegal actions during the strike.[13]

Two days before the labor board issued its official Kohler report, the agency announced the document would be released at 10:30 in the morning on August 26. Rauh anticipated that the UAW would prevail on most issues, but not all. The union would appeal some part of the board's order to a federal circuit court, and Kohler would do likewise. Legal victory would likely go to the party that first filed in a sympathetic federal court on August 26 because the law permitted an appeal either to the circuit where the decision came down or to the circuit of the company's location. Rauh's strategy insured that the Kohler case came before the appeals court in D.C., rather than a more conservative appeals bench in Chicago. He labored through the night with his partner John Silard, Pollitt, and Lou Pollock, future dean of Yale Law School, to prepare five separate petitions for review, each covering different grounds for appeal.

On the morning of the twenty-sixth, Silard manned the lone telephone in the hallway outside the NLRB offices. Pollock grabbed a copy of the official opinion at 10:30, scanned it quickly and shouted to Silard: "File number 2!" Silard dialed up Pollitt, stationed at the federal courthouse in D.C., who turned in the appropriate UAW petition five minutes later, at exactly 10:35. Lawyers for Kohler, who also anticipated a dash to the federal courthouses, filed their petition a half hour later in Chicago, but argued they had won the race because of the time difference, a proposition the courts rejected. "I may not be the world's greatest lawyer," Rauh told his confederates that day, "but I'm pretty good at logistics."[14]

On September 11, Judge Henry Edgerton, a Roosevelt appointee, and David Bazelon, a Truman appointee, took the bench with chief judge Wilbur K. Miller. Four months later, over Miller's angry dissent, Edgerton and Bazelon sustained all of the NLRB's rulings against Kohler and reversed the board on its refusal to order the reinstatement of seventy-seven strikers dismissed by the company. The majority remanded that issue to the NLRB with very explicit instructions that the agency should weigh the gravity of Kohler's unfair labor practices against the conduct of the dismissed employees.[15]

In 1965, over a decade after the strike at Kohler began, the same appeals court panel sustained an NLRB order reinstating fifty-seven of the final seventy-seven strikers, a decision that gave Rauh and his associates almost a complete victory.[16] When the final bill came due, Kohler had lost more than its reputation. Along with reinstatement, all the strikers received back pay and pension benefits totaling over $3 million.

The UAW and Race

Lower American tariffs, international competition in autos, the changing structure of the American economy, and racial conflict became the UAW's Achilles' heel in the years after the Kohler decision. About the first three problems, Rauh could do little. About the third he did a great deal, often with the support of Reuther and sometimes without. Few white labor leaders in the 1950s or 1960s spoke out with greater passion against racial segregation and discrimination or contributed more energy and money to their destruction than Reuther and the UAW. At the same time, deep racial fault lines within the union and a commitment to internal solidarity frequently compromised Reuther's ideals and his actions.

In the 1930s and 1940s the Communist Party had gained the loyalty of African-American autoworkers, many of whom had opposed Reuther's rise to power and continued to chafe under his leadership. Except for George Crockett and Horace Sheffield, few blacks held positions of influence on the union's staff, and no African-American sat on the UAW's executive committee. Reuther unequivocally supported the Supreme Court's decision in *Brown* and criticized the lack of enforcement by the Eisenhower administration, but he tolerated segregated UAW locals in the South. In Detroit and across Michigan, the UAW's white rank-and-file members voted against fair housing and fair employment laws, despite support for these measures by Reuther and the UAW leadership. In 1952 and 1956, when the Democratic Party and its presidential candidate Adlai Stevenson watered down the 1948 civil rights platform in order not to "put the South over a barrel," Reuther lobbied against those efforts at the convention, but ultimately swallowed the watered-down platform and the candidate.[17]

Mr. Randolph

Inside his own union, Reuther did not rock the boat on the issue of race. Outside the UAW, he gained much-needed credibility from Rauh's aggressive efforts on behalf of racial justice. None proved more significant than his lawyer's identification with Randolph, the Florida-born son of an itinerant Methodist preacher and the head of the Brotherhood of Sleeping Car Porters. With Reuther and Rauh it was always the intimate "Walter" and "Joe." Such informality never characterized the relationship between Rauh and the tall, dignified leader of the porters, who usually wore a pressed blue serge suit, a vest, and a clean, white pocket handkerchief. Randolph insisted on calling his attorney "Mr. Rauh," which he pronounced "Raw," and Mr. Rauh returned the compliment by calling him "Mr. Randolph."

They had met indirectly during the war, when Randolph's threatened march on Washington and Rauh's legal draftsmanship gave life to Roosevelt's decision to ban discrimination in federal contracts and to the creation of a Fair Employment Practices Committee in 1941. They first sat down face-to-face after the war, when Randolph launched an all-out attack on segregation and discrimination in the armed forces. He created the Committee Against Jim Crow in Military Service and Training and the League for Non-Violent Civil Disobedience Against Military Segregation. Through these organizations he made it clear that "Negroes are in no mood to shoulder a gun for democracy abroad so long as they are denied democracy here at home."[18]

General Eisenhower justified segregation in the army because, he claimed, it gave poorly educated blacks opportunities that would be denied them in competition with whites. Randolph challenged that idea when he organized a mock trial against the army at the Phyllis Sweetly YWCA in Washington. Arthur Garfield Hays of the ACLU served as counsel, and Rauh acted as his deputy. The YWCA trial, Randolph's new threat of civil disobedience against the military draft, and Truman's need for northern votes hastened desegregation of the armed forces between 1948 and the Korean War. Randolph, impressed by Rauh's performance at the mock trial, asked him to represent the Pullman porters in a series of jurisdictional battles to gain admission to the all-white Railway Labor Executives Association and to secure equal treatment for black firemen on the railroads.[19]

Fighting the White Brotherhoods

Until the major railroads adopted diesel locomotives in the 1940s, black firemen monopolized the dirty job of shoveling coal, although the all-white Brotherhood of Locomotive Firemen and Engineers barred them from membership. With the spread of diesel power, the white Brotherhood invoked its authority as an official bargaining agent under the Railway Labor Act of 1926 to sign contracts with the major carriers that stripped blacks of half of these positions despite their seniority. The contracts also barred the future employment of blacks in the craft and blocked their promotion to engineers.

Represented by Charles Hamilton Houston, the brilliant legal strategist of the NAACP, and supported *amici curiae* by the United States and the ACLU, the black firemen won a landmark victory in the Supreme Court in 1944 when the justices ruled unanimously that the Railway Labor Act imposed an affirmative duty on the Brotherhood to negotiate for all employees in a particular class, not only union members. The law also banned racial discrimination, the Court held, and for breach of this duty the Brotherhood could be enjoined from further discrimination and sued for damages.[20]

Rauh built upon Houston's success when he sought a similar injunction and damages for Leroy Graham and twenty other black firemen, organized by Randolph, who had endured similar discrimination by the Brotherhood in contracts negotiated with three railroads. On the merits, he had a strong case, but the Brotherhood and the carriers raised jurisdictional and statutory objections that threatened to derail the suit. Hoping to litigate the issues in the District of Columbia rather than in Ohio, location of the union's headquarters, Rauh named two local lodges of the Brotherhood as defendants. The court of appeals rejected his ploy and ruled that the federal venue statute required all of the defendants to reside in the appropriate judicial district. The Brotherhood also claimed that the Norris-LaGuardia Act, which barred federal courts from issuing injunctions in labor-management disputes, prohibited the relief sought by the black firemen.[21]

Rauh and Levy persuaded the Supreme Court otherwise. On the jurisdictional issue they pointed to another federal venue statute that permitted an action if the defendant was either "an inhabitant of" or "found within" the District of Columbia. A unanimous Supreme Court agreed that the suit could commence locally under that provision. Writing for the Court, Justice Jackson also made short work of the Norris-LaGuardia objection by noting that the general purpose of the law had been to secure the rights of labor, not to destroy them. An injunction was an appropriate remedy where the union had failed in its duty to represent employees under the Railway Labor Act.[22]

A year later, Rauh initiated a complaint with the Labor Department on behalf of Randolph that alleged that the Railway Labor Executives Association had illegally discriminated on grounds of race by excluding him from their organization. At first, Randolph's insistence on joining the all-white organization puzzled his counsel. The "Chief" had been a socialist his entire life, a man devoted to racial and economic justice. The heads of the railroad brotherhoods by contrast were notorious racists and economic conservatives. But for Randolph, principle and symbolism counted for a great deal. Like them, he was a railway labor executive, and he wanted a voice in their association.

Sensing that the Labor Department would rule against them, the executives surrendered without a fight and invited Randolph and Rauh to a meeting at the Hamilton Hotel in Washington to discuss the terms and conditions of the porters' membership. When they arrived in the hotel room, Randolph and his attorney found George Harrison, president of the association and head of the Railway Clerks Union, and two dozen other members already seated in stony silence around a large table. With every chair occupied, no one rose to offer Randolph or Rauh a place to sit. Instead, they were forced to stand for the entire meeting with their backs to the wall.

"I understand the porters want to become members of the association," Harrison intoned, barely looking at Randolph.

"Yes, Mr. Harrison, we do," Randolph replied.

Harrison then stated that the membership dues would be around $2,000 per year, a sum that Rauh immediately knew would strain the porter's meager budget. He and Levy had always given the porters a reduced fee and never complained when the bill went unpaid for months. The porters presently owed Rauh money. But Randolph didn't hesitate. In his deepest and most dignified voice, he said simply: "The porters will meet their financial obligations." Harrison quickly adjourned the meeting.

A few minutes later outside the hotel and under a streetlight at the corner of Fourteenth Street and J, Rauh stopped with his client.

"Mr. Randolph," he said, "we've got to have a drink and celebrate our victory," an offer that jumped out of his mouth before he reflected on the fact that racial segregation in D.C. would prevent such a celebration in public between a black man and a white man.

"Where do you think we can go to have a drink?" Randolph inquired.

Now aware of his gaffe, Rauh suggested that they go to his home or to Union Station, a small piece of interstate commerce that had been desegregated under court order. Mr. Randolph had a better idea, one that saved his dignity and Rauh's too.

"Mr. Rauh," he said, "let us consider that we have already had our symbolic drink." And with that remark, he turned and strolled off into the night.[23]

The drink that he and Randolph never had that evening and the humiliating experience with the railway labor executives infused Rauh with a new determination to mount other challenges to America's racial status quo and to secure from the courts and Congress a fresh commitment to civil rights, commitments that had too long lay dormant in the Constitution and laws of the United States.

CHAPTER ELEVEN

HHH, JFK, AND LBJ

Hubert Humphrey pushed through possibly
the worst bill of our time in an effort to
escape the wrath of the McCarthyites.

—JOE RAUH TO JOSEPHINE GOMON

FDR's Heirs

Hubert Horatio Humphrey, Lyndon Baines Johnson, and John Fitzgerald
Kennedy, each an heir to the political house FDR built, played critical roles
in Rauh's efforts to redefine the shape of liberalism and the Democratic
Party after 1945. The son of a Doland, South Dakota, pharmacist, Humphrey
embodied the virtues and grievances of the farmers, small shopkeepers, and
industrial workers of the upper Midwest, who formed the militant Minnesota Farmer-Labor Party in the 1920s. Entering politics in 1943, he lost his
first bid to become mayor of Minneapolis that year, but helped to unite the
Democrats and the Farmer-Laborites into the Farmer-Labor Party (DFL)
and purge Communists from the organization.

After winning the mayor's office in 1945, Humphrey helped found the
ADA, built a strong record in the city by combating racial and religious discrimination, and gained national recognition with his 1948 convention
speech on behalf of the minority civil rights plank. A year later, he became
the first Democrat since the Civil War to be elected to the United States Senate from Minnesota. By 1960 he ranked among that chamber's most liberal
members, sharing Rauh's vision of the party's future in civil rights, the role of
the ADA, and liberal anticommunism.[1]

Three years Humphrey's senior, Johnson had been born in a small farm-
house in Stonewall, Texas, the eldest of five children, a descendent of several

generations of Baptist preachers and local political notables. Like other Southerners of his generation, Johnson brought to Roosevelt's Democratic coalition a streak of economic populism and a desire to pull his state and region out of its grinding poverty with infusions of federal dollars. Sam Rayburn, a rising power in the House of Representatives, took Johnson under his political wing, and through Rayburn's influence, LBJ headed the Texas National Youth Administration, won a seat in the House of Representatives in 1937, and was elected to the Senate eleven years later.

In the Senate Johnson promoted the economic development of Texas via federal spending in military installations and on the state's infrastructure, especially dam construction and rural electrification. Reelected to the Senate in 1954, he soon became the youngest majority leader in history and, many said, the most powerful. In a state hostile to organized labor and devoted to maintaining the formal and informal segregation of African- and Mexican-Americans, LBJ's public record marked him as an enemy of both unions and civil rights. Civil liberties ranked even lower in his scheme of values. By 1960, Rauh considered Johnson his most cunning and determined enemy in the struggle to reshape the party's agenda in the direction of expanded economic justice, racial equality, and civil liberties.[2]

In 1956 Johnson was only one of three southern senators who did not endorse the so-called Southern Manifesto denouncing the Supreme Court's decision in *Brown v. Board of Education* as "contrary to the Constitution" and "a clear abuse of judicial power," but that same year he used his power as majority leader to torpedo a House-passed civil rights bill written with the encouragement of Eisenhower's attorney general. The measure would have created a civil rights commission with limited investigative powers and an expanded civil rights division in the Department of Justice, and would have authorized civil suits to protect voting rights. Johnson made certain the bill went to the hostile Judiciary Committee, dominated by southern segregationists, where it died.

A year later Johnson orchestrated passage of the first federal civil rights law since Reconstruction, but one that excluded House-passed provisions giving the attorney general power to file civil actions to enforce the Supreme Court's *Brown* decision and mandating jury trials in cases of civil contempt, a requirement that gave all-white juries an effective veto over federal district judges. LBJ warned Senator Richard Russell of Georgia that the legislation, which he called "the nigger bill," was necessary to counter the rising protests in the South by African-Americans, who had mounted a successful boycott of Montgomery buses. "These Negroes, they're getting pretty uppity these days," he told Russell, "and that's a problem for us since they've got something now they never had before, the political pull to back up their uppityness."[3]

As majority leader Johnson also took the lead in defending Senate Rule 22, the cloture rule, which required two-thirds of the entire Senate to vote to end debate, the most potent weapon southern Democrats used to block civil rights legislation. Johnson and the Southerners argued that the Senate was a perpetual legislative body whose rules carried over intact from one session to the next, a position that effectively blocked any change in Rule 22. Rauh believed the rule unconstitutional and had fought to change it beginning in 1953 with arguments advanced by Norma Zarkey, a researcher working for the UAW's legislative arm. The Rauh-Zarkey plan argued that each Senate became a new legislative body authorized by Article 1, Section 5 of the Constitution to "determine the rules of its proceedings."[4] With support from senators such as Clinton Anderson of New Mexico, Paul Douglas of Illinois, Wayne Morse of Oregon, Humphrey, and even Vice President Richard Nixon, who presided over the body, liberals in the Senate attempted to revise Rule 22 on several occasions between 1953 and 1958, but each time Johnson secured enough votes to block amendments and overrule the vice president.[5]

Kennedy, the youngest of the Senate trio in 1960, never served the New Deal, but his millionaire father, Joseph P. Kennedy, made rich in shipbuilding, motion pictures, and the stock market, had bought his way into FDR's political orbit. FDR rewarded him with the first chairmanship of the Securities and Exchange Commission and, later, appointment to the United States Maritime Commission. He was the first Irish Catholic ambassador to the Court of St. James. The Kennedy-FDR relationship went on the rocks during the early days of World War II, however, when the ambassador spoke kindly of the Nazi regime, predicted the defeat of England, and opposed Roosevelt's economic aid to the British. Kennedy's eldest son, Joe, lost his life flying bombers over Germany.

John, the second, became a hero in the Pacific War. Elected to Congress in 1946 from a safe Democratic district in Boston, JFK served three undistinguished terms in Congress before winning a Senate seat in 1952. In the Senate he won a Pulitzer Prize for *Profiles in Courage,* walked a fine line between labor and management in the passage of the Landrum-Griffin Act, and avoided the censure vote on McCarthy, an old family friend who had hired his brother Robert. That decision earned him the undying enmity of Eleanor Roosevelt and considerable skepticism from most liberal Democrats, including Rauh.

The Battle for Hubert's Soul

Rauh knew from the start of their relationship that he would have to live with two Hubert Humphreys. The first Humphrey was a stalwart, fiery progressive, often an eloquent fighter for civil rights and civil liberties. But there was a second Hubert, one more cautious, pragmatic, and ambitious, a man easily dominated by stronger personalities. This Hubert shrank from conflict and wanted desperately to join the inner circle of the United States Senate, where Richard Russell and Johnson served as gatekeepers. Beginning at the Democratic National Convention in 1948, Humphrey inspired Rauh's deepest admiration, but also left him at times in despair. The trick, Rauh learned, was always to have the last word with Hubert.

In the summer of 1954, faced with reelection in Minnesota, the loquacious Humphrey cosponsored an amendment to a Republican-drafted Communist Control Act that would have denied collective bargaining rights to any "Communist-infiltrated" labor union. This harsh amendment, backed by Wayne Morse and other liberals, declared the Communist Party of the United States (CPUSA) an agency of a hostile foreign power and a "clear and present danger to the security of the United States [that] . . . should be outlawed." The Humphrey amendment terminated all rights, privileges, and immunities enjoyed by the CPUSA under state and federal laws. A member of the Senate legal staff called the Humphrey amendment "unconstitutional and unconscionable," an opinion shared by Eisenhower's attorney general Herbert Brownell, but the upper chamber passed it without dissent, 85-0. A conference committee finally deleted the sanctions before the bill went to Eisenhower.[6]

Rauh denounced the failed amendment and its author. "Hubert Humphrey pushed through possibly the worst bill of our time in an effort to escape the wrath of the McCarthyites," he lamented to the ADA's Josephine Gomon.[7] A year later, however, Rauh stood up for Humphrey when another ADA member complained that the organization treated the senator with kid gloves. Its attitude, the member complained, seemed to be that "each time he gets out of line on a civil liberties issue he should be merely slapped on the wrist."[8] Asked to summarize and defend his friend's record, Rauh stressed that "year after year Humphrey would introduce bills supporting school desegregation, providing for fair employment practices, safeguarding voting rights, and strengthening other facets of civil rights, but to no avail."[9]

By 1958, Rauh hoped to move the Democratic Party away from the two failed campaigns of Illinois governor Adlai Stevenson, who had twice appeased the South on civil rights issues, but lost decisively to Eisenhower. In both 1952 and 1956, the Stevenson forces had accepted a watered-down party platform on civil rights that Rauh believed retreated from the commitment made in 1948. The 1956 platform, for example, said only that the *Brown* decision "brought consequences of vast importance to our nation," but did not endorse it. It condemned "all proposals for the use of force," which could be interpreted as a criticism of both white violence and the use of executive power to enforce school desegregation.[10]

In the hope of encouraging the liberal Humphrey and moving the Democratic Party away from the Stevenson legacy, Rauh signed on for the senator's run for the White House beginning in 1958–59. He soon found himself locked in a battle for Humphrey's political soul with two of the senator's other advisers, James H. Rowe Jr. and Max Kampelman, both of whom looked upon Humphrey's ties with the ADA as a major liability. Rowe, two years older than Rauh, a Montana-born and Harvard-educated attorney, always stressed his modest roots as someone who "came out of the depression-ridden copper town of Butte." But he had served as the last secretary of Oliver Wendell Holmes Jr. and worked in several New Deal agencies before becoming one of FDR's special White House assistants. In New Deal Washington he moved in circles that included Abe Fortas, William O. Douglas, Tom Corcoran, and Congressman Lyndon Johnson.

After the war, Rowe served as a technical adviser at the Nuremberg war crimes trials and then joined Corcoran's law firm. When LBJ became majority leader in 1950s, Rowe joined his Senate staff briefly before returning to the firm of Corcoran, Youngman, and Rowe. Given their New Deal roots and career aspirations, Rauh and Rowe often crossed paths and sometimes swords. Rauh declined to join Corcoran's firm, but Rowe became a younger version of the latter, absorbing his values and methods. After using his influence in the Senate to help Fortas secure legislation for Puerto Rico, Rowe remarked that in the future he hoped Fortas would "take care of my clients as well as I take care of his."[11]

New York–born Kampelman, a lawyer with a doctorate in political science from the University of Minnesota, first met Humphrey when both were aspiring academics in the Twin Cities. Humphrey soon abandoned the lecture hall for the campaign trail, but Kampelman finished a thesis and taught at Bennington College before joining Humphrey's Senate staff as legislative counsel. In that role he promoted the draconian amendments to the Communist Control Act of 1954. A conscientious objector during World War II, a former member of the ADA, and a zealous anticommunist, Kampelman's fund-raising prowess and political skills had earned him a sobriquet as the "Jewish Tommy Corcoran" by the time Humphrey launched his drive for the presidency.[12]

Rowe and Kampelman believed that Humphrey's success in the national political arena depended upon softening his image as an ADA liberal and maintaining good relations with southern leaders, especially Johnson and Russell. Rowe regarded Rauh and other ADA loyalists as a baneful influence. They were, he complained, starry-eyed utopians, always eager to crash and burn in political combat so long as they maintained the purity of their principles. Rowe saw himself, by contrast, as the political realist and the consummate professional.

As one of LBJ's confidants, Rowe regarded Rauh's "phobia about Lyndon" as a handicap to Humphrey's success. Rauh and the ADA, he told the senator, "have become inbred and doctrinaire; while they fight magnificently, they always lose." If he permitted Rauh to run the campaign, Rowe predicted to Humphrey, "you may lose graciously or you may lose ungraciously—but you will lose" because "they and their group are practically impossible to discipline at best and really impossible when they are 'suspicious' about Hubert's 'expediency.'"[13]

Rauh, of course, urged Humphrey to sail boldly under the liberal-ADA flag because "your strength lies in your ideas and idealism and in your position as the most articulate and dedicated spokesman of American liberalism." Taking Rowe into the campaign, he warned the senator, would give the appearance of compromising too soon with the Johnson forces and undermine that public image. "Down the road somewhere maybe it will be healthy to have it said that Humphrey is so big a man that he can win the support of all elements . . . from ADA and Reuther to Johnson—*but not now*," Rauh urged.[14]

When he tapped Rowe to be his official campaign manager, Humphrey triggered a revolt by Rauh and others, who questioned Rowe's loyalty and feared that conflict with him would ruin the campaign. "Any Rowe-directed campaign is not a possibility for any of us," Rauh told the candidate. "A campaign directed by Jim Rowe would be in many ways an antithesis of our ideas of how a Humphrey campaign should be run to be successful."[15] Rowe's claim to being a real pro, Rauh informed Bob Nathan, "is that he intensely dislikes liberals and labor people. . . . The best thing to do is to fight it out now—to get rid of him entirely."[16]

But loath to lose either man, Humphrey labored to keep both Rowe and Rauh on his team and to endure the inevitable battles that soon developed. He gave Rauh the principal task as speech coordinator, a job that made him the ideological filter for Humphrey's campaign and guaranteed that the senator's policies would not stray far from the liberal-ADA line. Although often marred by the simmering rivalry between Rauh and Rowe, Humphrey's presidential bid did not lack for enthusiasm or ideas and remained solvent thanks to New Yorker Marvin Rosenberg's fund-raising. The major obstacles to Humphrey's success lay elsewhere, in the candidacy of the dashing Senator Kennedy and the stealth efforts of Johnson, who calculated that bruising primary contests would weaken the others.

The Junior Senator

Kennedy's supporters claimed that he had saved organized labor by successfully diluting the Landrum-Griffin Act, but critics noted that Kennedy had begun his latest war on the Teamsters with the drastic Kennedy-Ives bill that prepared the way for Landrum-Griffin. According to columnist Jimmy Wechsler, Kennedy had once told an interviewer, "I'm not a liberal at all. . . . I never joined the Americans for Democratic Action or the American Veterans Committee. I'm not comfortable with those people." He might have matured since those comments, Wechsler concluded, "but I don't feel comfortable about Jack Kennedy."[17]

Rauh, usually the purist, gave JFK the benefit of the doubt. "I long since decided that Jack Kennedy's character cannot be judged by his reaction to McCarthy," Rauh wrote.[18] The Kennedy brothers always distinguished Reuther from Hoffa, he reminded critics. And finally, he told friends, Kennedy had fought hard in the Senate for progressive revisions in unemployment compensation. Stevenson had appealed to Rauh's head, his intellectual bent. Humphrey tapped into his reservoir of liberal idealism. In Kennedy he found another kindred spirit, someone who knew how to win the political game and who, like himself, always hated to lose.[19]

Rauh had repaid a portion of his debt to Kennedy during the senator's reelection campaign in 1958, when he countered the attacks by local leaders of the NAACP, who denounced Kennedy's tepid record on civil rights. A year later, when Rauh visited Kennedy's office on a legislative matter, the senator wanted to know why he had joined the Humphrey campaign, which he denounced as part of a "stop Kennedy movement." Rauh told Kennedy that Rowe and Kampelman harbored such views and hoped to promote a Johnson-Humphrey ticket, but he was not in that camp. If Humphrey dropped out of the race, Rauh promised, he would support Kennedy and never back Johnson.[20]

Wisconsin and West Virginia

Fearing that the Humphrey-Kennedy races could degenerate into personal rancor and open the door to more conservative candidates, Rauh and Arthur Schlesinger Jr. urged civility and moderation on the two contenders. Schlesinger, for example, cautioned Kennedy about the importance of "not allowing the primaries to get out of control" because "the emotions generated by [these] contests can carry people much farther than they ever intended to go." He hoped that both candidates would spurn the pressure of "your local people to take more and more antagonistic attitudes toward the other" and conduct the campaign "on a reasonably high level and without bitterness."[21]

Once the campaigns began, however, neither Humphrey nor Kennedy controlled themselves or their supporters. The Kennedy forces blamed Humphrey for a statewide newspaper ad in Wisconsin that claimed that five out of six Catholic voters in the state, normally Republicans, would cross over in the primary to support their coreligionist. This clumsy attempt to inflame the state's Lutheran voters had been financed by Hoffa and the Teamsters, but it backfired. The Kennedy brothers exploited the Hoffa issue relentlessly, with Robert Kennedy taking every opportunity to declare that Hoffa and the Teamsters indirectly backed the Minnesota senator. That attack infuriated Humphrey. "Bobby [Kennedy] didn't play fair on this," Rauh recalled. "This was just nonsense, and Bobby threw that implication all around [Wisconsin]."[22]

Humphrey raised the level of religious invective in a speech at the Jewish Community Center in Milwaukee two days before the vote when he made reference to the Catholic Church and the Inquisition, "the most organized thing that ever happened [and] almost destroyed civilization."[23] On election day, Catholic voters, including UAW members, carried the state's labor precincts for Kennedy. "The religious issue was murderous," Rauh reflected later. "All that John Kennedy had to do was to go to Mass in Milwaukee or Racine. . . . There was nothing we could say. We couldn't say he shouldn't go to Mass. Hubert couldn't go to Mass. There was no way out."[24]

In West Virginia, anxious to drive Humphrey out of the race, the Kennedy organization allowed matters to "get out of control." In the most egregious episode, Kennedy recruited Franklin Roosevelt Jr., who raised questions about Humphrey's military service. The son of the nation's most revered Democrat suggested that the Minnesotan had been a draft dodger by telling audiences, "I don't know where he was in World War II." Humphrey had received an initial deferment as a married man with an infant son and was later rejected because of color blindness, calcification of the lungs, and a double hernia. JFK exploited the theme of patriotism through-out the campaign, reminding West Virginians that the Purple Heart he won in the Pacific made him "as prepared as any man to meet my obligations to the Constitution of the United States." Lubricated by Kennedy dollars, West Virginia's Bible-reading Protestants gave the Massachusetts senator a re-sounding victory with 236,510 votes to Humphrey's 152,187, a margin that doomed Humphrey's White House bid.[25]

Seething over the tactics used against him, Humphrey refused to endorse Kennedy, but abandoned his campaign. He also issued a generous conces-sion statement that Rauh prepared and then read over the telephone to Bobby Kennedy. As they informed reporters of Humphrey's decision to quit the race, the telephone rang in the suite and someone announced, "Mr. Kennedy is on the way up." Rauh and other assumed it was the senator, un-til he appeared live on television from a Charleston station. "Oh, my God," Rauh thought to himself, "it's not Jack, but Bobby."

Moments later, the most hated man in the Kennedy camp walked through the door. "It was like the Red Sea opening for Moses," Rauh re-membered, as reporters and staff members cleared a wide path for Bobby, who walked slowly toward Hubert and his wife, Muriel. He leaned over and kissed Mrs. Humphrey on the cheek. For an instant, Rauh feared she would slap him, but the moment passed without incident. Turning on the charm, Bobby expressed his admiration for Humphrey's campaign and his gratitude for the concession statement, and invited him to their campaign headquar-ters. A good sport to the end, Hubert made the trip across town to meet Jack Kennedy, but Muriel, angry over the Kennedy's campaign tactics and the kiss, refused to go.[26]

Keeping Kennedy Liberal

With Humphrey out of the race, Rauh quickly turned his energies toward three goals: securing a strong civil rights plank in the party platform, winning the vice presidential nomination for the Minnesotan, and opposing Johnson's candidacy. "It seems to me it has to be Jack Kennedy," he wrote shortly after the West Virginia primary. "I don't think Stevenson can get it and, if he could, it would be as part of a stop-Kennedy move which would cost him the elec-tion in November." Our job, he concluded, "is to try to persuade Jack to stay liberal even though he is now fighting conservatives not Hubert, and it is to that end that Arthur [Schlesinger Jr.], Walter Reuther and the rest of us are now devoting ourselves."[27]

Within weeks of the West Virginia victory, the Kennedys took control of the planning for the Los Angeles convention by tapping Governor Leroy Collins of Florida as permanent chairman, Idaho senator Frank Church as keynoter, and Chester Bowles for chairman of the platform committee. "This thing is all set, stacked and planned," Humphrey complained to Rauh. "I am not disappointed. I just stand in constant admiration of the thoroughness of the Kennedy program. It is incredible, if at times not terrifying."[28] With assurances from Bobby Kennedy and Bowles that his views would dominate the civil rights platform, Rauh actively promoted Humphrey's vice presidential bid, despite the tepid enthusiasm of the Minnesotan. Humphrey, surrounded by many anti-Catholic supporters and still bitter over West Virginia, felt closer to Johnson, an emotional tie that proved fatal to his political ambitions in 1960 and later.

After a fund-raising luncheon for South Dakota Senate candidate George McGovern in June, Rauh shared a cab ride with Kennedy back to Capitol Hill. With the convention only weeks away, the stop-Kennedy forces, led by Johnson and Stevenson, had mounted a furious effort to derail his nomination. Former president Truman had expressed grave doubts about Kennedy's maturity and competence. Eleanor Roosevelt, unforgiving about Joseph P. Kennedy's attacks on her husband, reaffirmed her loyalty to Stevenson. Johnson's surrogate, Texas governor John Connally, suggested that Kennedy suffered from Addison's disease and took heavy doses of drugs to fight the illness, allegations soon repeated in the *New York Post* and elsewhere.

Kennedy denied these rumors and urged Rauh to persuade his friends at the *Post* to drop their coverage. Rauh said he would do what he could on that issue, and Kennedy turned the conversation to the vice presidency. He assured Rauh that in Los Angeles he would choose Hubert Humphrey "or another Midwestern liberal" as his running mate. He wanted to win the nomination with northern votes, he said, without making concessions to the South. Thrilled by this affirmation, especially the implied repudiation of Johnson, Rauh vowed that he would do his best to swing Humphrey and Stevenson delegates over to Kennedy.[29]

True to their word on the platform, the Kennedy organization put Rauh on the convention's large resolutions committee and made certain he sat on the smaller drafting committee that shaped the final document. They also kept the number of southern delegates on both committees to a minimum. "There's no question the drafting committee was stacked so we could get what we wanted," Rauh recalled. "It was the first time the Southerners were ever in a minority." Largely shaped by Rauh and the liberals, the 1960 platform declared that "the time has come to assure equal access for all Americans to all areas of community life, including voting booths, schoolrooms, jobs, housing, and public facilities." It vowed to use "the full powers" of the 1957 and 1960 civil rights laws to guarantee voting rights, including the elimination of literacy tests and poll taxes, and pledged to seek desegregation plans in all school districts covered by the *Brown* decision and to end racial discrimination in all federal and "federally-assisted" housing programs.

"Jack, Don't Do This"

Rauh dominated the civil rights platform, but he failed to secure the vice presidential nomination for Humphrey "or another Midwestern liberal" or to keep it away from Johnson. This turn of events flowed from a number of circumstances, but Rauh believed that Humphrey's own behavior helped doom his cause. On the Friday before the convention opened, Rauh attempted to see the senator in one last attempt to move him into the Kennedy camp. Failing that, he wanted to keep Hubert from joining any stop-Kennedy movement, an effort that now seemed hopeless in light of the delegate count. When the door opened to Humphrey's hotel suite, Pat O'Connor, a Minneapolis attorney and major fund-raiser, responded to Rauh's request to see the senator with a sudden fist that landed on Rauh's jaw. Reeling from the sharp blow, Rauh dropped his briefcase at the same moment Jim Rowe appeared, dragged O'Connor back inside the room, slammed the door, and turned the lock. Nursing a swollen lip, Rauh never saw Humphrey that day. Later he learned that another visitor had then been in the senator's suite: Lyndon Johnson. The next day, Humphrey threw his support to Stevenson, part of a last-ditch effort to block Kennedy, a futile decision that infuriated JFK and ended Humphrey's chances for the vice presidency.

Unable to stop Humphrey from destroying himself, Rauh trolled for Kennedy votes inside the Minnesota delegation with the support of the state's governor, Orville Freeman, another "Midwestern liberal" who had been touted as vice presidential material. He also fought for control of the D.C. delegation with Bob Nathan, who had spread the rumor that Kennedy would choose Johnson as his running mate. That story, if true, would have killed Kennedy's chances in the District and cost him votes among many northern delegates. In order to scotch it, Rauh asked Bobby Kennedy twice for assurances that LBJ would not be on the ticket. Bobby repeated these assurances to Rauh, even after the *Washington Post* ran several stories to the contrary as part of Phil Graham's efforts to keep Johnson's prospects alive.

But Nathan had been right. Kennedy betrayed Rauh by offering Johnson the vice presidency, despite a last-minute effort by Bobby Kennedy to have the majority leader decline the invitation for fear of a revolt by the liberals. Rauh expressed stunned disbelief when *Newsweek* reporter Hobart Rowan informed him that it would be LBJ. Like others, he felt used by JFK. "It was kind of feeling you have that you've done something dirty when you go to people and persuade them to vote for someone on a premise that you believe to be true but turns out false," Rauh remembered.[30] Delegates who had supported Kennedy based on Rauh's promises now swore at him. He avoided the Iowa delegation for fear that several of its African-American delegates would physically attack him. Unable to see Kennedy in person and encouraged by anti-Johnson Texans who shared his anger, Rauh vented his frustrations before television cameras on the convention floor and a national audience:

"Jack—don't do this! You're wrecking the party," he shouted over one microphone.

His anger rising, Rauh told a reporter for the *New York Times* that he had been "double crossed." He had harsh words for Johnson, whose civil rights record, he said, now threw doubt on the sincerity of the party's platform. Anticipating such reactions from Rauh and others, the Kennedy brothers sent forth people to pacify the rebels. When Rauh's name came up, Jack Kennedy turned to Phil Graham, who had promoted Johnson: "I guess he's hopeless, but you take him." A photographer soon caught Graham's pained expression as he attempted, without success, to soothe Rauh's feelings on the convention floor. The *Post's* publisher later sent the photograph to Olie Rauh with the inscription, "Sometimes when Mr. Rauh is exceedingly difficult, look at my saintly suffering face."[31]

Kenny O'Donnell from the Kennedy inner circle expressed sympathy with Rauh and attempted to cool his wrath. "I'm as sick about this as you are," O'Donnell said, "but in the morning we'll all feel better and we've got a job to do." On his way to Reuther's suite, Rauh encountered a shocked Leonard Woodcock of the UAW, who had tears rolling down his cheeks. Governor "Soapy" Williams and others in the Michigan delegation wanted to lead a floor fight against Johnson's nomination, an idea that had crossed Rauh's mind, too. Woodcock, however, his eyes still misty, urged calm and reminded everyone that he had voted for John Sparkman on the Stevenson ticket in 1952. "Lyndon Johnson isn't a John Sparkman, and Texas isn't Alabama," he said.[32]

Rauh and others in the D.C. delegation remained determined to register a protest against Johnson. After a brief caucus, they decided to nominate Governor Freeman, until the Minnesotan came down on the floor personally to decline the honor. Finally, the District delegates agreed that some of them would record their vote for Johnson, while others would dissent.[33] With the aid of Bobby Kennedy and Alex Rose, boss of the New York Liberal Party, however, Reuther put an end to the talk of a floor fight led by Michigan and rendered the D.C. protests academic. The younger Kennedy consoled Reuther with the thought that he had hoped for a different outcome. That evening without a roll call, but over a swelling chorus of "No," including the voice of Rauh, Lyndon Johnson became Kennedy's running mate.[34]

Rauh's feelings of disappointment did not soon ebb. As he told Harvard law professor Abe Chayes, a key staff member on the platform committee: "I received more vilification for supporting Kennedy over Stevenson than I ever got defending Bill Remington." If Kennedy had indicated his support for Johnson before the first ballot, he believed, Stevenson would have won the nomination. "There is something wrong with a ticket that couldn't openly be nominated," he lamented, but the platform remained a plus, "and my best service will be to spend the next four years reminding President Kennedy . . . that he is obliged to put it into effect."[35]

"We Don't Trust Kennedy and We Don't Like Johnson"

Johnson's conduct during the special session of Congress after the convention did nothing to ally Rauh's distrust. "As far as I am concerned," Rauh told Ronnie Dugger, the editor of the *Texas Observer*, "the Johnson nomination was and is an unmitigated catastrophe." When Johnson met with Kennedy to discuss strategy for the congressional session, Rauh complained that the majority leader expressed the view "that civil rights had no place on the . . . agenda" and that Kennedy had begun "putting the screws on the civil rights groups to accept this decision."[36] Along with Roy Wilkins, then chairman of the Leadership Conference, Rauh soon sat down with candidate Kennedy to urge his support for legislation in the special session. A strong stand on civil rights, he told the Democratic nominee, would help, not hurt, the ticket in November. "Joe, you made a terrific speech," Kennedy said, but he declined to endorse their position.[37]

Johnson and Kennedy were not alone in their desire to keep civil rights legislation out of Congress before the election. Rauh and Wilkins received no encouragement from Reuther, who told them to concentrate on defeating Richard Nixon. When Rauh and the Leadership Council still pushed legislation introduced by Senator Joe Clark of Pennsylvania, the Johnson-Kennedy-Reuther forces lined up votes against it. The Republicans eagerly exploited this hypocrisy. GOP minority leader Everett Dirksen and others called on Johnson and his party to enact several civil rights measures during the special session, but Johnson, "grinning," according to Rauh, tabled "the Republican civil rights efforts."[38]

Efforts to secure an endorsement of the Kennedy-Johnson ticket at the ADA board meeting in August triggered a fierce debate. As Schlesinger reported to Kennedy, at least half of the sixty chapter representatives opposed any endorsement. The other half voted to endorse the ticket reluctantly. As one member put it, "We don't trust Kennedy and we don't like Johnson; but Nixon is so terrible that we have to endorse the Democrats." With heavy pressure from the leadership, including Rauh, Schlesinger, and even Mrs. Roosevelt, the ADA officially backed the ticket, but only after refusing to include Johnson's name in the endorsement.[39]

On November 8, thanks to narrow victories in Texas and Illinois, Kennedy defeated Nixon in electoral votes, 303-219. His popular vote margin was much thinner, 118,574 out of 68.3 million ballots cast. When he took the oath of office in January 1961, Kennedy entered the White House with the most progressive civil rights platform ever adopted by a major party, thanks in large measure to Joe Rauh. But Kennedy's stirring inaugural address, a prelude to the next three years, had far more to say about winning the Cold War against the Soviet Union than achieving racial justice at home, even as young African-American college students continued to fight Jim Crow with sit-in demonstrations across the South. And for the next one thousand days, Rauh would be frustrated by the timidity of JFK's efforts to understand and respond to the escalating racial crisis in America.

CHAPTER TWELVE

A LIBERAL IN CAMELOT

In Albany you have indicted the oppressed . . .
rather than the oppressors.

— JOE RAUH TO JEROME HEILBRON

Glen Echo

In the summer of Kennedy's nomination, William Griffin and four friends walked boldly onto the grounds of the Glen Echo Amusement Park in Montgomery County, Maryland. Francis Collins, an off-duty special deputy sheriff working as the park's private security guard, ordered them to leave. The park, Collins said, did not admit Negroes. When the demonstrators refused to depart, Collins arrested them and charged them with criminal trespass. In the long struggle for civil rights, William Griffin, Marvous Saunders, Michael Proctor, Cecil T. Washington Jr., and Gwendolyn Greene are seldom mentioned with Rosa Parks, Medgar Evers, James Meredith, or Martin Luther King Jr. But what they did at Glen Echo that summer day in 1960 ultimately reached the Supreme Court of the United States and helped to change American law. Joe Rauh argued their case and found himself battling the administration he had helped to elect.

Rauh and his liberal ADA allies found much to cheer about during the Kennedy years. The administration ended the worst abuses of the loyalty-security program. JFK honored Dr. J. Robert Oppenheimer, branded a security risk in 1954, with the Atomic Energy Commission's own Enrico Fermi award. The new president hired Edward R. Murrow, one of Joe McCarthy's chief antagonists, to run the United States Information Agency. He defended State Department employees charged by reporters with being "well-known security risks" and ordered the Post Office Department to stop seizing the literature of foreign Communist organizations.

The president's brother, Attorney General Robert Kennedy, adopted a more aggressive posture on school desegregation. He brought the United States into two Louisiana school cases as a friend of the court. He intervened against Prince Edward County, Virginia, where the public schools had been shut down since 1959 to avoid integration. However, the Kennedy brothers remained prisoners of their party's southern wing, whose members dominated the major committees of Congress, where they held hostage other domestic initiatives. In the face of this reality, Kennedy lacked enthusiasm for pushing new civil rights legislation.

Rauh received a fresh hint of Kennedy's caution on civil rights early in 1961 when he and the Leadership Conference launched another assault on the filibuster prior to the president's inauguration. Rauh rejected the incoming administration's argument that another filibuster fight would undermine party unity on the eve of the election. Phil Graham, encouraged by Kennedy, deplored Rauh's effort as "a very great mistake . . . I am sad you are persisting in this." Responding to Graham, Rauh argued that the party's platform promises could not be achieved without new legislation. The best hope for overthrowing the present Rule 22, he added, would come with Vice President Nixon still presiding in the Senate. "The [Democratic] Party *is* split on civil rights," he told Graham. "The drawing of the issue on January 3rd will not worsen the split. . . . There will never be real unity in the Party as long as the Southerners can hold the filibuster pistol at the Party's head."[1]

At the opening of the Eighty-sixth Congress, with Nixon presiding, Humphrey and Republican senator Thomas Kuchel introduced the Rauh-backed resolution providing for cloture by a simple majority. New Mexico's Clinton Anderson, the tireless foe of the filibuster, pushed a similar measure to allow curtailment of debate by three-fifths of the senators present and voting. But without the active support from Kennedy and opposition from Majority Leader Johnson, neither resolution prevailed, despite Nixon's reaffirmation of his earlier ruling that a new Senate could adopt rules without a two-thirds supermajority. By a vote of 37-43, the senators refused to impose cloture to consider Anderson's modest modification.

The tide of battle against the filibuster shifted two years later, but without significant help from Kennedy's new vice president. Even before the vote, Rauh feared that Johnson would find it "distasteful" to follow Nixon's precedents. He urged Kennedy to intervene with the hope that "the Vice President would not do this if your position were made clear."[2] Kennedy remained silent. As Rauh feared, Johnson refused to build on Nixon's precedent. He declined to rule on the constitutional issue, which prevented a simple majority from changing the Senate rules. Instead, the vice president argued that the Senate decide the matter for itself as it had since 1803, a decision that perpetuated the southern veto.[3]

Waiting for Executive Action

Kennedy courted liberal support for his domestic initiatives, but excluded civil rights. When Rauh and three ADA board members met with the president at the White House soon after his inauguration, they immediately sensed Kennedy's defensiveness about the race issue. Bob Nathan opened the discussion by urging the president to act boldly on fiscal policy, including support for a $50 billion budget deficit in order to achieve full employment. Rauh shifted the focus to civil rights and inquired if the president wanted the ADA to advocate bold legislative initiatives there. Kennedy's face tightened. "Absolutely not," he fired back at Rauh. "It's a totally different thing! Your criticism on civil rights is quite wrong." Kennedy turned on Rauh "with great force" by pointing out the efforts his administration had made without confronting the white Southerners in Congress.[4]

Kennedy insisted progress on civil rights could be made through executive action independent of Congress, by appointing more African-Americans to high office, and by instituting more voting rights suits under existing law. But Rauh soon discovered that Kennedy's emphasis upon vigorous executive action produced few results. During the campaign, for example, the candidate promised "with a stoke of the pen" to end racial discrimination in housing programs administered or subsidized by the federal government, which included those financed by the FHA. But as president, it took Kennedy almost two years to fulfill that promise, although disillusioned citizens mailed him pens each week. And his final order exempted important sectors of the housing market, a decision that prompted Rauh to observe that "broader coverage would have made for more rapid progress toward housing integration."[5]

A Court Divided

Rauh's frustration with Kennedy intensified when he battled the administration over strategy in the Glen Echo sit-in cases. Rauh argued that the demonstrators' behavior at Glen Echo did not constitute a criminal trespass under the relevant Maryland statutes, but in addition he raised an important constitutional claim: their arrest had been an exercise of state power to enforce racial segregation, a violation of the Fourteenth Amendment. Judge James H. Pugh of the Montgomery County Circuit Court rejected all of these arguments, convicted the five, and fined them each a hundred dollars, a judgment predictably upheld by a unanimous Maryland Court of Appeals.[6]

The sit-in cases prior to *Griffin* had sharply polarized the Supreme Court between the views of Justice William O. Douglas and Justice Hugo Black. In the absence of state or federal laws banning racial discrimination, Black did not believe that the Fourteenth Amendment by its own force prohibited states from enforcing general trespass statutes in defense of property rights, even in cases where owners were motivated by racial prejudice. Douglas, on the other hand, read the Fourteenth Amendment more broadly as imposing on the states an affirmative obligation not to deploy their law enforcement machinery or judicial authority on behalf of private decisions to maintain racial segregation.

The Warren Court had managed to avoid these divisive constitutional issues in the earlier cases because the sit-ins had taken place in South Carolina and Alabama, where state laws or local ordinances clearly mandated segregation in restaurants and lunch counters. Maryland and Florida did not have similar state statutes affecting private property, which made *Griffin* and companion cases known as *Bell v. Maryland* and *Robinson v. Florida* more contentious to resolve. The justices would have to choose between Douglas and Black.

Teamed with Silard and Jack Greenberg from the NAACP, Rauh naturally favored the Douglas approach in their brief that stressed the Supreme Court's landmark ruling in *Shelley v. Kramer*, a 1948 decision where the justices held that judicial enforcement of a private racial covenant constituted "state action" prohibited by the Fourteenth Amendment. The arrest of William Griffin and others by a deputy sheriff and their conviction by the Maryland courts implicated the state in the discrimination. Rauh anticipated that Justice Black would resist extending *Shelley* to the sit-in cases. He therefore emphasized the illogic of Black's position on private property and criminal trespass laws. "The Court is dealing in *Griffin* and other cases with proprietors who claim no privacy at their establishments," Rauh advised, "and have retained the right of 'choice' *only* with respect to the exclusion of the Negro public. The point here is that the state's enforcement of this single racial choice is *uniquely* state aid to racial practices as distinguished from state protection of privacy of choice or of premises."[7]

Warren's Court, aware of the complexity of the issues, invited solicitor general Archibald Cox to prepare a brief and argue on behalf of the United States *amicus curiae*. Cox, on leave from his post at Harvard Law School, submitted a brief that ignored *Shelley* and the constitutional issues. On behalf of the United States, he urged that the convictions be reversed on narrow statutory grounds: the Maryland statute required prior warning by the owner before defendants entered private property, a condition ignored in both *Griffin* and *Bell*. In the companion Florida case, the solicitor general focused on another narrow point: the demonstrators had not been informed of the reasons why they were being asked to leave private property![8]

Rauh versus Cox

Cox hoped to avoid a polarizing conflict on the Court, but Rauh expressed outrage at this effort to avoid a broad constitutional challenge. He described the government's brief as "a monumental disgrace." The solicitor general had focused on a point not raised in any of the sit-in cases, he argued, and his approach would "throw doubt on *Shelley* and on every other . . . brief." In the Florida case, Rauh concluded, Cox advanced an argument "so weak . . . that everybody will know the Government's doubts on *Shelley* and the applicability of the Fourteenth Amendment generally." He sought a meeting with Robert Kennedy in order to put pressure on Cox "before the damage is compounded at oral argument."[9] The solicitor general's strategy did not please the justices either, who asked him to submit a supplemental brief that addressed "the broader constitutional issues."

Informed about Rauh's displeasure, Lee White, the president's special assistant for civil rights, cautioned Kennedy to tread lightly when dealing with the solicitor general. "There is some question of delicacy about pushing Archie Cox too hard on this point," White said, "without his exploding and resigning." White urged the president to tell Rauh and others that the attorney general and his two top assistants had met with Cox and they were convinced he "would come out with a very satisfactory position for the government on the Constitutional questions and . . . that we have assurances that the government will do a good job."[10]

But Cox's supplemental brief did not pacify Rauh. Further research by the Justice Department uncovered a Florida statute that required segregated restrooms in restaurants, which quickly disposed of the *Robinson* case, but Cox continued to urge reversal on narrow grounds in both *Griffin* and *Bell*, a position that put him at odds with Rauh and Greenberg. In the end, neither Rauh nor Cox won the battle. A badly splintered Court refused to accept Cox's narrow view in the *Griffin* case, but also declined Rauh's invitation to void the trespass statutes under the Fourteenth Amendment. Over dissents by Black, John Harlan, and Byron White, the newest Kennedy appointee, six justices found the involvement of Deputy Sheriff Collins sufficient to reverse the convictions on grounds of state action. Warren's opinion, however, studiously ignored *Shelley v. Kramer.*[11]

The justices also reversed Bell's conviction, although state involvement seemed tenuous. Justice Black had five votes for sustaining Bell's conviction and the validity of general trespass laws, until Justice William Brennan devised a solution that avoided a constitutional showdown. Brennan secured a majority for overturning Bell's conviction on the grounds that Maryland's own antidiscrimination laws, passed while his appeal had been pending, voided the convictions. This point had not been raised by the Rauh team or by Cox. The Warren Court never resolved the constitutional conundrum of the Fourteenth Amendment and the sit-in case, but passage of the Civil Rights Act in 1964 rendered the issue moot.[12]

Freedom Riders

William Griffin and his friends had been arrested and fined in Maryland. In Alabama and Mississippi, civil rights activists fared much worse. They faced an epidemic of white violence that the Kennedy administration seemed unable and unwilling to prevent. In the spring of 1961, Freedom Riders organized by the Congress for Racial Equality (CORE) attempted to desegregate bus terminals across the South. In Birmingham, Anniston, and Montgomery, Alabama, and McComb and Jackson, Mississippi, white mobs firebombed the buses and attacked passengers with clubs and chains while local law enforcement officials watched the carnage but did nothing to stop it. Only the presence of 500 federal marshals, dispatched by Robert Kennedy, prevented an attack on the Negro First Baptist Church in Montgomery, where Dr. King had begun to preach, but not before Kennedy's own representative from the Department of Justice, John Seigenthaler, had been savagely beaten. Upon petition by Kennedy, the Interstate Commerce Commission finally banned segregated bus and train terminals.

Rauh raised funds for the Freedom Riders in 1961 and joined Eleanor Roosevelt, Reuther, Randolph, Norman Thomas, and Telford Taylor as a committee of inquiry organized by CORE in May 1962 to take testimony from civil rights workers who had suffered harassment by local police, judges, and jailors.[13] Rauh wanted the FBI to fight white terror with the same weapons it had used against domestic Communism. The Bureau's infiltration of the Communist Party demonstrated its capacity to forestall criminal activity, Rauh told President Kennedy. "The failure to infiltrate the

Citizens Council, the Ku Klux Klan, and other racist organizations is inexcusable in this current crisis."[14] He also urged a radical reorganization of the Bureau or turning the task over to the Civil Rights Division of the Department of Justice, a suggestion likely to infuriate Hoover.[15]

When the Department of Justice indicted civil rights demonstrators in Albany, Georgia, for "conspiracy," but found insufficient evidence to prosecute white thugs who had violated their civil rights, Rauh expressed his anger to Robert Kennedy and Jerome Heilbron, chief of the Civil Rights Division. "It seems to me that the Department is in the position of having indicted the wrong party," he told Heilbron. "It is about like a little old lady being robbed on her way to the store to buy a load of bread and then being forced to steal the loaf of bread to eat. I rather doubt the Justice Department would think there was much equity in indicting the lady rather than the robbers. Yet, in Albany, you have indicted the oppressed . . . rather than the oppressors."[16]

Despite the Freedom Rides, white vigilantism, and the confrontation over James Meredith in Mississippi, no fresh legislative proposals came from the White House as Kennedy entered his third year in office. At a meeting of the Leadership Conference, Rauh launched a scathing attack on the administration and urged the organization to become more vocal in its criticism of the president. Roy Wilkins, reporting on a recent visit to NAACP chapters, cautioned against that approach. He, too, had denounced the administration in several speeches in North Carolina, but his predominately black audience "all sat on their hands" until he mentioned a few positive things Kennedy had done "and the place went up in smoke with everybody cheering." Wilkins doubted that rank-and-file blacks would support the Leadership Conference if it made war on the president, whose stature in the black community remained high even in the face of criticism.[17]

Birmingham

Dr. King and his allies, who spurned the advice of civil rights moderates and Robert Kennedy, turned the tide when they launched demonstrations in Birmingham in April to secure modest goals: an end to segregation in the city's stores and snack bars, nondiscriminatory hiring practices, and a biracial commission to develop proposals for future desegregation. Similar demonstrations had failed to dent segregation or generate intense national publicity the summer before in Albany. There, the police and local officials did not hesitate to fill up the jails with King and other protestors, but wisely avoided the use of greater force. In Birmingham, police commissioner Eugene "Bull"

Connor and segregationist mayor Arthur Hanes had been voted out of office the previous November, and prudence might have dictated a delay until they finished their remaining term and new white leadership had been installed.

But King and the Reverend Fred Shuttlesworth declined to wait and marched even in the face of growing apathy on the part of many adult protestors and an injunction forbidding demonstrations. King's arrest and his eloquent letter from the Birmingham jail focused the nation's attention on the struggle in Birmingham, but the behavior of Connor and his officers proved decisive. Frustrated by wave after wave of demonstrators, many of them teenagers who displayed more resilience than their parents, the police responded with nightsticks, powerful fire hoses, and snarling dogs. On May 12, a bomb blew off the front portion of the home of King's younger brother, the Reverend A. D. King, while a second blast ripped through the A. G. Gaston Motel, which had served as one of the headquarters of the protestors.

Alabama's new governor, George C. Wallace, who had vowed "segregation now, segregation tomorrow, segregation forever," completed his state's national isolation a few weeks later. The governor stood before the door of the Registrar's Office at the University of Alabama to block the admission of two twenty-year-old black students. In a well-choreographed scene, Wallace finally stepped aside when assistant attorney general Nicholas Katzenbach, supported by federalized Alabama guardsmen, returned to escort the students through the registration process. The Birmingham riots and Wallace's brief defiance exposed the weakness of administration's civil rights proposal, forced it to rethink pending legislation, and inspired the president's robust television address on June 11, 1963, probably the most important statement Kennedy made from the Oval Office. Moral outrage finally trumped political pragmatism.

"I hope that every American, regardless of where he lives, will stop and examine his conscience about this and other related incidents," Kennedy told the nation with reference to events in Tuscaloosa and Birmingham. "Who among us would . . . be content with the counsels of patience and delay? One hundred years of delay have passed since President Lincoln freed the slaves, yet their heirs, their grandsons, are not fully free. They are not yet freed from the bonds of injustice; they are not yet freed from social and economic oppression. And this nation, for all its hopes and all its boasts, will not be fully free until all its citizens are free." The time had come for action, the president concluded, action by Congress, by state and local governments, and by private citizens. "Those who do nothing are inviting shame as well as violence. Those who act boldly are recognizing right as well as reality."

Rauh had been engaged in trench warfare with the administration for over two years at the time of Birmingham. He had fought against housing discrimination, represented sit-in demonstrators, and raised money for the Freedom Riders, but he also found himself lumped with the Kennedys and denounced by many black intellectuals, notably the novelist James Baldwin. When Rauh hosted a small party after Kennedy's Nobel Prize dinner in 1962, for example, Baldwin, according to Schlesinger, "attacked Joe Rauh in his [own] house over civil rights. Baldwin's basic belief, I think, is that all whites hate Negroes and that, in consequence, all Negroes hate all whites. Feeling this, he finds white liberals the hardest of all to take because they are too hypocritical, in his view, to own up to their true feelings. That may be why he turned on Joe so savagely."[18] Baldwin's outburst foreshadowed the growing estrangement between white liberals like Rauh and many African-American radicals that would intensify over the next decades.

Restored to the White House

Rauh remained only a spectator when administration leaders first huddled with civil rights leaders in June to discuss a proposed civil rights bill. He had become persona non grata at the White House because of his ongoing struggle with Robert Kennedy and Cox over the sit-in cases and housing litigation. When he accused Robert Kennedy of indifference to integrated housing, that jab put him on RFK's blacklist and kept him out of legislative discussions until Schlesinger and others intervened after Birmingham. No one in Washington, they argued, could match Rauh's experience or mastery of detail with respect to civil rights legislation.[19]

Finally in strategy sessions at the White House, Rauh sat down with the president, the attorney general, Vice President Johnson, Wilkins, Reuther, Whitney Young of the Urban League, and others to discuss the administration's new bill. Everyone praised the new proposals that allowed the federal government to cut off funds from discriminatory programs, to initiate suits to desegregate public schools, and to ban similar discrimination in most public accommodations, including hotels, theaters, stores, and restaurants. But Rauh wanted stronger provisions, especially with respect to employment discrimination. In the bill's public accommodations section, the language contained numerous exemptions, including public swimming pools operated without restaurants. With the president out of the room, but the attorney general present, Rauh asked Johnson bluntly if he would regard their efforts to strengthen the bill as a hostile act. The vice president had declared in a recent Memorial Day speech at Gettysburg that "until justice is blind to color . . . emancipation will be a proclamation but not a fact." He now responded to Rauh's question by saying he did not see how pressure from liberals could hurt their chances. Rauh took that statement as a green light to expand the bill's coverage and sanctions, but he soon learned that Kennedy and Johnson would not go beyond certain limits.[20]

Rauh believed that the best bill could emerge from the House. He and Clarence Mitchell therefore concentrated their efforts on Manny Celler's Judiciary subcommittee, whose members, Rauh later recalled, "gave us the moon." The subcommittee version created an Equal Employment Opportunities Commission with authority to ban discriminatory hiring practices in the private sector; made the Civil Rights Commission permanent; broadened the public accommodations section to include virtually every facility operating under state license or charter; authorized the attorney general to file lawsuits in a broader range of civil rights cases; and extended the voting rights provisions to both federal *and* state elections.

Rauh believed that some or all of the Celler provisions—especially a permanent Equal Employment Opportunities Commission—could be traded away in final negotiations on the House floor or later with the Senate. Robert Kennedy and Katzenbach, the chief architect of the administration's measure, urged a more limited strategy: what can you get through Congress? The president also believed that Rauh and his overzealous allies had written off the House Republicans, a fatal mistake if they hoped to get the bill past the full Judiciary Committee and through the Rules Committee controlled by arch-segregationist Howard Smith of Virginia. Writing in the *Washington Star,* columnist William S. White, usually a spokesman for Vice President Johnson, declared that the White House had to fight southern reactionaries and "ultra-liberals pushing a violently punitive bill."[21] Robert Kennedy feared that Rauh and his allies were "in love with death. . . . they like it much better to have a cause than to have a course of action that's been successful."[22]

The March

The administration also expected the worst from a planned August 28 "March on Washington for Jobs and Freedom," the brainchild of Bayard Rustin and Randolph that had drawn support from ten organizations, including the Leadership Conference. King and other organizers hoped to draw 200,000 people to Washington both to dramatize the economic plight of African-Americans and to show support for Kennedy's proposed civil rights bill. The president and his advisers feared the march could degenerate into violence, poison public opinion against civil rights, and antagonize many legislators who remained on the fence about their bill.

Despite these fears inside the administration, the march became one of the transcendent moments in postwar America, but not without moments of crisis. On the morning of the event, when Rauh climbed into a bus at the Statler Hotel for a ride up to Capitol Hill where civil rights leaders were to meet with members of Congress, he found himself sitting next to Dr. King. He inquired how the minister's speech was coming along, an address scheduled for delivery in a few hours. "Not very well," King confessed. "I haven't had much time to work on it." Hours later, however, King's soaring "I have a dream" words rang out from the Lincoln Memorial before what one reporter described as "a vast army of quiet, middle-class Americans who had come in the spirit of a church outing. And instead of the tensions that had been expected, they gave this city a day of sad music, strange silences and good feeling in the streets."[23]

As they marched to the Lincoln Memorial, however, Rauh's anxiety rose in anticipation of one speech to be delivered by John Lewis of Nashville, the fiery chairman of the Student Non-Violent Coordinating Committee (SNCC). Lewis, one of the fourteen original Freedom Riders, had endured vicious beatings in South Carolina and Alabama, as well as brutal time spent in Mississippi's notorious Parchman Penitentiary. On the eve of the march, as Rauh, Randolph, and others huddled at the Statler, someone circulated a copy of Lewis's proposed speech that had been written largely by James Forman, SNCC's thirty-four-year-old executive director. The Lewis-Foreman draft denounced the administration, the president personally, and his proposed civil rights bill. They would march the next day, according to Lewis-Forman, to build a new society, not to support the pathetic legislative proposal now pending in Congress. Rauh had been working to strengthen the Kennedy bill, but Lewis's harangue threatened to disrupt the civil rights coalition, give the march an anti-Kennedy tone, and alienate several key senators.

Soon widely circulated, the Lewis-Foreman attack sparked angry words across racial lines, and no one, including Rauh, seemed able to propose a solution that did not border on censorship or appear to appease militants bent on savaging their white allies. Archbishop Patrick O'Boyle of Washington, scheduled to give the invocation, took the initiative when the speakers gathered on the platform to open the historic event. O'Boyle told Lewis bluntly he would walk out and not invoke the Lord's blessing for any speech contrary to the fundamental purposes of the march. Under this clerical pressure, Lewis relented and retreated to a back room in the Memorial, where he and Forman hastily rewrote his speech. His remarks still criticized the Kennedy administration, but he did not condemn the pending legislative effort. The president declined an invitation to join the marchers, but later met with the leaders at the White House for over an hour and issued a statement praising their "deep fervor and . . . quiet dignity."[24]

The Kennedy brothers could not stop the March on Washington or John Lewis from attacking their civil rights record, but they had enough influence to modify the House subcommittee's bill when Celler counted votes in the full Judiciary Committee. He became convinced that several of the provisions sponsored by Rauh and the Leadership Conference would not survive in his committee or on the House floor. Robert Kennedy also launched a blistering attack on Title III, which he declared would require the Department of Justice to file suits to vindicate every right mentioned in the Constitution. Celler and the administration also trimmed back the voting rights section to cover federal elections only and limited the public accommodations coverage to commercial establishments. Finally, the revised Celler bill stripped the Equal Employment Opportunities Commission of all independent enforcement powers.

On October 29, with Rauh and Mitchell standing watch outside the Judiciary Committee along with a platoon of clergymen, the members defeated the original subcommittee bill 19-15, and adopted the new Celler compromise 23-11, a result that Mitchell denounced as a sellout. The measure that now went to the House Rules Committee improved greatly on the original Kennedy-Katzenbach bill, although it was not the civil rights instrument Rauh had worked so hard to achieve. Even this watered-down bill, however, languished in Smith's southern-dominated Rules Committee throughout the remainder of October and John Kennedy's presidency.[25]

The defeat of the subcommittee bill added to the enormous sense of loss Rauh experienced in the horrific summer and fall of 1963. On August 3, released for a weekend from a Rockville, Maryland, psychiatric center where he remained under treatment for depression, Phil Graham, once the golden boy of the late New Deal, killed himself with a shotgun. On November 14, with his approval rating in the polls still high at 59 percent, John Kennedy predicted that Congress would pass his civil rights bill before it adjourned in the summer of 1964. "However dark it looks now," he told reporters, quoting Whitman, "I think that 'westward, look, the land is bright.'"[26] Eight days later he was dead. The fate of civil rights now rested with Rauh's old nemesis, Lyndon Johnson.

Joseph L. Rauh Jr., age 12, at the University School, Cincinnati. *Courtesy of the Estate of Olie W. Rauh.*

Rauh (*third from right, front row*) anchored the Harvard basketball team in the early 1930s. His roommate, William (Bill) Baskerville, the team's only African-American, is on the far left, front. *Courtesy of the Estate of Olie W. Rauh.*

Rauh (*top row, fourth from right*) led his class academically at the Harvard Law School and served on the coveted *Law Review* in 1934–35. *Courtesy of the Estate of Olie W. Rauh.*

Olie Westheimer became Mrs. Joseph L. Rauh Jr. on September 1, 1935. *Courtesy of the Estate of Olie W. Rauh.*

Benjamin V. Cohen, legal architect of many New Deal laws and Rauh's chief mentor. *Courtesy of the Estate of Olie W. Rauh.*

Lieutenant Colonel Rauh, aka "the Mayor of Manila," 1945. *Courtesy of the Estate of Olie W. Rauh.*

Rauh opens his legal practice in Washington, D.C., with Irving Levy, 1946. *Courtesy of the Estate of Olie W. Rauh.*

Rauh and President Johnson discuss legislative strategy for civil rights bill, 1964. *Courtesy of the Estate of Olie W. Rauh.*

Rauh (*third row, left*) joins President Johnson, Attorney General Robert Kennedy (*center*), Dr. King, and Roy Wilkins (*next to Johnson*), following signing of 1964 Civil Rights Act. *Courtesy of the Estate of Olie W. Rauh.*

Rauh turned against the Vietnam War and became a leading spokesman for Negotiations Now! in 1967–68. *Courtesy of the Estate of Olie W. Rauh.*

At Americans for Democratic Action convention in 1968, Rauh plotted antiwar strategy with Arthur M. Schlesinger Jr. (*center*) and John Kenneth Galbraith. *Courtesy of the Estate of Olie W. Rauh.*

Rauh accepts defeat of Senator Edward Kennedy's challenge to President Carter at 1980 Democratic National Convention. *Courtesy of the Estate of Olie W. Rauh.*

Rauh, age 80, in retirement. *Courtesy of the Estate of Olie W. Rauh.*

CHAPTER THIRTEEN

FREEDOM'S PARTY

This here fella is helping me on the civil rights bill.
— PRESIDENT LYNDON JOHNSON

The First Priority

Like two wary boxers, they had circled each other for years, often landing
sharp verbal blows. Lyndon Johnson regarded Joe Rauh as a shrill, dogmatic critic of everything he did. Rauh had come to expect the worst from
LBJ. Nine months before Kennedy's assassination, Johnson again fulfilled
Rauh's negative assessment. Presiding over the Senate, the vice president
declined to take a stand on revising Rule 22, the old procedural device that
sustained filibusters and blocked all civil rights legislation. Johnson's stand
drew the sharpest rebuke Rauh had ever directed at the Texan: "Vice President Lyndon Johnson," he told reporters, "has demonstrated once again
that his first loyalty is to the Southern racists."[1] Soon attacked for his choice
of words, Rauh responded without offering a clear apology: "I guess I feel
too deeply on the race issue to use the more cautious language that may
well be preferable."[2]

From Rauh's perspective, Johnson's failure to support the antifilibuster
majority in 1963 reconfirmed his role as a major obstacle to progress on civil
rights in Congress. Birmingham had transformed John Kennedy's approach
to that issue. Might the presidency do the same for Lyndon Johnson? Some
thought they had glimpsed another side to LBJ. Along with Tennessee's Albert Gore and Estes Kefauver, he had declined to sign the notorious "Southern Manifesto" that denounced the *Brown* decision. When his nomination as
vice president in 1960 stirred angry protests, Johnson met with black party
leaders and, according to Frank Reeves, a delegate from the District of Co-

lumbia, told them, "I'll do more for you in four years than anyone else has done for you in one hundred years."[3] He soon began to fulfill that boast.

Johnson wasted little time consolidating his authority as president and sending encouraging messages to those who might doubt his resolve on civil rights. One day after becoming president, Johnson told two of his closest aides that his "first priority is passage of the Civil Rights Act."[4] He surprised CORE's James Farmer with a telephone call at his home three days after Kennedy's assassination. "Now I'm going to need your help in the days and weeks and months and hopefully the years that lie ahead," Johnson told Farmer, "and I hope I'll have your help." He urged Farmer to "drop by and see me next time you're in Washington. . . . We've got to sit down and talk."[5] Two days later, on the eve of Thanksgiving, the new president electrified a joint session of Congress by vowing to continue what Kennedy had begun, with special emphasis upon the civil rights bill bottled up in the House Rules Committee. "We have talked long enough in this country about equal rights," Johnson said. "We have talked for one hundred years or more. It is time now to write the next chapter, and to write in the books of law."

The Johnson Treatment

Rauh's unexpected love feast with Johnson began soon after LBJ moved into the White House, when the president invited him abroad Air Force One to attend the funeral of former senator Herbert Lehman in New York. Johnson made certain Rauh felt at home on the trip by inviting other liberals, including his old Texas nemesis, Senator Ralph Yarborough.[6] During the flight to New York, Johnson urged Rauh to make an appointment with Kenny O'Donnell to discuss the civil rights measure. Then for two days, with Johnson expressing regret at their past differences, Rauh and the new president pored over the Judiciary Committee bill line by line and discussed strategy for the pending fights in Congress. At their second meeting, Rauh produced a recent report by the Civil Rights Commission that documented the deplorable figures on racial segregation in the Texas public schools.

"Your opponent next year will say you talk big, but the schools in Texas are heavily segregated," Rauh said, as Johnson eyed the figures and seemed genuinely shocked.

"I want you to write a memo for me on this and I'll give it to [Governor John] Connally," Johnson replied, a task Rauh carried out and one that inspired appreciation from a president ever on the alert for political potholes.[7]

Johnson continued their courtship by inviting the Rauhs to a White

House reception for the newly elected Italian prime minister, Aldo Moro. As they passed through the receiving line, Johnson took Rauh aside, threw an arm around his old adversary, and boasted to the Italian leader: "This here fella is helping me on the civil rights bill!" That gesture soon provoked a phone call from Reuther, who teased Rauh about his flourishing friendship with an old enemy.[8]

At a White House meeting several days before a crucial vote in the House Rules Committee, Rauh and Mitchell told Johnson they hoped to strengthen the bill on the floor by restoring some of the language on voting rights and public accommodations. Equally frank, Johnson said he could not support those revisions for fear of losing Republican votes, intensifying southern resistance in the Senate and complicating the problems of enforcement. Rauh and Mitchell finally relented and agreed to back what had now become a strong compromise between their ideal and the tepid Kennedy proposals of the previous spring.

"The Most Sweeping Civil Rights Measure"

True to its past, the House voted overwhelming on February 10 in favor of what the *Congressional Quarterly* called "the most sweeping civil rights measure to clear either house of Congress in the 20th century." Southern opposition, although strident and openly racist, had little impact, even when Congressman Smith, beaten in his own Rules Committee, asserted that the most terrible consequence of the measure would be to force white female manicurists to cut the toenails of Negro men. Smith's effort to kill the bill by offering an amendment to prohibit sex discrimination in employment backfired when enough southern congressmen voted with supporters of the National Women's Party to pass the provision, 168-133. Howard Smith had unintentionally initiated a legal revolution in gender relations that few imagined in 1964.

Although confident of victory, Rauh, Mitchell, and their Leadership Conference troops took nothing for granted as the House members marched through the chamber on individual teller votes. Under the command of Jane O'Grady of the Amalgamated Clothing Workers Union, they stationed monitors, whom Mitchell called "O'Grady's Raiders," on each floor of the House office building to make certain that pro–civil rights congressmen turned out for the crucial votes.[9] Rauh and Mitchell had barely begun to celebrate their triumph in the House gallery when thirteen-year-old Sandy Newman, a courier for the civil rights coalition, rushed in to tell them that they had to take a telephone call downstairs from the White House. To Rauh's amazement, the president came on the line and began barking orders about the next stage of the battle.

"What are you guys doing about the Senate?" he demanded.

LBJ then repeated the broad strategy already mapped out with Robert Kennedy and Katzenbach. "You tell Mike Mansfield [the majority leader] that I don't want another piece of legislation until this is passed. The way we're going to beat the filibuster is just letting it lie there forever." LBJ would sacrifice his other legislative initiatives in order to secure the civil rights bill, a choice Rauh called "the most crucial decision on civil rights in legislative history." The president also said that Mansfield should bypass the Senate Judiciary Committee, chaired by Mississippi's reactionary James Eastland. Instead, the Senate would immediately take up the House-passed bill and Humphrey, now the majority whip, should manage the floor debate.

Breaking the Filibuster

Johnson had devised a plan to break the filibuster that Rauh and the Senate leadership wisely rejected. He wanted to keep the Senate in twenty-four-hour sessions in order to exhaust the Southerners. Under the rules, no member could speak more than twice on the same subject during a single legislative day. Although outnumbered, it required only two southern senators to keep a filibuster alive for eight hours by demanding frequent quorum calls that required fifty-one of their opponents to answer a roll call, while other Southerners caught some shut-eye. If a quorum failed to appear, the Senate had to adjourn, a new legislative day officially began and the filibustering senators each gained another two speeches. As majority leader, Johnson had already tried this tactic once in 1960 and, failing to break the southern ranks, finally compromised on the legislation.[10]

Mansfield and Humphrey, caucusing with Rauh, Mitchell, and other civil rights leaders, vetoed this strategy. They feared a repetition of 1960 debate, which had worn down the antifilibuster forces and presented the embarrassing spectacle of senators sleeping on cots outside the chamber. Responding to endless quorum calls, the bleary-eyed, disheveled legislators stumbled onto the Senate floor. Instead, Mansfield and Humphrey agreed to keep the Senate's business focused exclusively on civil rights, but to maintain normal hours and delay a cloture vote until assured of at least sixty-seven supporters.

In order to counter the filibuster, Humphrey and Mansfield organized their supporters into teams, each one responsible for debating portions of the bill and responding to the anticipated quorum calls. But to gain sixty-seven votes, they needed Republican minority leader Everett Dirksen. As the president told Humphrey, "You get in there to see Dirksen! You drink with Dirksen! You talk to Dirksen! You listen to Dirksen!"[11] Humphrey told Marvin Rosenberg, "I promised to get the best damn civil rights bill I can out of this Congress, and if I have to kiss Everett Dirksen's ass every morning, I am going to do it."[12] At some point, the president and Humphrey predicted, Dirksen had to choose whether to allow the filibuster to continue or join the cloture forces and become a legislative hero.

Between May 6 and 13, as the filibuster droned on and Mansfield threatened to keep the Senate in daily sessions until midnight, the Democratic and Republican leadership, joined by Katzenbach, hammered out a new compromise package in Dirksen's office. The Republican leader had helped Mansfield defeat an effort by the Southerners to require jury trials in all cases of criminal contempt. But Rauh distrusted Dirksen's devotion to civil rights and objected to his amendments, a position that infuriated Humphrey. Rauh and the Leadership Conference people "are just up in arms, as they generally are," Humphrey complained to Johnson. "We had Joe all wired," he reported, but when he stepped out of the room for a moment, "Joe gave 'em a lecture about that we'd sold out," and finally declared, "Look, I'm not going to cause you any trouble, but I don't want to be here 'cause I'm not sure I want to agree yet, see."[13]

Furious that Rauh might break ranks and lead a revolt against the compromise, Johnson told Humphrey to speak bluntly to his friend about the threat of a "real revolution in this country when this bill goes into effect." Dirksen's support guaranteed cloture, and "unless we have the Republicans joining us and helping us put down this mutiny," LBJ added, "we'll have mutiny in this goddamn country. So we've got to make this an American bill and not just a Democratic bill." Rauh should be pleased that Republicans like Dirksen and William McCulloch of Ohio had participated, the president concluded, because it "doesn't do any good to have a law like the Volstead Act if you can't enforce it."[14]

After poring over the revised text with Mitchell and Tom Harris, the associate general counsel of the AFL-CIO, Rauh conceded that most of Dirksen's revisions seemed to be cosmetic. None would prove insurmountable, even a provision that required courts to find "intentional" racial discrimination before granting relief. In truth, Dirksen had betrayed his GOP's conservatives more than the civil rights forces. In public, however, Rauh and the Leadership Conference gave only grudging support for the changes because they feared that too much enthusiasm for the Dirksen-Humphrey compromise might provoke accusations of a retreat from some black leaders or ignite a rebellion by Republicans against their own leader.[15]

On June, 10, 1964, seventy-five days after Russell and the Southerners had launched their filibuster, the Senate voted to end debate on a civil rights bill for the first time in American history. The count was 71-49, with twenty-seven Dirksen-led Republicans joining forty-four Humphrey Democrats. Nine days later, after turning back 106 amendments offered by Russell's demoralized troops, the Senate finally passed the Civil Rights Act of 1964, to which the House concurred on July 2. At a nationally televised ceremony that evening in the White House, surrounded by Humphrey, Mansfield, Dirksen, and the other legislative leaders, the president signed the historic measure into law, an event Joe Rauh had always dreamed possible, but never from the hand of Lyndon Johnson.

Shortly after the ceremony, Johnson turned to Katzenbach and said, "What are we going to do next year in civil rights?" To which the tired assistant attorney general replied, "Jesus Christ, Mr. President, we just spent two years on this bill and practically nothing else happened." But Johnson persisted. "Let's get another bill," he said. "Let's get a voting rights bill." Joe Rauh would be in the thick of that battle, too, but his honeymoon with LBJ was about to end at the Democratic National Convention in Atlantic City. He had agreed to represent the Mississippi Freedom Democrats at the convention.[16]

Moses and Lowenthal

In an effort to redirect the energy of the Freedom Rides in 1961, Robert Kennedy had urged SNCC, CORE, and other groups to mount instead a voter registration effort in the South. With funds from the United Auto Workers and other liberal sponsors, SNCC workers launched a drive in Mississippi to register blacks under the 1957 and 1960 civil rights acts. Those who attempted to sign up faced white registrars brandishing guns, firebombs thrown into their homes, cars riddled with bullets, and the loss of employment as landowners evicted sharecroppers who sought the ballot. Faced with this intimidation, SNCC leaders hit upon the idea of organizing a mock election among Mississippi blacks in 1963, an event designed to take place at the same time as the state's official gubernatorial vote.

The Freedom Vote of 1963, the Freedom Summer of 1964, and ultimately the Mississippi Freedom Democratic Party sprang from the fertile imagination and tactical brilliance of Bob Moses, a Harvard-educated

African-American who had studied philosophy and Zen Buddhism, and Allard Lowenthal, a New York Jew, educated at the University of North Carolina and Yale, whose peripatetic career as an agitator earned him the label as the "world's oldest student activist." In an organization whose members had a well-earned reputation for heroism, SNCC's Moses stood out as a man of uncommon courage, a leader whose asceticism masked a will of iron in the struggle against southern racism. Assaulted by mobs, beaten by sheriffs, and thrown into jails where he passed the days reading Albert Camus, Moses inspired awe from both the rawest SNCC recruit and the most seasoned Justice Department veteran, like John Doar. Lowenthal's eloquence inspired scores of privileged white college students to head for Mississippi, where Moses trained them and put them to work running freedom schools and voter registration drives.[17]

In the middle of the struggle over the civil rights bill, Rauh spoke on a panel at the annual conference of the National Civil Liberties Clearing House in 1964. There he first met Moses, who stood up in the audience and posed a fascinating question: could a racially integrated delegation from Mississippi oust that state's all-white contingent at the coming Democratic National Convention? Rauh, who always relished a good credentials fight, said the prospects for success were better than fifty-fifty. He knew that as Reuther's lawyer he would likely have a place on the key committee. He encouraged Moses to go ahead with the Freedom Party challenge.

Four days later, Rauh and Moses met again in Atlantic City during the UAW annual convention, this time with Milly Jeffrey from the union leadership and Ella Baker, executive secretary of King's Southern Christian Leadership Conference, a woman regarded as the founding godmother of SNCC. Rauh both admired and distrusted Baker because of her devotion to civil rights and her longtime relationship with the Communist Party, but when Moses and Baker said the Freedom Party would go forward with the challenge, Rauh quickly agreed to act as their attorney. "I feel that the fight can be won at the Democratic Convention if everything is done correctly and if the fight is limited to Mississippi," Rauh told Albert Sayer, chairman of the New York ADA. As long as the insurgents focused on Mississippi, he emphasized, "I don't see why the Administration has to battle it." He had confidence that Moses would do a superb job "following the forms of Mississippi law . . . even more carefully than the lily white delegation will follow it." Liberals had failed to win similar challenges in 1948, 1952, and 1956, Rauh pointed out, because they lacked a real rival delegation, but the present situation "should be different and the odds should be on our side."[18] He was too optimistic.

By early May, Moses informed Rauh that in addition to forming an executive committee, the new Mississippi Freedom Democratic Party (MFDP)
planned to create precinct, county, congressional, and state conventions
"paralleling as closely as possible the regular party structure." Some MFDP
members intended to attend regular party precinct meetings, from which
they expected to be barred. "It sounds to me that you are doing everything
just right," Rauh told Moses and stressed the importance of having "many
Negroes seek to attend regular party precinct meetings so we can build up
the argument on exclusion."[19]

Checking the Lawyer's Guild

Rauh signed on with Moses and the MFDP both because he believed in
their cause and because he feared they would, under Baker's influence, employ more radical legal counsel if he declined. "I had little doubt," he
reflected later, "that were I ever to withdraw, the Lawyers Guild would have
taken over the representation of the Freedom Party." That prospect filled
him with dread even though the close ties between the guild and the Communist Party had been dissipated by 1964. He feared that Guild lawyers and
Baker would turn the legal challenge at Atlantic City into radical theater and
generally erode liberal influence in the civil rights movement. Rauh expressed great irritation when Baker encouraged Arthur Kinoy and other attorneys for the Lawyers Guild to file a suit that challenged the validity of the
lily-white Mississippi regulars. That decision, Rauh believed, should be left
initially to the convention and not dragged into the courts. He soon found
himself fighting off attempts by the Guild, the Johnson White House, and his
old liberal allies to control him and the destiny of the Freedom Party.[20]

When Rauh met with Walter and Roy Reuther and Jack Conway in early
May to discuss strategy on the civil rights bill, he told them about the potential Freedom Party challenge. No one raised an objection. A few weeks later,
the ADA went on record favoring the Mississippi challenge, an endorsement
followed in early July by the Central Committee of the Democratic Party for
the District of Columbia. Other state party organizations jumped on board as
well. But racial politics soon complicated Rauh's life that spring when Alabama's segregationist governor George Wallace did surprisingly well in the
Democratic primaries of Wisconsin, Indiana, and Maryland. Then in San
Francisco on July 15, the GOP nominated Arizona's Barry Goldwater, the
darling of conservatives, who had voted against the Civil Rights Act. That
same month, African-Americans rioted in Harlem, Rochester, and Philadel-

phia. Alarmed that white voters, especially in the South, would abandon him, Johnson and his advisers pushed the panic button over the Freedom Party.

A week after Goldwater's nomination, Rauh received a phone call from Kenny O'Donnell at the White House, who asked for an immediate meeting. O'Donnell came right to the point: "The President was very worried about the battle at the convention over the Freedom Party." Rauh responded with an equally blunt warning. The credentials fight would take place whatever his role, he said, but the president should realize "it was better to have it [the Freedom Party] represented by thoughtful people with the best interest of the Party at heart rather than by the Lawyers Guild crowd."[21] Keeping his options open, he also began to explore alternatives with O'Donnell, which appeared to boil down to the "seating of neither or both" of the delegations. A recent Mississippi law, Rauh told O'Donnell, could keep electors pledged to the president off the state's November ballot. In that event, the convention rules would bar the Mississippi regulars and open the door to seating the Freedom delegation, but if Mississippi allowed electors pledged to the president, then both might be seated in Atlantic City.[22]

By mid-July, Johnson's paranoia about the Freedom Party had taken over. He believed that "Joe Rauh and Martin Luther King and folks that normally run with that crowd are leading 'em [the Freedom Party]. Humphrey is trying his best to put an end to it, but he hasn't had much luck with 'em." The president also saw the hand of his archenemy Robert Kennedy behind the Freedom Party. "It may very well be that Bobby has started it," Johnson told Connally. Kennedy had nothing to do with the challenge, and SNCC leaders distrusted him, but Connally fueled the president's fears. If the convention ousted the Mississippi or Alabama regulars, Connally warned, "The impression around the country is going to be that they just got kicked out because the niggers wanted them kicked out."[23]

No Compromise

At the end of July, the White House rejected any compromise and threw its support to the Mississippi regulars, even though the lily-white state convention declined to give Johnson the official Democratic Party endorsement. At the same time, Rauh learned through various UAW sources that Reuther "had exploded against the Mississippi [Freedom] Democratic Party" when civil rights veteran Bayard Rustin warned him that "white liberals had to make a good showing at this Convention or life would become intolerable for those Negroes who believed in cooperation with the white liberals." On the day before the Freedom Party's convention opened in Jackson, Bill Moyers, a special assistant to the president, attempted to console Rauh by saying that he personally favored seating both delegations, but "the President felt that too many Southern delegations would walk out if both were seated."[24]

Rauh flew to Jackson on August 5, a day before the MFDP convention opened in the city's Masonic Temple. He received his introduction to Mississippi when Moses picked him up at the airport and drove him to a hotel while looking every minute into the rearview mirror at the car tailing them. Two days earlier at the Olen Burrage dam in Neshoba County, FBI agents had recovered the bodies of three young Freedom Summer volunteers, one black, two white—James Chaney, Mickey Schwerner, and Andrew Goodman. Last seen while in the custody of Sheriff Lawrence Rainey and his deputy, Cecil Price, they had been shot to death and Chaney savagely beaten before his execution.

The three murders cast a pall of gloom over the Masonic Temple, but also infused the nearly all-black gathering with moral fervor. Rauh described it to Tom Carvey of the California Democratic Council as "inspirational . . . I am proud to be able to represent the group at Atlantic City." The Freedom Party presented a striking contrast to the Mississippi regulars: Moses; Aaron Henry, a pharmacist from Clarksdale; the Reverend Ed King, banned by the all-white Mississippi Methodist Conference for his support of Medgar Evers; Fannie Lou Hamer from Ruleville, the gospel-singing twentieth child of sharecroppers; as well as schoolteachers and sailors from Beloxi.

Introduced by Henry, Rauh gave the delegates a rousing oration, what he later called his "Eleven and Eight" speech, but he also touched on Johnson's civil rights record in the faint hope of gaining the president's neutrality at Atlantic City. They would need eleven votes, or 10 percent of the credentials committee, to file a minority report, he told them; the support of eight states could also force a roll call on the floor of the convention to oust the regulars. That evening after the convention elected its delegates, Rauh drafted a letter to party chairman John Bailey of Connecticut declaring their intention to mount the historic challenge.[25]

"Tell Him I'm Just a Son-of-a-Bitch"

Johnson wasted little time after the Jackson convention in mobilizing his troops against Rauh and the MFDP. "If you and Hubert Humphrey have got any leadership, you'd get Joe Rauh off that damn television," he stormed at Reuther. "The only thing that can really screw us good is to seat that group of challengers from Mississippi. . . . Now there's not a damn vote that we get by seating these folks." If Rauh and his challengers succeeded, Johnson told the UAW president, Georgia and Texas might bolt the convention. He could lose states like Oklahoma and Kentucky in November as well as congressional seats that would endanger the recently enacted Civil Rights Act. "We don't want to cut off our nose to spite our face," Johnson concluded. "If they give us four years," he promised, "I'll guarantee the Freedom delegation somebody representing views like that will be seated. . . . But we can't do it all before breakfast."[26]

Over the next few days, as the Atlantic City showdown approached, Rauh heard directly and indirectly from Reuther, Kampelman, Rowe, and Bill Connell of Humphrey's staff. They all conveyed the same message and warning: the president had become "very concerned" about the Freedom Party challenge; unless it was resolved to his satisfaction, Humphrey would not be on the ticket. Feeling the heat from the White House, Humphrey told the president on the morning of August 14, "I've been just working the devil out of that Joe." When the two old political friends met later that same afternoon, Humphrey expressed understanding of Rauh's position: "I know, Joe, you've got to go on," the senator said, "but what do I tell the president?" Returning the sympathy, Rauh advised, "Well, you tell him I'm just a son-of-a-bitch nobody can do anything with." Humphrey shook his head and said, "The President won't like that as an answer."[27]

Unmoved by the accumulating threats, Rauh led the charge for the Freedom Party. With the assistance of Eleanor Holmes Norton, a recent law school graduate, he wrote a powerful brief on their behalf and submitted it to the credentials committee. When California governor Edmund G. Brown, his arm twisted by Johnson, attempted to pressure his delegation to reconsider their support for the insurgents, Rauh leaked the story to reporters for the *Los Angeles Times* with the result that the governor retreated under attack from many Democrats in the Golden State. Despite Brown's opposition, California's Central Committee reaffirmed its backing of the Freedom Party.

In a meeting with Bailey, Governor David Lawrence, chairman of the credentials committee, and Harold Leventhal, the committee's attorney, Rauh threatened to walk out when the party leaders proposed limiting the challengers' presentation to a half hour. He demanded two hours, and finally settled for one. On the afternoon of their scheduled appearance before the committee, Rauh learned that the convention managers proposed to hold the hearing in a cramped room large enough for only one television camera. The networks protested, and, Walter Jenkins told Johnson, "Joe Rauh is rais-

ing hell." Fearing that "Rauh will storm the room," the president finally relented and allowed the hearing to be moved to a larger ballroom with additional television cameras.[28]

LBJ successfully interrupted their television coverage with a meaningless
press conference, but Rauh and his Freedom Party witnesses offered the credentials committee harrowing accounts of life under Mississippi's regime of
white political terror. Mrs. Hamer, in words as plain as the cotton dress she
wore, recounted her eviction from the plantation when she refused to withdraw her voter registration; the gunshots fired into the homes of others who
had dared to register; and her arrest and beating in the Winona jail, where a
Mississippi highway patrolman had forced another black prisoner to beat her
with a blackjack. After Fannie Lou, the testimony of James Farmer, Roy
Wilkins, and even Dr. King on behalf of the Freedom Party was anticlimactic.

"Are you going to throw out of here the people who want to work for Lyndon Johnson," Rauh asked the credentials committee in summation, "who
are willing to be beaten in jails, to die for the privilege of working for Lyndon
Johnson?" It came down to fundamental things, he concluded: "Will the
Democratic Party stand for the oppressors or for the oppressed? Will it stand
for loyal people like those who testified, or for the disloyal 'regular' party?"[29]

Fearing eventual defeat that would serve no one, Rauh argued openly for
the ouster of the Mississippi regulars, but continued to float the idea of a
compromise that would seat both delegations. As he pointed out many times
to O'Donnell and Lee White on the president's staff, the Democrats had
faced a similar situation in 1944 with respect to two delegations from Texas.
The party decided then to seat both, and Johnson had been a member of one
of them. But the president, as Moyers had indicated earlier, rejected that
precedent and refused to support such an arrangement for Mississippi.
"There's no compromise," Johnson told Humphrey. "You can seat one or the
other. You can't seat both of them because if you do, then the other one walks
out. There's just no justification for messing with the Freedom Party at all in
Mississippi."[30]

Johnson also kept close watch on Rauh and the Freedom Party's strategy
through FBI wiretaps placed on the phones of Dr. King and Rustin, illegal
surveillance that continued throughout the convention. Filing their reports
under the heading "Communist Party, United States of America—Negro
Question—Communist Influence in Racial Matters—Internal Security,"
Hoover's electronic spies learned that Rauh advised Rustin on how King
should negotiate with the president at a meeting scheduled for the White
House, a gathering that King finally declined to attend. King should push for
seating both delegations, Rauh urged, and if LBJ refused, "then he is looking

for trouble." King should be "forceful," tell Johnson there would be "an explosion if he did not . . . just grab the ball and say you've got to seat them
both, Mr. President."[31]

Honored Guests of the Convention

When the credentials committee convened for a showdown on Sunday afternoon, August 23, Rauh learned what compromise would be acceptable to
Johnson. Chairman Lawrence declined to give him the floor and instead entertained a motion to seat the regulars if they pledged loyalty to Johnson and
the platform. The Freedom Party delegates would be named "honored
guests of the convention." Again ignoring Rauh, Lawrence recognized Congressman Al Ullman of Oregon, the point man for the administration, who
moved to amend the motion by giving the Freedom Party two seats and to
accord the rest of their forty-person delegation status as honored guests.
When finally recognized by the chair, Rauh spoke against both the original
motion and Ullman's amendment. He received sufficient support in the
room to force Lawrence into a strategic retreat instead of an immediate vote.
The chairman appointed a subcommittee of five, including himself and Minnesota attorney general Walter Mondale, to hammer out another compromise and report back on Monday before the convention opened.

That night as Rauh reviewed the day's events with Freedom Party delegates in the sitting room of Martin Luther King's hotel suite, SCLC leaders
caucused in the adjacent bedroom with Moses and Lowenstein, whose later
versions of those conversations conflicted sharply. Moses and Dr. King, according to Lowenstein's account, did not reject the two-seat compromise.
"Well, God, if that's the best we can get, that's the best we can get," Moses
said, a concession he soon denied making. Rauh left King's suite and went to
bed, unaware of those discussions, thoroughly exhausted, and worried about
the health of his son Carl, who had taken ill in Atlantic City with a high
fever.[32]

When he met the next morning in Humphrey's suite with Dr. King,
Moses, Lowenstein, Mrs. Hamer, other MFDP leaders and Congresswoman
Edith Green of Oregon, one of their supporters on the credentials committee, Rauh faced a continuing stalemate. Humphrey now put forward a new
plan: the Freedom Party would be seated as nonvoting guests, and the regulars would have to pledge to support the party's candidate and civil rights
platform. Furthermore, the Democratic Party would go on record to disqualify any future delegations tainted by racial discrimination. Humphrey
pleaded for their endorsement, but Mrs. Hamer offered him only her

prayers and the admonition "to do what you know is right," a flat rejection of his compromise.[33]

On the convention floor Monday night, Rauh began to sense the tide moving away from the Freedom Party. He made the rounds of many northern delegations in search of prominent Democrats who would speak on behalf of a minority plank the next evening. At the Illinois delegation, he cornered Paul Douglas, an old friend and a champion of civil rights. Douglas, like others, begged off making a speech. "Don't ask me to do this," Douglas pleaded, "I'm up for reelection in '66. I can't do it." Stunned by Douglas's refusal, Rauh retired for the night to care for Carl, but he sensed that few liberals now relished a floor fight. He and Congresswoman Green might be alone.[34]

The next day as Rauh entered the meeting of the credentials committee, Congressman Charles Diggs of Michigan, the lone African-American on the subcommittee, handed him a scrap of paper and told him to call the phone number he had scribbled down. Walking down a floor to the public phones where television reporters huddled, Rauh dialed the number and listened as Reuther came on the line and began barking out commands. The convention, said the UAW president, had made its decision, by which he meant Johnson had now made a final offer: the Mississippi regulars would be required to take a loyalty oath and, failing that test, tossed out. The Freedom Party could have two at-large seats. The convention rules would require integrated delegations in the future.

"I think it's a good deal," Rauh told Reuther, but added, "I can't support it until I talk with Aaron Henry and my clients. I need time. I need to see Aaron." Reuther promised to secure a delay for such consultation, but he then reminded Rauh that he was the UAW's general counsel. This decision, he said, was an order. Reuther was so angry, Rauh recalled later, "you could have fried an egg on his heart." Without raising his voice, Rauh told Reuther that he was not acting as general counsel for the UAW. "I've never used my UAW connections," he told Reuther. "I'm speaking here as a political figure for the District of Columbia and you cannot give me orders." The discussion ended abruptly. Reuther, clearly annoyed, did not speak to Rauh for several months.[35]

"That Illiterate Woman"

Reuther had trapped Rauh into leaving the committee. When he returned to the meeting, Mondale had already introduced "the decision of the convention," the same one outlined minutes earlier on the phone by Reuther. But now Rauh would not be given the time to meet with Henry and the other

MFDP leaders. They had been locked up in Humphrey's suite with Dr. King and Rustin, all of them subject to intense pressure from Reuther to accept the two-seat compromise that excluded Mrs. Hamer. "The President will not allow that illiterate woman to speak from the floor of the convention," Humphrey told them bluntly. Back at the credentials committee, Rauh's call for a postponement fell on deaf ears. Led by Sherwin Markman of Iowa, a member of the subcommittee of five, cries of "Vote! Vote! Vote!" swept the room. Rauh demanded a roll call but was ignored, and the Mondale compromise won by voice vote. The Freedom Party supporters fell three short of the eleven needed for a minority report.

When Mondale, Rauh, and other members of the committee emerged to face television cameras, disaster struck. As a reporter declared, "I understand it was unanimous for the position you took," Mondale either did not hear the statement or failed to grasp its significance. He launched into a summary of what the reporter and others took to be a unanimous decision. Watching Mondale's televised statement in Reuther's suite, Moses and others believed Rauh had capitulated. The SNCC leader bolted from the room before Rauh took the microphone several minutes later to explain that he had been unable to consult with MFDP leaders and had voted against the Mondale compromise. The Freedom Party's lawyer also complained that intense pressure from the Johnson administration had doomed their effort to secure eleven votes for a floor debate.

By the time the Freedom Party delegates and their supporters assembled that evening and the following Wednesday morning at Union Temple Baptist Church, Moses knew the truth of Rauh's dissent in the credentials committee, but that did not soften his opposition to the compromise. Rauh shared their anger about the slap at Mrs. Hamer. He believed her deliberate exclusion from the compromise had been a fatal blunder, produced, he told Humphrey, by "the dumb bastards on your side." He also criticized Reuther's strong-arm tactics with Dr. King and the SCLC leaders, who had been reminded that much of their financial support depended on the UAW.

Rauh made one last attempt to persuade the administration to allow the Freedom Party to select their two delegates, but then spoke in favor of the compromise. So did others, including Aaron Henry, James Farmer, Rustin, Senator Morse, and Dr. King. King attempted to have it both ways when he said, "Being a Negro leader, I want you to take this, but if I were a Mississippi Negro I would vote against it." SNCC leaders didn't attack King, but denounced Rustin as a traitor. Heeding King's advice and the eloquence of Moses and Mrs. Hamer, the Freedom Party delegates voted against the compromise. "We're not here to bring politics to our morality," Moses told them, "but to bring morality to our politics." Mrs. Hamer, speaking for the majority, said emphatically, "We didn't come all this way for no two seats."[36]

Fallout

Johnson, Humphrey, Reuther, and the party leaders had manipulated the compromise badly. Security guards dragged MFDP delegates from the convention floor when they attempted to take the seats of the regulars who bolted. Despite that fiasco and others, Rauh believed Atlantic City represented an important turning point that would forever transform the Democratic Party by eradicating white supremacy. His party would be more open and inclusive than ever before. "Furthermore," he told Ed Gray of the UAW, "even though Aaron Henry and Ed King did not take their delegate seats, the fact that they were offered delegate status was at least partial recognition of the Freedom Party."[37] "When the smoke finally cleared," John Lewis recalled, "Joe Rauh would be seen as a villain, a traitor, a back stabber. And that was a shame. He was a good man who worked incredibly hard to bring this moment about. It's ironic that the situation he had worked so hard to create wound up skewering his reputation, at least among the black community."[38]

The Freedom Party challenge inflicted other wounds. Johnson and Humphrey crushed Goldwater and the emerging Republican right wing in November, but the Arizonan took the electoral votes of five southern states, a clear statement of the region's continuing racial divide and a harbinger of the growing white migration to the party of Lincoln that would transform American politics in the next two decades. Atlantic City drove a sharp wedge between leaders like Rustin and King, who pushed for compromise, and those like Moses, who regarded it as a sellout by people who valued their white allies more than their brothers and sisters in the movement. SNCC soon expelled its white members and adopted the demand for "Black Power," a call that signaled the unraveling of the civil rights coalition and difficult days ahead for white liberals like Joe Rauh.

CHAPTER FOURTEEN

VIETNAM AND THE LIBERAL CRISIS

Joe, it's a very frustrating, unhappy, miserable world. I wish
I could be as pure of heart as you.
—MARVIN ROSENBERG TO JOE RAUH

High Tide of Reform

Rauh knew Lyndon Johnson would win and win big, but he also feared that
his victory might prove to be a curse, not a blessing. On the eve of the Democrats' greatest electoral sweep since 1936, he became pessimistic about the
consequences of LBJ's anticipated landslide over Senator Goldwater. "What
does worry me about the campaign," Rauh told Reinhold and Ursula
Niebuhr, "is that it really isn't a campaign at all—no issues, no education, no
leaps into the future. Goldwater and [William] Miller have made the campaign into a farce and no one (not even Hubert) is discussing all the things
that ought to be done in the country during the next four years." In his bid
for consensus, LBJ avoided proposing "needed radical programs because
some of his supporters wouldn't like them." Rauh doubted Johnson, after
winning, could run the country "trying to appeal to both Walter Reuther and
Henry Ford."[1]

On the domestic scene, Rauh's fears proved premature. As predicted, despite losing five southern states to Goldwater, the Johnson-Humphrey ticket
rolled to one of the most crushing victories in the history of presidential elections, massing a popular vote majority of 43 million to 27 million in addition
to a 486-52 advantage in electoral votes. Huge Democratic majorities rode
Johnson's coattails into Congress, where they gave him the leverage to drive
through Congress the most far-reaching program of domestic reform since
1935. Johnson fulfilled the New Deal and with respect to civil rights broad-

ened it beyond anything contemplated by FDR. In Johnson's War on Poverty and Great Society, American liberalism reached its zenith with the creation of Medicare, adoption of the radical Voting Rights Act, massive federal aid to education, two new cabinet-level positions, revision of the old, racist immigration laws, and the founding of the National Endowments for the Arts and Humanities.

But even as Congress neared a final vote on Johnson's Economic Opportunity Act, the centerpiece of his War on Poverty, the president and his national security advisers escalated another war in Southeast Asia. Johnson's commitment to civil rights had ruptured the old New Deal–Democratic Party coalition in the South. Within four years the war in Vietnam dealt his party another blow by driving a wedge between the president and the liberals who had supported his domestic initiatives. Joe Rauh's Democratic Party lay mortally wounded by 1968.

Johnson claimed that American destroyers, the USS *Maddox* and *C. Turner Joy,* had been attacked without provocation by North Vietnamese patrol boats in the Gulf of Tonkin. He then launched the first air attack against bases and oil storage facilities in North Vietnam and quickly sent a resolution to both houses of Congress that authorized him "to take all necessary measures to repel any armed attack against the armed forces of the United States and to prevent further aggression." The administration, speaking through secretary of defense Robert McNamara, never informed Congress that the destroyers had been engaged in electronic espionage ten miles off the North Vietnam coast and had monitored South Vietnamese gunboats as they fired on coastal installations. The administration also withheld from Congress the administration's own doubts about whether a second attack had even taken place.

The signing of the Voting Rights Act became the final triumph for postwar American liberalism, a movement soon shaken by unprecedented social upheaval in the nation's cities, bitter racial divisions, and Johnson's escalation of the war in Vietnam. From a position where they had shaped the agenda of change, Rauh and other liberals now found themselves thrown on the defensive by those who affirmed the bankruptcy of their ideas and who preached either the necessity of revolution or restoration of the status quo. Less than a week after Johnson signed the Voting Rights Act, an altercation between police and a young black man over a speeding ticket in the Los Angeles community of Watts sparked six days of rioting, looting, and fire-bombing that left thirty-four dead and property damage estimated at $35 million before police and National Guardsmen quelled the disturbance.

The Making of a Quagmire

Every American president since Truman had pursued an unwavering policy with respect to Vietnam, where the people had struggled for centuries to create a nation free of foreign domination by the Chinese, French, or Japanese. The Vietnamese Communist Party and its indefatigable chief, Nguyen Sinh Cung, later known at Ho Chi Minh, seized leadership of this struggle immediately after World War I. A dedicated Marxist, trained in Moscow, Ho had one fundamental goal: to defeat foreign imperialism and unify Vietnam under his party. The United States gave Ho military equipment in their common war against the Japanese, who had ousted the French in 1941, but American presidents from Truman forward could not accept a united, Communist-dominated Vietnam in the context of rising Soviet power and the triumph of Mao Tse-tung in China.

American administrations opposed Ho and the Communists by various means, first by giving military and economic support to the French in their effort to crush the Vietminh and restore France's imperial role, a strategy that ended with the military defeat of the French in 1954. Then faced with the near certainty that Ho Chi Minh and the Communists would win a mandate in elections scheduled for 1956 under the terms of so-called Geneva Accords that concluded the French-Vietminh war, the Eisenhower administration repudiated elections for national unification and created an anticommunist regime south of the seventeenth parallel, led by Ngo Dinh Diem, whose American patrons included John Kennedy, Cardinal Francis Spellman, archbishop of New York, Lyndon Johnson, and Supreme Court justice William O. Douglas.

By 1963, Diem's police state in the south resembled Ho's Communist Party dictatorship in all but its efficiency. With a nod from President Kennedy and the American ambassador, Henry Cabot Lodge, Diem's generals ousted him. To Kennedy's shock, they also murdered the president and his brother. The collapse of the Diem regime, the perpetual political instability in South Vietnam, and the incompetence of its military, where desertions reached 11,000 soldiers a month in 1965, exhibited the fundamental defect in the policy of the United States: South Vietnam was not a nation, but an artificial geopolitical construction of America's anticommunist zealotry in Asia, a make-believe country incapable of surviving without a continuing infusion of external aid, military and economic, from the United States. As Johnson confessed to Senator Russell in the spring of 1965: "There's no sense of responsibility there on the part of any of their leaders.

. . . It's a hell of a situation. It's a mess. And it's going to get worse. And I don't know what to do."[2]

Escalation

Until Johnson's escalation of the bombing war and the deployment of marines, the conduct of American foreign policy had not loomed large on Rauh's political agenda. Along with other Democratic liberals he had endorsed the Marshall Plan, the Berlin Airlift, and Truman's decision to repel North Korea's attack against the south. "I had made up my mind never to say a word on foreign policy," he recalled, "because I don't know anything about it, and besides I wanted to save what good will I would have to the civil rights things."[3]

Vietnam began to change Rauh's perspective because it threatened to tear apart the Democratic Party and the liberal coalition. But the growing division among his own friends and allies in the liberal movement over the war confronted him with painful choices. "In the field of foreign policy," he told Philip Potter of the *Baltimore Sun* in early 1966, "I am an ADA follower rather than a leader. . . . I cannot help, however, having personal views on so vital a subject as Vietnam and . . . I side with the critics of the Administration policy rather than with Vice President Humphrey." At the same time, Rauh wished Potter to know that he and the ADA, while disagreeing with the administration, "do not believe in unilateral withdrawal [from Vietnam]." Moreover, he added, we "are not peaceniks . . . [and our] criticism of the Administration has been responsible and constructive."[4]

The ADA Divided

Within the ranks of the ADA, support for the war ran strong among labor leaders such as Gus Tyler and David Dubinsky of the International Ladies Garment Workers Union and I. W. Abel of the Steelworkers Union. Political science professor John Roche, ADA chairman in 1964, backed the administration. So did Paul Douglas, the veteran Illinois senator, who believed the ADA had compromised its principles with respect to diplomatic recognition of Red China "and resistance to aggressive communism in Southeast Asia."[5]

Rauh's closest ADA allies, Arthur Schlesinger Jr. and economist John Kenneth Galbraith, opposed American bombing, but also believed that the United States could not unilaterally withdraw from Vietnam, although it had been a mistake to reject the Geneva Accords. In the spring of 1966, Schlesinger advocated "a holding strategy" in South Vietnam, as opposed to offensive military operations, and participation of the Vietcong "in the future political life of South Vietnam," a position that Vice President Humphrey condemned as "putting the fox in the chicken coop." Like Rauh and other admirers of the vice president, Schlesinger hoped in 1966 that "intellectual disagreement over Vietnam" could be contained within rational, liberal discourse and not be "transformed into an emotional estrangement."[6] Such discourse became increasingly difficult after 1966.

In alliance with the Tyler forces, the Rauh-Schlesinger wing of the ADA prevented the adoption of a minority resolution at the organization's 1965 convention that condemned the expansion of America's military presence in Vietnam. They also blocked ADA endorsement of a march on Washington in 1965 organized by Bayard Rustin, Norman Thomas, and Dr. Benjamin Spock that called on the administration to stop the bombing and abide by the Geneva Accords, including the removal of all foreign troops and self-determination for the Vietnamese people. The proposed march, Rauh and other ADA leaders said, would undermine efforts to achieve a negotiated settlement and indicate a collapse of support for the administration, a judgment Hanoi had begun to make even without Dr. Spock's endorsement. By 1966, however, convinced that Johnson had begun to sacrifice domestic reforms for war and that his peace overtures lacked sincerity, Schlesinger and others called for a negotiated settlement that included a role for the Vietnamese Communists.[7]

Reflecting the mood of the country, opposition to the war intensified within the ADA by 1965–66, led by local chapters in California and by younger members such as Curtis Gans, a veteran of the civil rights movement. Congressman Don Edwards of California, elected ADA chairman in 1965, openly criticized the administration on the war. These ADA rebels gained additional support from the irrepressible Allard Lowenstein, who had been voted onto the executive board in 1966 with the support of Rauh and the Schlesinger-Galbraith faction. Unwilling to join the draft-card burners or those who urged direct civil disobedience against the war machine, the Gans-Edwards-Lowenstein faction wanted the ADA to condemn the war outright and repudiate Johnson, including a threat to support a peace candidate in 1968. "If a president is wrong but popular," Lowenstein often said, "political realities may make opposing him difficult, however right; if a president is right but unpopular, supporting him may be a duty, however difficult. But when a president is both wrong and unpopular, to refuse to oppose him is a moral abdication and a political stupidity."[8]

Vietnam tormented Rauh's liberal soul in 1965–66. His heart remained with the Gans-Edwards-Lowenstein faction because they had the better ar-

guments, but he hesitated to sever the ADA's ties with the Johnson administration or to oppose the president's reelection without an alternative candidate. He feared Vietnam would drive a wedge into the liberal coalition, already weakened by the civil rights battles. Wilkins and Young, for example,
supported the president on Vietnam, while King had become a vocal critic.
In the summer of 1965, when King first spoke out against the war at an
SCLC meeting, Rauh attacked him and declared it was wrong to be "mixing
the civil rights forces and the peace movement." Until Johnson's State of the
Union message in 1967, Rauh maintained the fragile hope that Vietnam
would not overwhelm domestic programs. After that message, he knew that
civil rights and the War on Poverty had become other casualties of Vietnam.[9]

Rauh also feared the destruction of the ADA as a result of the increasingly bitter polarization between LBJ stalwarts like Tyler and the peace faction headed by Lowenstein and Gans. Even the Reuther brothers went their
separate ways on the war, with Walter maintaining a discreet silence and Vic
actively opposed. Dubinsky had abandoned the ADA over its mild criticism
of Johnson and cut off ILGWU funding of the organization. If other labor
leaders followed his example, it would further weaken the liberal movement
and plunge the organization into serious financial difficulty. Rauh searched
futilely for some middle ground, but one increasingly tilted toward the
doves. The president and Humphrey left him little choice.[10]

"That's Shit and You Know It"

Rauh's meetings with Humphrey were dispiriting. When he and other ADA
leaders first met with the vice president at the home of his personal physician, Edgar Berman, they found him depressed over his relationship with
Johnson. At one point Humphrey broke down in tears when Rauh told him
they understood his ordeal, but that he should "stop being a cheerleader for
the war." A few months later, Humphrey asked Rauh to arrange another
gathering, this one at Rauh's home, with the guests to include Schlesinger,
Galbraith, Jimmy Wechsler, Robert Bendiner of the *Nation*, and Gilbert
Harrison and Alex Campbell from the *New Republic*.

When the drinks, food, and pleasantries ended, the discussion became
heated on Vietnam. Humphrey claimed that America's resolve in Vietnam
had saved the rest of Southeast Asia from succumbing to Communism, a restatement of the old "domino theory" that if Vietnam fell, so eventually
would other nations in the region. Even Schlesinger had touted the theory at
one time. Now the former Kennedy adviser said, "Hubert, that's shit and you
know it." When Schlesinger complained about the bad advice coming from

the Department of State, the vice president shot back: "Arthur, these are your guys. . . . Don't blame them on us." As the level of hostility rose, Olie Rauh, who had been entertaining Secret Service agents in the next room, burst into the dining room and lectured Schlesinger: "You can't talk that way to the Vice President in my house!"[11]

After tempers cooled, Humphrey admitted that Vietnam remained a "morass" and even agreed with Rauh and the others that the United States should stop bombing. But, he added, "the President's advisers don't agree," a statement that indicated his isolation from the inner circle of decision-making at the White House. Any hope Rauh entertained that Humphrey might distance himself from Johnson soon vanished when the vice president continued his attacks upon administration critics, especially Robert Kennedy, who had come out in favor of broad peace negotiations that included the National Liberation Front (NLF), Communist insurgents in the south allied with North Vietnam.

Breaking with Johnson

Faced with the intransigence of Johnson and Humphrey, Rauh became a principal organizer of Negotiations Now!, an effort to broaden the antiwar movement by stressing the need for United Nations participation, an end to the bombing, a cease-fire, and, like Kennedy, full participation in peace talks by all parties, including the NLF. Rauh now welcomed Dr. King to his side at the New York news conference that launched the organization. He no longer believed it possible to separate the civil rights movement from the peace movement. In the wake of the New York rally, John Roche, now working at the White House, denounced the gathering to Johnson. Dr. King, he told the president, "in desperate search of a constituency—has thrown in with the commies. . . . The Communist-oriented 'peace' types have played him (and his driving wife) like trout. . . . He is painting himself into a corner with a bunch of losers."[12]

In the spring of 1967, Rauh joined Lowenstein by firing a loud warning shot across Johnson's bow. The ADA convention blamed the administration for escalating the war "in size, scope and barbarity," called for an end to the bombing, and urged participation of the NLF in peace negotiations. It also offered a resolution, written by Jimmy Wechsler, that declared the ADA's support for "a serious liberal challenge to the administration's course in the ranks of the Republicans." That resolution provoked protests from Tyler and other Johnson supporters who argued it did not represent the dominant view within the organization and would destroy the ADA. Lowenstein made the final appeal for the resolution, one that Rauh later called the most powerful spontaneous speech he had ever heard. "You were the best thing at the convention," he told Lowenstein, "and I think a great many people knew it." In the face of Tyler's opposition, however, the Rauh-Lowenstein forces settled for a less provocative statement: the ADA remained "pledged to no man and no party; our commitment is to a sane peace and the advance of the cause of human justice and equality."[13]

A bigger explosion took place following a rump ADA board meeting in May, where Rauh and others engineered the election of Lowenstein as vice chairman and then rammed through an even stronger anti-Johnson resolution. Lowenstein's election as vice president by a single vote also stirred doubts even on the part of those who had supported him. "I do think that it is time for us to bring in the younger men even if some of us are not going to be very happy about what they say and do," Marvin Rosenberg told Rauh after the vote. "I have an uncomfortable feeling that I may regret it sometime before the '68 elections." He would not be the only one.[14]

Rauh versus Lowenstein

Although he backed Lowenstein's election and the May resolution, Rauh began to have second thoughts when "the younger men" demanded more direct opposition to the president. Rauh parted company with the insurgents at this point. Any attempt to beat Johnson would be doomed, he believed, without a viable candidate, and none had yet appeared willing to challenge the president. At the July ADA board meeting, when Lowenstein introduced a new resolution that put the organization clearly on record against Johnson, Rauh's opposition helped defeat it, but the intrepid Lowenstein never gave up easily. Hoping to win a convert before the next scheduled board meeting in September, Lowenstein carried the debate to Rauh's backyard patio.

"Joe, we've got to dump Johnson," Lowenstein said.

Rauh countered, "We need a candidate."

"No, we don't," Lowenstein insisted.

Rauh replied, "An organization can't be for dumping somebody without somebody to dump him for."

"You're wrong," Lowenstein retorted. "We'll do it in Wisconsin."

In the Wisconsin primary, Lowenstein pointed out, the ballot contained a provision for voting "none of the above." "We're going to beat Johnson with 'none of the above,'" he concluded.[15]

Rauh thought Lowenstein's plan brilliant, but he remained skeptical that

Johnson could be defeated without a flesh-and-blood opponent. At the same time he sensed that the "dump Johnson" campaign had grown large within the ADA and some alternative would be necessary if he hoped to thwart Lowenstein at the next board meeting. He proposed instead the election of antiwar delegates to the convention and creation of a "peace caucus," pledged to support platform language that repudiated the war and Johnson if he chose to run again. But the ADA would hold off any endorsement or rejection of a candidate until after both party conventions.

The Lowenthal-Gans faction regarded Rauh's "peace plank" idea as far too mild, but others in the ADA attacked it as a recipe for dividing the party and opening the door to a Republican victory. "Joe, it's a very frustrating, unhappy, miserable world. I wish I could be as pure of heart as you," Rosenberg told him. Eugene Wyman, the powerful national committeeman for California, offered a blunter assessment. "I do not believe that the Democrats can afford the chance of a Reagan or a Nixon or others of their ilk to be President."[16] Rauh made it clear to Wyman and others that he, too, feared "the disaster . . . Reagan or Nixon would portend," but a peace caucus at the convention could express their disagreement with Johnson over Vietnam while still offering him full support "if the Republicans were to put up Reagan or Nixon rather than a moderate."[17]

Taking heat from all sides, Rauh remained determined to head off Lowenstein's "dump Johnson" resolution. At lunch with Lowenstein on the day before the September ADA vote, he emphasized that once a candidate came forward to oppose the president, he would immediately join the effort to dump Johnson. They again went over the list of the possible alternatives—Kennedy, George McGovern, Frank Church—when Lowenstein suggested that Senator Eugene McCarthy should be considered as well. After a moment's reflection, Rauh seconded the idea. McCarthy, he told Lowenstein, might be a better candidate than Senator George McGovern because "as a Catholic, he [McCarthy] can't be charged with being soft on communism, whereas that charge could be brought against McGovern." When Rauh spoke against Lowenstein's position the following day, he added McCarthy to the list of candidates who would have his support if they entered the race against Johnson.[18]

Lowenstein and his allies ridiculed Rauh's "peace caucus" as a defeat for the antiwar movement, but with support from the Tyler faction, the caucus idea easily defeated the Lowenstein resolution. The president's Vietnam policy "is as wrong politically as it is morally and practically," he told a Yale Law School audience later, but "the worst possible political strategy is the over-personalization of the issue against President Johnson. Virulent attacks on an individual in America bring sympathy for the attacked rather than votes for the attackers. The issue is peace, not personalities."[19]

The Rauh-Lowenstein rift gave much pleasure to some old ADA board members, who noted that Rauh had been nearly beaten by his own candidate. "It was nice of him [Lowenstein] to have a fight with you the first meeting after you made him a vice chairman," one quipped. The tension briefly escalated when Harold Ickes Jr. told a reporter that Lowenstein had described Rauh as "a Johnson man." Rauh hit back. "I rebuked quite sharply a few who were unkind about you," Rauh heatedly told Lowenstein. "I consider your explanation of my position hitting below the belt." Lowenstein denied that he or Ickes had made such a statement, cautioned that some people hoped "to make mischief between us," and noted that "the tone of your letter suggests they may succeed in doing so."[20]

The Alternative

Lowenstein had not prevailed within the ADA, but he proved to be a better judge of the volatile political future. He estimated that antiwar sentiment ran deep among campus youth, who could form the shock troops of a campaign, and that Johnson would be vulnerable to a challenger in the primaries, especially in states such as Wisconsin. Like Rauh and others, Lowenstein struck out with Kennedy, McGovern, and Church. At the end of October, following a speech on Vietnam in Los Angeles, however, McCarthy and his top staff aide, Jerome Eller, sat down for a discussion about money and volunteers with Lowenstein and Gerald Hill of the California Democratic Council. Hill's group had helped to finance and organize something called the Conference of Concerned Democrats, an offshoot of the dump Johnson effort now headed by Lowenstein and Gans. McCarthy listened to them and suddenly said he would run. Lowenstein had his alternative.

A week later, Rauh pledged his support to McCarthy with the additional understanding that he and Galbraith would work for an ADA endorsement. On the morning of November 30, 1967, in the historic Caucus Room of the Old Senate Office Building, McCarthy reconfigured the political landscape when he announced that he would enter four Democratic presidential primaries in the coming campaign season. American politics would soon be transformed by the senator's decision and by others made in Vietnam.

CHAPTER FIFTEEN

1968

There is only one thing to do—take it to the country.
—SENATOR EUGENE MCCARTHY

The Other Senator from Minnesota

They were an odd couple in American politics, despite shared revulsion against the Vietnam War, distrust of Lyndon Johnson, and a desire to channel the growing antiwar fury into electoral protest. Eugene McCarthy, long in the shadow of Hubert Humphrey, had been known as the other senator from Minnesota. He had been one of two northern Democrats who voted against a strong anti-poll tax provision in the Voting Rights Act. On economic issues, McCarthy sided more often with the Republicans than with his own party. But in 1968 he dared to do what others had been too timid to do—challenge President Johnson—and Rauh would stick with him to the end.

McCarthy was an unlikely candidate to carry the flag of rebellion against Johnson. When he came to the Senate in 1959, the first Roman Catholic elected to that office in Minnesota, he enjoyed the favor of LBJ, who gave him choice committee assignments, including Public Works and Finance. The Minnesotan had dropped his membership in the ADA, he said, because the organization had become stridently anti-Johnson. If Lady Bird Johnson and Texas governor John Connolly had prevailed at Atlantic City in 1964, McCarthy, not Humphrey, would have become LBJ's running mate.

McCarthy had not been among the earliest critics of the war. He had voted for the Gulf of Tonkin Resolution. As late as the spring of 1966, he endorsed the use of American ground troops in Vietnam with the observation that "the kind of escalation we now have . . . is defensible on the part of the administration." That same year, however, McCarthy signed a public letter to

Johnson along with fourteen other senators that urged a pause in the bombing of North Vietnam, and he soon joined four other senators who voted for an amendment to a military appropriations bill to rescind the Gulf of Tonkin Resolution. He warned that "if we move from this kind of escalation to . . . bombing civilian areas in North Vietnam, this is a change of substance . . . and one which I think should be challenged."[1]

"The Wildest Testimony I Have Ever Heard"

McCarthy became an outright opponent of the war when undersecretary of state Katzenbach told the Foreign Relations Committee on August 17, 1967, that the Gulf of Tonkin Resolution constituted a "functional equivalent" to a declaration of war. Under modern circumstances, he continued, Congress became "compelled" to support any president who unleashed military force. Shaken and angry, McCarthy left the hearing room and told a reporter, "This is the wildest testimony I have ever heard. There is no limit to what he says the president can do. There is only one thing to do—take it to the country."[2]

Rauh, alarmed by the rising tide of street protests and violence, hoped that McCarthy's candidacy would become the vehicle for restoring faith in the political process, especially among the young, and would head off those in the administration who demanded a crackdown on dissent. If liberals did not lead an electoral challenge to Johnson, Rauh feared, more radical elements would dominate the antiwar movement, as they had done with respect to civil rights. "We disapprove of civil disobedience, draft-card burnings and Pentagon assaults," he said, echoing McCarthy. "We say you can change the war through political action. But having said that," he added, "we're obligated to try to do it."[3] Electoral politics might save democratic institutions from "the violent and illegal protests against the war [that] wrack the country with division and hostility." McCarthy's candidacy, he believed, "by offering a political alternative to the war, may yet make some dent even into that aspect of the political spectrum."[4]

On the day before McCarthy's official announcement, Rauh visited Humphrey at his office in the Capitol. The meeting proved to be the saddest in their long personal and political friendship.

In the presence of his top aide, Bill Welsh, Humphrey launched into a rapid, thirty-minute lecture defending the administration's policy in Vietnam, his remarks peppered with military jargon and statistics. When the monologue ended, the vice president cautioned Rauh he had conveyed some information that remained top secret and should not be repeated.

"Don't worry, Hubert," Rauh replied, "you went so fast I didn't get much of it." Humphrey's fervor for Johnson and the war strengthened Rauh's conviction that his old ally had lost all independence and that he had made the right decision in joining McCarthy's insurgency.[5]

ADA and Tet

Rauh turned his immediate attention to securing a quick ADA endorsement of McCarthy and convincing the senator to enter the New Hampshire primary in February. Their chances of defeating Johnson's supporters in the ADA would be enhanced if McCarthy ran in the Granite State. Rauh found a potent ally for the New Hampshire decision in Blair Clark, a former CBS vice president and assistant publisher of the *New York Post,* whom McCarthy had chosen to run his campaign and who lived out of a suitcase for a month at the Rauhs' home in Washington. In order to put further pressure on the senator, Rauh leaked a story to journalists Rowland Evans and Robert Novak suggesting that liberal support for his candidacy would depend upon a debut in New Hampshire. Early in January, McCarthy entered the fateful primary.

    The ADA endorsement proved more challenging. As Rauh noted in early December, "The ADA is nostalgically for Humphrey, ideologically for McCarthy, realistically for Johnson and actually for [Robert] Kennedy."[6] He hoped initially to move the organization's regular board meeting forward to January, when a vote could be taken in favor of McCarthy. But chairman Ken Galbraith, although strong for McCarthy, refused to cut short his European skiing vacation in Switzerland, and Johnson's allies, uncertain of their strength, demanded a delay until February. Face with what he called Galbraith's "damn laziness" and foot-dragging by Johnson's supporters, Rauh took the initiative. He went on television, represented himself as an ADA vice chairman, and urged McCarthy's nomination. He also promoted McCarthy's candidacy at a special meeting on equal rights hosted by the Democratic National Committee in Chicago. Johnson's partisans in the ADA protested that Rauh had abused his official post, and in Chicago he found himself alone among the Democratic committeemen and women, all of whom said they opposed the war but still favored Johnson's reelection.[7]

    In a sudden twist of fate, the delay in the ADA board vote boosted McCarthy's candidacy. Shortly after midnight on January 30, 1968, the Tet holiday, Vietcong and North Vietnamese regular troops began surprise, coordinated attacks on thirty-six of the forty-four provincial capitals and five of the six major cities in South Vietnam, including the U.S. embassy in Saigon. The Tet offensive was a military disaster for the Communists, who suffered staggering casualties, but it proved to be an even greater political defeat for the

Johnson administration, which had continued to claim that American military power would soon force Hanoi to accept a noncommunist regime in South Vietnam.

The ADA board meeting on February 10, two weeks after Tet, became the most rancorous in the organization's history. By Rauh's early count, Johnson could rely on at least one-quarter of the board, mostly labor representatives led by Gus Tyler and Jack Conway, plus additional votes rounded up by Humphrey. Despite enormous pressure from the White House, however, the president's lines cracked on the eve of the showdown. A tormented Bill Dodge, the UAW's political director, told Rauh he had been ordered by Walter Reuther to vote against McCarthy.

"Jesus, Joe," Dodge said. "They'll fire me if I don't support the president."

"What are you going to do?" Rauh asked.

"I'm going to call in sick on Saturday," Dodge replied. He kept his word and never showed up for the meeting, but Reuther sent an alternate, who backed Johnson.[8]

Rauh, Galbraith, and Lowenstein carried the day for McCarthy by a vote of 65-47 with a resolution proclaiming, "When you follow an idea, you follow the man who created it." Led by Tyler and John Roche, the Johnson supporters argued that the ADA had now become an absurd, one-issue organization. It had endorsed a candidate with a weaker liberal record than the president. Roche declared that McCarthy's candidacy would prove ephemeral and that the ADA should wait until its official convention in May to make a decision. "By then," he added, sarcastically, "McCarthy might have retired to a monastery or given up politics for Lent. I don't know." Roche soon resigned from the ADA and castigated it for practicing "the politics of Disneyland."[9]

Tyler, equally bitter, reminded Rauh and other McCarthy supporters that the organization had made a terrible error in 1948 when it voted to draft Dwight Eisenhower to replace President Truman. He had gone along with that decision, "the greatest mistake I ever made," but he would not repeat it now. Tyler also quit the board with the lament that the vote had destroyed a historic liberal coalition. The United Steel Workers and the Communication Workers of America followed Tyler out of the ADA. So did other Johnson loyalists, including Leon Keyserling and Congressman Henry Gonzales of Texas.[10]

Gene versus Bobby

The ADA endorsement moved McCarthy's campaign from the back pages of major newspapers to page 2 or 3 for the remainder of February. The fallout from Tet and the energy of young volunteers put him on the front pages on March 13 when the senator received 28,791 votes (42 percent of the total) in the New Hampshire primary, only 230 short of defeating Johnson. Not all of those who cast their ballot for the Minnesotan shared his views on Vietnam. Exit polls indicated that many confused him with the long deceased Senator McCarthy from Wisconsin; others believed he supported a quick, decisive military stroke to crush the Communists. Two days after McCarthy's near upset in New Hampshire, Robert Kennedy announced that he was reconsidering his decision, and on March 16 he entered the race.

Rauh received Kennedy's decision with mixed feelings. When told by Schlesinger and Kenny O'Donnell that the senator had reconsidered his options, Rauh urged RFK to endorse McCarthy. In private, Rauh believed that Kennedy would be a stronger campaigner and a better president than McCarthy, but he immediately declared his unwavering support for the Minnesotan. In this case as in others, loyalty trumped convictions. "I am for McCarthy as long as he is in the race," he told the press and added that he hoped "a way can be found to maximize the cooperation and minimize the confrontation" between Johnson's two opponents.[11] Cooperation proved impossible between the two campaigns, although the ADA leaders occupied key roles in both campaigns. As expected, Schlesinger and Dick Goodwin quickly joined Kennedy. Rauh and Galbraith remained with McCarthy, as did Lowenstein, the latter more out of a sense of honor than passionate devotion to a candidate he ridiculed privately. But Lowenstein soon abandoned McCarthy's campaign to run for a congressional seat in New York.

For Rauh the test of cooperation came in the D.C. primary. On the Friday before the New Hampshire vote, he told McCarthy frankly he had little chance of defeating Johnson in the District because of the heavy African-American vote. "I've told you this before, but I'll say it again," Rauh declared. "There isn't one Negro in your headquarters over at the Transportation building. You're just silly. The problem with coming into the District is that you don't have any Negro support." Despite this warning, McCarthy announced he would contest the District in order to keep the Johnson forces off balance, and he asked Rauh, a veteran of D.C. primary battles, to lead the effort.[12]

Rauh cobbled together a joint slate with Kennedy supporters in the District, but did not consult his candidate, who said he would not make a deal with Kennedy under any circumstances. McCarthy's rejection of the alliance brought a sharp rebuke from Rauh, who warned him that he would then run third in the primary and perhaps "a very bad third." Twenty-four hours later, on March 18, McCarthy finally relented and agreed to the joint slate—Citizens United for Peace—with Rauh and Channing Phillips as co-chairmen, but McCarthy's delegates would hold a seven-to-five majority. The joint slate seemed poised for victory when Johnson suddenly pulled out of the race on March 31 and McCarthy swept to a decisive win in Wisconsin's primary two days later. Johnson's retreat and McCarthy's victory in Wisconsin brought Humphrey into the presidential contest. These stunning developments encouraged an optimistic McCarthy to believe that any compromise with Kennedy signaled weakness and was now unnecessary to his eventual victory. McCarthy suddenly pulled out of the joint slate agreement for the District, without consulting Rauh. Dumbfounded, Rauh quickly reaffirmed his support for the Minnesotan, but vented his wrath at Clark and Curtis Gans, whom he blamed for the decision. In addition to his investment of time and energy in the joint slate, he knew that McCarthy's decision forecast a brutal trench war against Kennedy and a further splitting of the liberal forces.

At the regular ADA convention on May 19, little more than a month after Dr. King had been assassinated in Memphis and riots ripped through the District, Rauh pushed through a resolution that reaffirmed the organization's primary commitment to McCarthy, but paid respect to Kennedy and Humphrey as well. "McCarthy is the man who has rescued the Democratic Party from the worst error in modern times," Rauh wrote. "He is, in consequence, the man our people want and whom we can elect." Humphrey, by contrast, "is the candidate of the past and of a policy that the people have rejected. . . . We watch with sadness as he even now fails to support proposals that could end the war." As an effort to keep peace in the ADA house, Rauh's resolution sparked criticism, but McCarthy could count it a victory in the wake of losing primaries to Kennedy in D.C., Indiana, and Nebraska, while nursing the hope of rebounding in Oregon and California.[13]

McCarthy defeated Kennedy in Oregon, a state noted for its political independence, small minority population, and few big cities with festering social problems. Fearful that Kennedy might drop out of the race completely if McCarthy won California, Rauh flew back to Washington on the day of the primary to meet with William Shannon, editor of the *New York Times*, a longtime Kennedy friend from Massachusetts who shared his concerns. Shannon agreed that he would urge RFK to continue the fight for delegates through the convention whatever happened in the Golden State. Kennedy defeated McCarthy in California, but shortly after midnight on June 5, Olie Rauh awakened her husband with the news that RFK had been shot and lay dying in a Los Angeles hospital.

"There Must Be Some Other Way"

Without Kennedy in the race, Rauh feared that McCarthy's hopes had vanished, although Humphrey had not won a single primary. Hundreds of delegates, loyal to either Johnson or his surrogate, had been chosen months, even years before. An assassin's bullets had nominated the vice president. Kennedy's death also plunged McCarthy into an emotional trough from which he never recovered. "Maybe we should do it a different way," he told a reporter after hearing the news. "Maybe we should have the English system of having the cabinet choose the president. There must be some other way." Arriving in Chicago two months later for the convention, he told reporters, "Well, it looks like all my friends have come to witness the execution."[14] Despite his belief that their cause had become hopeless, Rauh gamely carried on the fight for McCarthy while other Kennedy loyalists shifted to Humphrey or searched in vain for some alternative candidate. In the summer following Kennedy's death, Rauh made his greatest contributions as a fund-raiser, corralling delegates in nonprimary states and leading the challenge to delegations controlled by Johnson and Humphrey. At rallies from coast to coast, he became McCarthy's chief pitchman and solicitor of campaign money, notably in Madison Square Garden, where 20,000 faithful greeted his word of the ADA endorsement with wild cheers and filled shoeboxes with nearly $1 million for the Minnesotan.

Rauh also learned during these fund-raising events to endure the candidate's quixotic behavior. At Boston's Fenway Park, with Leonard Bernstein scheduled to make a speech on McCarthy's behalf, Rauh begged the candidate not to take the rostrum first for fear of losing the huge audience before they collected any money. McCarthy ignored the advice, gave his standard stump speech, and then exited quickly through the centerfield gate before Rauh could woo the thinning crowd from a makeshift podium at second base. He estimated that McCarthy's quick exist had cost them thousands. The only consolation had been that he realized one of his life's desires—he reached second in a major league ballpark.[15]

Rauh's efforts in Chicago before the credentials committee and on the convention floor failed to slow the Humphrey-Johnson juggernaut. Apart from Mississippi and Georgia, the anti-McCarthy forces prevailed on all the delegate issues. They also turned back a McCarthy-sponsored peace plank in the platform and easily nominated the vice president and his running mate, Senator Edmund Muskie of Maine. The only suspense inside the Chicago Amphitheater arose over a brief and futile effort to promote the candidacy of

Ted Kennedy, the junior senator from Massachusetts, whose entrance might have derailed Humphrey on the first ballot. At this point in the political soap opera, McCarthy hinted he might step aside if the youngest Kennedy chose to run. But undecided himself and doubting McCarthy's sincerity, Kennedy bowed out. His exit left Humphrey's path clear to a first-ballot victory.

Johnson, undercutting Humphrey, insisted on platform language that any bombing halt "not endanger the lives of our troops in the field" and "take into account the response from Hanoi," a version that became the official position of the platform committee. Humphrey swallowed it. Early on the evening of August 28, the Johnson-endorsed platform won by a vote of 1,567 to 1,041, after which McCarthy, Kennedy, and delegates pledged to George McGovern put on black armbands and sang the old civil rights anthem "We Shall Overcome." Many of Rauh's old allies from that struggle deserted the peace forces and supported Humphrey and the administration on Vietnam, including Bayard Rustin, Clarence Mitchell, and Roy Wilkins.[16]

Exhausted from the credentials fights and nursing a sore back, Rauh left Chicago for Washington in the late afternoon on Wednesday before the vote on the peace plank. At home that evening, he witnessed on television Humphrey's nomination, the Chicago police run amok, and the death of the Democratic Party. Rauh watched the Chicago carnage in disbelief, especially as cameras inside Humphrey's suite caught the vice president kissing the television screen when he secured the nomination at the same moment policemen beat demonstrators senseless on the streets below. His anger rose when told that aides to Humphrey had refused to awaken the vice president later that night as the violence continued in the streets of Chicago. Both the Sunday *Post* and *Times* reported that Humphrey, asked about the melee, responded, "I think we ought to quit pretending that Mayor [Richard] Daley did anything wrong. He didn't."[17]

Humphrey versus Nixon

Rauh had barely turned off the television on the night of the Chicago catastrophe when his phone rang with calls from ADA members who urged an immediate endorsement of the vice president. That would not be possible, he knew, until the wounds of Chicago healed and Humphrey reaffirmed his liberal credentials, especially on Vietnam. He therefore urged Humphrey to adopt a drastic new course in late September—the vice president should sever all nonconstitutional ties with President Johnson and become the peace candidate by supporting an unconditional end to the bombing in Vietnam. Influenced by Rauh's advice, trailing Nixon by fifteen points in some polls, and campaigning in the face of raucous antiwar demonstrations, Humphrey took a half-step in that direction with a major television address on Vietnam from Salt Lake City on September 30.

Humphrey's campaign chief, Larry O'Brien, agreed with Rauh and urged an unconditional bombing halt, but the candidate's more cautious advisers, Jim Rowe and Bill Welsh, played upon his usual fear of a rebuke from Johnson. As a result, the vice president's Salt Lake City speech satisfied no one, except perhaps the candidate himself. He declared a halt in the bombing an "acceptable risk for peace," but "before taking action" he would require evidence "by deed or word" from Hanoi of reciprocal steps, including a restoration of the demilitarized zone between North and South Vietnam. O'Brien and Rauh thought the statement a meaningless gesture. Johnson, however, regarded it as a betrayal that undermined his negotiations with Hanoi in Paris. He snubbed Humphrey until the closing days of the campaign and, in the opinion of a recent biographer, finally opposed Nixon only after he received reliable intelligence that the Republican candidate had himself sabotaged the Paris negotiations by encouraging South Vietnamese leaders to boycott the talks.[18]

Rauh dismissed the Salt Lake City speech as too tepid, but he used it to secure a mild endorsement for Humphrey from the ADA board. Against those who attacked the vice president as "a passionate defender of our vicious policy in Vietnam," Rauh argued for a limited commitment on the grounds that Humphrey had moved "substantially" closer to the ADA's position on the war. The final resolution hoped the vice president would "separate himself from the Johnson-Rusk errors of the past." Die-hard Humphrey supporters denounced Rauh's language, but Humphrey expressed appreciation for the endorsement and pleaded with his old friend to join the campaign. In the hope that Humphrey might eventually support his position on the war and fearful of Nixon in the White House, Rauh finally joined the vice president's campaign plane.

The seat proved to be an unpleasant one. Humphrey refused to go beyond his Salt Lake City statement or to cut his ties with the most reactionary leaders of the party. Rauh became the campaign's peace ambassador to disaffected McCarthy-Kennedy Democrats, most of whom received his message with ridicule. Even when he spoke about Humphrey's strong civil rights record to black voters in the South, the boos and catcalls drowned out the applause. California's Democrats, passionately against the war, remained the most bitter and hostile.

Despite his gaffes and cowardice, Humphrey nearly pulled the election out of the fire in the closing ten days of the campaign. George Wallace as a third party threat faded; Johnson stopped the bombing of North Vietnam and spoke up for his vice president with enthusiasm. Angry and disillusioned Democrats returned to the fold, frightened more of a future Nixon presidency than of a man still identified with a war they loathed. The Minnesotan lost the popular vote by less than 0.01 percent, 31,783,000 to 31,271,000, but lost the electoral college when he failed to carry major states such as California, Illinois, Ohio, and Florida. The Democrats retained control of Congress, but Nixon and Wallace, sweeping all of the South except Texas, received nearly 57 percent of the national popular vote, while Humphrey garnered barely one-third of the white electorate in the former Democratic heartland of the North. Liberalism, beaten in Chicago, had now been repudiated nationwide. Theodore White called it "a negative landslide . . . undeniably a swing to the right."

In his postmortem, Rauh blamed Humphrey's inner circle of advisers for the defeat—Rowe, Connell, Welsh—rather than the vice president, who, he claimed, "would be President if he had gone with the minority [Vietnam] plank, if he had criticized Daley, or if he had started to be himself a fortnight earlier." The "real Hubert," according to Rauh, "wanted to do all those things." Unfortunately, he concluded, Hubert was "the best guy with the biggest jerks around him that I have ever met."[19] The candidate himself did not share this assessment. Reflecting on the election later, Humphrey placed the blame on his own weakness. "I ought not to have let a man who was going to be a former President [Johnson] dictate my future."[20]

CHAPTER SIXTEEN

JOCK AND THE MINERS

When ye be an anvil, lie ye very still.
When ye be a hammer, strike with all thy will.
—JOSEPH (JOCK) YABLONSKI

Tony Boyle's UMW

Shortly before his Salt Lake City speech on Vietnam in September 1968, Vice President Humphrey appeared at the forty-fifth annual convention of the United Mine Workers of America (UMW) in Denver. There he received the union's endorsement, the first offered by the miners since its legendary former president, John L. Lewis, supported Wendell Willkie against FDR in 1940. Tom Kennedy succeeded Lewis, but the latter assumed that the mantle of leadership would soon pass ultimately to his brother, R. O. Lewis. However, William Anthony "Tony" Boyle, who now stood on the platform with Humphrey, engineered the ouster of R. O. Lewis and took control of the UMW.

His hands locked with Boyle's, Humphrey, effusive as ever, bathed in the applause and showered praise on "the one and only" Tony Boyle, a short, balding man with a taste for elevator shoes, colorful suits, and a fresh rose in his lapel each day. "I am mighty glad to rub shoulders with this fellow Tony Boyle," Humphrey told the delegates. "He has been giving me advice and counsel for a long time." Before the campaign ended, the mine workers' political arm, Labor's Non-Partisan League, poured $30,000 into the vice president's bid for the White House.[1]

Eight months later, Joe Rauh, whose prounion labor politics had usually antagonized conservatives, fought to topple Tony Boyle from the leadership of the United Mine Workers. Representing insurgent presidential candidate

Joseph A. "Jock" Yablonski, a high-ranking union official whose loyalty to Boyle had been unquestioned, Rauh's efforts on behalf of the UMW reformers in the early 1970s plunged him into a world of violence and put his own life at risk. Eventually, it propelled him into similar campaigns for union democracy among steelworkers and those demanding change even from Reuther's successors inside the UAW. Once an opponent of the Landrum-Griffin Act, he became its most creative litigator on behalf of rank-and-file unionists who believed their leadership had become ossified and, in some cases, hostile to their interests.

In his pursuit of civil rights, Rauh had often antagonized both old liberal allies like Reuther and younger African-American radicals. In the case of Vietnam he helped to lead an insurgency that shattered the liberal wing of the Democratic Party. Now in the union democracy wars, Washington's premier labor lawyer found himself condemned and ostracized by the barons of big labor, branded as antiunion and unfit to represent them. The pursuit of reforms inside unions like the UMW cost Rauh and his firm dearly. "The union practice went down," he told a reporter in 1988, "and the union democracy practice went up!"[2]

Two months after the Boyle-dominated Denver convention endorsed Humphrey, lengthened the UMW president's term to five years, and made it more difficult for candidates to challenge incumbent union officials, seventy-eight miners died in a massive underground explosion at the No. 9 coal mine of the Consolidation Coal Company near Farmington, West Virginia. Although other blasts had killed coal miners in 1954 and 1965, Farmington was the worst disaster since a similar explosion at Monongah, West Virginia, in 1907 had claimed 361 victims. West Virginia governor Hulett Smith consoled relatives of the dead with the cold observation that "this is a hazardous business and what has occurred here is one of the hazards of mining." Boyle echoed the governor and praised Consolidation as "one of the best companies to work with as far as cooperation and safety are concerned."[3]

Lewis's Legacy

Issues of mine safety, highlighted by the Farmington disaster, constituted but one strand in a dense web of financial corruption, callousness, nepotism, and tyranny that characterized relationships between UMW leaders and the union's rank and file. While the flamboyant Lewis had created the Mine Workers' machinery of benevolent entrepreneurial unionism prior to his retirement in 1959, Boyle, former president of the UMW's District 27 in Montana, perfected it after he assumed the presidency.

In the 1950s Lewis negotiated contracts with the major companies that gave mechanization and higher coal output to the operators in exchange for fewer coal miners with higher wages and benefits, a strategy that cost 300,000 jobs and left many communities devastated. While the number of pensioners rose, their pensions did not, but with the largess from royalty payments (40 cents per ton by 1952) flowing into the Welfare and Retirement Fund, Lewis bought a controlling interest in the National Bank of Washington, where the UMW fund began to deposit its money, which grew to $145 million by the end of the decade, one-third of which rested in a general checking account that drew no interest. Fueled by UMW money and guided by officers beholden to Lewis, the National Bank gobbled up other financial institutions and invested in or made loans to coal companies that financed their mechanization and unionization. At the same time, Lewis entered into secret "sweetheart" contracts with nonunion producers that by shaving royalty payments and wages allowed them to remain in business and produce coal cheaper than other UMW mines.[4]

Mechanization raised company profits, enlarged the UMW's Welfare and Retirement Fund, and increased wages for miners able to find work, but the giant machines that ripped out coal produced an epidemic of pneumoconiosis, or black lung disease, among the men who inhaled it. By one estimate, at least 125,000 miners suffered from the incurable malady by 1968, but most of the victims did not receive compensation under existing state laws, such as those in West Virginia, because of the difficulty of diagnosis, the confusion of black lung disease with silicosis by many physicians, and the statute of limitations.

Boyle and his assistants did not put much energy into the effort against black lung until a group of rank-and-file miners in West Virginia organized the Black Lung Association in 1969. They began to pressure the state legislature to reform West Virginia's antiquated workmen's compensation law. The insurgents drew support from Congressman Ken Hechler and the rising star of consumer advocacy, Ralph Nader, whose volunteers had begun to expose the union's lethargic efforts with regard to safety and black lung disease. Much to the displeasure of Boyle and the coal companies, miners throughout West Virginia rose up in wildcat strikes in support of the reformers' proposal and marched on the capitol at Charleston to back up their demands, a protest that finally produced a more progressive compensation statute. Boyle and the UMW hierarchy denounced this spontaneous uprising, referred to its leaders as the "black tongue" people, and accused the Black Lung Association leaders of the mortal sin of "dual unionism." When Congress made black lung disease compensable in the Federal Coal Mine Health and Safety

Act of 1969, this reform owed more to the dedicated West Virginia doctors and Congressman Hechler than to the UMW's own leaders.

Privileges and Power

Boyle regarded any initiative taken by those outside the union's headquarters in Washington as a threat to his authority and privileges. He dismissed criticism of the UMW leadership by Hechler or Nader as antiunion propaganda spread by employers. Along with his relatives and the top UMW officials in Washington, Boyle enjoyed bountiful benefits. UMW pensioners received only $115 a month from a Welfare and Retirement Fund running huge surpluses, while Boyle drew upon an unlimited expense account plus an annual salary of $50,000 a year. International officers such as John Owens, the secretary-treasurer, received $40,000 in compensation and the ability to retire at full pay after ten years in office. Boyle's brother received $27,000 a year as president of the union's District 27 in Montana, while his daughter, Antoinette, had a post in the legal department at $40,000 a year. Owens likewise had one son on the UMW legal staff and another on the international executive board. The secretary-treasurer maintained a suite at the Sheraton-Carlton Hotel in Washington paid for by the union at the rate of $11,000 a year.[5]

The UMW's formal and informal organizational machinery gave Boyle, like Lewis before him, ample means to crush any opposition and silence critics. The union's official organ, the *United Mine Worker's Journal,* published twice a month, served as the personal public relations instrument of Boyle and his regime and seldom gave voice to any doubts about the leadership's sagacity and compassion. Of the union's twenty-three districts, only four elected their own officers, despite provisions of the Landrum-Griffin Act of 1959 that mandated such local control in an effort to limit the authority of distant union hierarchies. And although mechanization and retirements had decimated many UMW locals, these "ghost locals" of less than ten active miners continued to send delegates to conventions despite provisions in the union's own constitution banning the practice.

If all else failed, Boyle and his allies did not hesitate to use violence. At the union's 1964 convention in Bal Harbour, Florida, miners from District 19 in Middlesboro, Kentucky, wearing "Loyal to Boyle" on their white helmets, savagely attacked a delegate who protested the presence of coal company officials on the convention floor prior to a vote. When Steve "Cadillac" Kochis, a candidate for president, and other delegates criticized these tactics, they, too, encountered physical threats and dead microphones. In the election that year, Boyle defeated Kochis by 77,000 votes and carried some districts in Kentucky and Tennessee by margins of 1,000 to 1.

Establishment Rebel

Fifty-nine-year-old Jock Yablonski, the eldest son of a Polish coal cutter, had followed in his father's footsteps and entered the mines of the Jones and Laughlin Steel Company at the age of fifteen. He seemed an unlikely challenger to Boyle's regime in 1969. From that beginning at Jones and Laughlin in 1925, Yablonski had risen to become a major presence in Local 1787, District 5, which extended over twelve counties in western Pennsylvania, and belonged to the union's governing council, the international executive board. A single incident when he was twenty, one that returned to haunt him three decades later, marred an otherwise exemplary life. Believing that he had been cheated by a slot machine at the Moose Club in Monongahela, Yablonski broke into the building, smashed the machine, and helped himself to the coins. Arrested and convicted in 1930, he served eight months in a Pennsylvania workhouse.

The union had been good to Jock, as part of the UMW establishment. In addition to an unlimited expense account, he earned $26,000 a year, lived in a spacious fieldstone farmhouse set on 365 acres outside Clarksville, Pennsylvania, played golf, and had investments in real estate, stocks, and a harness racing track. His two sons, Ken and Joseph "Chip," had become successful attorneys. His daughter, Charlotte, had earned a master's degree in social work from West Virginia University and directed the Office of Economic Opportunity in Monongalia County. His wife, Margaret, the driving intellectual force in the family, had attended college for three years, wrote short stories, and subscribed to *The New Yorker* and *Punch*.

Few union leaders had displayed more outward fealty to Boyle and the UMW's hierarchy. When miners in District 5 launched wildcat strikes in 1964 to protest the modest two-dollar wage increase that Boyle had negotiated with the major companies, Yablonski's eloquence and arm-twisting sent them back to work. In the 1964 election, he supported Boyle, not Kochis. At the 1968 Denver convention, no one exceeded Yablonski in showering praise on the incumbent leader. "I lack the words," he said, "which would enable me to describe the love, the devotion, and the respect that I have."[6] Beneath the surface of this alliance, however, Yablonski often seethed with anger over Boyle's methods and his apparent callousness with respect to safety and black lung. The UMW president in turn resented the District 5 leader's flashes of independence. Yablonski threatened to take his delegation out of the 1964 Bal Harbour convention unless Boyle put a stop to his bullying tactics. He opposed Kochis's candidacy for the presidency that year, but did not extend himself on behalf of Boyle's reelection either, with the result that the incumbent enjoyed a smaller margin of victory in District 5 than elsewhere, an outcome that rankled the president.

Enter Nader and Rauh

In an attempt to curb Yablonski's influence, Boyle forced him to step down as District 5 president in 1965 on the pretense of irregularities in expenditures and under the threat of placing the district in trusteeship, an outcome that would have given Boyle authority to choose new officers. Yablonski retained his seat on the international executive board, but found himself otherwise exiled from influence. Boyle briefly sought to bring Yablonski back into the establishment fold during the spring of 1969 by naming him acting director of the union's lobbying arm, Labor's Non-Partisan League. By then, however, Yablonski had decided to bolt. With the encouragement of his nephew Steve, a young Washington attorney, Yablonski met Nader, who told him that he could secure the best legal assistance in town, a promise he kept by arranging a meeting with Rauh.

On the morning of May 28, 1969, Yablonski and Nader set forth for Rauh an emotional case for challenging the UMW leadership and their need for his legal skills in what promised to be a no-holds-barred election campaign. Rauh had normally represented labor unions in litigation directed against employers and the government. Only once had he represented an insurgent faction, a rank-and-file group inside the Paperworkers Union. Those clients immediately provoked a phone call from Reuther, who complained that such representation caused him and the UAW embarrassment with other union leaders. Rauh had also known personally union reformers who faced violence and death. In 1966, Dow Wilson and Lloyd Green, leaders of a reform movement in the Painters Union, had been gunned down in San Francisco. And, finally, the labor leaders he most admired—Randolph and Reuther—had always been models of financial probity and personal integrity. Rauh took an immediate liking to Yablonski and his cause, agreed to become his attorney, and joined him at a news conference the next day.

At the Mayflower Hotel, with Rauh at his side and Nader lurking in the background, Yablonski announced his candidacy. He would run on a platform that stressed greater attention to mine safety and black lung disease, the restoration of elections for district leaders, mandatory retirement at sixty-five for all union officers, and the end to rule by what he called "inaccessible bureaucrats." Admitting that he had been a part of Boyle's UMW administration, Yablonski quoted John L. Lewis and the poet George Herbert when asked why he had decided to become a reformer: "When ye be an anvil, lie ye very still. When ye be a hammer, strike with all thy will."[7]

Rauh and his client soon discovered that Boyle and the UMW hierarchy would spare little effort, expense, or scruple to crush the rebellion. In order to qualify for the election, Yablonski needed the endorsement of at least 50 of the 1,200 UMW locals. On the surface this did not appear to be an insurmountable task until one realized that nineteen of the twenty-three districts containing these local units were so-called trusteeships whose officers had been appointed by Boyle. They remained loyal to him through a system of loans and payoffs for bogus organizing work. The Labor Department had filed suit in 1964 to overturn the UMW trusteeships, a device outlawed by the Landrum-Griffin Act, but the case had not even come to trial by 1969. Boyle's control of the nineteen trusteeships gave him a powerful tool for blocking Yablonski's nomination and ultimately defeating his election campaign, although ninety-six locals finally voted to put the reformer on the December ballot.

Landrum-Griffin Revisited

Qualifying Yablonski for the ballot proved to be the least of Rauh's problems. On June 11 at his Alexandria, Virginia, home, Lewis died at the age of eighty-nine without giving Yablonski an endorsement. Even worse, Boyle immediately stepped into Lewis's position on the board of trustees for the union's pension fund, a post that gave him a new opportunity to influence the votes of the UMW's 70,000 retirees. Barely a week after Yablonski announced his campaign, Boyle discharged him from his post as director of Labor's Non-Partisan League. When Yablonski requested a list of union members and asked the UMW to distribute his campaign literature, the Washington headquarters turned him down. The union's official publication, the *United Mine Workers Journal*, continued at the same time to tout Boyle's achievements and reelection while ignoring Yablonski's candidacy. Rauh immediately challenged these actions in federal court under Landrum-Griffin and thereby launched the first of a half-dozen lawsuits on behalf of his client and the UMW insurgents.

Rauh saw the irony of invoking Landrum-Griffin. It had passed Congress in the wake of scandals involving the Teamsters Union, backed by conservatives in both political parties. On behalf of the UAW, which regarded its reporting and governance provisions as an assault on union power, Rauh lobbied against it in 1959.[8] Now it gave Yablonski a fighting chance to contest the UMW presidency. Landrum-Griffin prohibited retaliation against a union member who challenged an incumbent, obliged the union to make membership lists accessible, and banned the use of union funds, such as an official publication, in support of any candidate. Rauh quickly won judicial support for all of these propositions.[9]

A federal district court could keep Yablonski on the UMW payroll and open up the union's membership lists, but it could not protect him from physical violence or dirty tricks in the campaign. In late June as the candidate left a meeting with a small group of miners in Benton, Illinois, an unknown assailant attacked him from behind with a karate chop that rendered him unconscious and nearly paralyzed. At about the same time, Boyle administered another blow to his opponent's hopes by ramming through the pension fund board an increase in the monthly benefit for retirees from $115 to $150. The increase, largest in UMW history, depleted the fund's reserves and virtually guaranteed Boyle the support of 292 locals made up entirely of retired miners.[10] In early July, the Boyle camp published an election broadside that included a photograph of Yablonski clad in a prison uniform for his 1930 offense. Branding him "the ex-convict, the thief," the publication accused Yablonski of attempting to destroy the UMW by delivering it into the hands of outsiders, notably Nader and Rauh.

"Long-Established Policy"

Yablonski's prison photo and his restricted travel schedule after the Illinois assault disillusioned Nader, who virtually disappeared from the campaign, a desertion that the candidate and his family neither understood nor forgave in light of the crusader's earlier enthusiasm and grandiose promises of financial support. Rauh stayed the course and launched an aggressive effort to bring the federal government into the conflict under Section 601 of Landrum-Griffin, a provision that gave the secretary of labor authority to conduct "an immediate and continuing investigation" if the secretary "believes it is necessary in order to determine whether any person has violated or is about to violate any provision" of the law. In two letters and a face-to-face meeting at the end of July, Rauh presented labor secretary George Shultz with a long list of illegal UMW activities that had already taken place during the nominating period. He urged Shultz to invoke Section 601 and to conduct a formal inquiry in order to head off what promised to be a rigged and violence-filled election.[11]

Shultz and his chief counsel, Laurence Silberman, did not contest Rauh's interpretation of the secretary's powers under law, but they declined to intervene based on what Shultz called the department's "long-established policy" not to undertake such an investigation "without having a valid complaint . . . *after* an election has been completed."[12] Under a barrage of new complaints from Rauh, Schultz finally warned Boyle and the UMW leadership that renewed allegations might force his department to intervene "before the balloting occurs." That threat proved empty. Boyle swept to a lopsided victory on December 9, defeating Yablonski by over 30,000 votes in a contest the insurgent described as "the most dishonest election in the history of the American labor movement."

In two notorious Kentucky districts, 19 and 30, where Yablonski could not deploy poll watchers, he lost by margins of 3,725 to 87 and 5,433 to 860. Two dozen UMW locals failed to return official tally sheets. Three others reported more votes than members. Some locals held the election without notifying members. Boyle supporters carted off ballot boxes in two West Virginia polling places and counted the votes elsewhere. When Yablonski's poll watchers made an appearance there on December 9, they faced expulsion by Boyle partisans. According to one report, coal operators cast votes at Local 7692 in West Virginia, and the president of Local 975 in Pennsylvania filled out twenty-five ballots on behalf of absent pensioners.[13]

Even before the balloting, Rauh had filed a separate civil suit in federal district court on behalf of Yablonski and other UMW miners accusing Boyle and the union hierarchy of misappropriation of funds, negligent administration of UMW assets, and defrauding the organization. That suit, combined with the prospect of a new election and a federal grand jury inquiry into UMW election expenditures, gave renewed hope to Yablonski and Rauh that their campaign to clean up the union would bear fruit in 1970. Unknown to them, however, Boyle had already set in motion a plan to eliminate his principal tormentor. On the day before he orchestrated the pension increase in June, Boyle met briefly with District 19's president, William Turnblazer, and secretary-treasurer, Albert Pass, the latter well known throughout the union as an expert in mayhem against coal operators and UMW dissidents. "We are in a fight," Boyle told them. "Yablonski ought to be killed or done away with." Pass assured him that if no one else took care of that assignment, "District 19 will. District 19 will kill him."[14]

Cold Blood

Not long after the election, Yablonski responded to a knock on the door of his Clarksville home and encountered two strangers who claimed to be unemployed miners from West Virginia looking for work. His suspicions raised, Yablonski and his older son Ken tracked the visitors' car into town and discovered that it bore Ohio license plates. They asked the police who owned the car, and Yablonski wrote on a legal pad next to an Ohio license plate number: "Paul Gilly, painter." Then, early in the morning on New Year's Eve, as Yablonski, his wife, and daughter Charlotte lay sleeping, three men armed with a .38 caliber pistol and an M-1 rifle entered his home and shot all three to death. Ken Yablonski found their bullet-riddled and bloated bodies on January 5 when his father failed to appear at a scheduled swearing-in ceremony for new Washington County officials.

On the afternoon of January 5, Rauh accompanied Chip Yablonski, his wife Shirley, and five-year-old son Jeffrey on a mournful flight from Washington to Pennsylvania. A state trooper took them immediately to the Yablonski home for an interview, an experience Rauh never forgot because the stench of death remained in the old fieldstone structure. He spent that night at Ken Yablonski's house, packed with grieving relatives, and slept fitfully in a room with young Jeffrey, now aware that something terrible had happened to his grandfather. Although bone tired, Rauh comforted the youngster who crawled, crying, into his bed. Shortly after midnight, Ken awakened Rauh with the news that a radio broadcast indicated the Federal Bureau of Investigation had decided not to enter the case, describing it as a local homicide outside federal jurisdiction. A quick call by Rauh to the nearest FBI field office in Pittsburgh confirmed that the decision not to intervene had been made in Washington by the attorney general, John Mitchell.

Outraged by Mitchell's decision, Rauh took the morning plane to Washington and arranged to meet with the attorney general that afternoon. Clarice Feldman, a young attorney recruited to assist in the legal struggles, joined him for the meeting. A battery of television cameras and reporters gathered outside the attorney general's office at the Department of Justice when Mitchell emerged to welcome his visitor with a jovial "Hi, Joe," although the two had never met.

Rauh insisted that the FBI enter the case. Mitchell noted that Ed Carey, general counsel to the UMW, had described Yablonski as "a pretty rough character." He didn't see any grounds for federal intervention. The attorney general then quoted George Shultz, who had assured him the union could not have been involved in the murders since Boyle had won the election. Rauh retorted that Section 609 of Landrum-Griffin made it a federal crime to use violence or the threat of violence against anyone exercising rights protected by that statute, a provision that clearly applied to Yablonski, who had earlier been attacked in Illinois. Mitchell jotted some notes on a legal pad, told Rauh he would review the matter, and abruptly ended the meeting.[15]

Outside Mitchell's office in the glare of television cameras, Rauh recited his arguments about the mandate of Section 609, laced with a sharp attack on the attorney general and the Nixon administration's dismal record during the UMW elections. NBC's reporter Carl Stern, covering the event, took Rauh aside and told him: "Joe, your eloquence will never make the six o'clock news." When asked why, Stern gave him a dose of political reality: "Mitchell knows what you've said here, and he's not going to let that go on the evening news. Instead, he'll be on at six o'clock saying that he's decided to send in the FBI."[16]

Stern's prediction proved correct. Mitchell dominated the evening news with an announcement that the FBI would investigate the Yablonski murders at the request of Pennsylvania governor Raymond Shafer. Internal FBI documents on the Yablonski case tell a different story. Shafer had been pressured to ask for federal assistance by Mitchell. According to Carla (Deke) DeLoach, Hoover's second-in-command at the FBI, the attorney general "did not want it to appear that he was ordering the FBI to enter this investigation simply because of pressure brought on by Joseph Rauh, Jr." On the day following Rauh's confrontation with Mitchell, assistant director Alex Rosen urged that Yablonski's attorney be interviewed for possible leads in the case, although, he added, "Rauh has a poor reputation and since 1950 has been on the list of persons not to be contacted without prior Bureau authority."[17]

The Yablonski murders sparked fears that others associated with his campaign, including his lawyer, might be targets for violence. Acting on this suspicion, Carl Rauh, then a United States attorney in D.C., attempted to secure FBI protection for his father, but received a flat rejection from the agency. Any protection, he was told, should come from the local D.C. police. After learning of this intervention, Hoover complained to Mitchell that he regarded Rauh as a personal enemy who should be kept at arm's length, even when he attempted to provide the Bureau with possible assistance in the Yablonski case. "We simply cannot waste personnel at the whims of Rauh," Hoover told his subordinates.[18]

Keeping the Struggle Alive

Rauh returned to Clarksville on a frigid Friday morning in early January 9 for the Yablonski funerals. That afternoon, following a graveside ceremony, Mike Trbovich, one of Yablonski's loyal lieutenants, gathered a hundred miners in the church basement to decide the future of the UMW rebellion, the air thick with rumors of possible violence against those who continued the struggle. Emotionally drained, Rauh kept back tears by looking at the men's feet as he spoke. He explained in great detail how they could seek a new election and continue the corruption suit in order to secure restitution and damages for Boyle's financial peculations. If they wanted to continue the fight, he would go on with them, words that brought the miners to their feet, cheering and clapping.[19]

Over the next three years, the FBI and Pennsylvania's relentless special prosecutor Richard Sprague tracked down, arrested, and prosecuted the three men who murdered the Yablonskis, and those in the UMW, including Boyle, who organized and financed the killings. At the same time, Rauh successfully hounded the union's corrupt leadership in the civil courts. Beyond his creative use of Landrum-Griffin, he kept the struggle for reform alive with an aggressive fund-raising effort that made it possible to hire other attorneys like Feldman and to match the legal resources of the UMW.

"A Monumental and Inexcusable Blunder"

Rauh believed Shultz and Silberman bore major responsibility for Yablonski's murder because they had refused to intervene before the balloting. This conviction grew stronger as evidence mounted that the assassination plot had been organized and financed from inside the UMW. A federal presence during the election might have forced Boyle and his conspirators think twice about assassination. When Shultz finally decided in March 1970 to file suit under Landrum-Griffin to upset Boyle's election, that action increased Rauh's frustration, which soon boiled over into anger when Shultz testified before the Senate Labor Committee in May that he was "required by the statute" to file suit, a mandate he had rejected prior to the election. The secretary told the committee he had decided not to intervene during the campaign because "there had been no hard evidence that anything more than internal union politics was involved." He also told the senators his department possessed "no evidence that the murders were connected with the election," a conclusion that defied common sense since five individuals, including the president of a UMW local in District 19, had already been indicted by a federal grand jury for conspiracy to violate Yablonski's civil rights.[20]

Speaking to reporters after the secretary's testimony, Rauh and Chip Yablonski accused him of "false statements, innuendoes and other concealment of wrong-doing." Shultz's comments on Yablonski's murder, Rauh told reporters a few days later, contradicted the FBI, the United States attorney, and a grand jury. "Only a guilt-stricken man would deliberately undercut the enforcement efforts of his own government."[21] Summarizing his legal efforts for the reformers in the *Georgia Law Review* a year later, Rauh blasted Shultz's inaction during the election as "a monumental and inexcusable blunder" that led to Yablonski's defeat and murder.[22]

In the early spring of 1970, Rauh and his team of attorneys filed suit on behalf of Mike Trbovich and Miners for Democracy, who wished to intervene in the Labor Department's action to overturn Boyle's election. Their motion for intervention came before federal district judge William Bryant, who rejected their motion and ruled that Congress had given the secretary of labor "exclusive" jurisdiction to bring such election suits under Landrum-Griffin.[23] In a terse, two-paragraph *per curium*, the court of appeals affirmed Bryant's judgment six months later, which left Rauh without much hope that the Supreme Court would grant certiorari.[24]

To his surprise, the justices agreed to hear the case, and Rauh found himself arguing the intervention issue against solicitor general Erwin Griswold in November 1971. His confidence rose sharply during oral argument, when Justice Douglas taunted Griswold about the Miners for Democracy: "General, you don't want these people to have any rights, do you?" Two months later, in an opinion written by Thurgood Marshall, the Supreme Court reversed Bryant and the circuit court. The justices gave Rauh a partial victory: Miners for Democracy could intervene in the election suit, but only on the basis of presenting additional evidence to support the Labor Department's original complaint. The ruling also held that Miners for Democracy would be permitted to offer the district court additional advice if the court ordered a new election and imposed specific remedies. Those remedies, later crafted by Rauh's legal team and imposed by Judge Bryant, represented the most extensive control and oversight by the Department of Labor in the history of the Landrum-Griffin Act. Because of them, reformer Arnold Miller defeated Boyle for the presidency of the UMW a year later in the new election.[25]

Sorting through his father's papers, Chip discovered a cache of letters from the union's Non-Partisan League indicating that Boyle had dipped into UMW dues to make direct contributions to political candidates, including $30,000 to Humphrey in 1968. Soon indicted and convicted under the Federal Corrupt Practices Act for making illegal donations and embezzlement, Boyle received a three-year prison sentence on March 31, 1972, one of the stiffest ever handed down for the offense. The indictment and conviction not only branded Boyle a felon prior to the new UMW election, but ousted him from his directorship at the union-run National Bank of Washington.

At Rauh's urging, disabled miners and widows filed a civil case against Boyle, the UMW, and the National Bank of Washington for breach of their fiduciary duty to protect the union's pension funds. At its conclusion, Judge Gerhard Gesell ordered the defendants to pay damages of $11.5 million. The defendants' conduct, Gesell observed, constituted a breach of trust "deeply ingrained by a long continuous course of improper dealing and the momentum of the violation was never arrested by the affirmative conduct of any of the conspirators before the Court."[26]

"The Ethics of a Pig Sty"

Beginning with the initial lawsuits he filed on behalf of Yablonski, Rauh went into court against the union's in-house legal staff, headed by Ed Carey, as well as the formidable Washington law firm of Williams and Connolly, whose senior partner, Edward Bennett Williams, many regarded as one of the nation's most successful criminal defense lawyers. Williams had represented mobster Frank Costello and Teamsters president Jimmy Hoffa, whose acquittal he secured on charges of bribing a staff investigator for the United States Senate. Paul R. Connolly's clients included, among others, the Central Intelligence Agency.

Williams and Connolly fought Rauh's effort to limit Boyle's use of the official UMW journal during the campaign; they remained passive when Carey ordered an expedited printing of election ballots to avoid both observers and a possible injunction; two days after the discovery of Yablonski's body, they served Rauh with papers arguing that his death had terminated all rights under the several preelection suits; and they defended the legitimacy of Boyle's election before Judge Bryant. When it became clear that Williams and Connolly would also attempt to represent both Boyle and the UMW in the corruption suit brought under Section 501 of the Landrum-Griffin Act, Rauh moved to disqualify the firm on grounds of the conflict of interest between Boyle and the UMW members suing him.

Federal district judge Howard Corcoran denied Rauh's motion to disqualify Williams and Connolly from the corruption suit, but a three-judge court of appeals reversed that decision in late July 1971 and found ample grounds for barring the firm from representing either the UMW or Boyle. In a stinging rebuke to Williams, the panel noted "that in 18 months of representation . . . counsel has not brought forth a single issue on which the UMWA and the Boyle individual interest have diverged."[27] That damning opinion would have produced a grievance before the bar association, Rauh told Congressman Robert Drinan, had the attorneys been political radicals "rather than pillars of the bar." In representing Boyle, he added, Williams and Connolly had displayed "greedy and irresponsible conduct."[28]

Evidence of Boyle's role in the plot to murder Yablonski accumulated in the spring of 1972 with the arrest and indictment of three District 19 officials, Silous Huddeleston, a retired organizer, Pass, the secretary-treasurer, and William Prater, the field representative. All three were charged with laundering over $19,000 in union funds used to pay the triggermen. Boyle, desperate to keep Pass quiet, asked Harrison Combs of the UMW legal staff if he could keep Pass and Prater on the union payroll while in jail without bond and awaiting trial. Combs told Boyle such payments would violate Landrum-Griffin, but Jeremiah Collins, on behalf of Williams and Connolly, found no such legal obstacle. Collins argued that Pass, like any other union employee, could continue to receive his salary for "temporary absences . . . due to illness or when he is on vacation."[29]

Boyle cited the Williams and Connolly memo to Turnblazer and instructed him to pass the information along to Pass and Prater. When Judge Bryant learned of the payments, however, he exploded at Collins and the UMW officials, and ordered the Department of Labor to stop the flow of money immediately. Bryant, who had often opposed Rauh's efforts in the past, now expressed special contempt for the government's argument when its lawyers declared the payment issue very complicated and declined to take a position on the matter. "I could call in any old lady off the street to resolve this," he told them. "It's clear to me what's going on here."[30]

For his part, Rauh minced few words about the Williams and Connolly memo endorsing payments to Pass. "Bennett Williams," he told reporters outside the courtroom, "has the ethics of a pig sty and if he sues me for libel, I'll plead the truth." Several months later in the wake of the reformers' victory in a new election, Rauh encountered Jeremiah Collins on a street corner. In jest, he asked if Collins and others in the Williams firm had missed him since the UMW cases. "Oh, no," Collins responded, "I've been too busy working on the disciplinary committee for the bar association." The irony of that assignment was not lost on Rauh, who strolled on without comment.[31]

Falling Out

Growing conflict among the reformers tempered Rauh's pleasure at the election of Arnold Miller as UMW president in December 1972, followed by the indictment and conviction of Tony Boyle for the murder of Jock Yablonski two years later. Rauh declined Miller's offer to become general counsel for the union, but persuaded the new president to turn instead to Chip Yablonski. Soon, however, Miller began to cut his ties with the Yablonski faction and others who had led the legal crusade. An honest and decent man, hardened by the long struggle and plagued by bouts of paranoia, Miller instituted a series of reforms, but spurned Rauh's warning when he chose Sam Church as his vice president, an old Boyle loyalist who later turned against the new president.

Church's successor at the UMW, Rich Trumpka, continued the reform efforts begun by Miller, but also put increasing distance between himself, Rauh, and the memory of Jock Yablonski, whose courage had made reforms possible. When he visited UMW headquarters from time to time, Rauh often chided Trumpka about the absence of any commemorative plaque or photographs honoring Yablonski. Finally, one day he noticed that a photograph of the fallen insurgent had appeared, very small and inconspicuous in a side hallway.[32]

CHAPTER SEVENTEEN

UNION DEMOCRACY

If we lose this case most other unions will follow suit
and that will be the end of union democracy.

— JOE RAUH

Attorney for Dissidents

In twenty years of practice he had become accustomed to phone calls from strangers and unannounced visitors to his office, most of whom brought him tales of legal woe. Many were political dissenters, rebels, and outsiders, and some were not entirely rational. One man believed the FBI bombarded him with a death ray from outer space and wanted the harassment stopped. Rauh said his jurisdiction did not extend that far. In the wake of the Yablonski case, others now arrived, mostly ordinary union members, bearing stories of repression and corruption. Like the miners who rallied behind Yablonski, they wanted more democracy in their unions.

When thugs in the National Maritime Union savagely beat reformer Jim Morrissey, Rauh arranged for Jimmy Wechsler to expose the affair in the *Post* and raised funds that permitted Morrissey to win a substantial judgment. For others, such as Selina Burch, a staff member purged by the Communications Workers for criticizing union leaders, he found attorneys willing to take up her cause. Chip Yablonski represented Burch, who received her job back with lost pay and $100,000 in damages. While helping Burch, Rauh simultaneously represented the officials of the Communications Workers and nine other unions in their suit against the National Right to Work Legal Defense and Education Foundation, which financed individual employee legal actions against unions to whom they owed dues.[1] As his efforts on behalf of union dissidents increased, however, he found it more difficult to carry such litigation for the labor establishment.

Rauh often worked behind the scenes to aid insurgents. When three locals of the Federation of Government Employees (AFGE) joined in antiwar demonstrations, their national leaders put the units in trusteeship and threatened to revoke their charters. Rauh mobilized Jerry Wurf, the maverick president of the American Federation of State, County and Municipal Employees, and several other union leaders who pressured the AFGE to back down. In a 1975 profile *Business Week* hailed Rauh as "Attorney for the Dissidents." That article encouraged more dissenters, including carpenters from the union's local in Fairbanks, Alaska, whose members had been excluded by their own international from work on the giant oil pipeline to Valdez.[2]

Each time Rauh took one of these cases he called down the wrath of the labor barons, especially AFL-CIO president George Meany and the head of the United Steelworkers Union, I. W. Abel, who had hoped to unite his union with the UMW. Yablonski's rebellion and the election of Arnold Miller scotched those plans, and Abel blamed Rauh. Meany and others did not bother to hide their resentments. When he came to the funeral for Senator Wayne Morse at the National Cathedral in 1974, the AFL-CIO chief greeted him with an icy stare, quickly turned his back, and loudly railed to other union leaders present about Rauh's treachery.[3]

Sadlowski

Weary after the UMW battles, Rauh hoped for a respite from union democracy wars in 1973, but he could not refuse an old friend and ADA stalwart from Chicago, Leon Despres. A prominent labor and civil rights attorney, Despres wanted him to meet a new client, steelworker Ed Sadlowski, who had been defeated recently in a campaign to become director of District 13, the largest local in the union's hierarchy. Over dinner, Despres and Sadlowski gave Rauh a fact-laden account of how, in old-fashioned Chicago style, the leadership of the Steelworkers had stolen the election for their handpicked candidate, Sam Evans. One international staff member had already resigned in the face of evidence he had stuffed ballot boxes against Sadlowski.

The thirty-three-year-old Sadlowski won over Rauh with his charm, lack of guile, and intellectual curiosity. The son of a steelworker, he had moved quickly from the production floor to a union staff position with his brains and sociability. His candor and ambition to head District 13, however, irritated Abel and the union's national officers, who had become accustomed to anointing candidates and guaranteeing their victory. Sadlowski broke the union's code: he did not wait his turn. Unlike Boyle and his gang, Abel and the Steelworkers' officers did not steal from their members or employ violence, but they did not tolerate opposition to their candidates.

After listening to Sadlowski's account, Rauh agreed to join his effort to force a new election in District 13 either by pressuring the union to take that action or by encouraging the Department of Labor to intervene under Landrum-Griffin. Sadlowski's case looked like a mini mineworkers struggle, but without mayhem and murder. He never imagined after their initial meeting that this case would dominate a large portion of his life for the next decade. He had committed himself, moreover, at a time when the established union leaders and many in the rank and file felt especially vulnerable to massive structural changes in the American and global economy. From the perspective of many union leaders, all rebellions at the grass roots and demands for greater union democracy served only to destroy the solidarity required to protect their power and American jobs.

The Department of Labor, still in Republican hands but with a new secretary, Peter Brennan, did not relish Rauh's intervention in the aftermath of his successful role in the Yablonski campaign. In 1971 he had written a scathing attack on the department in the *Georgia Law Review* that accused the agency of "abysmal failure . . . to enforce the LMRDA [Landrum-Griffin] with respect to Boyle and the UMWA." Under the leadership of George Shultz, he added, the department "has been in the neighborhood . . . only to place roadblocks and obstacles in the path of reform."[4]

Rauh had also defeated the department's lawyers in the *Trbovich* case when he won from the Supreme Court the right to intervene for union members in Title IV suits under Landrum-Griffin.[5] One legal scholar called that victory "a landmark decision" in American labor law, but it rankled the Labor Department brass.[6]

Rauh made his presence felt immediately in the department, where the Sadlowski case had been languishing for several months. He demanded that they remove from the inquiry a former employee of the Steelworkers, a demand the agency met before it filed suit under Title IV to overturn the old election in District 31. That gave Rauh the right under the *Trbovich* case to intervene on behalf of Sadlowski, an opening he quickly seized to launch his own investigation and to depose the union's leadership, including Able.

In addition to Despres, Rauh gained the assistance of Judith Schneider, the youthful legal director of the Association for Union Democracy (AUD). That organization, now one of Rauh's chief passions, had sprouted from Norman Thomas's efforts in the late 1950s to reinstate two Chicago machinists expelled from their union. After Thomas's death, the leadership of the AUD passed to Clyde Summers, a law professor at Yale, who had advised Senator Kennedy on the Landrum-Griffin Act. Herman Benson, an original member of Thomas's team, joined Summers and became the AUD's executive director and the publisher of *Union Democracy in Action,* the organization's newsletter.

Grilled on the stand by Rauh, Abel admitted that the Steelworkers' leadership, what he called "the official family," took a dim view of those like Sadlowski who challenged their decisions about district candidates. In the face of mounting evidence of voting fraud in District 13, gathered by Rauh and the Labor Department, Abel and the union agreed to hold another election in District 13. This election would be supervised by the department with Rauh's team monitoring the proceedings. In November 1974, a year after he had been counted out, Sadlowski swept to victory by a two-to-one margin and took his seat as a member of the Steelworkers' powerful international executive board.

Bachowski

With Sadlowski nearing vindication, Rauh became entangled simultaneously in a second Steelworkers' election case, one that again broke new legal ground for union democracy and raised the stakes in his ongoing battle with the Department of Labor and the leadership of big labor. Like Sadlowski, Walter Bachowski had challenged the "official family" in 1973 when he ran for the directorship of District 20 and lost by 907 votes out of 24,000 returns. He complained to the Labor Department about numerous irregularities in the voting and violations of the Steelworkers' constitution, but following an inquiry, Secretary Brennan declined to file suit to upset the election. Rauh believed the Labor Department continued to support the status quo whenever possible and that Bachowski's case presented an ideal test case for contesting erratic and arbitrary bureaucratic decisions. When he learned of Rauh's decision to help Bachowski, however, Sadlowski objected:

"He's a bum," Sadlowski said. "He's not one of us," by which he meant that Bachowski's credentials as a reformer remained suspect.

"But he got screwed, too," Rauh shot back. "From what I've seen of his election it was as bad as yours. How can I take yours and not his?"

Over these objections, Rauh and Ken Yablonski filed suit on behalf of Bachowski in federal district court in Pennsylvania. In refusing to order a new election, they argued, Secretary Brennan had acted in an arbitrary and capricious manner. He should be compelled to disclose all evidence bearing on the department's investigation and required to bring suit to set aside the election. This full-bore assault on the discretion of the department under Landrum-Griffin received a chilly reception from the district court, which threw out the suit for lack of jurisdiction. The law, according to the court, did not authorize judicial review of the secretary's decision.[7]

Seldom one to bow before a district court decision, Rauh appealed to the Third Circuit and gained a major victory in the summer of 1974 when that tribunal ruled that judicial review should be available to ensure that the secretary's decisions were not "arbitrary, capricious, or an abuse of discretion." The appeals court ordered Brennan and his department to provide Bachowski with a specific statement of reasons for the secretary's decision, with the district court to determine on discovery what materials should be disclosed by the department to assure "a fair determination of the issues."[8]

One year later, with only Justice William Rehnquist dissenting, the Supreme Court gave Rauh and his allies a partial victory against the Labor Department. In a carefully drawn opinion, Justice Brennan sustained all of the appeals court decision with the exception of the portion allowing a mini-trial of the secretary's decision. The department would be obliged to provide Bachowski with a clear statement of reasons for not filing suit, but the Court would be required to sustain the department unless it found those reasons "so irrational as to be arbitrary and capricious." In short, Rauh lost his bid for a full trial to challenge the factual basis of the department's actions.[9]

What Justice Brennan and the Supreme Court refused to do in theory, a federal district judge did in fact when Bachowski's case went back to the Western District of Pennsylvania. Rauh and Yablonski now had the good fortune to appear before Edward Dumbauld, an old-time New Deal Democrat appointed to the bench by President Kennedy. Within earshot of all the attorneys present, the judge looked at Rauh and said flatly, "I've admired you work in the liberal movement for years." Dumbauld reviewed the Labor Department's explanations and then ordered the agency to explain in detail why it had awarded the plaintiff all disputed ballots in some cases, but not in others.[10] He also invoked Justice Brennan's language by ruling that the department's decision had been "so irrational as to be arbitrary and capricious." Bachowski got his new election, won it, and took his seat on the Steelworkers' governing board.[11]

Walter Bachowski's case became an important weapon in the arsenal of those fighting for union democracy, but the plaintiff proved to be a disappointment inside the Steelworkers. He cleaned up the worst abuses in District 20, but soon joined the union's "official family" and voted regularly against Sadlowski and other dissidents on the international board. He snubbed Rauh and Yablonski, too, by refusing to ask the court for attorneys' fees, which left them to foot the bill for all his litigation expenses.[12]

Counted Out in Canada

Sadlowski also faced problems in his home district apart from Bachowski's defection. The rank and file supported him, as did the celebrated Chicago writer Studs Terkel, but Sadlowski had little leverage against the Steelworkers' central bureaucracy in Pittsburgh, which appointed most of his staff and controlled his budget. He fought a long battle with his own local counsel, who also served as general counsel to the union and remained loyal to Abel, until Rauh found a way to remove him. In the face of this constant harassment from Pittsburgh, Sadlowski decided to run for the presidency of the union when Abel stepped down in 1976–77. The "official family" regarded that as an affront since Abel had already anointed his successor, Lloyd McBride.

Rauh and his client quickly learned that a run for the union presidency against its entrenched leadership presented far more formidable obstacles than winning a district election. Votes would be cast in 4,000 locals, 827 of them located in Canada beyond the jurisdiction of American law, but not beyond the influence of the union's headquarters in Pittsburgh. Sadlowski and his allies could not possibly monitor every election site or begin to compete against a Pittsburgh staff of over 800 workers loyal to the Abel-McBride machine. Former union president David McDonald predicted openly that even if Sadlowski carried the American locals, he would be counted out by the returns from Canada. In an effort to counter McBride's advantage, Rauh raised funds from various foundations to help defray litigation and monitoring expenses.[13]

Once Sadlowski announced his challenge, the "official family" mobilized to crush it. Abel announced that he would turn in his union card if Sadlowski won. The president then attempted to disband the local union of Ignacio "Nash" Rodriguez, a Latino candidate running for international secretary on the Sadlowski slate. Rauh went to court and quickly stopped that crude attempt to eliminate Rodriguez as a candidate. In an effort to prevent defections by black steelworkers to Sadlowski, the leadership also created a new international office and named an African-American to the post, the first time this racial barrier had been breached in the union's history.

When Rauh offered to turn over their evidence of preelection violations of Landrum-Griffin to the Labor Department, the agency spurned it. Bruce Miller, attorney for the union, accused him of making false and unsubstantiated charges and demanded that he provide his proof to the international board. Rauh told him, "You're about as subtle in your effort to work a cover up . . . as a rhinoceros!" Turning over their files to Abel and other officials, he noted, "would only make it possible for your crowd to use the staff representatives working full time for you to help alter or destroy the evidence."[14]

In addition to the Labor Department, Rauh reserved special anger for Michael Gottesman and his law firm, which took large fees from the union to represent its leadership and defeat Sadlowski. In his opinion, Gottesman, Cohen & Weinberg had violated the spirit if not the letter of the law by pocketing union dues. "You talk about your ethical responsibility to take the position of your clients," he told Gottesman. "The trouble is you don't know who your client is. Your client is the union membership not its Official Family. . . . You have the instincts of a bully. . . . You can prate about equal rights in public, but you are trying to deny Sadlowski any semblance of equality in this election."[15]

Backed by the financial resources and staff of the international and without monitoring by the Labor Department, McBride swept to victory over Sadlowski in February 1977 by 328,861 to 249,281, a margin of 79,580 votes. Irregularities in the voting plagued many of the locals, including instances where more ballots had been cast than enrolled union members or where tally sheets had been filled out before the polls closed. Rauh and his staff believed the worst abuses had taken place in Canada, where the results put McBride over the top. Sadlowski's team deployed only token observers north of the border, and Lynn Williams, an avid McBride supporter, ran the district with an iron fist. Williams soon became the official family's designated successor to McBride.

Rauh's efforts to overturn the election results through appeals to the union, the Labor Department, and the courts proved fruitless. The department mobilized 250 investigators to probe complaints by the loser, but this inquiry covered only the United States and less than 25 percent of the union membership. Rauh told the new labor secretary, F. Ray Marshall, that he had condoned a sham investigation. The probe did not include local union officials, and staff representatives were not placed under oath. "In a union the size of the steelworkers," he complained, "two hundred and fifty persons without questionnaires is a joke."[16]

The federal courts proved no more responsive. Both the district court and the appeals court declined to extend the *Bachowski* decision that would further undercut the Labor Department's discretion in Landrum-Griffin cases. They accepted the department's findings on the election as conclusive and rejected Rauh's claims that the limited nature of the investigation meant that the agency had failed in its duty to the membership. A year later, without comment, the Supreme Court allowed those decisions and McBride's election to stand.[17]

Rauh's campaigns for Sadlowski incurred more hostility from union officials, some of whom feared they might be the next target of their insurgents. At the Steelworkers' 1974 convention, Abel denounced what he called "outside meddlers," and in an obvious jab at Rauh, those "high-priced lawyers—and I mean really high—who have an eye on the considerable assets of this great union."[18] The AFL-CIO leaders drafted a letter that ridiculed Rauh's "self-proclaimed sainthood" and his "broad-scale propaganda . . . against reputable leaders of labor like I. W. Abel." They ordered Jacob Clayman, secretary-treasurer of the Industrial Union Department, a former chairman of the ADA executive committee and one of Rauh's oldest friends, to sign the document and send it to the *Washington Post*.[19]

Slamming the Door on Insurgents

Early in 1980 Rauh signed on for one last legal battle on behalf of Sadlowski and other potential union insurgents. In anticipation of a new round of elections, the leadership of the Steelworkers had pushed through the 1978 national convention a so-called outsider rule, a provision designed to cut off external campaign funds to union rebels. Complete with detailed reporting requirements, the new rule prohibited any candidate for national union office from soliciting or accepting any direct or indirect financial contributions from nonmembers of the union. The rule even included the candidate's own family members, unless they happened to be members of the union. The rule would have killed both the Yablonski and the Sadlowski campaigns, where Rauh had raised outside financial support.

The new leaders of the Steelworkers, of course, justified the rule as an effort to preserve the autonomy of their organization. The labor movement would repel what its leaders regarded as a sinister plot by American business and liberal reformers to divide and conquer the labor movement. "The union belongs to the members," intoned McBride, "and we're not going to expose our internal election campaign to interference from outside persons or agitators, including foundations, most of which are heavily supported by American corporations." Rauh saw the rule otherwise when he filed suit to overturn it in November 1979. "If we lose this case," he said, "most other unions will follow . . . and that will be the end of union democracy."[20]

Two lower courts agreed with Rauh's challenge to the "outsider" rule and struck it down as a violation of Landrum-Griffin. District judge George L. Hart, a senior jurist in Washington who had not often found Rauh's arguments compelling, declared the rule in violation of the broad "right-to-sue" provisions of Landrum-Griffin. It would, he wrote, prevent union members from raising the funds necessary to protect their legal interests, and he permanently enjoined the Steelworkers from enforcing the rule.[21] In the hope of winning on appeal, the union issued a convoluted interpretation of the rule with the claim that it only barred financing litigation "designed to extract political benefit" for a candidate.

Two months later, a unanimous panel of the Court of Appeals for the District of Columbia, led by Judge George MacKinnon, affirmed the district court and its interpretation that the outsider rule violated "right-to-sue" provisions. "One would go a far distance to find any lawsuit brought during the heat of a campaign that was not designed to extract political gain," MacKinnon noted tartly. The court also broadened Hart's decision when it found the rule also violated rights of free speech and association protected by Landrum-Griffin. MacKinnon cited with approval portions of the Supreme Court decision in *Buckley v. Valeo,* which struck down expenditure and contribution limits on campaigns for federal office. "A restriction on the amount of money a person or group can spend on political communication," McKinnon concluded, "necessarily reduces the quantity of expression by restricting the number of issues discussed, the depth of their exploration, and the size of the audience reached."[22]

During the final days of the Supreme Court's 1981 term, however, in a decision that baffled and infuriated Rauh for years, a bare majority of the justices reversed both lower courts. The High Court sustained the union's rule as a "reasonable" method for achieving the dominant purpose of the Landrum-Griffin statute, which it read as one protecting union autonomy. Thurgood Marshall, who had earned a reputation for supporting underdogs and the First Amendment, cast the decisive vote and wrote for the majority.

In his *Sadlowski* opinion, Marshall cast aside other important provisions of Landrum-Griffin, including the right-to-sue provision and MacKinnon's strong conclusion about the importance of freedom of speech. Marshall concluded that the outsider rule only limited "somewhat" the ability of members to wage effective campaigns. That modest restriction, he argued, did not trump Congress's desire to prevent the infiltration of unions by what he called "racketeers . . . thugs and hoodlums" and to guarantee that unions remained controlled by members.[23]

Rauh could take some comfort in a stinging dissent written by Justice Byron White, joined by Brennan, Harry Blackman, and the chief justice. White dismissed the conclusion that Congress had placed a higher value on union autonomy than the right to sue and freedom of expression. "It is incredible to me that the union rule . . . can be found to be a reasonable restriction on the right of Edward Sadlowski Jr. to speak, assemble, and run for union office in a free and democratic election," he wrote. The dissenters endorsed MacKinnon's conclusions because "the scope and stringency of the rule cannot be doubted."[24]

Rauh remained long mystified by Marshall's vote and opinion in the Sadlowski case and once raised the question with one of the justice's former law clerks from the 1981 term. Marshall, the clerk told him, had been swayed by the union's long financial support for his old employer, the NAACP, and its support of affirmative action programs in the steel industry. The justice had remarked: "They [the United Steelworkers] were with us when we needed them." Rauh could appreciate those commitments, but could not understand how they conflicted with efforts to advance greater democracy in the union.[25]

"A Flagrant Violation of the UAW Constitution"

The union democracy movement began inside one of nation's most corrupt regimes in the 1970s, but within a decade, thanks to Rauh, it had spread even to those unions with glowing reputations for integrity and openness. It soon rocked Rauh's old client, Reuther's UAW, when he took up the cause of UAW rebel Jerry Tucker.

A legacy of Reuther's regime came back to haunt Rauh in the Tucker case as union officials invoked the UAW's "ninety-day rule" when the insurgent challenged incumbent Ken Worley for the leadership of District 5, which embraced Kansas-Missouri and the Southwest. The ninety-day rule required any union staff member who challenged an incumbent to declare his candidacy at least ninety days before the election and to take an unpaid leave during the campaign. The rule had been put in place by Reuther's old anticommunist faction after it had taken control of the union and been used to ward off any resurgence by his left-wing opponents. It had become an anachronism by the middle of the 1950s, and Rauh had occasionally urged Reuther to get rid of it. Buried in the bylaws, the rule lived on, although no one could find a record of its formal adoption by the UAW executive board or at its national convention.

By 1986 Tucker and other local leaders in District 5 had become disenchanted with Worley's timid stewardship and with the international in Detroit. They organized New Directions, a movement dedicated to tougher collective bargaining methods against companies such as Ling-Temco-Vought and more aggressive efforts at organizing and political action. Two months before the scheduled election at the UAW convention in Anaheim, California, Tucker announced his challenge against Worley. Four days later, instead of granting Tucker a leave, UAW president Owen Bieber fired him as assistant director of District 5 for violating the seldom-used ninety-day rule. Bieber's actions denied Tucker access to the floor of the annual convention and tarred him with the brush of disloyalty.[26]

At the Anaheim convention, despite support from Bieber and the other international leaders, Worley barely defeated Tucker by less than one vote under the union's complex fractional voting system based on delegates in attendance. Some delegates later claimed they had been offered staff jobs if they voted for Worley. Charlotte Consiglio, a Tucker supporter, signed an affidavit that she had been physically attacked by men who wore "Ken Worley" emblazoned on their jackets. Following UAW bylaws, Tucker took his complaints first to the union, where he protested illegal voting by five locals, Bieber's decision to fire him, and Worley's use of staff resources. The UAW rebuffed these challenges as unfounded.[27]

Tucker and his attorney, Chip Yablonski, next filed their complaint with the Department of Labor, alleging various violations of Landrum-Griffin. They also initiated a civil action against Bieber for breach of contract and unlawful termination. In response to Tucker's complaints and after an inquiry, labor secretary William Brock filed three suits against the UAW that endorsed Tucker's claims on his termination, the ninety-day rule, and the use of staff personnel by Worley. On March 30, 1988, district judge Richard Suhrheinrich ruled in favor of the Labor Department and ordered a new election in District 5, although he declined to consider the validity of the ninety-day rule, then under reconsideration by the union's executive board and the UAW's own public review board. In the new election, Tucker defeated Worley, 362.2 votes to 327.8.[28]

Recuperating from hip surgery that almost took his life, Rauh had advised Yablonski on legal strategy and hailed Tucker's victory, but not the UAW's handling of the ninety-day rule or the leadership's response to the outcome in District 5. Judge Suhrheinrich had suggested that the rule might withstand legal challenge as a reasonable election provision "if . . . the restriction is contained in the UAW's Constitution or bylaws." The union seized on those words. In April 1988, without a written record, and relying only on verbal recollections, the union's public review board declared the rule to be part of the UAW's official constitution. That decision brought a stinging rebuke from Rauh to board member Monseigneur George C. Higgins of Catholic University. The union's constitution, he pointed out, required all formal actions to be recorded, but no such record existed for the ninety-day rule, a rule that "strikes at the very heart of union democracy."[29]

The contents of Rauh's letter found its way to Jordan Rossen, the union's general counsel, who accused the man who had hired him in 1964 of "unfairness and hypocrisy" and attempting to improperly influence the public review board. The ninety-day rule, he told Rauh, would be governed by the union constitution, the convention, and elected officers, "and not by former officials, even if they are concerned."[30] Rauh did not respond in kind to those remarks, but Yablonski pointed out to the general counsel that the public review board reached its decision behind closed doors, without cross-examination of witnesses, and kept no record of its own proceedings.[31] When Rauh spoke at the annual ACLU dinner in Detroit that fall, Rossen and the union legal staff boycotted his presence—the first time union lawyers had not appeared at that traditional venue.

Official UAW attacks on Tucker, Yablonski, and anyone associated with the New Directions movement, including Vic Reuther, reached a new low at the union's national convention in the summer of 1989. UAW staffers distributed a four-page unsigned broadside that Rauh described as "false and vicious . . . gutter-snipe activities." The document accused Tucker of fronting for a "Trotskyist group" dedicated to sowing discord between the rank-and-file members and the leadership. It condemned Reuther as someone who had never been elected to a union post or been involved in contract negotiations. As for Yablonski, he had "made a fortune in legal fees from Jerry Tucker." Both Reuther and Yablonski were accused of trading on the names of their famous brother and father."[32]

When Rauh protested the broadside to his friend and former UAW president Doug Fraser, the latter claimed not to have seen it on the convention floor, but confessed that it went "beyond the limits and . . . crosses the line." The entire Tucker affair, he added, had been "a sad one in the history of the U.A.W.," but he put the blame on Tucker and Vic Reuther for fomenting discord and for costing the union a victory in a recent representation struggle at Chrysler.[33]

That same summer, Tucker lost his bid for reelection in District 5 to Roy Wyse, a staff member, who honored the ninety-day rule. Before the district court, the UAW later argued that the rule had become a well-known, customary standard within the union, although never incorporated into the constitution. On that basis the court sustained the rule, rejected Tucker's arguments that it violated Landrum-Griffin, and upheld his termination for violating it. The court of appeals affirmed this ruling on the grounds that the issues had become moot, a blow to Rauh's vision of union democracy inside the UAW.[34]

Tucker's defeat stung, but beginning with Yablonski and Sadlowski, Rauh had drawn up the legal blueprint for advancing union democracy through the courts. In large measure because of his efforts, the movement spread, even to the Teamsters Union, when the Department of Justice required Jimmy Hoffa's old union to adopt a one-person, one-vote standard for elections. Ron Carey, the reform candidate, enjoyed the preelection benefits of a "battle page" in the Teamsters' official magazine, a benefit derived from Rauh's success in the UMW election case. Carey won the Teamsters' presidency and then cast his union's 1.4 million votes for a new regime at the AFL-CIO headed by John Sweeney and Rich Trumka. When Sweeney took the post once occupied by George Meany, a bit of union democracy arrived at AFL-CIO headquarters, courtesy of Meany's old nemesis, Joe Rauh.

CHAPTER EIGHTEEN

CARDOZO'S SEAT

If Haynsworth is a laundered segregationist, then
Rehnquist is a laundered McCarthyite.
—JOE RAUH

Warren's Legacy

William Cushing, nominated by George Washington, first held the seat in
1789. Joseph Story occupied it on John Marshall's Court. Benjamin Curtis,
who dissented in *Dred Scott*, graced it before the Civil War. In 1902 the seat
passed to Oliver Wendell Holmes Jr., then to Benjamin Cardozo, Felix
Frankfurter, Arthur Goldberg, and, finally, Abe Fortas. Over time it had become known as both the "Jewish seat" on the Supreme Court of the United
States and the "liberal seat," the one often occupied by a justice of intellectual distinction. In 1969, President Richard Nixon nominated court of appeals judge Clement Furman Haynsworth from South Carolina to fill the
seat. Haynsworth counted as his close friend and political sponsor Senator
Strom Thurman, who had led the segregationist Dixiecrat revolt in 1948. Joe
Rauh, who had clerked for both Cardozo and Frankfurter, regarded the
nomination as a disaster, and he set out to prevent it. Beginning with the
Haynsworth fight, Supreme Court confirmations would consume a major
portion of his life for the next two decades.

By 1969 Rauh knew the crucial importance of each Supreme Court appointment to the success or failure of the liberal project. Led by Earl Warren, the Court had become responsive beginning in 1954 to the claims of
countless minorities and accelerated the direction of liberal change in America. Warren's majority handed down decisions attacking racial segregation,

banning sectarian religious exercises in public schools, mandating the reapportionment of state legislatures, extending provisions in the Bill of Rights to the states, and articulating a new constitutional right of privacy.

Johnson's nomination of his old friend Fortas to replace Warren floundered in 1968 when senators learned that while on the Court the justice had accepted a $15,000 honorarium, raised by his former law partner and friends, for teaching a summer course at American University. *Life* magazine published an article a year later disclosing that Fortas had also received $25,000 as a consultant to a charitable foundation headed by a former client, Louis Wolfson, twice indicted and convicted for stock manipulations. Abandoned by his colleagues on the Court, Fortas resigned.[1]

In 1968 Republican candidate Nixon claimed in *Reader's Digest* that Warren and his colleagues had "weakened law and encouraged criminals."[2] He vowed to tame the judiciary. When Warren retired, he began by appointing a new chief justice, Warren Burger, who received the reward for his conservative opinions on the Court of Appeals for the District of Columbia and his faithful service in the Department of Justice during the Eisenhower years.

Rauh deplored Burger's record, but knew his confirmation could not be stopped in the wake of Nixon's victory and the Fortas fiasco. For all of his denunciations of judicial activism, Burger had no skeletons, financial or otherwise, in his closet. Confirmation hearings before Senator James Eastland's Committee on the Judiciary lasted barely two hours on June 3, 1969, with Southerners Harry Byrd Jr., William Spong, John McClellan, and Sam Ervin leading the brief parade of enthusiastic supporters, aided by Republicans Everett Dirksen and Roman Hruska. Burger waltzed into his new post, but his would be the last perfunctory confirmation of a Supreme Court justice for over thirty years.

Three months later, Nixon nominated Haynsworth to replace Fortas. The president tapped a member in good standing of the white establishment in South Carolina, the fifth generation of Haynsworths to practice law. He had been appointed to the Fourth Circuit Court of Appeals by Eisenhower in 1957, and at the time of Nixon's nomination served as its chief judge. He enjoyed the endorsement of the American Bar Association and his colleagues on the Fourth Circuit, including Simon Sobeloff, a former solicitor general of the United States, who vouched for his integrity. The *Washington Star* hailed Nixon's choice as "both a logical and an excellent one" because the president intended "to bring the Court back to a more balanced, a more central position."[3]

Organizing Opposition

Rauh didn't accept the press clippings. Even a cursory examination of the judge's opinions on the circuit court convinced him that Haynsworth's views on civil rights and labor would turn back the judicial clock. In 1963, for example, Haynsworth had dissented in *Simkins v. Moses H. Cone Memorial Hospital* when Sobeloff and his colleagues ordered a hospital receiving federal funds to end its official practice of denying staff positions to African-Americans or serving them as patients. Despite a landmark Supreme Court ruling two years earlier to the contrary, Haynsworth found insufficient state involvement under the Fourteenth Amendment to require the hospital to end its blatant racial discrimination.[4] That same year, over a powerful dissent by Judge J. Spencer Bell, he permitted the public schools of Prince Edward County to remain closed for seven months while a defiant county and State of Virginia continued to subsidize private, racially segregated schools and its courts debated whether or not the state constitution required operation of public schools. The United States Supreme Court put a quick end to this example of massive resistance by Prince Edward County. "The time for mere 'deliberate speed' has run out," wrote Justice Hugo Black.[5]

In the seven labor-related cases that came before Haynsworth on the Fourth Circuit, all later reviewed by the Supreme Court, he voted against the unions and the National Labor Relations Board in all seven, and the Supreme Court reversed him on each occasion. Only a single justice—the inept Charles Whittaker—found any merit in Haynsworth's views. In sixteen other labor cases where the Fourth Circuit remained divided, he favored employers in all but one. In 1963, for example, he cast the deciding vote that gave Deering Milliken the right to shut down one of its textile plants, discharging five hundred workers who had voted in favor of union representation, an action condemned by the NLRB and later by the Supreme Court as an unfair labor practice designed to "chill unionism" throughout the company's factories.[6]

After reviewing Haynsworth's stance in *Simkins* and *Griffin*, civil rights organizations quickly enlisted in the fight against his confirmation. Labor leaders, smarting from the *Darlington* opinion, soon joined the opposition. Rauh wanted a united front from the Leadership Conference on Civil Rights, not a simple task, because some of its one hundred constituent organizations had refused in the past to become involved in confirmation battles. At a crucial meeting in August prior to the confirmation hearings, with Rauh leading the charge, the Leadership Conference voted without open dissent to oppose Haynsworth. Rauh gained another important ally when Marian

Edelman at the Washington Research Project assigned Rick Seymour to help with research on Haynsworth's judicial record.[7]

The legacy of the Fortas confirmation had created a major obstacle for those who now opposed Haynsworth. Fortas's supporters, such as Senator Philip Hart of Michigan, rested their case on the proposition that a nominee's ideological persuasion or judicial philosophy should carry less weight than paper qualifications. Rauh had cautioned Hart about this argument because he believed the Senate should pay close attention to a nominee's judicial philosophy, especially his attachment to the Bill of Rights. He feared that Hart's defense of Fortas would now be thrown back against them if they made Haynsworth's civil rights and labor opinions the basis of opposition. At the same time, the Fortas episode worked in Rauh's favor. Many Senate Democrats, angry over that defeat, had an appetite for revenge and remained eager to exploit any conflict-of-interest charges against a new nominee.

"Mr. Southern Textile"

When the confirmation hearings began, the AFL-CIO rolled out its heavy artillery against Haynsworth, with president George Meany, associate general counsel Tom Harris, and legislative director Andy Biemiller attacking the nominee. "Briefly stated," Meany told the committee, "this record [Haynsworth's] is one of insensitivity to the needs and aspirations of workers and to the plight of unorganized employees working for an antiunion employer in a local environment hostile to unions."[8]

Stephen Schlossberg, Rauh's successor as general counsel to the UAW, referred to the judge as "Mr. Southern Textile," whose "lifetime close association with socially backward, irresponsible, and reactionary economic interests in the South raise very serious doubts concerning his ability to administer justice objectively and impartially." Haynsworth opposed civil rights, Schlossberg concluded, his decisions supported segregation, and the UAW found it "unthinkable that such a man should be appointed to the Supreme Court in 1969."[9]

On behalf of the Leadership Conference, Rauh led the committee through a meticulous review of the judge's opinions touching racial discrimination and paid special attention to the decisions where he remained out of step with his own colleagues on the Fourth Circuit and the Supreme Court. He took direct aim at Haynsworth's dilatory tactics in the Prince Edward County case, where the nominee held the case for seven months awaiting a ruling by the Virginia courts on the question of the state's obligation to operate public schools. "Now why would anyone, in the spring of 1963, want to wait to hear what the courts of Virginia had to say about the facts of this case?" Rauh asked. "Schools were open everywhere else in Virginia. They were open in every other county, but in this county they were closed, and they were getting help from the State."[10]

Senator Bayh asked Rauh if he believed Haynsworth was a segregationist. "I think . . . the appointment of an admitted segregationist is not within the realm of practicality," Rauh replied. "In other words, almost no judge in America today says 'I am a segregationist.'" But, he added, "Judge Haynsworth . . . is sort of a laundered segregationist . . . a man who seeks to continue segregation in the present form and for the longest time possible in this country." Rauh's description of the judge as a "laundered segregationist" earned a prominent place in Richard Nixon's memoirs when he deplored the "pack mentality [that] took hold in Washington" against his nominee.[11]

Vend-A-Matic

Despite his dismal judicial record and the united opposition of civil rights and labor groups, Haynsworth would have been confirmed had it not been for conflict-of-interest issues. The Textile Workers of America first charged the judge with unethical conduct in the *Darlington* case, where his vote reversed a labor board decision in favor of the union. Their complaint focused on the judge's relationship to a vending machine firm, Carolina Vend-A-Matic. Since its founding in 1950, Haynsworth served as a vice president and director of that company, whose president and secretary were also his former law partners. But most of the union's initial complaint proved groundless. Deering Milliken had sought competitive bids from a number of vending machine firms for three of its factories, and Carolina Vend-A-Matic had secured only one of them

There the issue would have died except for William Eaton, an enterprising reporter for the *Chicago Daily News*, whose examination of public records at the Securities and Exchange Commission indicated that Haynsworth owned stock in Carolina Vend-A-Matic at the time of the *Darlington* case, an investment he had not disclosed to the union and which he refused to confirm or deny until Eaton published the record. Moreover, when Automatic Retailers of America bought Vend-A-Matic in 1964, the judge swapped his stock and immediately sold the 14,173 shares of ARA for about $450,000. Vend-A-Matic had been capitalized originally at $30,000, with Haynsworth owning 15 percent.[12]

Haynsworth had not broken the law or technically violated the canons of judicial ethics by participating in the *Darlington* case while owning stock in the firm, but in the shadow of the Fortas resignation, the revelation proved fatal. As Meany pointed out to the Judiciary Committee, when the Darlington dispute finally reached the Supreme Court on appeal, Justice Goldberg, who had once represented the Textile Workers Union of America, did not participate, thereby offering a striking contrast to Haynsworth's behavior.[13]

The judge's supporters argued that his critics had provided "insufficient evidence to brand [him] as anti-Negro, anti-labor or unethical in his financial dealings," but seven of the seventeen members of the Judiciary Committee voted against his confirmation, and a delegation of Republican senators, headed by Robert Griffin of Michigan, who had led the charge against Fortas, urged Nixon to withdraw the nomination. So did Nixon's chief legislative adviser, Bryce Harlow, but the president refused to retreat and forced a Senate vote where Haynsworth went down to defeat, 55-45, with seventeen Republicans voting against the candidate. No nominee in history had suffered a worse rejection by the Senate.[14]

"A Good Clean Conservative Southerner"

A few of the president's advisers believed the defeat of Haynsworth might work to Nixon's advantage if, as H. R. Haldeman expressed it, they could "find a good clean conservative Southerner to put in."[15] But enraged over the defeat, Nixon chose instead to escalate the judicial war with the Senate. In mid-January 1970 he nominated George Harrold Carswell, a fifty-year-old Georgia native and a judge on the Fifth Circuit Court of Appeals. As Haldeman and others soon learned, Carswell hardly fit the description of a good clean conservative Southerner.

The White House had barely announced the Carswell nomination when Rauh opened fire. The president, he told reporters, had again proposed "an unknown, whose principal qualification for the post seems to be his opposition to Negro rights. While this may be good politics in the suburbs and the South, it can only add to already dangerous racial tensions in America."[16] When Rauh went into battle, however, he did not know how many weary troops from the Haynsworth engagement might follow. Leon Shull, ADA director, gave him quick support, but even Clarence Mitchell expressed hesitation, and Tom Harris, apparently speaking for Meany and the AFL-CIO leadership, initially told reporters that the labor coalition would not fight the nomination.

"We need to be careful on this one," Mitchell cautioned. Rauh said they had no choice. "How would you like it said," he told his longtime ally in the Leadership Conference, "that Joe Rauh and Clarence Mitchell were responsible for Harrold Carswell because they whipped Haynsworth?" That argument ended Mitchell's doubts. But a number of senators who had joined the fight against Haynsworth expressed hostility to another confirmation battle. Senator Joe Tydings of Maryland became so furious that he threatened to throw Rauh and other opponents of Carswell out of his office.

"You can't ask us to march up that hill again," Tydings stormed. "We will look terrible."

"You would look worse if you didn't oppose Carswell," Rauh shot back.[17]

On the merits, Rauh knew he had a strong case. By comparison with Nixon's new nominee, Haynsworth was a racial moderate and a judicial giant. Running for a seat in the Georgia legislature in 1948, Carswell had declared himself to be "a Southerner by ancestry, birth, training, inclination, belief and practice. I believe that segregation of the races is proper and the only practical and correct way of life in our states. I have always so believed, and I shall always so act. . . . I yield to no man as a fellow candidate, or as a fellow citizen, in the firm, vigorous belief in the principles of white supremacy, and I shall always be so governed."

The speech had been delivered twenty-two years in the past and six years before the historic *Brown* decision. Carswell might have survived it given the political fatigue that gripped many senators in the wake of the Haynsworth fight. But he had since compiled a lamentable civil rights record as a district judge and an unusually high rate of reversal by the Fifth Circuit Court of Appeals, and engaged in numerous examples of hostility to civil rights attorneys who appeared before him. The American Bar Association had also given him a tepid endorsement.[18]

A Golf Course in Tallahassee

And then there was a golf course in Tallahassee. Dispatched to Florida, Rick Seymour uncovered a cache of documents indicating that Carswell, then a United States attorney, had been one of the incorporators in 1956 of the Tallahassee Country Club when its status changed from a public to private course in order to circumvent the Supreme Court decision banning segregation in similar recreational facilities. Others soon supplemented Seymour's discoveries, notably Fred Graham of the *New York Times*.[19] Rauh recognized the importance of the incorporation papers and turned them over to an old New Deal friend, Charles A. Horsky, a member of the ABA's Committee on the Judiciary.

That committee, dominated by Lawrence E. Walsh, a Nixon confidant, had given Carswell a grudging "qualified" rating without dissent. Armed with the Seymour documents, however, Horsky and Norman Ramsey, another member of the ABA committee, confronted Carswell prior to his testimony before the Judiciary Committee. In his later appearance before the senators, Carswell made fatal mistakes when he claimed limited knowledge of the documents, denied his role as an incorporator, and asserted that the project had not been designed to thwart desegregation. These statements cast the judge as either a liar or a fool and hastened the defection of several Republicans who had been inclined to support Nixon's nominee.[20]

"Haynsworth with a Cutting Edge"

In his own appearance before the Judiciary Committee on behalf of the Leadership Conference and the ADA, Rauh mounted a blistering attack on Carswell's ethics, fairness, and competence. The judge's 1948 "white supremacy" speech, he said, "is certainly the worst statement made by a candidate for the U.S. Supreme Court in this century" because it expressed views even contrary to *Plessy v. Ferguson,* the infamous "separate but equal" case of 1896. *Plessy* condoned racial separation, he pointed out, but still rested on the proposition that all men were created equal and entitled to equal facilities, although segregated ones. The judge's participation in the scheme to perpetuate segregation of a municipal golf course, months after such segregation had been ruled unconstitutional, may have constituted a criminal conspiracy under the 1870 Civil Rights Act, Rauh suggested, because it deprived black citizens of rights and privileges secured by the Fourteenth Amendment.

Rauh also took the committee on a tour of fifteen civil rights cases where Carswell had been reversed and often rebuked by the Fifth Circuit. Without a hearing, for example, he had dismissed the complaint by African-Americans against motion picture theaters and city officials in Tallahassee who conspired to maintain segregation, a ruling that prompted the appeals court to observe that the case presented "a classical allegation of a civil rights cause of action" and that Carswell's orders "were clearly in error."[21] In the three largest school desegregation cases that came before him from Pensacola, Tallahassee, and Bay County, Carswell had been reversed, sometimes twice, by the appeals court for approving inadequate integration plans in conflict with established Supreme Court decisions.[22]

Carswell's supporters pointed out that the judge had applied the 1964 Civil Rights Act to his own barbershop in Tallahassee's Duval Hotel, but that provoked Rauh's sharpest retort: "If Judge Carswell is confirmed, God help us, it will be the first time in history that a man ever was confirmed for writing an opinion that his racist barber ought to cut a Negro's hair." Two revolutions now gripped the South, Rauh said, one seeking positive change in race relations, the other attempting to turn back the clock. "What you are doing is fanning the flames of that negative revolution and killing the good revolution by putting Judge Carswell there [on the Supreme Court]." The president's nominee, he concluded, "is Judge Haynsworth with a cutting edge. He is Judge Haynsworth with a bitterness and a meanness that Judge Haynsworth never had. A Senate that would not confirm Judge Haynsworth cannot confirm Judge Carswell."[23]

Rauh also worked the halls of the Senate office buildings in search of votes against the nominee, a task that proved frustrating. After presenting a detailed memorandum on Carswell's record to Senator William Saxbe, a Republican who had gone on record as undecided, he learned that Saxbe had ridiculed the document in a meeting with other senators and attempted to use it to discredit the opposition's case. Republican John Sherman Cooper of Kentucky, who had voted against Haynsworth and was often called the conscience of the Senate, proved the biggest disappointment when he announced support for Carswell.

In the hope of changing Cooper's mind, Rauh called a number of his Kentucky friends, including Wilson Wyatt, Ed Prichard, and Barry Bingham of the *Courier-Journal*. They all told him not to worry. Cooper's decision would make it easier for Marlow Cook, the state's other Republican senator, to vote against Carswell because the two men hated each other and Cook had already expressed serious reservations about the nominee's devious testimony before the Judiciary Committee. Cook fulfilled that prophecy when he cast a crucial vote that gave Carswell's opponents a 51-45 majority against confirmation in early April.

In the short run, Rauh and his allies frustrated Nixon's attempt to roll back the judicial revolution of the Warren era by filling the Holmes-Cardozo seat with a southern reactionary. Twice humiliated in the Senate, the president soon nominated Harry A. Blackmun of Minnesota, a judge on the Court of Appeals for the Eighth Circuit, to fill the Fortas vacancy. A graduate of both Harvard College, *summa cum laude* in mathematics, and Harvard Law School, Blackmun won confirmation without opposition in the Senate. "This is icing on the cake," Rauh quipped to a reporter, "we have gone all the way from Haynsworth and Carswell to *summa cum laude*."[24] Blackmun, although a close friend of Chief Justice Burger, with whom he was soon linked as "the Minnesota Twins," evolved into one of the Court's most liberal members over the next twenty-six years on the bench. He authored the landmark abortion decision in 1973, defended the right of homosexuals to be free of criminal prosecution, and opposed the death penalty.[25]

Nixon's Court

In 1971 Nixon enjoyed his greatest opportunity to reconstruct the Court when Hugo Black and John M. Harlan retired less than a week apart. After canvassing a number of possibilities, including at least one woman and Senator Howard Baker of Tennessee, Nixon nominated Virginia attorney Lewis Powell and assistant attorney general William Hobbs Rehnquist. Rauh prepared for another confirmation fight against Rehnquist, whom Biemiller of the AFL-CIO characterized as "a right-wing zealot . . . one of the prime theoreticians of and apologists for this administration's root and branch assault on the constitutional system of checks and balances."[26]

A courtly Southerner, Powell bore little resemblance to Haynsworth or Carswell. A former chairman of the Richmond School Board, he did not have an extensive public record of either speeches or judicial opinions. No glaring examples of conflict of interest dogged his career. In the face of this evidence, Rauh urged the Leadership Conference to remain neutral on Powell, but to marshal all of their forces against Rehnquist, a decision that disappointed Congressman John Conyers and other African-American leaders, but received support from organized labor. It also proved realistic when Powell easily won Senate confirmation, 89-1.

More than the president who nominated him, Rehnquist represented the dogmatisms of right-wing conservatives from the Sunbelt who had waged a guerrilla war against liberalism since the 1950s. In Rauh's opinion, the nominee's intellect and ideological fervor made him a far greater threat to the Warren Court's legacy than either Haynsworth or Carswell. First in his Stanford Law School class of 1952, Rehnquist had brains and stamina. At age forty-seven he was likely to remain a force on the Court for a very long time. After graduating from Stanford, Rehnquist had clerked for Justice Jackson in 1952–53, the first term during which the Court considered *Brown v. Board of Education*. He returned to Phoenix to practice law between 1953 and 1969, entered Republican politics, and earned the highest rating of lawyers from Martindale-Hubbell, the bible of the profession.

Rehnquist had not made a speech openly defending white supremacy in Arizona, but in the summer of 1964 he appeared before the city council in Phoenix to oppose a local public accommodations ordinance designed to root out racial discrimination.[27] Three years later, he denounced efforts by the superintendent of the Phoenix public schools to overcome *de facto* racial segregation in that district with the observation that "the school's job is to educate children. They should not be saddled with a task of fostering social change which may well lessen their ability to perform their primary job."[28] In the same year he spoke against the Phoenix ordinance, Rehnquist joined the presidential crusade of Senator Goldwater. Leaders of the NAACP in Arizona accused him of intimidating and harassing minority voters over many years, beginning in 1958.

As chief of the Office of Legal Council, Rehnquist led the Justice Department's offensive for Haynsworth and Carswell and defended Nixon's decision to invade Cambodia, a neutral country. The president, he claimed, had far-ranging powers as commander-in-chief beyond the control of Congress. He invoked what he called "qualified martial law" to justify the wholesale arrest and detention of 7,200 citizens in the District who protested the Cambodia invasion. Federal judges flatly rejected that broad assertion of executive power and threw out most of the arrests.

Rehnquist, in short, stood for everything Rauh had fought against for four decades. Appearing before the Judiciary Committee following the nominee, he did not flinch from expressing his opposition with such vehemence that it provoked criticism from Senators Birch Bayh and Edward Kennedy, two of Rehnquist's major critics. Contrary to the president's public statements, Rauh declared, his nominee would be a judicial activist, someone bent upon imposing his conservative philosophy upon the Court, a man "who has lived roughly his whole adult life in the milieu of anti-human rights and anti–Bill of Rights." The Senate should reject Rehnquist based on his long-standing and public resistance to racial equality, his dismal record on civil liberties, his belief in unchecked presidential authority, and his lack of candor. If Haynsworth had been a "laundered segregationist," Rauh said, then Rehnquist was a "laundered McCarthyite."[29]

Most members of Eastland's committee, who had neither the resources nor the inclination to investigate further in 1971, accorded greater credibility to the nominee's responses than to sworn statements from members of the Arizona NAACP. And even a last-minute disclosure by *Newsweek* magazine of a memorandum Rehnquist had written in 1952 as a law clerk at the time of *Brown* failed to derail confirmation. The memo, which Senator Bayh called "dynamite," endorsed *Plessy v. Ferguson*. Rehnquist claimed he wrote it to express the views of Justice Jackson, but he had signed it with his initials "WHR," and the claim that it expressed the views of Jackson struck most observers as absurd. So did the testimony of another Jackson clerk, Donald Cronson, who alleged that he and Rehnquist had jointly composed an earlier memorandum recommending against "separate but equal." Jackson's official biographer could find no evidence of such a document in Jackson's court papers.[30]

In the wake of the memo defending segregation, Bayh and his allies forced the Senate to debate the nomination for four days. Administration efforts to invoke cloture and silence Rehnquist's critics failed by eleven votes, but Bayh's attempt to postpone a final decision until January 1972 went down to defeat, 70-22. The Senate then confirmed Rehnquist, 68-26. Unlike Haynsworth and Carswell, only three Republicans—Edward Brooke, Jacob Javits, and Clifford Case of New Jersey—broke ranks with the administration, while several liberal Democrats, including Tom Eagleton, William Proxmire, and Adlai Stevenson III, voted to confirm Rehnquist.

Despite the efforts of Rauh and others, Nixon successfully reconstituted the Supreme Court, but the results were not what either the president or Rauh might have anticipated. In the summer of 1974, by a vote of eight to nothing, with Rehnquist not participating, Burger's Court helped to topple Nixon's presidency when it ordered the president to deliver to a federal district judge and a special prosecutor tape recordings of secret White House conversations. Those tapes demonstrated that Nixon and his chief aides had obstructed the investigation of a burglary at the Democratic Party headquarters in the Watergate complex, a break-in authorized and carried out by those running the president's reelection campaign, including his former attorney general, John Mitchell.

The Nixon-Burger Court proved disappointing to those who hoped to reverse the judicial activism of earlier decades. While often divided, Burger's Court struck down criminal abortion statutes, invalidated laws that discriminated against women, declared existing death penalty laws unconstitutional, and upheld affirmative action programs. As Rauh had predicted, Rehnquist usually dissented.[31]

Republican domination of the White House after 1968 meant that each new appointment to the High Court threatened to tip the ideological balance further to the right. That situation drew Rauh into new and protracted confirmation battles. Choosing when to fight became a critical problem given the Leadership Conference's limited resources and its need to engage other issues touching school desegregation, voting rights, and affirmative action. Rauh and the Leadership Conference elected not to oppose Gerald Ford's choice of John Paul Stevens and Ronald Reagan's nomination of the first woman, Sandra Day O'Connor.

Rehnquist and Scalia

Rauh did not give Reagan a pass on his next Court appointments five years later when Burger accepted the president's call to head the commission organizing the American Bicentennial celebration and announced his retirement. To no one's surprise, Reagan sent Rehnquist's name to the Senate as the next chief justice. At the same time, the president nominated Antonin Scalia, one of the most aggressive conservatives on the federal bench, to fill Rehnquist's seat. Rauh urged the Leadership Conference and its allies to marshal all of their energies against Rehnquist. If he could be defeated, no vacancy existed for Scalia, a situation that argued for reserving their attack on the appeals judge. But women's organizations regarded Scalia as an enemy to efforts to eradicate sex discrimination, and they wanted immediate and vocal opposition to both candidates. With some reluctance, Rauh backed that decision, not because he found Scalia acceptable, but because he doubted the stamina of his troops in such a protracted war.

Rauh's strategy had much to recommend it. Rehnquist had more than fulfilled the hopes of those who put him on the Court. He had become the anti-Warren. In fourteen cases involving racial discrimination from 1971 to 1985, the justice rejected the plaintiff's claims each time. In 1983, he alone on the Burger Court voted to sustain federal tax exemptions for Bob Jones University, an institution whose avowed policy condoned racial segregation.[32] Since 1971, Burger's Court had also struck down fourteen state laws on grounds of sex discrimination, while Rehnquist had joined only three of those opinions, and dissented alone in six of them.[33]

The son of a Sicilian immigrant who taught romance languages at Brooklyn College, Scalia had graduated *magna cum laude* from Harvard Law School in 1960, served briefly in the Department of Justice during the Ford administration, joined the American Enterprise Institute as one of their scholars-in-residence, and taught at the University of Chicago before Reagan nominated him to the Court of Appeals for the District of Columbia. Scalia combined the intellectual firepower and scathing tongue of a Frankfurter with a libertarian philosophy that made him the archenemy of government affirmative action programs for women and minorities and of judicial efforts to curb the influence of sectarian religious values in public life.

The day before Rehnquist made his appearance before the Judiciary Committee, Ted Kennedy arranged for Rauh and an opposition contingent to hold a large press conference in the Dirksen Office Building. In a room packed with TV cameras and reporters from the major networks and newspapers, Eleanor Smeal of NOW, Ben Hooks from the Leadership Conference, and Irene Natividad of the National Women's Caucus attacked the nominee's record on civil rights and civil liberties. Rauh, as usual, batted cleanup.

"Oh, sure, he's got a high I.Q.," he told reporters in response to a question about Rehnquist's legal acumen. "So what? Let them appoint Roy Cohn. He's got a high I.Q. Everyone I know has a high I.Q. This man [Rehnquist]

is disqualified for the job because he doesn't believe in individual rights!"
When someone asked Rauh whom he would name to the bench, the response came back: "Ben Hooks, he's a lawyer."[34]

The Memo

Rauh believed he now had incontrovertible evidence that Rehnquist had lied
in the past about both the Phoenix election charges and the *Brown* memorandum in the Jackson files. Five new witnesses came forward in addition to
the six who submitted affidavits in 1971 to declare that Rehnquist had challenged minority voters in the early 1960s and that his behavior constituted
harassment and intimidation.[35] Richard Kluger had challenged Rehnquist's
statements about the *Brown* memo in his exhaustive study of the case, *Simple Justice*, published in 1975. On the basis of his research, Kluger concluded
that Rehnquist had expressed his own views upholding "separate but equal,"
not those of Jackson.

Rauh also persuaded Elsie Douglas, Jackson's former secretary and mis-
tress, to enter the controversy with a letter to Kennedy that refuted the nominee's account. Rehnquist's version, she wrote, "is a smear of a great man.
. . . Justice Jackson did not ask law clerks to express his views. He expressed
his own and they expressed theirs. That's what happened in this instance."[36]
Further scrutiny of Jackson's court papers produced two other Rehnquist
memos, including one for the case of *Terry v. Adams*, a challenge to the exclusion of African-American voters from primary elections. Rehnquist had
written that he had "a dim view of this pathological search for discrimination," and that "it is about time the court faced the fact that the white people
in the South don't like the colored people."[37]

In his appearance before the Judiciary Committee, Rauh made his most
passionate plea in any confirmation fight. Rehnquist's nomination, he said
flatly, "is a desecration of the Supreme Court of the United States." He
feared that the committee and the Senate were about "to reward a lifetime
of opposition to individual rights . . . with the highest judicial and legal post
in the country." From his *Brown* memo in 1952 to his dissent in *Bob Jones*,
Rauh argued, Rehnquist had consistently displayed opposition to civil liberties and civil rights. He would never change. The justice might or might not
be a bigot, Rauh concluded, but he was a justice who consistently glorified
the power of the state. "He thinks the State is always right. Whether it is
women, blacks, Hispanics, homosexuals, aliens, people on welfare, the State
always is right when it denies them their rights. That is no position for a Chief
Justice. That is no view for him to hold."[38]

As Rauh had feared, once the Rehnquist hearings concluded with a sense of his inevitable confirmation, opposition to Scalia withered. A panicky call from Eleanor Smeal of NOW, who did not wish to be the only witness against Scalia, sent Rauh back into battle as a spokesman for both the ADA and the Leadership Conference. Judge Scalia, he told the committee, had "ice water in his veins, when a Supreme Court Justice ought to have a feeling of compassion." Scalia's sarcastic views on affirmative action especially outraged Rauh, because "he makes jokes about things we believe in deeply. He laughs at affirmative action. . . . I cannot understand putting on the Supreme Court someone who laughs at affirmative action."[39]

On September 17, 1986, however, the Senate confirmed Scalia without a single negative vote. Earlier, it put Rehnquist into the chief justice's seat, 65-33, with seven more senators voting in the negative than fifteen years earlier. The thirty-three votes against Rehnquist, the largest negative for any chief justice in history, represented a moral victory of sorts for Rauh, but President Reagan and the conservatives of his counterrevolution now stood a single vacancy away from dominating the Supreme Court. That goal seemed in reach when Justice Powell retired at the end of the court's term a year later and Reagan nominated Robert Bork, Scalia's former colleague on the appeals court.

CHAPTER NINETEEN

SAVING THE COURT

Why should we hide? Why are you ashamed
to be called liberals?

—JOE RAUH

Paper Trail

Judge Robert Bork probably saved Joe Rauh's life. President Reagan's nomination of the former Yale law professor to the Supreme Court in the summer of 1987 rekindled Rauh's spirit after a brush with death and gave him enthusiasm for another confirmation battle. This one surpassed in intensity those he had earlier fought against Haynsworth, Carswell, Rehnquist, and Scalia. Now, slowed by illness, the aging lion of legal liberalism accepted a more modest role, one he continued to play in the final Court struggles of the Reagan-Bush years.

Early in 1987, his hip weakened by many years of competition on the tennis courts and softball fields, Rauh checked into Johns Hopkins Medical Center for a replacement. The operation went well, but three days after surgery, he suffered a heart attack. Faced with internal bleeding, he underwent an additional operation that took a heavy physical toll. "I nearly croaked," he joked to friends. Not until May did he find the stamina to travel and accept accolades at a Common Cause dinner in Washington. When Herman Benson, his old ally from the union democracy wars, saw him a year later in Los Angeles, he noted that Rauh "has the old crusading spirit. But physically he is obviously weakened by the long ordeal he suffered last year. He walks painfully with a cane and gets tired, but when he gets up to the platform, the spirit is still there."[1]

Robert Bork, with his scraggly red beard and rumpled appearance, looked every bit the part of a professor, his profession before joining the Nixon administration as solicitor general fourteen months before the president resigned. A graduate of the University of Chicago and its law school, Bork's intellectual journey had taken him from youthful support for the New Deal (he voted for Adlai Stevenson in 1952), through the free-market libertarianism of the Chicago school of economics, to the extremes of cultural conservatism in the 1980s.

In 1963, for example, he condemned Kennedy's proposed civil rights bill on grounds that "having the state coerce you into more righteous paths . . . is itself a principle of unsurpassed ugliness."[2] He attacked the Court's 1948 decision outlawing restrictive racial covenants as lacking "neutral principles" because it "converts an amendment . . . aimed only at governmental discrimination into a sweeping prohibition of private discrimination. There is no warrant anywhere for that conversion."[3] Bork also denounced Supreme Court decisions striking down the poll tax and sustaining a congressional ban on literacy tests as "very bad, indeed pernicious, constitutional law."[4] He ridiculed *Griswold v. Connecticut,* which affirmed a constitutional right to privacy and the right of married couples to use contraceptives, as "an unprincipled decision."[5] *Roe v. Wade* drew his fire as "an unconstitutional decision, a serious and wholly unjustifiable judicial usurpation of state legislative authority."[6]

"Saturday Night Massacre"

Bork's role during the Watergate crisis also raised serious questions concerning his candor and judgment as solicitor general. On October 20, 1973, after special prosecutor Archibald Cox won an appeals court ruling ordering President Nixon to turn over to his office potentially incriminating tape recordings of White House conversations, the president instructed attorney general Elliott Richardson to fire Cox. When Richardson refused and resigned, Nixon next ordered William Ruckelshaus, the deputy attorney general, to oust the special prosecutor. He, too, refused and resigned, but Bork, third in command at Justice, carried out the president's orders and fired Cox, an event soon labeled the "Saturday Night Massacre." Bork insisted at his confirmation hearings for the appeals court that he intended for the Watergate investigation to continue without delay, but he did not appoint a new special prosecutor, Leon Jaworski, until early November following intense criticism of his inaction in Congress and the press.

Former members of the special prosecutor's office, especially Henry Ruth, questioned Bork's version of events. They noted he had long opposed the special prosecutor post and that the president had ordered him to fire Cox and also "to abolish the Office of Special Prosecutor." On October 23 Bork carried out Nixon's order by rescinding the regulation that had created Cox's post, and he then ordered its functions transferred to the Criminal Division in the Department of Justice. Bork, some critics noted, must have known that the president hoped to further obstruct the criminal investigation. Federal district judge Gerhard Gesell later ruled that Bork's firing of Cox had been illegal because it came prior to rescinding the regulation. Moreover, the regulation permitted removal only for cause.[7]

Rauh believed he needed a smoking gun, something similar to Haynsworth's vending machines, Carswell's country club, or Rehnquist's *Brown* memorandum. Bork's role in the firing of Cox might prove his undoing. And Rauh believed that William Coleman, a former Frankfurter clerk and chairman of the NAACP's Legal Defense Fund, held a key piece of evidence. If he testified, Coleman could be an impressive witness against Bork.

Bill Coleman was no radical. The first African-American law clerk hired at the Supreme Court, he belonged to the American legal establishment. As a member of the American Bar Association's committee that probed Bork's fitness to serve on the court of appeals, Coleman had asked him many questions in 1982 about Watergate, the firing of Cox, and the abolition of the special prosecutor's office. Coleman had taken notes of that hearing, but had never made them public. And despite Rauh's probing, he declined to reveal their content, although Rauh believed Coleman did not entirely accept Bork's version of the Cox firing.

Before the Judiciary Committee, despite Rauh's pleading, Coleman avoided a direct confrontation over details of Watergate, but proceeded to attack Bork on ideological grounds.[8] Judge Bork read certain provisions in the Constitution broadly, Coleman said, but "when it comes to the great clauses dealing with human rights, for some reason Judge Bork says such rights are not there." He pointed to Bork's often-stated denunciation of the privacy decisions from *Griswold* to *Roe.* He also reminded senators that Bork had hesitated on the question of Congress's enforcement of the Fourteenth and Fifteenth Amendments, "which gives you the power to correct things that the Court does not correct. I think that when someone's writings put that in jeopardy, you should look at that person carefully."[9]

"Why Should We Hide?"

Two weeks into the hearings, with several platoons of lawyers, law deans, and law professors on record against the nominee, Rauh entered a sharp debate among the opposition organizations. Many leaders of those organizations wanted to avoid oral testimony for fear that their presence would further inflame Bork's supporters, push some senators into the undecided camp, and destroy their chances of victory. When Rauh learned of their caution from Ralph Neas, now the head of the Leadership Conference, he angrily objected. From the perspective of beating Bork, he said, the strategy might be correct, but the integrity of the liberal movement remained at stake, too. Such timidity, he argued, would confirm right-wing stereotypes about the negative influence of liberalism. "Why should we hide," Rauh demanded. "Why are you ashamed to be called liberals? This is the same crap now destroying the Democratic Party." But only Molly Yard from the National Organization for Women and Ralph Nader backed his defense of the liberal cause with enthusiasm.[10]

Reluctantly, Rauh bowed to the majority. Anxious to leave for France on a recuperative barge trip, he submitted only a written statement of opposition to the Judiciary Committee on behalf of the ADA. Bork's devotion to judicial restraint, he argued, meant he would uphold actions of the government he agreed with and strike down those he opposed. If confirmed, Bork would turn back the clock "on widely-accepted constitutional rights." Bork's role in the Saturday Night Massacre, he argued, had been illegal, and he continued to shade the truth about Watergate.[11]

On October 5, a day before the scheduled vote in the Judiciary Committee, chairman Joe Biden informed the White House that nine of the fourteen members would recommend against Bork's confirmation, a vote guaranteed to produce rejection by the full Senate. Biden urged Reagan and his advisers to withdraw the nomination, but they declined. On his French barge, Rauh kept score by means of the Voice of America as senators lined up for and against the nominee. Bork, like the White House, refused to bow out before the full Senate rejected his nomination, 58-42, a more humiliating defeat than the ones suffered by Haynsworth or Carswell.[12]

"Bork without a Paper Trail"

With the corpse of the Bork nomination still warm, President Reagan went before a crowd of reporters in the East Room of the White House on October 29 to present his new candidate, forty-one-year-old judge Douglas H. Ginsburg. A member of the Court of Appeals for the District of Columbia for less than a year, Ginsburg stood by as the president denounced Bork's defeat as "a disservice to the Court and to the nation." The president dared opponents to repeat the performance by declaring that "the American people will know what's up" if the Senate did not promptly agree to his new choice.[13]

Rauh took up the challenge. Ginsburg, he knew, had been anointed by the administration's far-right cabal in the Department of Justice led by attorney general Ed Meese, assistant attorney general William Bradford Reynolds, and spokesman Terry Eastland, who had written speeches for Bork. Speaking before the Women's Democratic Forum of Greater St. Louis, Rauh denounced Ginsburg as "a closet Bork" and called for his defeat, a position also adopted by Ted Kennedy, who called the judge "an ideological clone of Judge Bork, a Judge Bork without a paper trail." Rauh reminded his St. Louis audience that Reagan had promised that if the Senate defeated Bork, he would nominate someone equally objectionable. "Why shouldn't we believe him [Reagan] for once?" Rauh quipped.[14]

Rauh anticipated long, exhaustive hearings before Biden's committee. He hoped the process might be extended into the next year, Reagan's last in the White House. With a presidential election arriving in 1988 the possibility seemed to grow that Reagan would be unable to fill the vacant seat, but then Nina Totenberg, judicial reporter for National Public Radio, altered the course of Supreme Court history. On NPR she announced that witnesses at Harvard Law School saw Ginsburg smoke marijuana at a party there while an assistant professor.[15] The day after Totenberg broke the story, Ginsburg withdrew, pressured by education secretary William J. Bennett and with the president's blessing. As Rauh had feared, Reagan and his advisers now had a fresh opportunity to send a third nominee to the Senate, where the Bork ordeal and the Ginsburg collapse had left tempers and patience frayed. Ginsburg's self-destruction had not improved the mood.[16]

Another Bork?

To no one's surprise, Reagan sent the name of Anthony Kennedy, a judge on the Ninth Circuit Court of Appeals, to the Senate at the end of November. A bridesmaid in the contest with Ginsburg a month earlier, Kennedy had neither the paper trail of a Bork nor the conflict-of-interest problems that would have plagued Ginsburg. A native Californian, born and raised in Sacramento, Kennedy had graduated from Stanford and Harvard Law School.

Republican and Catholic, Kennedy caught the eye of Governor Reagan and later President Gerald Ford, who nominated him for the Ninth Circuit in 1975. After a quick review of Kennedy's opinions on the court of appeals, Rauh knew that the nominee would likely march with Rehnquist and Scalia, not Justices Brennan and Marshall. In a major school desegregation case from Pasadena, California, Kennedy had voted to terminate federal court supervision despite evidence that the local school board had not complied with previous orders, and favored restoring so-called neighborhood schools, likely to result in the resegregation of minority pupils.[17]

When the Ninth Circuit, *en banc*, threw out an airline regulation that fired flight hostesses above a certain weight, but not obese male employees, Kennedy joined a dissent that argued against the finding of discrimination on the grounds of gender, because the flight hostesses were all female.[18] He voted to reverse a district court that had ruled wages paid by the State of Washington for work performed overwhelmingly by women discriminated on the basis of gender, a violation of Title VII of the Civil Rights Act, but he sustained the navy's rule requiring the termination of homosexuals.[19]

Rauh lacked support for opposing Kennedy both within the Leadership Conference and the judiciary committee, where few members relished another round against Reagan. The Leadership Conference declined to take a position for or against Kennedy and did not send chairman Neas to testify. Even opponents of Bork, including Harvard professor Larry Tribe, came forth to endorse Kennedy for his "great intelligence and fair-mindedness . . . the essence of true judicial restraint, and potentially, of genuine judicial greatness."[20]

Discouraged by the lack of allies, Rauh gave little thought to testifying until he received a plea from Molly Yard at NOW, who feared that she and Susan Deller Ross, a Georgetown law professor, would be forced to appear alone before the committee. Moved by Yard's appeal, Rauh wrote a statement and secured the approval of Congressman Ted Weiss and others in the ADA to appear on the organization's behalf. He stressed the cases involving school desegregation and sex discrimination as well as the nominee's past membership in San Francisco's all-male Olympic Club. Rauh also sharply condemned the committee for its hasty scheduling of confirmation hearings that limited inquiry into Kennedy's judicial record. "Somebody had to bell the cat," he wrote in a note accompanying the statement. "But we don't seem to have any votes."[21]

Rauh spared no one in his testimony, including the nominee, the committee, the American Bar Association, and others who had endorsed the nominee. Biden's committee, he said, had rushed to judgment by scheduling hearings so near the end of the congressional session. They had failed to probe the nominee's views, especially what he may have told students in his law school classes at McGeorge School of Law about cases such as *Roe v. Wade*. "You played patty cake with Judge Kennedy," he added. "I don't think you found out what he really thinks."[22] Biden and whole committee, he feared, seemed poised to play "Russian roulette" with the Bill of Rights. He ridiculed the ABA endorsement by noting it had never flatly opposed a Supreme Court nominee, including Haynsworth, Carswell, and Bork.

Biden expressed irritation that Rauh and others dared to question Professor Tribe's praise for Kennedy's concurring opinion in a Los Angeles case brought by Mexican-Americans who protested at-large elections. Tribe had his facts wrong, Rauh retorted. Kennedy's opinion, Rauh noted, affirmed a summary judgment against the plaintiffs and rejected all of their arguments. His concurrence slammed the door more tightly against such suits than did the views of the majority on the Ninth Circuit.[23] The exchange with Biden became rancorous.

"Do you think that Professor Tribe is less committed to the Bill of Rights than you are?" Biden demanded.

Rauh answered, "I plead the Fifth Amendment."

Biden tried another tack: "Do you think I am less committed to the Bill of Rights than you are?"

Rauh responded, "That is a question. Are you asking a question?"

Biden said, "I did."

Rauh replied, "And you insist on an answer, my answer has to be yes."[24]

Prior to the Senate vote, Rauh made one final effort to rally opposition against Kennedy. In an opinion piece for the *Washington Post,* he called on Biden's committee to reopen the hearings, invite Kennedy back, and ask the nominee what he had said in the past to students, faculty colleagues, and Ninth Circuit judges about public school prayers, abortion, affirmative action, and other civil rights issues. He reminded *Post* readers that Reagan and his administration had been attempting for seven years to roll back civil freedoms. "At a time when we are pressing other countries on human rights," he concluded, "retreat at home should be unthinkable."[25] Early in February 1988, by a vote of 97-0, however, the Senate put Anthony Kennedy on Rehnquist's Court.

The Brennan Seat

When he turned eighty in 1990, Rauh knew that age also stalked the shrinking liberal bloc on Rehnquist's Court led by Brennan, Marshall, and Blackmun. And when Brennan, the elder statesman of the Warren era, stepped down in the summer of 1990, his retirement opened the way for President George Bush's first appointment. Anyone chosen to fill Bill Brennan's chair would suffer close scrutiny from Rauh. Bush's choice of David

Hackett Souter, an obscure federal appeals judge from New Hampshire, guaranteed it.

An authentic Yankee, Souter professed great admiration for Oliver Wendell Holmes Jr., but other entries on his resume raised Rauh's doubts. A graduate of Harvard College and Harvard Law School, as well as a Rhodes Scholar at Oxford, he had practiced law in Concord, New Hampshire, and moved through the ranks of the state's Department of Justice to become attorney general in 1976. Souter later served as a superior court judge before his seven-year tenure on the New Hampshire Supreme Court, where he authored over 200 opinions. Nominated by Bush to the Court of Appeals for the First Circuit in February 1990, he had barely warmed that seat when Brennan retired.

Soft-spoken, scholarly, and a bachelor who inhabited a reclusive world dominated by study of the law, the narrowness of Souter's life experience stirred alarm, especially in the women's movement, where issues of reproductive rights had assumed transcendent importance following several restrictive decisions. Was Souter a kinder, less abrasive version of Robert Bork? His opinions as attorney general, on the state supreme court, and before the Judiciary Committee raised serious questions in Rauh's mind. As New Hampshire's attorney general from 1976 to 1978, Bush's nominee joined Governor Meldrim Thomson in opposing legislation that in part would have repealed the state's strict ban on abortions dating from 1848. "I don't think unlimited abortions should be allowed," Souter wrote, "[and] I presume we would become the abortion mill of the United States."[26]

From Rauh's perspective, Souter's views on race and civil rights seemed equally objectionable. In testimony before the Judiciary Committee on September 13, the nominee responded with a resounding no when asked by Senator Simpson if he were a racist. He then added: "In a way, I think that answer might have been impressive to some people if I had grown up in a place with racial problems, and some people have pointed out that I did not." The State of New Hampshire, Souter concluded, "does not have racial problems."[27] That statement infuriated Rauh.

When he appeared on behalf of the Leadership Conference before Biden's committee with Antonia Hernandez of the Mexican-American Legal Defense Fund and Joan Bronk from the National Council of Jewish Women, Rauh lashed out at a nominee who "cannot see what is right under his nose: the terrible racial problems in New Hampshire." Judge Souter might not be a racist, Rauh said, but "he has done nothing about it. He has over and over again tried to brush it under the rug." New Hampshire remained one of two states, the other being Montana, that refused to honor Dr. King with a holiday. Beyond that symbolic declaration, however, Rauh filed with the committee a list of cases and news reports documenting the state's racial phobias:

> Governor Thomson had praised the black ghetto of Soweto in South Africa as a "wonderful place," while proclaiming the head of its all-white government, John Vorster, a "great world statesman."
>
> Minority students at Daniel Webster College reported racial threats and harassment, including other students dressed in Klu Klux Klan regalia and the words "niggers sucks" scrawled on dorm room walls.
>
> Daniel Webster College, where Souter had spoken against affirmative action, could be described as "the Bob Jones University of the North."

The committee, Rauh urged, should recall the judge to answer some tough questions concerning his knowledge of racial bigotry at Daniel Webster. "Now, if you want that insensitive a man on that Court, why, I am only one citizen," Rauh concluded. "But I tell you that the most frightening thing is to put people on that Court who have no sensitivity to the race problem in this country."[28]

Rauh's critique had little impact, with the Leadership Conference divided, the NAACP joining the opposition late, and most labor unions remaining neutral. Few senators felt the pressure of earlier confirmation fights. When the Judiciary Committee finally took up the Souter nomination, only Kennedy dissented. And when the full Senate voted in the early evening of October 2, only nine members—all Democrats—voted not to confirm the nominee.

"A Model for All Americans"

In the spring and summer of 1991, Rauh suffered two loses, one private, the other public. His sister Louise, who had provided medical care to the indigent in Ohio for over half a century, died in Cincinnati. He mourned her death and missed their regular Sunday morning telephone chats. Then, when the Supreme Court's term concluded in June, Thurgood Marshall, eighty-two years old, announced his retirement. "What's wrong with me?" Marshall responded to the queries from reporters. "I'm old. I'm getting old and coming apart."[29] Marshall was the living embodiment of the struggle for racial justice in America. Perhaps anticipating what President Bush might do, the justice cautioned that race should not be used as "an excuse" for picking the wrong person to take his seat. "There's no difference between a white snake and black snake," he said. They'll both bite."[30]

Rauh predicted to friends that Bush would nominate Clarence Thomas, an African-American who had been on an appeals court for little more than a year. Thomas, he believed, had been groomed for the Marshall seat by the Reagan and Bush administrations since his days as an assistant secretary for civil rights in the Department of Education and chairman of the federal Equal Employment Opportunity Commission. Bush fulfilled this prophecy on July 1, when, Thomas by his side, the president announced his choice to reporters at his summer home in Kennebunkport, Maine. Thomas's life, the president told reporters, "is a model for all Americans."[31]

Thomas's nomination sent Rauh into his last confirmation war against a candidate who had minimal judicial qualifications and represented the repudiation of the civil rights legacy he and Marshall had helped to create over half a century. The eldest of two sons and a daughter born to Leola Thomas, a woman who picked the meat from crabs for a nickel a pound at a factory in Pin Point, Georgia, Clarence Thomas grew up in a wooden house without an indoor toilet, lit by kerosene lamps, its water drawn from a common pump.

In Savannah, under the watchful eye and strict discipline of Franciscan sisters at St. Benedict's school who rode at the back of the bus with their black students, Thomas acquired an educational foundation, a sense of self-esteem, and a spiritual commitment that sent him to Catholic seminaries in Savannah and later at Conception Junction, Missouri. In 1968, a year that changed many lives in America, Thomas abandoned study for the priesthood and entered Holy Cross College, one member of the school's first significant class of African-American students recruited through an affirmative action program.

At Holy Cross, decked out in army fatigues and a Black Panther beret, Thomas helped to found the Black Student Union and protested against the war in Vietnam, at one point leading a demonstration against recruiters from General Electric. That behavior brought disciplinary action from campus officials and his temporary resignation from the school. Soon reinstated and displaying a strong academic record, in 1971 he entered Yale Law School, where the faculty and administration had also begun a major effort to recruit minority applicants. When Thomas graduated three years later, he found a major patron in Republican senator John C. Danforth, then attorney general of Missouri, who offered him a job as an assistant attorney general and brought him to Washington in 1979 as his legislative assistant.

In Jefferson City, before moving to Washington, Thomas soaked up the writings of Thomas Sowell, the black libertarian economist, who attacked government poverty programs and affirmative action. The problems of the black underclass, Sowell argued, would be best solved through self-help and the free market. Armed with these ideas that fit the Reagan-Bush agenda for dismantling federal programs and backed with the patronage of Danforth, Thomas moved steadily up the ladder in these two Republican administrations. He became a consultant to the Office of Civil Rights in the Education Department, then an assistant secretary of education for civil rights, and finally, chairman of the Equal Employment Opportunity Commission. Confirmed for the court of appeals in 1990, although he had never practiced law, Thomas had authored only eighteen opinions when Bush introduced him to the press as Marshall's replacement.[32]

As the author of Roosevelt's original executive order banning racial discrimination in employment, Rauh had special reason to deplore Thomas's views on race and affirmative action and his role as chairman of the Equal Employment Opportunity Commission. The *Brown* decision, Thomas wrote in 1988, had spawned "a disastrous series of cases requiring busing and other policies that were irrelevant to parents' concern for a decent education." He ridiculed the voluntary affirmative action program upheld by the Court in *United Steel Workers v. Weber* as an "egregious example" of "creative interpretation" of federal civil rights laws, while the minority set-aside adopted by Congress for allocating highway construction funds indicated that "there is [not] a great deal of principle in Congress itself." And in a 1987 panel discussion at the Center for the Study of Democratic Institutions in Santa Barbara, Thomas claimed that "any race-conscious remedy is no good."[33]

Confronted by his own writings, speeches, and policy declarations before the Judiciary Committee, Thomas sought refuge in the separation of powers by arguing that his prior statements had been made while stationed in the executive branch and did not necessarily reflect how he might rule as the justice. He also dodged specific questions about natural law, privacy, affirmative action, and property rights by shifting attention to his own background and heroic rise out of poverty, a narrative that brought tears to the eyes of Senator Orrin Hatch, who noted that he, too, "was born into a family and we didn't have indoor facilities."

Rauh appeared before Biden's committee on a panel that included John Buchanan from People for the American Way, Julius Chambers of the NAACP Legal Defense Fund, Antonia Hernandez of the Mexican-American Legal Defense and Education Fund, and William Lucy from the Coalition of Black Trade Unionists. He placed special emphasis upon the ABA's divided endorsement, Thomas's evasiveness under questioning, and the threat he posed to the Bill of Rights. A few days later, he echoed these same criticisms in a debate with William Bennett, the administration's leading conservative intellectual, before a packed luncheon audience at the Washington Hilton. Given the ABA report, Rauh argued, the claim that Bush had found "the best man" offended common sense and history. "Even Carswell had a better record," he pointed out. "Thomas has a worse record than even Carswell. I can't see how the Senate can confirm somebody who has a worse record than Carswell."[34]

Miss Hill's Complaint

Despite opposition as large and determined as the one against Bork, Thomas appeared on the brink of confirmation at the end of the hearings in mid-September. Then Timothy Phelps, a reporter at *Newsday,* and the redoubtable Nina Totenberg at NPR, broke the story of sexual harassment charges leveled against the judge by a former EEOC employee, Anita Hill, currently a law professor at the University of Oklahoma. Thomas, according to Hill, had often raised questions about her sexual behavior, commented on pornographic films he had seen, and even remarked about pubic hairs on a soft drink can.

For three days, Americans stayed glued to their television screens as the Thomas hearings reopened with Hill restating her charges in public and Thomas denying them. Republican senators denounced the accusations as a liberal conspiracy based on the words of a woman scorned, while Democrats hesitated to probe too deeply for fear of being branded as racists. Republican Arlen Specter, whose interrogation wounded Bork, led the assault against Hill, going so far as to accuse her of perjury. Privately, Spector told Rauh he attacked Hill because he feared a right-wing challenge in a future Pennsylvania primary. Democratic leader George Mitchell warned his colleagues not to ignore the support for Thomas among many African-Americans, many of whom condemned Hill's accusations, not the judge's alleged conduct.[35]

Despite pressure from Rauh and others, Biden and the Democrats declined to call other witnesses from Thomas's EEOC tenure who might support Hill's account. With that decision to stop the probe, Hill's sexual harassment charge—potentially as fatal as Haynsworth's vending machines, Carswell's golf course, or Ginsburg's marijuana use—deflated. Thomas shrewdly backed the Democrats into a corner when he played the sexually charged race card that had been used historically by white supremacists. The entire proceeding, he raged at the committee, had been "a high-tech lynching for uppity blacks."

A divided and demoralized Judiciary Committee could not report a recommendation to the full Senate, which engaged in another lacerating debate before confirming Thomas by a vote of 52-48, the narrowest margin for any Supreme Court nominee in the twentieth century. Senators, especially in the South, who had relied on black votes to win their seats turned the tide against Bork. A sharply divided African-American community saved Clarence Thomas. As the Columbia historian Manning Marable later noted, "The majority of the African-American community has supported the wrong person for the wrong position for the wrong reasons."[36]

Rehnquist's Court

Joe Rauh did not live to see the opening of the Supreme Court's term in October 1992, but many of his worst fears were then realized when Thomas voted consistently with Scalia in all but two cases, a record that prompted the *New York Times* to brand him "the youngest and the cruelest" justice. Even the Southern Christian Leadership Conference, the only significant civil rights organization that supported his confirmation, publicly regretted its endorsement by 1992.

Now in command of the Court, Rehnquist's majority, usually including O'Connor, Scalia, Thomas, and Kennedy, limited the remedies federal judges could employ against the persistent forms of racial segregation in public schools,[37] all but abolished affirmative action programs for both the states and federal government,[38] and sharply curtailed the creation of electoral districts that favored minority candidates.[39]

Had Thomas's views prevailed in voting rights case, the 1965 law and its amendments would have been restricted to formal voting qualifications, leaving other forms of discrimination outside federal protection.[40] When the issue touched questions of criminal justice, Thomas could be counted on to endorse the views of Rehnquist or adopt an even more punitive position. The constitutional ban on cruel and unusual punishments, he wrote, did not apply to postsentencing incarceration, including the rape of prison inmates.[41]

As Rauh had predicted, Rehnquist triumphed also in the arena of federalism by forging a majority following the departure of Brennan and Marshall that sharply curtailed the authority of Congress under the commerce clause for the first time since the Great Depression.[42] Had he lived, however, Rauh would have been pleasantly surprised by the behavior of Souter and Kennedy, who once again demonstrated that one could never predict how an appointee would vote in the future. Much depended upon the personal chemistry inside the Court. As the Rehnquist-Scalia-Thomas faction attempted to drive the Court sharply to the right on many issues, other justices shifted to the center, including Sandra Day O'Connor.

Souter, who firmly rejected the chief justice's cramped version of congressional power, soon broke ranks with him on other issues as well. Kennedy and Souter refused to overrule *Roe v. Wade* when presented with the opportunity in 1992, and they joined to strike down a Colorado initiative that sought to deny homosexuals the right to litigate discrimination claims in the state's courts.[43] In 2003, Kennedy also authored the majority opinion striking down criminal sodomy laws.[44] Joe Rauh's tireless efforts had delayed and frustrated the attempts by Nixon, Reagan, and Bush to reverse the constitutional course charted during the Warren years, but he could not finally turn the conservative tide that reshaped the federal courts and other American institutions after 1968.

CHAPTER TWENTY

THE LIBERAL IN CONSERVATIVE TIMES

Liberalism is not a dirty word.
— JOE RAUH

Defeat and Victory

Rauh had been there before. He had been a liberal in other conservative times. McCarthy once terrorized the Senate. Fred Vinson had led the Supreme Court. Southern racists had controlled Congress. But beginning with Nixon's victory in 1968, confirmed by Reagan's in 1980, there were new, troubling political configurations shaking America, including deep divisions in the old liberal coalition. None pained him more than the growing chasm between Jews and African-Americans over affirmative action programs. The entire political and legal landscape drifted to the right. Mean times for liberals. The word itself became a pejorative, cast off by all but the most dedicated.

The confirmation of Clarence Thomas had sealed the immediate triumph of the conservative counterrevolution against the jurisprudence of the Warren Court. Since 1969 Rauh and his allies in the Leadership Conference, the ADA, NOW, and People for the American Way had delayed that revolution, but they could not turn it back when liberal voices weakened in the White House, the Senate, and the nation. During these same years, against the rising conservative tide, Rauh fought to preserve the civil rights and civil liberties gains of the 1960s, to maintain the historic cross-racial alliances that had supported those advances, to redress the injustice done to Japanese-Americans during World War II, and to keep the liberal flag flying in the Democratic Party. He faced an uphill struggle in the face of forces pulling the party of FDR in the opposite direction.

The bruising confirmation fight over Thomas produced one huge triumph for Rauh and the Leadership Conference when President Bush signed into law the Civil Rights Act of 1991, a statute that reversed twelve previous rulings by Rehnquist's majority on the Supreme Court. A year earlier Bush had vetoed almost identical legislation, but in the wake of the Thomas-Hill imbroglio, congressional Republicans and the president capitulated. The new law placed the burden on employers to justify hiring practices as nondiscriminatory against minorities; prohibited racial and gender discrimination in all phases of employment from hiring to termination; and mandated jury trials for victims of discrimination, including a provision for punitive damages. The number of employment discrimination cases filed by women and minorities tripled under the statute during the next decade.[1]

The Civil Rights Act of 1991 climaxed two decades during which Rauh and his firm waged trench warfare against Republican attempts in the White House, Congress, and the Court to roll back the civil rights revolution. Rauh's firm went to court to block successfully attempts by the Nixon administration to slow down the pace of school desegregation in the South.[2] Led by Rauh and the Leadership Conference, the civil rights forces defeated an attempt by the president and House Republicans in 1970 to water down the 1965 Voting Rights Act by repealing provisions that required southern states to seek approval from the Department of Justice before changing suffrage requirements.

But Rauh found himself aligned with Nixon on a major affirmative action initiative. As part of his War on Poverty, President Johnson had issued an executive order in 1965 requiring all federal contractors and institutions receiving federal funds to take special steps, affirmative action, to recruit and hire more women and racial minorities. Rauh, who had written Roosevelt's original executive order in 1941 banning discrimination in federal contracts, applauded this program and its extension by the Nixon administration with the so-called Philadelphia Plan, which required labor unions subject to federal law to train African-American apprentices and bring them into their organizations.

Some critics argued that the Philadelphia Plan was a cynical attempt on the part of the Nixon administration to sow discord in the ranks of two key Democratic voting blocs, labor and African-Americans. If so, it succeeded. The AFL-CIO leadership pushed an amendment through the Senate in 1969 to cut off appropriations for the plan. Unions affiliated with the Leadership Conference forced the organization to remain on the sidelines when the House took up the issue, and Clarence Mitchell refused to testify against the amendment. Rauh, however, lobbied against it with the active support of the ADA and Nixon's top lawyer, Leonard Garment. They received passive help from Ken Young, the AFL-CIO's chief lobbyist, who confided to Rauh that he supported the Philadelphia Plan even though his bosses did not. The House killed the Senate amendment.[3]

Mr. Affirmative Action

As the Nixon-Watergate era ended, Rauh often broke ranks with many of his old allies over issues that threatened to rip apart the civil rights coalitions that had fought segregation and discrimination for three decades. The Philadelphia Plan exposed sharp divisions between unions and African-Americans inside the Leadership Conference, the split became wider between Jews and African-Americans over affirmative action, and renewal of the Voting Rights Act drove a wedge between African-Americans and Mexican-Americans. Rauh struggled to keep the coalitions together while refusing to compromise his own principles, a balancing act that usually proved difficult to maintain. When the Voting Rights Act came up for its second renewal in 1975, the debate disrupted the civil rights organizations when Hispanic leaders insisted on amendments to combat the systematic discrimination they faced in the Southwest, especially in Texas.

Rauh found himself again aligned against Mitchell and NAACP officials who argued that inclusion of those provisions would dilute enforcement of the 1965 law and make its renewal more difficult. At a rancorous Leadership Conference meeting that Mitchell boycotted, Rauh sided with the Hispanics, but the session became so heated that the organization could not take a position when the legislation reached the House and Senate. Rauh finally testified in the Senate, but only on behalf of the ADA, while Mitchell spoke for the NAACP. Congress passed the renewal with the Hispanic amendments, but deep wounds had been opened in the coalition.[4]

Rauh and Arnold Aaronson, one of the founders of the Leadership Conference, attempted to repair the wreckage left in the wake of the voting rights fight by bringing the two camps together, but the peace conference dissolved into name-calling. Hispanic leaders claimed that the Leadership Conference cared more about the fate of African-Americans and had been dominated too long by their aging spokesmen, Wilkins, Mitchell, and Ben Hooks. Mitchell then launched into a tirade. "Where were you guys when we were dying for the right to vote," he shouted. "You guys could not decide whether you were Caucasians or not," a remark that ended any hope of reconciliation then and inflamed ethnic tensions until African-American and Hispanic leaders found common enemies during the Reagan-Bush years.[5]

Even before the major affirmative action cases such as *DeFunis* and *Bakke* reached the courts, Rauh chastised Jews and Jewish organizations, which, he said, had been "largely on the wrong side of the great civil rights issues of the day." Jews had fought open housing efforts in Forest Hills, New York, and led school boycotts in Brooklyn where they taunted black children about wearing clothes provided by welfare workers. These episodes and others, he told one Milwaukee audience, "disgraced the heritage of those courageous Jews who helped form the NAACP early in this century and participated in all the daring struggles of the blacks right down through the sixties."[6]

Rauh sharply criticized those in the Jewish community who invoked the concept of "quotas" to oppose affirmative action programs such as the Philadelphia Plan. He often reminded Jewish audiences that elite universities such as Harvard once had "real quotas," a fixed ceiling on educational opportunities for Jews. He, too, opposed such restrictive quotas, but it was simply false to equate them to affirmative actions efforts that stressed goals and timetables, "standards for the measurement of progress . . . in overcoming past discrimination."[7]

Only two Jewish organizations joined the brief he wrote with Marian Edelman of the Children's Defense Fund in defense of the University of Washington's affirmative action program for its law school in 1974. "The question here is whether the Court will now take that tool [affirmative action] from the hands of those who have been using it for almost half a decade now. We urge the Court not to do so, and let the progress along this historic path continue." Although the Washington Supreme Court had sustained the program, a bare majority of the justices on the United States Supreme Court ruled the lawsuit moot because the plaintiff had been admitted to another law school and was scheduled to graduate.[8]

No Jewish organization supported Rauh's legal efforts in the *Bakke* case three years later when, in addition to his own brief in support of the medical school admissions program at University of California, Davis, he worked behind the scenes to strengthen the amicus brief initially proposed by officials in the Carter administration, who attacked the Davis program as a quota system and failed to meet the claims of opponents that it violated both the Fourteenth Amendment and the Civil Rights Act of 1964. Disillusioned when he read a purloined copy of the administration brief, Rauh urged Mitchell and Nat Jones, general counsel for the NAACP, to put pressure on solicitor general Wade McCree and HEW secretary Joe Califano through the Black Caucus in the House of Representatives. After Califano told the president that the proposed brief was "bad law and pernicious social policy," Rauh and Jones were able to channel their suggestions to McCree and his staff. The administration's revised brief did not condemn the Davis set-aside of sixteen out of one hundred seats in the first-year class, but endorsed what it called "minority-sensitive" admissions plans.

Rauh's intervention, coupled with a strong oral argument by McCree and Archibald Cox, who represented the university, helped to save affirmative action in higher education. Justice Lewis Powell crafted a narrow opinion for the five-to-four majority that ordered Allan Bakke's admission and struck down the rigid set-aside, but endorsed the use of race as one of the factors that academic institutions could consider in seeking a diversified student body to promote a more robust educational environment. Many critics on the right and left condemned Powell's hair-splitting, but Rauh counted it a major victory that kept affirmative action alive in a critical sector of American life.[9]

In the same year the Court decided *Bakke,* a group of American Nazis prepared to march through the village of Skokie, Illinois, a heavily Jewish suburb where many survivors of the Holocaust lived. Local officials adopted ordinances and secured a court injunction to ban the Nazis' demonstrations until the American Civil Liberties Union successfully overturned them in state and federal court. Rauh faced an agonizing choice between his devotion to the ACLU and the First Amendment and his contempt for the Nazis, but he finally signed a letter in support of the organization, whose lead attorney in the Skokie case was David Goldberger. So doing, he called down the wrath of his old mentor, Ben Cohen, normally a stout civil libertarian, who denounced the ACLU, the judicial decisions favoring it, and Rauh's endorsement.[10]

Redress

Rauh often tangled with Jewish leaders and organizations over affirmative action and civil liberties in the 1970s and 1980s, but he counted many of them on his side, including the Anti-Defamation League, in the long and frustrating struggle to gain financial reparations for Japanese-Americans sent to relocation camps during the war. Since 1942, when he and others failed to find a compromise between those demanding relocation and those resisting even a curfew, Rauh had carried a heavy burden of responsibility for the fate of the internees. He began to discharge this emotional debt beginning in the 1950s when he worked with the Japanese American Citizens League (JACL) representatives on the Leadership Council.

Through the JACL he agreed to represent more than 4,000 Japanese-American claimants whose certificates of deposit in a Japanese-owned bank had been confiscated by the United States government during the war under the Trading with the Enemy Act. The Rauh firm won a major victory for their clients at the Supreme Court when the justices ruled for an equitable tolling of the statute of limitations and ordered millions of dollars refunded to the depositor-claimants. Before the justices he prevailed in oral argument against the advocate for the Solicitor General's Office, future appeals court judge Richard Posner.[11]

Throughout the 1970s and 1980s he outlined various legal strategies for securing reversal of the infamous Supreme Court decision in *Korematsu v. United States* that had sanctioned exclusion, and he endorsed the creation of the Commission on Wartime Relocation and Internment of Civilians (CWRIC), which finally recommended redress legislation to Congress in 1983. The CWRIC proposals included a joint resolution of apology from Congress, presidential pardons for persons convicted under the evacuation orders and statutes, and a one-time payment of $20,000 to each survivor who had been sent to a relocation camp. But legislation to implement those recommendations languished in Congress until 1988 due largely to a penny-pinching Congress and opposition from the Reagan administration.

"Nothing can ever adequately compensate the Japanese-Americans for the wrongs done them," Rauh told a House subcommittee in 1986, "but we can demonstrate that a great nation can recognize and give recompense for the severest blow it ever inflicted upon the civil liberties of its people and thus give new vitality to its commitment to civil freedom." Two years later, although his own Justice Department still testified against the legislation, Reagan suddenly came out in favor of the redress bill, known as the Civil Liberties Act, which he signed into law.[12]

Despite passionate testimony from Rauh, Eugene Rostow, members of the CWRIC, and others, Congress refused to authorize payments in either 1988 or 1989. "I thought my 1986 testimony on redress would be the last," he told Congressman Neal Smith's subcommittee, "and I am deeply saddened that there should be this new appropriations roadblock." More eligible internees would die while Congress continued to deny funding. "This is a matter of national integrity."[13]

Seven months after Rauh's testimony, President George Herbert Walker Bush, shot down by the Japanese as a young navy pilot in the Pacific War, signed an appropriations bill authorizing redress payments. And on October 9, 1990, nearly a half century after the relocation began, attorney general Richard Thornburgh presented the first checks to a few of the oldest internment survivors. Rauh could not recall a finer day in Washington.[14]

With McGovern

Rauh loved the party that FDR built, but few Democrats escaped his criticism when they departed from what he regarded as true liberalism. Truman's loyalty-security program drew his unrelenting opposition. He pilloried the

Johnson-Rayburn leadership on civil rights during the Eisenhower years, and Kennedy received similar negative reviews prior to Birmingham. He deserted Johnson over Vietnam. Even his closest friends were not immune to attack. When Senator Tom Eagleton supported legislation to restrict school busing in desegregation cases, Rauh condemned the effort as "walking on quicksand" because the Missouri senator "seemed to be siding with the segregationists on this issue."[15]

The 1970s and 1980s tested his loyalty to the party, as many of its leading presidential candidates and congressional leaders tacked to the right in response to the Nixon-Reagan victories that signaled a public weary of New Deal–Fair Deal–New Frontier–Great Society liberalism. Vietnam and the 1968 election left deep wounds within the ADA and the liberal movement, as many party leaders blamed McCarthy and his supporters for Humphrey's defeat and the resurrection of Nixon. The Chicago convention debacle, however, contained seeds of a potent liberal resurgence, a resolution of its Special Equal Rights Committee.

That resolution mandated that each delegation to future national conventions be broadly representative of the state's racial, ethnic, and gender demography. Rauh had pushed for that standard as early as 1964 when he served as counsel to the original equal rights committee. The party codified Rauh's vision in 1972 when it adopted the recommendations of a commission headed by Senator George McGovern and Congressman Don Fraser. By the 1980s, thanks in part to Rauh's efforts, the proportion of African-Americans at national conventions rose from 5 percent to 15 percent, Hispanics from less than 1 percent to 4 percent, and women from 13 percent to over 40 percent. Both the party's 1972 platform and candidate, McGovern, represented the high tide of post–New Deal liberalism.

The Rauh-McGovern relationship went back to the South Dakotan's days in the House of Representatives, when Humphrey brought his Maryland neighbor over to the Rauhs' home one evening. After they departed, Rauh's sister-in-law, Grace, unmoved by Humphrey's volubility, remarked: "I like the other one better." Dismayed by Humphrey's increasingly conservative rhetoric, Rauh signed on with McGovern's campaign for the presidency in 1972 when the scandal at Chapaquiddick in 1969 destroyed Ted Kennedy's bid and after flirting briefly with a possible run by John Lindsay, the former mayor of New York City, who had switched his party allegiance to the Democrats. Lindsay, who had been a young lawyer in Beth Webster's firm, had worked with Rauh in the Remington case. His campaign collapsed in the 1972 Florida primary, however, when ex–New Yorkers took their revenge for his crisis-ridden administration.[16]

McGovern owed his first-ballot victory at the 1972 convention to Rauh's legal strategy that defeated Humphrey's attempt to reverse the results of the crucial California primary vote, which McGovern had won handily. Under existing California law the contest had been winner-take-all, a formula that Rauh opposed because it conflicted with the party's reform agenda, but he defended it when Humphrey, who had previously endorsed the formula, changed his mind and decided to challenge McGovern's 271 delegates, enough to give him the nomination at the Miami convention. Rauh headed McGovern's legal team before the party's credential committee, where Burke Marshall, a former assistant attorney general in the Kennedy administration, took testimony on the California challenge and upheld McGovern's victory on the simple theory that you do not change the rules after the game has been played. The full committee, however, chaired by Patricia Harris, voted to split the California vote among the seven candidates, which left McGovern well short of a first-ballot victory.

At the heated meeting at McGovern's home on the Sunday before the convention opened, Rauh argued for an immediate appeal to the federal courts to block the credentials committee's decision, a solution the candidate finally endorsed. Rauh and his legal team filed appropriate papers that afternoon with district judge George L. Hart Jr., and he argued the case a day later against Joe Califano, counsel for the party's national committee. Hart expressed sympathy for McGovern's cause, but refused to intervene on the grounds that the court lacked jurisdiction to meddle in the internal affairs of a political party. "It might not be cricket to change the rules," Clark said. "It might even be dirty pool, but is it unconstitutional?"[17]

On Independence Day, Rauh faced Califano again before an emergency session of the Court of Appeals for the District of Columbia, where a three-judge panel of David Bazelon, Charlie Fay, and George MacKinnon heard his plea to stay the decision of the credentials committee. Fay, an old New Dealer but a notorious hawk on the Vietnam War, expressed hostility to Rauh's arguments, but MacKinnon, a Minnesota Republican who had been nominated by Nixon, joined Bazelon in an opinion affirming judicial relief and striking down the credential committee's decision. Califano immediately appealed to the Supreme Court.[18]

Rauh's heart sank when news leaked from the Supreme Court that Chief Justice Burger opposed holding oral argument and hoped to overturn the appeals court. Justices Douglas, Marshall, and White resisted Burger, but lacked a fourth vote from Brennan, who refused to leave Nantucket, where he stood vigil over his ailing wife. Without Brennan, Burger won the battle inside the Court with a short *per curiam* opinion that stayed the court of appeals pending a future decision on the merits by the Supreme Court. That became moot when the Democrats gathered in Miami, where the full convention, influenced by Rauh and others, overturned the credentials committee and gave McGovern all of California's delegates.

Rauh lobbied many delegations to secure votes for McGovern prior to the convention vote, including Missouri's, where he spent considerable time persuading Senator Tom Eagleton to back his position on the California challenge. He applauded McGovern's initial decision to tap Eagleton as his vice presidential running mate and became furious when the South Dakotan made the feckless decision to drop Eagleton from the ticket after it was disclosed that the latter had twice undergone shock treatment for depression. But Rauh's influence could not match the panic generated by the Eagleton disclosure among McGovern's chief fund-raisers and harsh attacks leveled against the Missouri senator by journalists such as Jimmy Wechsler.[19]

The Eagleton debacle did not prove decisive in the end as Nixon carried every state except Massachusetts and the District of Columbia by a larger margin than Johnson in 1964. The most broadly based Democratic National Convention in history had sent forth its most progressive candidate with an ultraliberal platform, but suffered a stinging rebuke from an electorate increasingly polarized over issues of race, gender, and war. The 1972 defeat hastened the party's resolute march to the right side of the political spectrum and blocked Rauh's renewed efforts to prevent that steady drift to conservatism. Even as the Nixon administration crumbled under the weight of Watergate and as his successor, Gerald Ford, stumbled through a series of economic crises, the leaders of Rauh's party lowered the flag of liberalism. They ousted McGovern's national chairwoman, Jean Westwood of California, and replaced her with Texas businessman Robert Strauss, an old ally of Texas governor John Connally. Strauss found a perfect candidate for 1976 in former Georgia governor Jimmy Carter, a onetime supporter of George Wallace who had become enamored more recently with Dr. King. That ideological trajectory raised Rauh's suspicions and his vigorous opposition.

Rauh versus Carter

On the eve of the ADA annual convention in 1975, without a Kennedy, Humphrey, or McGovern in the race, chairman Leon Shull proposed that the organization invite all the leading candidates to a special session where they would make a prepared speech and meet the membership. Rauh agreed to the format and secured the participation of three candidates, former Oklahoma senator Fred Harris; Terry Sanford, former governor of North Carolina and president of Duke University; and his own favorite, Moe Udall, the Arizona congressman. All three expressed some hesitation about appearing before the ADA, but they came on a Friday night, made their speeches, and answered questions from the audience. Carter, although invited with the others, declined to appear that evening. He turned up on Saturday night, however, as the ADA members downed cocktails and prepared for dinner. Vice chairman Don Fraser pulled Rauh aside and announced that Carter would make a speech.

"The hell he will," Rauh exploded. "We had an agreement. I gave my word to the other guys that everyone would have a chance to speak last night."

Fraser protested that he knew nothing of the agreement and that it would be impolite not to let Carter say a few words. Rauh relented, but in his load baritone made his displeasure known to all. "He [Carter] didn't come when we invited him, and we don't want to hear him. I'm not in favor of breaking the ground rules for anyone, but especially not for a Wallace-ite!"[20]

The Rauh-Carter relationship never fully recovered from that first encounter. When Rauh and his wife met Andy Young, the future U.N. ambassador, outside Ford's Theatre following Carter's surprise victory in the Iowa caucuses, Dr. King's former aide announced that he and other African-American leaders were going to get the nomination for Carter.

"What does he stand for?" Olie Rauh asked, tartly.

"I haven't the vaguest idea," Young responded, but noted that two-thirds of the African-American doctors and lawyers in America had been trained in Atlanta and were now mobilized for Carter, enough to erase the old stigma of supporting Wallace.[21]

On the eve of the national convention that nominated him, Carter and his chief advisers raised the level of vitriol. Carter reminded reporters of the ADA incident and affirmed that he didn't "feel at home" with the liberals in the organization. "I don't understand Joe Rauh," he added, "and he doesn't understand me." Jody Powell, the candidate's press spokesman, snapped that "if Joe Rauh wants to come to the White House, let him take the public tour."[22]

When the Carter-Ford race tightened in the fall, however, Carter briefly changed his mind about Rauh and the ADA. Pressured by NBC president Bob Kintner, whose relationship with Rauh went back to the 1940s, Carter attempted to secure the support of the ADA's vice president with a phone call late at night. Rauh at first thought it was a crank call until Carter said, "I've known and admired your work for a long time. I think you are a great American. I'm sorry about what's happened in the past and I want to let bygones be bygones. I need your help and I hope you will help me."

Rauh told Carter that he would be eager to talk "any time that is conve-
nient for you . . . any place, any time, if that is your wish." He urged Carter
to arrange such a meeting through his staff and assured him that "as far as
I'm concerned there will be no press knowledge of this." But neither Carter
nor his key aides followed up on that conversation. Carter wanted Rauh's endorsement without a discussion; Rauh would not campaign without one. In
November he worked only for congressional candidates and cast an absentee
vote for Carter while visiting the Soviet Union. Olie Rauh reversed the
names on her Carter-Mondale bumper sticker and left her presidential ballot unmarked.[23]

The next four years intensified the feud. Rauh testified against Griffin
Bell, Carter's friend and nominee to become attorney general, who had sat on
the federal appeals court from 1961 to 1976. Rauh recalled that Bell had
given "a lyrical endorsement" to Harold Carswell and displayed on the bench
"a lack of sensitivity to the rights of blacks, other minorities and women." Bell,
he concluded, "gave aid and comfort to the segregationists of this country."[24]

Carter's presidency fared little better. He launched a domestic program
with much fanfare touted as "New Foundations," but Rauh ridiculed it at the
1977 ADA convention as little more than "the conservative doctrine of
donothingism dressed up in five-dollar words. It's not a New Deal, or a Fair
Deal, or even a Square Deal. It's a Bum Deal for the nation." A year later,
writing "Who Says Liberalism Is Dead" for the *Washington Post,* he argued
that the hardest time for men and women of his convictions came "when
there is a middle-of-the-road Democrat in the White House" who creates "a
sort of no-man's land with maximum uncertainty as to whom is doing what to
whom."[25] At its 1979 convention, with Rauh leading the charge, the ADA declared that Carter had "ignored the principles that are at the very heart of the
historic commitment of the Democratic Party," and that his record was one
of "broken promises and abandoned principles . . . conservative domestic
policies and Republican Party economic programs."[26] He told Montgomery
County Democrats, "We do not need a second 'does nothing' party in the
White House. . . . We want to put the Democratic Party back together again
and Ted Kennedy is the man to get us moving toward that goal." When
Kennedy announced he would challenge Carter for the nomination, Rauh
jumped on board his campaign.[27]

Bolting the Party

Rauh had fought Humphrey's attempt in 1972 to strip McGovern of pledged
primary delegates, but in 1980 he helped to organize a last-ditch effort to re-

lease similar delegates from their primary obligation to Carter. Accused of
hypocrisy by the president's supporters, he argued that Carter now demanded a new convention rule binding all delegates, one never considered
or formally adopted by the party. He lost a spirited debate on that issue before the convention rules committee dominated by Carter's troops. His
hopes blasted, Kennedy withdrew as a candidate ninety minutes before the
convention opened. On the night Democrats crowned Carter again to face
former California governor Reagan in the fall, Rauh and seventy-five other
disillusioned refugees from Madison Square Garden met across town at a
private club to hear Mary Crisp, the former co-chair of the Republican Party,
urge them to support Illinois congressman John Anderson, who had announced his independent campaign.

Unlike many others who had backed Kennedy's abortive challenge, Rauh
did not hesitate to join Anderson, who had built a liberal record on abortion,
civil liberties, gun control and the reduction of nuclear weapons, despite his
conservative district. "I am 70 years old," Rauh told reporters, "and I have
never voted for anyone but a Democrat in a presidential election in my life.
I'm a little tired of Democrats and Republicans. I think Anderson is simply
the best candidate." Then he added, "I'd rather support a man who is moving to the left than a man who moves in circles."[28]

He raised money for Anderson, spoke on his behalf, and tried to block an
ADA endorsement of Carter when the leadership, headed by Patsy Mink,
Winn Newman, and Leon Schull, argued that the president needed all the
support he could muster against Reagan. That did not persuade Rauh and
Schlesinger, who told the ADA board that backing Carter "would undermine
ADA's credibility [and] demonstrate that we never really meant what we said
about him these past four years." At the most acrimonious board meeting
since the Vietnam era, Rauh and Schlesinger lost the fight when Mink, Newman, and Schull rounded up a bare majority for Carter, but 43 percent of the
board voted for no endorsement. Schlesinger became so furious over the result that he drafted a letter of resignation and was about to post it until Rauh
cooled him down.[29]

When he read the organization's press release endorsing Carter, Rauh
told Schull it constituted a "sell out to Carter and the Democratic Party. . . .
but nothing matches the obscenity of the statement . . . that Carter 'has often
promoted our domestic agenda . . . and pursued a generally enlightened foreign policy.'" He had kept many people from resigning from the ADA, he
concluded, "but I am beginning to wonder why."[30]

On election night, when Reagan buried both Carter and Anderson in a landslide, Rauh served as toastmaster at a cheerless Anderson headquarters. When Anderson floated the idea a year later of mounting a third party, Rauh demurred on the grounds that it would be impossible to yoke together his fiscal conservatism with his liberal stand on issues such as abortion and gun control. "I supported your candidacy in 1980 despite that incongruity because of your granite-like integrity and because you and your views appeared more likely to move America forward," he told Anderson, "but I cannot see building a new party on that incongruity."[31]

"Liberalism Is Not a Dirty Word"

The Reagan tidal wave in 1980 also ended the Senate career of McGovern in South Dakota, the bitterest defeat of the evening for Rauh because it symbolized the rout of liberalism. The 1980 election and the ADA's endorsement of Carter also marked a turning point in his long relationship to the mainstream of the Democratic Party and the liberal organization he had helped to found in 1948. Reagan's reelection in 1984 and George Bush's defeat of Massachusetts governor Michael Dukakis four years later hastened the party's rush to the right-center of the political spectrum. The ADA, once the voice of dissent and opposition even in the Democratic Party, became little more than an adjunct of the party, held hostage to the labor unions who kept it solvent. "The trouble with ADA," he complained to Schlesinger, "is that it is in the pocket of the Democratic Party and the labor movement, whereas I thought it ought to be independent, critical, and out front, of both."[32]

Rauh did not attend another ADA board meeting until 1984, when he rose up to oppose its mechanical endorsement of Walter Mondale, whom he regarded as the most conservative candidate in a field that included Jesse Jackson, Colorado senator Gary Hart, California senator Alan Cranston, and McGovern. "If ADA is true to its role of liberalism," he told the board, "it will endorse from the left, or it won't endorse at all." That drew a bitter response from Barney Frank, leading the Mondale supporters. "If this is therapy, then vote for McGovern," he said. "If you're trying to elect a president, then vote for Walter Mondale."[33] Rauh lost the vote for no endorsement before the primaries, when the other candidates failed to combine to stop Mondale. Four years later, when candidate Dukakis declared during one debate with George Bush that the election should focus on "competence, not ideology," Rauh rebuked him. "Liberalism is not a dirty word," he told a reporter, "but Dukakis made a tragic mistake when he denied being a liberal. . . . If a liberal presidential candidate runs away from the word, why shouldn't others?"[34]

Dukakis hid from the liberal label, but Rauh cast his last presidential ballot for him anyway as he had done for Mondale four years before. Shortly before his death, he favored Tom Harkin of Iowa, a feisty Midwestern liberal in the tradition of the young Hubert Humphrey. He expressed skepticism about Al From, the Democratic Leadership Conference, and the governor of Arkansas, Bill Clinton, who became the party's nominee in 1992. Clinton's "new Democrat" rhetoric, he complained, sounded too similar to the "New Foundations" slogans touted by another former southern governor.

CHAPTER TWENTY-ONE

CLOSING ARGUMENT

They [the Canadians] were made guinea pigs in hazardous
experiments funded with $60,000 of CIA money.
— JOE RAUH TO WILLIAM WEBSTER

Elder Liberal Statesman

By 1992 he could not display them all—the plaques, the parchment scrolls,
the medallions—tributes to the man some called "the personal embodiment
of American liberalism," or "the liberals' elder statesman" or "one of the last
New Dealers." To make room on the wall of his study for the new awards
would have meant taking down too many other treasures, photographs of
Cardozo, Frankfurter, and Dr. King, even one with Lyndon Johnson. So the
awards kept arriving, but usually were left in boxes, seldom displayed, much
as he had kept secret his class ranking at Harvard Law School.

In retirement, Rauh had no desire to become an aging liberal icon, the
passive recipient of accolades. He moved his activities from downtown Far-
ragut Square to a small upstairs office on Appleton Street. The new venue
did not significantly diminish his zeal for preaching the liberal gospel or reduce his active engagement in causes that remained close to his heart. He labored tirelessly to create and sustain a new law school in the District, affiliated initially with Antioch College, a school he hoped would both recruit
lower-income students and train lawyers with a social conscience. When Antioch abandoned the project for financial reasons, he provided the vision and
energy to realize the dream of the District of Columbia School of Law as a
member of its board of governors. "Heaven knows there ought to be at least
one law school which trains lawyers to represent the poor," he reasoned.[1]

Before he stepped down as general counsel to the Leadership Conference in the spring of 1991 and formally passed that baton on to Ralph Neas, he remained active in the confirmation fights against Bork, Ginsburg, Kennedy, Souter, and Thomas. His voice rang out in support of financial redress for Japanese-Americans, in support of the Americans with Disabilities Act of 1989, which extended civil rights protection to 43 million Americans, and for the Civil Rights Act of 1991 that rebuked the Rehnquist-led Supreme Court.[2] Historians and political scientists, most of them baby boomers with little firsthand memory of events before the 1960s, arrived at his office and became the beneficiaries of his wit and wisdom about FDR, Frankfurter, Tommy the Cork, Reuther, Randolph, Humphrey, Kennedy, King, and LBJ.

In 1988 he made a New Year's resolution to stop sending opinion pieces to the *Washington Post's* editor-in-chief, Meg Greenfield, because "my rejection rate . . . hardly warrants the effort I have to put into writing." Three years earlier, Greenfield had refused to publish as too "offensive" his attack on the Senate confirmation of Ed Meese, Reagan's choice to become attorney general. Washington's major paper, he believed, had strayed far from the influence of Phil Graham and the robust civil liberties views of writers like Alan Barth. He blamed Greenfield's "ideological trip" for the newspaper's "swing to the right" that made life increasingly difficult for "the very people, organizations and issues you [the *Post*] once espoused."[3]

At the same time, he endured the usual attacks from conservatives who called him a "knee-jerk liberal." And he suffered the occasional barbs fired by journalists such as Victor Navasky at the *Nation,* who continued to fight the ideological battles of the McCarthy era. Navasky called him "the quintessential anti-communist liberal," a pejorative label, but one that Rauh wore proudly.[4]

Brainwashing, CIA Style

Apart from rescuing the District of Columbia School of Law, Rauh devoted the final years of his life to a case begun in 1979–80 on behalf of nine Canadian citizens who had been subjected during the height of the Cold War to devastating CIA-initiated brainwashing experiments at the Allan Memorial Institute at McGill University in Montreal. This epic legal battle, formally known as *Orlikow v. United States,*[5] equaled in complexity, length, and public significance any in his long career as a civil liberties lawyer. *Orlikow* became his closing argument on behalf of liberalism, his final pursuit of individual justice in a life devoted to that ideal.

When David Orlikow, a member of the Canadian Parliament, asked Rauh and his firm to begin a civil action on behalf of his wife Velma in 1979, he told a story to rival John Frankenheimer's 1962 Cold War fantasy *The Manchurian Candidate*. But Velma Orlikow and fifty-three other Canadians had been victimized by the Central Intelligence Agency of the United States of America, not sinister Communist agents in Red China and the Soviet Union. The CIA had paid for and promoted experiments by Dr. D. Ewen Cameron at McGill University on human beings, experiment that included intensive electroshocks to the brain, injections of lysergic acid diethylamide (LSD), and "psychic driving," a procedure in which tape-recorded messages were played hundreds of thousands of times.

Velma Orlikow and the other Canadians went to the McGill psychiatrist hoping to receive treatment for maladies ranging from depression, anxiety, and alcoholism to chronic leg pain. Dr. Cameron and his CIA sponsors had another, less healthy agenda: brainwashing experiments with funds from the "Society for the Investigation of Human Ecology," a CIA front based at Cornell University Medical School in New York City. One plaintiff, Louis Weinstein, a successful Montreal businessman, received from Cameron intensive electroshock and LSD, months of sensory isolation and psychic driving, and long periods of drug-induced sleep. Rita Zimmerman, who came to Cameron seeking treatment for alcoholism, received thirty electroshock sessions that produced incontinence of the bowel, in addition to almost two months of drug-induced sleep. Florence Langleben, suffering from anxiety attacks, was given LSD and intensive electroshock and some forty-three days of drug-induced sleep.

These and other stories from Cameron's records confirmed earlier revelations of massive CIA abuses at home and abroad documented by the 1975 Rockefeller Commission and the Senate Intelligence Committee. Its chairman, Frank Church, had branded the agency "a rogue elephant." The CIA's specific brainwashing program, code-named MKULTRA, had been initiated in 1953 by the head of its Operations Directorate, Richard Helms, with the approval of then director Allan Dulles, who ordered the effort mounted without "the usual contractual arrangements," highly "compartmented," and with "exacting control . . . maintained . . . by TSS [Technical Services Section]." But as journalist John Marks and his researchers discovered and as Rauh and his colleagues would further expose in discovery efforts over the next several years, the MKULTRA activities of Dr. Cameron resembled a "rogue elephant," not the "exacting control" mandated by Mr. Dulles.[6]

Dr. Cameron's pseudotreatments, condemned by the eminent psychiatrists Leon Salzman and Robert Jay Lifton, violated the Nuremberg Code in failing to protect the health and welfare of patients, and ignored the rule of "informed consent" for brainwashing experiments. Cameron's experiments alone offered the possibility of holding the CIA negligent under the Federal Tort Claims Act. But, in addition, further acts of commission and omission had been committed by two CIA agents, Sidney Gottlieb and Robert Lashbrook, who ran the MKULTRA program, approved Camerson's grant, paid his bills, but also failed to monitor his activities.

Based on the agency's own internal investigation, the Church committee concluded that Gottlieb and Lashbrook had been responsible in 1953 for the death of Dr. Frank Olson, an army chemical and biological warfare expert. Olson had been given LSD surreptitiously, suffered severe depression, and fell to his death from a tenth-story room at the New York Statler Hotel that he shared with Lashbrook. The agency's general counsel, Lawrence Houston, called Olson's death "culpable negligence" by those in charge of MKULTRA. The CIA's own inspector general in 1957 condemned the same activities as "professionally unethical . . . unorthodox . . . and in some instances border[ing] on the illegal."[7]

Given the CIA's lamentable record already in the public domain by 1979, including admission of Frank Olson's death, one might have expected a quick settlement to a civil action by Velma Orlikow and eight others whose lives had been ruined by Dr. Cameron. When Rauh filed administrative claims as required by the Federal Tort Claims Act before bringing suit, the agency's general counsel, Daniel B. Silver, reaffirmed that the spy agency would not "shirk responsibility for the unfortunate acts that occurred in the course of the MKULTRA program." Silver also denounced the research carried on at McGill by the late Dr. Cameron as "repugnant."

Changing the Guard

Reagan's presidency changed the guard at the CIA. By 1980 the new president had turned up the heat on the Cold War and installed William Casey as director of Central Intelligence with a mandate to use whatever means necessary to prevail over the nation's Communist adversaries. That year, too, the Supreme Court ruled that a former CIA agent, Frank Snepp, violated the terms of his employment by failing to clear his book manuscript with the agency, although he had disclosed no classified information.

Larry Houston and Daniel Silver in the agency's office of legal counsel had voiced distress at the lawlessness of the past, but Casey and those who now headed the CIA's Operations Directorate declined to compromise. The ethical values of Richard Helms, who had lied to a Senate committee in the early 1970s and then bargained his offense down to "refusal to answer," again dominated Reagan's Central Intelligence Agency. The CIA refused to settle with Mrs. Orlikow and the other Canadians. The agency, it claimed, bore no legal responsibility for what had taken place at McGill because it had not initiated Dr. Cameron's experiments, a defense soon exposed as fallacious.

But Rauh and his colleagues initially underestimated the ferocity of CIA resistance, the hostility of the Canadian government under prime minister Brian Mulroney, which supported the Reagan administration's delaying tactics, and the sheer incompetence of federal district judge John Garrett Penn, whose refusal to rule on motions in a timely fashion aided the CIA. Two years elapsed between the initial filings and the first depositions, because the agency refused to allow discovery while Penn pondered for a year its unmeritorious motion for summary judgment.[8] Nor did Rauh anticipate the stubbornness of David Orlikow, bent on political gain, who had initiated the case of behalf of his wife.

Once Penn threw out the CIA's motion for summary judgment in January 1988, Rauh and his partner Jim Turner hit a gold mine of CIA culpability. They put John Gittinger under oath in Norman, Oklahoma. As the chief assistant to Gottlieb and Lashbrook and the actual project manager of MKUL-TRA, Gittinger admitted that he initiated contact with Dr. Cameron after reading one of his articles in the *American Journal of Psychiatry* in 1957. From that point forward, Gittinger admitted under oath, he had orchestrated Camerson's grant application to the Society for Human Ecology and made certain Gottlieb and Lashbrook secured funding from the CIA. Gittinger's deposition destroyed a basic CIA defense.

Not all depositions proved so productive, thanks in part to Judge Penn, who usually genuflected every time the agency uttered the magic words "national security." The CIA finally agreed to produce former director Richard Helms for a deposition. They deployed a team of four lawyers to protect "the man who kept the secrets" from interrogation by seventy-seven-year-old Rauh, then leaning somewhat unsteadily on a cane. The agency insisted the deposition of Helms continue for eight hours without any break for rest or food. The next morning, after Rauh and Turner had received a copy of the deposition, agency lawyers filed a motion with Penn to suppress portions of it on the grounds that Helms had made a serious security breach during the interrogation.

Neither Rauh nor Turner had the slightest idea what slip Helms might have made, but they soon received a letter from the CIA informing them they could be prosecuted for espionage if they failed to hand over the deposition. Rauh could not recall a worse example of official intimidation. "I've often fought the U.S. government," he told a reporter later. "I fought the loy-

alty oaths, the McCarthy stuff, Arthur Miller and Lillian Hellman. Compared to this, they were rather simple. They had parameters, there was some
stage when it was clear where you were going."[9]

Smoking Gun

Using civil discovery and Canada's version of the Freedom of Information
Act, Rauh and Turner soon learned that sometime in the late 1970s CIA
officers in Canada had tendered an official apology to the Canadian government. When they attempted to confirm this damaging evidence by deposing
the former CIA chief of station and his successor in Ottawa, the agency filed
motions to bar this testimony on grounds that it would compromise national
security. Judge Penn, criticized by the administrator of the federal courts for
his dilatory behavior, ruled on these motions after a long delay and finally upheld the agency's national security claim. The Canadian government abetted
the cover-up. It bowed to CIA lawyers and prohibited the chief of its own intelligence service from identifying the source of the American apology. At
the same time, the Canadians admitted that such an apology had been made.

A more serious blow to national sovereignty is difficult to imagine, but the
Canadian government under Mulroney consistently aided the CIA's delaying
tactics in a case involving the physical and emotional abuse of its own citizens. The Canadians refused to bring a complaint before the International
Court of Justice. Canada's external affairs minister, Joe Clark, did not raise
the issue with secretary of state George Shultz until 1984. Even then, Clark
refused to meet with Rauh. He later dispatched two of Canada's top government lawyers—Mark Jewett and Lewis Davis—to meet with their CIA counterparts in addition to Rauh and Turner. The Canadian lawyers turned over
many of their investigative files. The CIA, however, gave Jewett and Davis
only an oral briefing at which one of the agency's attorneys denounced the
brainwashing charges as "a red herring." Finally, facing allegations that it had
also funded Cameron's experiments, the Mulroney government sponsored
an "independent study" of the brainwashing accusations by a former member of the Tory government, John Cooper.

Cooper's report absolved the Canadian government of any role with
Cameron and attempted to vindicate the CIA by repeating the "red herring"
charges made by the agency's own counsel. The report's conclusions denied
that Cameron had inflicted physical or psychological injury (without inter-
viewing the plaintiffs or reviewing their medical records), but it recommended that Canada make *ex gratia* payments of $100,000 to each of Rauh's
plaintiffs. Lawyers in the Canadian Department of Justice reduced this

figure to $20,000, the same paltry sum offered by the CIA. Rauh's clients turned down the offer once Judge Penn ruled against the agency's motion for summary judgment.

Despite Penn's ruling, the CIA attempted to avoid discovery and an immediate trial date by invoking an obscure section of the U.S. Code that provided for an "interlocutory appeal" of the district court's decision *prior* to trial. This ploy consumed more weeks of brief writing and argument before the Court of Appeals for the District of Columbia denied the agency's motion. Then, two weeks before a June 1988 trial date, Judge Penn found reason to delay the opening. "Damn," Rauh wrote, "the Judge postponed the trial again—till October."[10]

Dear Bill

By the time of Penn's last delay, Rauh knew he did not have the physical stamina for a trial and turned over leadership of the case to Turner, who drew support from others in the old firm, Elliott Lichtman and Mary Levy. By then, too, one of the plaintiffs had died and others remained in serious financial straits. Rauh faced a difficult choice: Should he pursue another avenue for settlement that would immediately benefit his clients or wage a public trial that might dramatically vindicate the public interest? He chose the first course with a personal letter to the new head of the CIA, William Webster, a former federal judge in Missouri and past director of the FBI. He barely knew Webster, although they had met on a few social occasions in Washington. When he raised the idea of writing to Webster with Turner, Lichtman, and Levy, they raised an immediate ethical objection that such correspondence had to be channeled through the CIA's lawyers. But Rauh pointed out that he had ceased to be counsel of record for the Canadians. A personal letter to Webster, he believed, would not cross the line of legal ethics, a position endorsed by his son, Carl, a former United States attorney, who floated the idea with his previous employers. Much to their surprise, United States attorney Jay Stephens both encouraged a letter to Webster and hinted that his office favored a settlement, despite the vehement opposition of their legal counterparts at the CIA.[11]

Rauh's letter to Webster broke the stalemate. In seven concise, passionate pages he reviewed for Webster the horrors visited upon the Canadians by Cameron. "Instead of the expected medical treatment, they were made guinea pigs in hazardous experiments funded with $60,000 of CIA money. In various ways and to various degrees, these experiments adversely affected the course of their lives. . . . None can function normally and all lead lives shattered by these experiments." Drawing upon depositions and internal CIA documents, he quoted the agency's own lawyers who had called Cameron's project "repugnant" and doubted that "any meaningful form of consent . . . [was] involved in this case." He also cited former CIA director Admiral Stansfield Turner, who had denounced the entire MKULTRA program before Congress as "totally abhorrent."[12]

Rauh's letter stirred Webster's thinking, but did not bring an immediate positive response from the CIA's new chief, who acknowledged that he knew about the case only by reputation "and the representations made to me." The CIA contributed funding to the Cameron project, he admitted, but the research itself "was not in any way under the Agency's control," a conclusion consistent with the CIA's long-held defense, but flatly contradicted by the overwhelming weight of the evidence.[13] Two weeks later, however, Webster told Rauh that he had instructed the CIA's general counsel Russell Bruemmer "to meet with you and explore the available alternatives," a task Rauh quickly turned over to Turner and Lichtman, who concluded a settlement agreement that secured over $100,000 for each of the surviving Canadian plaintiffs.[14]

Judge Penn was about to sign off on the agreement—the largest financial settlement ever won from the Central Intelligence Agency—when Rauh's team encountered reluctance on the part of Orlikow. Turner speculated that this hesitation arose from the pending Canadian elections in November 1988, when Orlikow's party, the New Democrats, hoped to gain ground against Mulroney and the Conservatives. Publicity from a public trial might aid in that effort, especially in Orlikow's own Winnipeg constituency, where his party had not run well in the past. For two weeks in early October, Rauh negotiated constantly with Orlikow over the telephone, first securing his backing for the settlement, later learning that the Canadian had pressured other plaintiffs not to settle, and finally, receiving a plaintive thank-you and acceptance message on his answering machine.[15]

In November 1992, four years after Orlikow relented and the CIA settled, the Canadian government finally lived up to its responsibilities by agreeing to pay eighty of the former patients at Dr. Cameron's institute $80,000 apiece. "It's a sad episode that happened more than 30 years ago, and the case is closed," said a spokesman for the CIA. The agency, he added, had "nothing to add concerning the decision in Canada."[16] Joe Rauh, the old lion of American liberalism, won his last civil liberties case and gained vindication for the Canadians from the United States and their own government, but he did not live to see that final victory.

Farewell and Legacy

They came in a steady September rain in 1992 to say good-bye to Joe Rauh: seven hundred men and women who had benefited from his dedication to the law and liberalism or simply admired him from afar. The mourners included Justice Brennan, Arthur Miller, *Post* chairwoman Katharine Graham, and former presidential candidate John Anderson. They gathered on Sunday afternoon at the University of the District of Columbia, a few blocks from where he and Olie lived for half a century. He had dedicated a large portion of his life in his final years to keeping the institution's fledgling law school afloat financially in the hope it would train lawyers devoted more to public service than to making money.

Family and friends delivered eulogies and heard Rauh praised as someone who "lit the candle that gave hope for so many" and "a liberal with a capital 'L' first, last and always," in the words of former United States senator Thomas Eagleton. With more smiles than tears, they departed to the strains of his favorite songs that seemed to summarize his life and spirit: "Sweet Survivor" and "Weave Me the Sunshine."

The year of his death had not been a good one for the things Joe Rauh cared about. In April, an all-white jury in Los Angeles found four police officers not guilty of using excessive force when they pummeled Rodney King, a black resident stopped for a traffic violation. Los Angeles soon erupted in the worst racial violence since Watts in 1965, with firebombings, looting, and general mayhem that left fifty-five people dead, 18,000 arrested, and property damage totaling over $700 million. The racial divide he had labored so hard to close was as wide as ever.

But he remained a man of hope and optimism who cheered the summer meeting of President George Bush and Russian president Boris Yeltsin that proclaimed an official end to the Cold War and concluded a chapter of hysterical anticommunism that warped the fabric of America's constitutional values in the 1950s. Had he lived, he would have voted for Bill Clinton in November and welcomed, despite serious doubts, the return of a Democrat to the White House. He would have given Clinton about six months in office before filing his first dissent against the president's policies. One can only imagine his hostile response to Clinton's later abandonment of Aid to Families with Dependent Children, a historic part of FDR's original Social Security Act.

Rauh would have been more elated by the November election results that returned two women to the United States Senate from California, Dianne

Feinstein and Barbara Boxer, and the first African-American woman, Carol Mosley Braun from Illinois. And he would have been among the first to praise justices David Souter and Anthony Kennedy for voting with Sandra Day O'Connor to reaffirm the core of abortion rights in *Planned Parenthood of Southeastern Pennsylvania v. Casey.* In the course of fifty years, he had come to know that there were no final victories for human dignity and freedom, only a long march fraught with disappointment and setbacks.

At the White House a year later after his death, Clinton awarded Rauh the Medal of Freedom in a ceremony that also honored Brennan, Thurgood Marshall, federal appeals judge John Minor Wisdom, and environmental crusader Marjory Stoneman Douglas. Even in death, Joe Rauh kept good company. That day, he became only the second American to receive the Medal of Freedom posthumously—the other, tennis legend and civil rights activist Arthur Ashe.

In his eighty-one years, Joe Rauh never did anything indifferently or at half speed, whether playing tennis, defending a client, managing a political campaign, lobbying a congressman, writing a law review article, or bouncing a grandson. He had a thousand best friends who loved and worshiped him as a tireless champion of equality and social justice. He had more than his share of enemies who regarded him either as a subversive or as a stubborn, unyielding idealist for lost causes. But Clinton had made the right choice. How could you not give the Medal of Freedom to someone who had made freedom his life's work?

Of course, Joe Rauh had made his share of mistakes and miscalculations. His search for a compromise solution to anti-Japanese hysteria after Pearl Harbor proved futile and doomed American citizens to relocation camps, an outcome he lamented and spent forty years attempting to rectify. Hoping to salvage the civil rights coalition already in disarray, he misjudged the depth of public sentiment against the war in Vietnam and held back too long against the full-throttled attack on Lyndon Johnson's reelection in 1968. Dr. King's assessment was more correct on this issue, as were the views of Lowenstein and the other young doves in the ADA.

When he fought on behalf of union insurgents in the United Steelworkers and UAW, he usually saw an entrenched leadership as self-serving reactionaries and enemies of democracy, which some of them were, but he failed to appreciate the fear and insecurity spreading through their ranks as a result of sweeping structural changes in the global economy. He correctly saw that the judicial nominations of Nixon, Reagan, and George H. W. Bush, especially those of Rehnquist, Bork, Scalia, and Thomas, threatened to turn back the constitutional clock on racial justice and civil liberties. He was right to insist that the Senate take its advice-and-consent role more seriously, probe the ideology of nominees thoroughly, and insist on evidence that they had consistently supported the Bill of Rights. But he sometimes failed to recall the lesson offered by his own mentor, Frankfurter: a judicial nominee's past record was not always a reliable guide to a justice's future behavior.

Since its colonial beginnings, America has been blessed by many lawyers who rose to defend the liberty and dignity of individuals against arbitrary power. Andrew Hamilton challenged the common law of seditious libel on behalf of the publisher John Peter Zenger in 1735 and won a victory for freedom of the press. James Otis Jr., opposing general search warrants in Boston before the Revolution, could justly claim to be the architect of the Fourth Amendment. James Madison labored to end government coercion of religious practices in Virginia and shaped the First Amendment in the first Congress. Francis Scott Key, author of "The Star Spangled Banner," defended African-Americans facing the ordeal of the federal fugitive slave acts. Joseph Franklin Rutherford and Hayden C. Covington won thirty-six cases defending the religious freedom of Jehovah's Witnesses between 1940 and 1955. All deserve induction into a mythical American Lawyer's Hall of Fame—alongside the "knee-jerk liberal," Joe Rauh.

NOTES

Prologue

1. "The President's Hero," *New Yorker*, February 2, 2009, 23.
2. John Lewis with Michael D'Orson, *Walking with the Wind: A Memoir of the Movement* (New York, 1998), 277.
3. Thomas G. Corcoran to Ben Cohen, December 18, 1946, telephone conversation. President Truman, in the belief that Corcoran led efforts to oppose his nomination in 1948, secretly ordered a wiretap on the latter's phone. The transcripts are housed in the Truman Library, Independence, Missouri.
4. Lillian Hellman, *Scoundrel Time* (Boston, 1976), 60.
5. Arthur M. Schlesinger Jr., *A Life in the 20th Century: Innocent Beginnings, 1917–1950* (Boston, 2000), 410.
6. Hellman, *Scoundrel Time*, 60.
7. Author's notes, September 13, 1987; *Washington Post*, September 14, 1987.
8. Maggie Rauh, interview, September 27, 1992; Olie Rauh, interview, February 9, 1993.
9. *New York Times*, September 4, 1992.
10. Ben Cohen to Joe Rauh, n.p., n.d., Box 12, Benjamin V. Cohen Papers, Library of Congress.

Chapter One

1. Response of Joseph L. Rauh Jr. to Maurice N. Eisendrath Bearer of Light Award, November 3, 1985, copy in Rauh Papers (Library of Congress).
2. Remarks of Joseph L. Rauh Jr. before the Milwaukee Jewish Council dinner, July 26, 1973, copy in Rauh Papers.
3. The case was *DeFunis v. Odegaard*, 416 U.S. 312 (1974). Marco DeFunis claimed that he had been denied admission to the law school's first-year class of 150 students, although black applicants with lower test scores had been admitted. The Supreme Court ruled the suit moot when DeFunis had been provisionally admitted while the litigation advanced and was due to graduate at the time of the decision. See also *DeFunis v. Odegaard, Landmark Briefs and Arguments of the Supreme Court of*

the United States, 80, ed. Philip B. Kurland and Gerhard Casper (Arlington, Va., 1975), 287.

4. *New York Times,* September 25, 1977, 15. In this case, *University of California Regents v. Bakke,* 438 U.S. 265 (1978), the Court ordered Bakke's admission and condemned the specific quota in the plan as unconstitutional, but Justice Lewis Powell's opinion for a plurality of the justices also held that universities were not prohibited from making race one factor among many in judging admissions.

5. Author's notes of Los Angeles meeting with Joe Rauh, November 3–4, 1985.

6. Benjamin Hooks et al. to Joseph L. Rauh Jr., August 21, 1979, Rauh Papers. On Young's resignation and its impact on black-Jewish relations see *New York Times,* August 16, 1979, A1.

7. Joseph L. Rauh Jr., interview, August 28, 1986, Washington, D.C.

8. Joe Rauh, draft of statement on Andrew Young resignation, August 22, 1979, Rauh Papers.

9. Quoted in Victor Lasky, *Jimmy Carter: The Man and the Myth* (New York, 1979), 340–42.

10. Statement by NAACP Board of Directors, August 22, 1979, copy in Rauh Papers.

11. See James Wechsler's column in the *New York Post,* August 24, 1979; and "Black Leadership Meeting, August 22, 1979, Rauh Papers.

12. When Rauh later opposed attorney Morris Abram, whom President Reagan had nominated to the U.S. Commission on Civil Rights, an angry Abrams accused Rauh of "kowtowing to the blacks" by remaining outside the 1979 board meeting.

13. Louise Rauh, interview, September 4, 1986, Cincinnati, Ohio.

14. Quoted in Barnett A. Bricker, "The Jewish Community of Cincinnati: Historical and Descriptive, 1817–1933" (Ph.D. diss., University of Cincinnati, 1933), 279. See also Henry D. Shapiro and Jonathan D. Sarna, eds., *Ethnic Diversity and Civic Identity: Patterns of Conflict and Cohesion in Cincinnati since 1820* (Urbana, 1992), 131–64.

15. Quoted in Jonathan D. Sarna and Nancy H. Klein, *The Jews of Cincinnati* (Cincinnati, 1989), 6.

16. Bernard Bailyn, ed., *Glimpses of the Harvard Past* (Cambridge, Mass., 1986), 79.

17. Quoted in Marcia Graham Synnott, *The Half-Opened Door: Discrimination and Admissions at Harvard, Yale and Princeton, 1900–1970* (Westport, Conn., 1979), 49–50.

18. Joseph L. Rauh Jr., interview, August 9, 1985, Washington, D.C.

19. See Synott, *The Half-Opened Door,* 51.

20. Theodore H. White, *In Search of History* (New York, 1978), 41–43.

21. Joseph L. Rauh Jr., interview, August 9, 1985.

22. Ibid.

Chapter Two

1. Joseph L. Rauh Jr., interview, August 10, 1985.

2. Ibid.

3. Joseph L. Rauh Jr., interview, September 9, 1985.

4. His Cincinnati boyhood friend, Tom Freiberg, who attended Yale at the same time, recalled many of Rauh's escapades in an interview with the author, December 18, 1985.

5. Olie Rauh, interview, August 17, 1985.

6. Quoted in Arthur E. Sutherland, *The Law at Harvard: A History of Ideas and Men, 1817–1967* (Cambridge, Mass., 1967), 248.

7. Quoted in Sutherland, *The Law at Harvard*, 297.

8. *Buck v. Bell*, 274 U.S. 200 (1927), at 207. Joseph L. Rauh Jr., interview, August 10, 1985.

9. Liva Baker, *Felix Frankfurter* (New York, 1969), 13, from Francis Plimpton's *Reunion Runes*.

10. Joseph L. Rauh Jr., interview, August 10, 1985.

11. *Muskrat v. United States*, 219 U.S. 346 (1911). In this celebrated example of the limitations imposed by "the cases and controversies" requirement of Article III of the Constitution, the Supreme Court refused jurisdiction in a case involving claims brought by Cherokee Indians, including David Muskrat, on the grounds that Congress had manufactured a friendly suit that lacked any genuine clash of legal interests.

12. 294 U.S. 103 (1935).

13. Joseph L. Rauh Jr., interview, August 10, 1985.

14. Quoted in Joseph P. Lash, *From the Diaries of Felix Frankfurter* (New York, 1975), 54–55.

15. Joseph L. Rauh Jr., interview, August 11, 1985; Olie Rauh, interview, August 17, 1985.

Chapter Three

1. George Peek, "In and Out: The Experiences of the First AAA Administrator," *Saturday Evening Post*, May 16, 1936, 7.

2. *Norman v. Baltimore & Ohio Railroad Co.*, 294 U.S. 240 (1935); *Nortz v. United States*, 294 U.S. 317 (1935); and *Perry v. United States*, 294 U.S. 330 (1935).

3. Alpheus T. Mason, *Harlan Fiske Stone: Pillar of the Law* (New York, 1956), 391n.

4. *Retirement Board v. Alton Railroad Co.*, 295 U.S. 330 (1935).

5. *Louisville Joint Stock Bank v. Radford*, 295 U.S. 555 (1935).

6. *Humphrey's Executor v. United States*, 295 U.S. 602 (1935).

7. *Schechter Poultry Co. v. United States*, 295 U.S. 495 (1935).

8. Michael E. Parrish, *Securities Regulation and the New Deal* (New Haven, 1970), 42–178.

9. George Peek with Samuel Crowther, *Why Quit Our Own* (New York, 1936), 20.

10. Joseph P. Lash, *Dealers and Dreamers: A New Look at the New Deal* (New York, 1988), 9–53.

11. Ibid., 142.

12. Joseph L. Rauh Jr., interview, August 11, 1985.

13. Katharine Graham–David Ginsberg conversation, January 1, 1986, copy in Rauh Papers.

14. Joseph L. Rauh Jr., interview, August 11, 1985.

15. See *Muskrat v. United States*, 219 U.S. 346 (1911).

16. In February 1936, the Supreme Court upheld various provisions of the Tennessee Valley Authority Act but did so in a suit brought by minority stockholders against the directors of their own utility, which sought to buy electricity from the government agency. Justice Brandeis filed a famous concurring opinion reminding his brethren that they should not decide constitutional questions in a number of circumstances, especially in a nonadversary proceeding. See *Ashwander v. Tennessee Valley Authority*, 297 U.S. 288 (1936).

17. Joseph L. Rauh Jr., interview, August 11, 1985.

18. Ibid.

19. Olie Rauh, interview, August 17, 1985.

20. *Burco v. Whitworth*, 12 F. Supp. 667 (1935).

21. *Burco, Inc. v. Whitworth et al.* (Lautenbach et al., Interveners, 81 F.2d 721) (1936).

22. 297 U.S. 288 (1936).

23. 297 U.S. 724–25 (1936).

24. *North American Co. v. Landis et al.*, 85 F.2d 398 (1936).

25. *Landis et al. v. North American Co.*, 299 U.S. 248 (1936).

26. *Electric Bond & Share Co. v. SEC*, 303 U.S. 419 (1938).

27. *Butler v. United States*, 297 U.S. 1 (1936); *Carter v. Carter Coal Co.*, 298 U.S. 238 (1936).

28. *Morehead v. New York ex rel. Tipaldo*, 298 U.S. 587 (1936).

29. Joseph L. Rauh Jr., interview, August 15, 1985.

30. Joseph L. Rauh Jr., "A Personal View of Justice Benjamin N. Cardozo: Recollections of Four Cardozo Law Clerks," *Cardozo Law Review* 1 (Spring 1979): 10.

31. Katharine Graham–David Ginsberg conversation, January 1, 1986, Rauh Papers.

32. Joseph L. Rauh Jr., interview, August 15, 1985.

33. *Valentine, Police Commissioner of New York City, et al. v. United States ex rel. B. Coles Neidecker*, 299 U.S. 5 (1936).

34. Joseph L. Rauh Jr., interview, August 16, 1985.

35. 302 U.S. 319 (1937). Affirming the death sentence of a Connecticut prisoner convicted after a second trial under a state statute that permitted the prosecution to appeal procedural errors in the first proceeding, Cardozo rejected the argument that the double jeopardy provision of the Bill of Rights applied to the states through the concept of due process in the Fourteenth Amendment. While conceding that the same provisions of the Bill of Rights—notably speech, press, and religious liberty—had been "incorporated" in the due process clause, he placed double jeopardy in a second category of rights "not of the very essence of a scheme of ordered liberty." Critics at the time and later, including Rauh, rejected Cardozo's incremental approach to extending the Bill of Rights to the states, but others saw *Palko* as another important milestone on the road to eventual incorporation.

36. Katharine Graham–David Ginsberg conversation, January 1, 1986, Rauh Papers.

37. Joseph L. Rauh Jr., interview, August 16, 1985; *Smyth v. United States*, 302 U.S. 329 (1937).

38. Rauh, "A Personal View of Justice Benjamin N. Cardozo," 10.

Chapter Four

1. See Orme W. Phelps, *The Legislative Background of the Fair Labor Standards Act* (Chicago, 1939), passim; Irving Sloan, ed., *The Fair Labor Standards Act of 1938* (Dobbs Ferry, N.Y., 1984), passim.

2. Frances Perkins, *The Roosevelt I Knew* (New York, 1946), 265–67.

3. Quoted in Lash, *Dealers and Dreamers*, 339.

4. Joseph L. Rauh Jr. to Albert Steiner, April 3, 1939, Box 4, Rauh Papers. Steiner, a Cincinnati soap manufacturer, sought Rauh's support for a committee to defend the Bill of Rights, a laudable objective Rauh noted, but he cautioned that the committee was "going to be put in the position of spreading meaningless shibboleths" unless it also confronted the nation's social and economic inequalities.

5. *Congressional Record*, 76 Cong., 3rd sess., March 21, 1940, 4953.

6. Joseph L. Rauh Jr., interview, August 18, 1985. At least one member of the House, Congressman Cochran of Missouri, rose to Rauh's defense following Cellar's attack. While laboring at Wage and Hour on Washington's birthday, Rauh had assisted Cochran and his constituents in the interpretation of FLSA provisions, for which the congressman remained very grateful. "True, he is a young man," Cochran told the House, "but if they had looked into his background they would have found, young as he is, his brilliant record does not warrant criticism." *Congressional Record*, 76 Cong., 3rd sess., March 27, 1940, 5377.

7. Joseph L. Rauh Jr., interview, August 21, 1985.

8. Ibid.

9. Harlan Phillips, ed., *Felix Frankfurter Reminisces* (New York, 1960), 280–81; Samuel Spencer's notes of Frankfurter–Grenville Clark conversation, Summer 1947, Box 195, Frankfurter Papers, Harvard Law School.

10. Harold Ickes, *Diary*, January 2, 1939, and January 7, 1939, Library of Congress; Eugene Gerhart, *America's Advocate: Robert Jackson* (Indianapolis, 1938), 166; Phillips, *Frankfurter Reminisces*, 334; Joseph L. Rauh Jr., interview, August 18, 1985.

11. Joseph L. Rauh Jr., interview, August 17, 1985.

12. Thomas Reed Powell to Frank W. Buxton, December 10, 1945, Box A, File 28, Powell Papers, Harvard Law School; John Mason Brown, "The Uniform of Justice," *Saturday Review*, October 30, 1954, 11.

13. *Hale v. Bimco Trading, Inc.*, 306 U.S. 375 (1939). The Florida law imposed a fee of 15 cents per 100 pounds upon cement imported from any foreign country, but exempted all locally produced cement. In *Keifer & Keifer v. R.F.C.*, 306 U.S. 381 (1939), Frankfurter and the Court held that the agency could be sued for negligence although its charter did not contain a specific "sue and be sued" provision similar to those contained in the charters of other federal corporations.

14. Frankfurter to Powell, February 27, 1939, Box A, File 7, Powell Papers.

15. Joseph L. Rauh Jr., interview, August l8, 1985.

16. Ibid.

17. *Opp Cotton Mills v. Administrator*, 312 U.S. 126 (1941).

18. Joseph L. Rauh Jr., interview, August 19, 1985; *New York Times*, April 9, 1940, 26.

19. Ibid.

20. *Union Terminal Company v. Pickett,* 1 Wage and Hour Cases, 113; *Williams, et al. v. Jacksonville Terminal Company,* 1 Wage and Hour Cases, 109; and *Williams, et al. v. Jacksonville Terminal Co.,* 315 U.S. 386 (1942).

21. Peter Irons, *The New Deal Lawyers* (Princeton, 1982), 137–39, 142–44, 210.

22. Joseph L. Rauh Jr., oral history for James Lawrence Fly Project, Columbia Oral History Office (1971), 2–3.

23. Federal Communications Commission, *Report on Chain Broadcasting* (Washington, D.C., 1941); Rauh, Fly Oral History Project, 4–5.

24. Joseph L. Rauh Jr., interview, August 19, 1985. When Fly later appeared at an NBC convention for its affiliates, he suffered a scathing attack from Ethridge, but held his own: "It's like a mackerel in the moonlight," he said, quoting John Randolph, "it shines and stinks." Rauh, Fly Oral History Project, 9. See also "The Impact of the FCC's Chain Broadcasting Rules," *Yale Law Journal* 60 (January 1951): 78–111.

25. See Otha Wearin and Alfred D. Kirchhofer, "Joint Ownership of Newspapers and Radio Stations," *Public Opinion Quarterly* 2 (April 1938): 300–308.

26. See William B. Ray, *The Ups and Downs of Radio-TV Regulation* (Ames, Iowa, 1990); and Ben H. Bagdikian, *The Media Monopoly* (Boston, 1983).

27. *Nardone v. United States,* 302 U.S. 379 (1937); *Weiss v. United States,* 308 U.S. 321 (1939); and *Nardone v. United States,* 308 U.S. 338 (1939).

28. Joseph L. Rauh Jr., interview, August 20, 1985.

29. Rauh, Fly Oral History Project, 18–20.

30. Christine M. Marwick, "Warrantless National Security Wiretaps," *First Principles* 1 (October 1975): 6–7; Victor Navasky and Nathan Lewin, "Electronic Surveillance," in *Investigating the FBI,* ed. Pat Watters and Stephen Gillers (New York, 1974), 291. According to Rauh's recollection, Fly's opposition to wiretapping was rooted both in his tepid support for FDR's internationalist foreign policy and his "absolute detestation of [J. Edgar] Hoover." See Rauh, Fly Oral History Project, 27.

31. Lash, *Dealers and Dreamers,* 408–10.

32. Michael E. Parrish, *Anxious Decades: America in Prosperity and Depression, 1920–1941* (New York, 1992), 470–71; Joseph L. Rauh Jr., interview, August 21, 1985.

Chapter Five

1. David S. Wyman, *Paper Walls: America and the Refugee Crisis, 1938–1941* (Amherst, Mass., 1968); and David S. Wyman, *The Abandonment of the Jews: America and the Holocaust, 1941–1945* (New York, 1984).

2. On Ed Prichard see the penetrating biography by Tracy Campbell, *Short of the Glory: The Fall and Redemption of Edward F. Prichard, Jr.* (Lexington, 1998), 7–78.

3. This portrait of Graham is drawn from David Halberstam, *The Powers That Be* (New York, 1979), 224–49.

4. 320 U.S. 586 (1940). See also Richard Danzig, "How Questions Begot Answers in Felix Frankfurter's First Flag Salute Opinion," *Supreme Court Review* (1977): 257–74.

5. Joseph L. Rauh Jr., interview, August 15, 1994; Campbell, *Short of the Glory,* 65–68.

6. Gary N. A. Botting, *Fundamental Freedoms and the Jehovah's Witnesses* (Calgary, 1993); David R. Manwaring, *Render unto Caesar: The Flag Salute Controversy* (Chicago, 1962); *West Virginia State Board of Education v. Barnette*, 319 U.S. 624 (1943).

7. Ibid.

8. Victor Reuther, *The Brothers Reuther and the Story of the UAW: A Memoir* (Boston, 1976), 228. See also *New York Times*, December 23, 1940, 1; and December 24, 1940, 7.

9. Two years after Pearl Harbor, K. T. Keller, the head of the Chrysler Corporation, told a Senate committee that 89 percent of his company's machine tools had been converted to war production. Hearing this, Phil Graham remarked that Reuther had been 89 percent correct. See John Barnard, *Walter Reuther and the Rise of the Auto Workers* (Boston, 1983), 178–79.

10. Joseph L. Rauh Jr., interview, August 14, 1985.

11. Ibid.

12. Joseph L. Rauh Jr., interview, August 14, 1985.

13. Ibid. See also Herbert Garfinkel, *When Negroes March: The March on Washington Movement in the Organizational Politics for the FEPC* (Glencoe, Ill., 1959); Darryl Pickney, "A. Philip Randolph: Pioneer of the Civil Rights Movement," *New York Review of Books*, November 22, 1990, 29–35; and Jervis Anderson, *A Philip Randolph: A Biographical Portrait* (New York, 1973).

14. Henry L. Stimson, Diary, February 3, 1941, Yale University Library.

15. Joseph L. Rauh Jr., interview, August 14, 1985.

16. Memorandum, "The Japanese Situation on the West Coast," File 146-13-7-2-0, Records of Alien Enemy Control Unit, Department of Justice.

17. Ibid.

18. John McCloy to Felix Frankfurter, April 1, 1942, McCloy Papers, Amherst College.

19. See the devastating indictment in Peter Irons, *Justice at War: The Story of the Japanese American Internment Cases* (New York, 1983), especially 253–310.

20. Ibid., 55.

Chapter Six

1. Rauh, Fly Oral History Project, 23; Joseph L. Rauh Jr., interview, August 14, 1985.

2. Frankfurter to Rauh, April 24, 1942, Box 4, Rauh Papers.

3. Rauh to Frankfurter, April 24, 1942, Box 4, Rauh Papers.

4. Frankfurter to Rauh, April 24, 1942, Box 4, Rauh Papers.

5. John McCloy to Felix Frankfurter, May 21, 1942, McCloy Papers, Amherst College.

6. On the relationship between British investors and the mine see William Giles Nash, *The Rio Tinto Mine: Its History and Romance* (London, 1904).

7. *P.M.*, February 17, 1942, 12; and I. F. Stone, *The War Years* (Boston, 1988), 110–11.

8. S. K. McKee to J. Edgar Hoover, February 19, 1942, Rauh FBI File.

9. Ibid.

10. S. K. McKee to Hoover, February 24, 1942, Rauh FBI File. Sixteen years after the event, Roy Cohn, the enfant terrible of the McCarthy Committee, told radio commentator Fulton Lewis that he had been in the Department of Justice at the time of the *PM* "leak" and took Rauh "before a grand jury but that the matter was never followed up." FBI officials quickly scotched the rumor by reporting that "Cohen is wrong in this regard . . . and it appears to be a matter which was handled administratively by Lend Lease." G. A. Nease to Clyde Tolson, March 28, 1958; and Nease to Tolson, March 29, 1958, Rauh FBI File.

11. In August 1941, Hoover informed Matthew McGuire, an assistant to the attorney general, that the bureau had received information "from a highly confidential source" indicating that Rauh's name appeared on "the active indices of the Washington Committee for Democratic Action." Hoover to McGuire, August 26, 1941, Rauh FBI File. A later FBI memo notes an earlier report of January 21, 1941, that identified Rauh on a card index maintained by the committee. D. M. Ladd to Hoover, February 24, 1942, Rauh FBI File.

12. Richard Polenberg, "Franklin Roosevelt and Civil Liberties: The Case of the Dies Committee," *Historian* 30 (1968): 165–78.

13. FBI Memorandum, File 101-1193, March 25, 1942, Rauh FBI File.

14. Ibid.

15. Ibid.

16. Ibid.

17. Joseph L. Rauh Jr., interview, March 12, 1942, FBI File 101-1193, Rauh FBI File.

18. Wayne Coy to John Edgar Hoover, April 6, 1942, Rauh FBI File.

19. Hoover to Coy, April 11, 1942; and Hoover to S. K. McKee, April 21, 1942, Rauh FBI File.

20. Henry Frei, *Japan's Southward Advance and Australia: From the Sixteenth Century to World War II* (Melbourne, 1991), 245–303; Ann Howard, *Australia and World War II* (Sidney, 1984).

21. See Dick C. Horton, *Ring of Fire: Australian Guerilla Operations against the Japanese in World War II* (London, 1983), 1–164.

22. Joseph L. Rauh Jr., interview, August 18, 1985. A number of incidents marred relations between American and Australian military units, especially the so-called Battle of Brisbane on Thanksgiving Day, 1942, when rioting erupted following the shooting death of an Australian private by an American MP. See E. Daniel Potts and Annette Potts, *Yanks Down Under 1941–45: The American Impact on Australia* (Melbourne, 1985), 302–15.

23. Edgar G. Crossman, "My Experiences in World War II," November 18, 1966, 5, typescript in Rauh Papers.

24. Joseph L. Rauh Jr., oral history, June 21, 1989, Harry S Truman Library.

25. Cornelia Spencer, *Romulo: Voice of Freedom* (New York, 1953), 188–89.

26. Rauh, oral history, Truman Library.

27. C. Vann Woodward, *The Battle for Leyte Gulf* (Nashville, 1989); John D. Ahlstrum, "Leyte Gulf Remembered," *U.S. Naval Institute Proceedings* 110 (1984): 45–53; M. Hamlin Cannon, *Leyte: The Return to the Philippines* (Washington, 1954); Samuel Eliot Morison, *Leyte, June 1944–January 1945* (Boston, 1958).

28. Crossman, "My Experiences in World War II," 32.

29. Joseph L. Rauh Jr., interview, August 18, 1985.

30. Confessor, the prewar governor of Iloilo, became a national hero when he defied his Japanese-appointed successor, F. M. Caram, and refused to abandon his guerrilla campaign "for the sake of peace and tranquility." See A. V. H. Hartendorp, *The Japanese Occupation of the Philippines* (Manila, 1967), 2:610–11.

31. Joseph L. Rauh Jr., interview, August 18, 1985.

32. Rauh, oral history, Truman Library.

33. See Bernard Asbell, *When FDR Died* (New York, 1961), 119; Joseph L. Rauh Jr., interview, August 19, 1985.

Chapter Seven

1. William A. Leuchtenburg, *In the Shadow of FDR: From Harry Truman to Bill Clinton* (Ithaca, 1991), 14–15. According to Clark Clifford, Truman detested the words *progressive* and *liberal* and described the people around Roosevelt as "crackpots and lunatic fringe."

2. David Halberstam, *The Powers That Be* (New York, 1979), 250–51; and see the letter to the editor from Rauh, Cox, Lloyd Cutler, and others, *Washington Post*, December 29, 1945.

3. Gregg Herkin, *Winning Weapon: The Atomic Bomb in the Cold War, 1945–1950* (New York, 1981), 129–30.

4. Joseph L. Rauh Jr., "Emergency Committee for Civilian Control of Atomic Energy—Statement of Purpose," March 1946, Rauh Papers.

5. Joseph L. Rauh Jr., "Set-Back for Civilian Control of Atomic Energy," June 23, 1946, Rauh Papers; Herkin, *The Winning Weapon*, 148.

6. Joseph L. Rauh Jr., "The Bill Protects the 'Secret,'" July 15, 1946, Rauh Papers; Herkin, *The Winning Weapon*, 135–36.

7. Victor Reuther, *The Brothers Reuther and the Story of the UAW* (Boston, 1976), 254.

8. M. E. Gurnea to D. M. Ladd, January 10, 1946, Rauh FBI File.

9. Hoover to SAC, Washington, "Re: Joseph L. Rauh, Jr. Registration Act," May 8, 1946, Rauh FBI File.

10. Guy Hottel, SAC, to Hoover, October 28, 1946, Rauh FBI File. Rauh's reported perspective on the use of the atomic bomb anticipated the arguments of later revisionist historians who also argued that Japan's surrender could have been achieved prior to the planned invasion of its home islands in December through a combination of other incentives, especially conventional bombing, continuation of the naval blockade, modification of the "unconditional surrender" terms to preserve the position of the emperor, and the Soviet's declaration of war. See especially Gar Alperovitz, *Atomic Diplomacy: Hiroshima and Potsdam* (New York, 1965); and Barton J. Bernstein, "The Atomic Bomb and American Foreign Policy, 1941–1945: An Historiographical Controversy," *Peace and Change* (Spring 1974). For a recent interpretation that stresses the importance of Soviet intervention, not the bomb, in achieving Japan's surrender in August 1945 see Murray Sayle, "Did the Bomb End the War?" *New Yorker*, July 31, 1995, 68.

11. Ibid.

288 NOTES TO PAGES 82–89

12. Ibid.

13. Hoover to SAC, Washington, October 31, 1946, Rauh FBI File.

14. Guy Hottel to Hoover, December 31, 1946; and Hoover to Hottel, January 23, 1947, both Rauh FBI File.

15. Ibid.

16. Ibid.

17. FBI Report, "Re: Joseph L. Rauh, Jr.," September 3, 1947, Rauh FBI File.

18. Alonzo Hamby, *Beyond the New Deal: Harry S. Truman and American Liberalism* (New York, 1973), 159–60.

19. Ibid., 158–59.

20. *New York Times,* January 4, 1947, 5; Loeb to *New Republic,* January 27, 1947, 3, 46. Rauh remained angry about how the "red-baiting" label had been misapplied to ADA by its opponents on the left. In his view, it was not "red-baiting" to single out as communists those who were in fact communists. "Red-baiting," on the other hand, involved unfounded accusations of party membership, which, he believed, ADA leaders had never practiced. Joseph L. Rauh Jr., interview, August 18, 1985.

21. Arthur M. Schlesinger Jr., "The U.S. Communist Party," *Life,* July 29, 1946, 84–96.

22. Joseph L. Rauh Jr., interview, August 15, 1985.

23. See *PM,* January 9, 1947; Freda Kirchwey, "Mugwumps in Action," *Nation,* January 18, 1947, 61–62; Hamby, *Beyond the New Deal,* 165. Several leading members of ADA, including Loeb and Paul Porter, joined the Truman administration after the 1948 election, which gave weight to Victor Navasky's later criticism that "these anti-Communist liberals identified with not the left but the center, with not the masses but the intellectual elite. They celebrated rather than criticized the social order and had given up the old ideal of the perfectibility of man." See Victor Navasky, *Naming Names* (New York, 1980), 52. Rauh came to believe that ADA too quickly lost its independence by becoming financially dependent on the unions and too eager to support a liberalized Democratic Party.

24. At about the same time, Loeb brought into the ADA fold another Roosevelt Democrat, the star of *Kings Row,* Ronald Reagan. See Ronnie Dugger, *On Reagan* (New York, 1983), 10–11; and Rauh, "Memories of Jim," Rauh Papers.

25. In Chicago, Rauh failed to recruit an aspiring gubernatorial candidate, Adlai Stevenson, whom he had known during the pre–Pearl Harbor days in the Office of Facts and Figures. Stevenson came to an ADA reception but otherwise kept his distance from the organization. Joseph L. Rauh Jr., interview, August 15, 1985.

26. Rauh to Willard Hurst, May 21, 1947, Rauh Papers.

27. Hamby, *Beyond the New Deal,* 171.

28. "Well honest to God, I almost went through the goddamn floor," Rauh recalled later. "I didn't know what to say I was so nonplused. I thought this was a democracy, and you had to have a race for president. They were nuts." Joseph L. Rauh, oral history, January 31, 1978, Franklin D. Roosevelt Library, 24.

29. "The Democrats: The Line Squall," *Time,* July 26, 1948, 12.

30. Arthur M. Schlesinger Jr., *Journals 1952–2000* (New York, 2007), 445; Joseph L. Rauh Jr., oral history, January 1992, Harry S Truman Library, 60–61.

31. Joseph L. Rauh Jr., interview, August 16, 1985.

Chapter Eight

1. Executive Order No. 9835, 12 Fed. Reg. 1935 (1947). The text of Truman's executive order can be found as well in the *New York Times*, March 23, 1947, 11.

2. Joseph L. Rauh Jr., "NonConfrontation in Security Cases: The Green Decision," *Virginia Law Review* 45 (1959): 1175; *New York Times*, December 28, 1947, 28.

3. Daniel Pollitt, interview, August 13, 1985.

4. Ibid.

5. Joseph L. Rauh Jr., interview, August 17, 1985.

6. Joseph L. Rauh Jr., "Revised Loyalty Article," 4–6, n.p., n.d., Rauh Papers.

7. Ibid.

8. *New York Times*, October 14, 1948, and May 2, 1949.

9. Pollitt also described the poorly educated Kutcher as "a slob," shamelessly exploited by the Trotskyites for propaganda purposes. Rauh held his nose through the showing of a documentary film about the case sponsored by the Socialist Workers Party and later when Kutcher praised the North Koreans and Chinese. Pollitt, interview, August 13, 1985.

10. *Kutcher v. Gray*, 199 F.2d 783 (1952). The court refused, however, to pass on Rauh's constitutional challenge to the entire program and specifically affirmed the legality of the attorney general's listing of organizations without a hearing.

11. *Kutcher v. Higley*, 235 F.2d 505 (1956), at 507; *New York Times*, June 21, 1956; Joseph L. Rauh Jr., interview, August 18, 1985.

12. Joseph L. Rauh, interview, August 15, 1985; *New York Times*, December 31, 1955, and January 9, 1956.

13. Gary May, *Un-American Activities: The Trials of William Remington* (New York, 1995), 82–85.

14. Ibid., 89–93.

15. Ibid., 98–100.

16. Ibid., 15–29.

17. Ibid., 44–57.

18. Ibid., 107–8, 113, 120.

19. Joseph L. Rauh to Gary May, April 10, 1981, Rauh Papers.

20. Joseph L. Rauh to James Allen, July 6, 1949, Rauh Papers.

21. Rauh to May, April 10, 1981, Rauh Papers.

22. Rauh to James Allen, July 21, 1948, Rauh Papers.

23. May, *Un-American Ac*tivities, 127–30. Richardson did not believe Remington had dealt with Bentley "as part of his official permissive duty." Their relationship struck him as "off-color," but like Rauh he concluded that Remington "was very young and immature, the times were different, and his work since has been above criticism."

24. *Washington Post*, February 11, 1949; Daniel Lang, "The Days of Suspicion," *New Yorker*, May 21, 1949, 37–54.

25. Guy Hottel to J. Edgar Hoover, May 5, 1950, Rauh FBI File; and Rauh to Seth W. Richardson, May 6, 1950, Rauh Papers.

26. The FBI had commenced an investigation of the Robert Marshall Founda-

tion in 1944, after the organization made grants to the Southern Conference for Human Welfare; the Workers Defense League; and Tom Mooney, the chairman of the Citizens' Committee to Free Earl Browder, the former head of the American Communist Party. All of these groups, the bureau noted, had been cited by either HUAC or the attorney general as communist fronts or communist dominated. When Rauh and Chanler denied that Remington's defense expenses had been paid by the communists, the FBI suggested otherwise based on the Marshall Foundation's gifts. D. M. Ladd to Hoover, January 17, 1951, Rauh FBI File.

27. May, *Un-American Activities*, 161–64, 210–15.

28. When Rauh and Chanler asked Noonan at one point in the trial to define "membership" in the communist party, the judge snapped back: "Ask him [Remington]; he knows." A three-judge panel on the circuit court, Thomas Swam, Gus Hand, and Learned Hand, promptly reversed Noonan on the bail issue. In a crowded elevator as they left the court that day, Learned Hand said to his cousin, "That's the most outrageous thing I have ever heard." Joseph L. Rauh Jr., interview, August 15, 1985.

29. Saypol had learned of the Brunini-Bentley connection before the Devin-Adair employees came forward to testify. He had urged the attorney general to seek a fresh indictment, fearing that this secret would be exposed and ruin the prosecution's case. He was overruled. At the time, even Saypol did not know that the grand jury proceedings had been further compromised by the fact that Donegan and another prosecution witness, Joseph Egan, also had prior legal relationships with Bentley. See May, *Un-American Activities*, 204; and *United States of America, Appellee, v. William Walter Remington, Appellant,* Brief for Appellant, United States Court of Appeals for the Second Circuit, 36–37, Rauh Papers.

30. *United States v. Remington*, 191 F.2d 246 (2d Cir., 1951); and *New York Times,* August 23, 1951.

31. May, *Un-American Activities*, 273; Sidney Zion, *The Autobiography of Roy Cohn* (New York, 1988), 50–51.

32. Three justices, Frankfurter, Hugo Black, and William O. Douglas, voted to hear the case, but only Black and Douglas publicly expressed their dismay with the Court's refusal to grant certiorari. Black believed that the Bentley-Brunini connection and the prosecution's failure to disclose it constituted conduct "abhorrent to a fair administration of justice" and probably denied Remington due process of law. Supreme Court of the United States, No. 387, October Term, 1951, *William Walter Remington v. The United States of America,* March 24, 1952; Joseph L. Rauh Jr., interview, August 16, 1985.

33. Rauh to William C. Chanler, April 21, 1952, Rauh Papers; Joseph L. Rauh Jr., interview, August 16, 1985.

34. Remington reaffirmed to Rauh his innocence on both perjury counts: he had never knowingly engaged in espionage with Bentley or belonged to the communist party. An undated memorandum in Rauh's papers, "Spy Rings and Riddles," notes that since the FBI had Bentley and Jacob Golos under surveillance from 1940 until the latter's death in 1943, the bureau either believed any information they received was of little value or the bureau bungled its responsibilities to protect the nation's secrets. William Remington to Rauh, March 16, 1953, Rauh Papers; "Spy Rings and Riddles," n.d., n.p., Rauh Papers.

35. *United States v. Williams*, 341 U.S. 58 (1945).

36. Brief for Appellant, United States Court of Appeals for the Second Circuit, *United States of America v. William Walter Remington,* Rauh Papers; *Silverthorne Lumber Co. v. United States,* 251 U.S. 385 (1925); *Nardone v. United States,* 308 U.S. 385 (1941).

37. Gerald Gunther, *Learned Hand: The Man and the Judge* (New York, 1994), 614–22.

38. Gunther, *Learned Hand,* 623; Joseph L. Rauh Jr., interview, August 16, 1985; Joseph L. Rauh Jr., "Felix Frankfurter: Civil Libertarian," *Harvard Civil Liberties Review* 11 (Summer 1976): 510–13. Rauh believed that Frankfurter's intense dislike of Black in 1954 blinded him to Jackson's own complicity in the Remington tragedy. A year earlier during the final appeals in the *Rosenberg* case, Jackson had behaved in a similar manner by refusing to hear their appeal when Justice Douglas's behavior offended him. See Michael E. Parrish, "Cold War Justice: The Supreme Court and the Rosenbergs," *American Historical Review* 82 (October 1977): 805–42.

39. May, *Un-American Activities,* 3–9; Zion, *Autobiography of Roy Cohn,* 52. Morton Sobell, the convicted atom spy, believed that persons connected with the Bureau of Prisons engineered Remington's murder, a theory demolished by Lee Jones, a historian, who first secured the Bureau of Prisons files through a Freedom of Information Act lawsuit. See *Nation,* April 16, 1988, 518.

40. "Revised Loyalty Article," Rauh Papers.

41. 341 U.S. 918 (1951).

42. Rauh's old mentor Justice Frankfurter advanced this narrow approach of resolving the *Peters* case during oral argument and persuaded Warren to adopt it for the majority. Neither the government nor Peters's attorneys had raised the issue, prompting Arnold to protest the Frankfurter gambit. Justices Black and Douglas believed the Court should have decided the constitutional problem. Joseph L. Rauh Jr., interview, August 18, 1985; *Peters v. Hobby,* 349 U.S. 331, at 349 and 350–52.

43. *Greene v. McElroy,* 360 U.S. 474 (1959).

44. *Taylor v. McElroy,* 360 U.S. 709 (1959); Rauh, "Nonconfrontation in Security Cases," 1182.

Chapter Nine

1. David Caute, *The Great Fear: The Anti-Communist Purge under Truman and Eisenhower* (New York, 1978), 487–518; Navasky, *Naming Names,* 78–96.

2. Carl Rollyson, *Lillian Hellman: Her Legend and Her Legacy* (New York, 1988), 41–316.

3. Arthur M. Schlesinger Jr., *Journals 1952–2000* (New York, 2007), 413–14.

4. Lillian Hellman, Typewritten statement No. 1 to Rauh, n.d., n.p., Rauh Papers.

5. Hellman, *Scoundrel Time,* 43.

6. Hellman, Statement No. 1 to Rauh, n.d., n.p., Rauh Papers.

7. Hellman, Statements No. 1 and No. 2, Rauh Papers. In both of her own draft statements, Hellman offered as proof of her "independent direction" the fact that the communist press attacked her play *Watch on the Rhine* during the period of the Nazi-Soviet Pact but praised it once the Germans invaded Russia. In 1976, however, she alleged that Rauh had first suggested raising this point and that she had rejected it: "I

said that I didn't want them used in my defense, that my use of their attacks on me would amount to my attacking them at a time when they were being persecuted and I would, therefore, be playing the enemy's game." *Scoundrel Time*, 61.

8. Joseph L. Rauh Jr., Draft of Statement by Miss Lillian Hellman, April 14, 1952, Rauh Papers.

9. Joseph L. Rauh Jr. to Lillian Hellman, April 30, 1952, Rauh Papers.

10. Ibid.

11. Ibid.

12. Lillian Hellman to John S. Wood, May 19, 1952, Rauh Papers.

13. John S. Wood to Hellman, May 20, 1952, Rauh Papers.

14. Hellman, *Scoundrel Time*, 101–2. In 1985, Rauh had no recollection of the call from Arnold and dismissed the idea that he would have placed much credibility in his opinion. "Arnold was a brilliant man, but a man whose judgment I would put after Little Orphan Annie's," he remarked. Joseph L. Rauh Jr., interview, August 18, 1985. But correspondence between Hellman and Rauh in 1975 suggests that her recollection of the call from Arnold may be more correct. See Hellman to Rauh, June 2, 1975, and Rauh to Hellman, June 27, 1975, Rauh Papers.

15. See Herbert Monte Levy to ACLU Board of Directors, December 18, 1952; Joseph L. Rauh Jr. to Levy, January 2, 1953, both Rauh Papers.

16. Hellman, *Scoundrel Time*, 109.

17. Rauh to Hellman, June 27, 1975, Rauh Papers.

18. *New York Times*, May 22, 1952; Rollyson, *Lillian Hellman*, 328.

19. Hellman to Rauh, May 29, 1952, Rauh Papers.

20. United States House of Representatives, Committee on Un-American Activities, *Investigation of the Unauthorized Use of United States Passports*, part 4, 4659.

21. Ibid., 4661.

22. Ibid., 4686.

23. Ibid., 4687–88.

24. Ibid., 4688.

25. Ibid., 4689.

26. *New York Times*, July 8, 1956, sec. 1, 25.

27. Joseph L. Rauh Jr., interview, August 18, 1985; *New York Times*, February 19, 1957, sec. 1, 5.

28. Carl Rauh, interview, August 19, 1985.

29. Joseph L. Rauh Jr., interview, August 18, 1985.

30. Schlesinger, *Journals*, 162.

31. *New York Times*, June 1, 1957, sec. 1, 1; June 29, 1957, sec. 1, 4.

32. Nelson Lichtenstein, *The Most Dangerous Man in Detroit: Walter Reuther and the Fate of American Labor* (New York, 1995), 325; Hearings before the House of Representatives Committee on Un-American Activities, *Investigation of Communist Activities in the Chicago Area*, part 3, 83rd Cong., 2nd sess., 4268.

33. Hearings before the House of Representatives Committee on Un-American Activities, *Investigation of Communist Activities in the Chicago Area*, part 3, 83rd Cong., 2nd sess., 4275.

34. *Watkins v. United States*, 98 U.S. App. D.C. 190, 233 F.2d 681.

35. *Watkins v. United States*, 354 U.S. 178 (1956), 214.

36. Ibid., 215, 205.

37. *Miller v. United States,* Brief for Appellant in the United States Court of Appeals for the District of Columbia Circuit, 30–31, Rauh Papers.

38. Daniel Pollitt, Memorandum, June 11, 1958, Rauh Papers. Rauh told Lloyd Garrison, also acting as Miller's attorney, "I must say I am optimistic about the outcome, even in this Court." Rauh to Garrison, June 12, 1958, Rauh Papers.

39. *Miller v. United States,* 259 F.2d 187 (1958), at 188.

40. Rauh to Alan R. Howe, August 11, 1958, Rauh Papers.

41. Miller to Rauh, August 9, 1958, Rauh Papers. Miller also told Rauh that Spyros Skouras, president of Twentieth Century–Fox, who urged Kazan to name names and required his actors to send him letters explaining why their politics did not threaten the studio, sent his congratulations on their legal victory. " Such are the pillows of society," Miller wrote, "AND I'LL BET YOU THE SON OF A BITCH FEELS PROUD OF HIS MAGNANIMITY . . . This usher for the Committee! Joseph, we must give him a demerit." On Skouras see Navasky, *Naming Names,* 89–90, 201.

42. *Barenblatt v. United States,* 360 U.S. 109 (1959). Frankfurter, who had joined the majority in both *Watkins* and *Sweezy* to curb such legislative inquiries, now switched sides and voted with Justice Harlan to sustain the contempt conviction.

43. Arthur Miller to Joe Rauh, June 12, 1959; Rauh to Miller, June 15, 1959, Rauh Papers.

Chapter Ten

1. Reuther earned the first label from American Motors president George Romney during the General Motors strike of 1945 and the second from Arizona senator Barry Goldwater a decade later. See Lichtenstein, *The Most Dangerous Man in Detroit,* 230, 347.

2. Ibid., 1–45.

3. Hearings before the Subcommittee on Constitutional Rights of the Committee on the Judiciary, *Security and Constitutional Rights,* 84th Cong., 2nd sess., 1955, 544.

4. Harold Cranefield to Walter Reuther, August 6, 1959, Rauh Papers.

5. Ibid., 545.

6. Ibid., 558–59.

7. Joseph L. Rauh to Harold A. Cranefield, August 26, 1959; Rauh to Cranefield, August 28, 1959; Cranefield to Rauh, August 7, 1959; and Cranefield to Walter Reuther, August 6, 1959, all Rauh Papers.

8. *Washington Post,* March 5, 1958, and March 7, 1958.

9. Joseph L. Rauh, oral history, December 23, 1965, John F. Kennedy Library, 21.

10. *New York Times,* March 5, 1958, sec. 24, 3.

11. Joe Rauh to Arthur M. Schlesinger Jr., October 16, 1975, Rauh Papers.

12. *New York Times,* March 7, 1958, sec. 10, 4.

13. Kohler Company, 128 N.L.R.B. 1062 (1960).

14. Joseph L. Rauh Jr., interview, August 19, 1985.

15. *Local 833, UAW-AFL-CIO, International Union, United Automobile, Aircraft & Agricultural Implement Workers of America v. National Labor Relations Board; Kohler Company v. National Labor Relations Board,* 300 F.2d 699 (1962).

16. *Kohler Company v. National Labor Relations Board*, 345 F.2d 748 (1965).

17. Kevin Boyle, *The UAW and the Heyday of American Liberalism* (Ithaca, 1995), 83–91, 123–26.

18. Paula F. Pfeffer, *A. Philip Randolph, Pioneer of the Civil Rights Movement* (Baton Rouge, 1990), 138.

19. Joseph L. Rauh Jr., interview, August 19, 1985.

20. *Steele v. Louisville & Nashville Railroad Co., et al.*, 323 U.S. 192 (1944). Concurring separately, Justice Murphy would have imposed these conditions as a matter of constitutional right as well.

21. *Brotherhood of Locomotive Fireman and Enginemen v. Graham et al.*, 175 F.2d 802 (1948).

22. *Graham v. Brotherhood of Locomotive Firemen & Enginemen*, 338 U.S. 232 (1949).

23. Joseph L. Rauh Jr., interview, August 19, 1985. For a slightly different version of that evening, see Jervis Anderson, *A. Philip Randolph: A Biographical Portrait* (New York, 1972), 9–10.

Chapter Eleven

1. On Humphrey I have relied on Carl Solberg, *Hubert Humphrey: A Biography* (New York, 1984); and Timothy Thurber, *The Politics of Equality: Hubert H. Humphrey and the African-American Freedom Struggle* (New York, 1999).

2. On Johnson see Robert A. Caro, *The Years of Lyndon Johnson: The Path to Power* (New York, 1982); Caro, *The Years of Lyndon Johnson: Means of Ascent* (New York, 1990); and Caro, *The Years of Lyndon Johnson: Master of the Senate* (New York, 2002). Also Randall Woods, *LBJ: Architect of American Ambition* (New York, 2006).

3. Quoted in Robert Mann, *The Walls of Jericho: Lyndon Johnson, Hubert Humphrey, Richard Russell and the Struggle for Civil Rights* (New York, 1996), 204–5.

4. Joseph L. Rauh Jr., interview, Civil Rights Documentation Project, August 28, 1967, 34–35; Joseph L. Rauh Jr., interview, August 19, 1985.

5. Joseph L. Rauh to Richard Nixon, January 9, 1957, Rauh Papers. Rauh praised Nixon's "splendid opinion," which he said, brought closer the day "when the Senate will throw off the manacles which have permitted the minority, in the name of tradition, to dominate its procedures."

6. Congressional Quarterly, *Congress and the Nation* (Washington, D.C., 1965), 1:1645–70; Solberg, *Hubert Humphrey*, 157–58; Alfred H. Kelley et al., *The American Constitution: Its Origins and Development*, 7th ed. (New York, 1991), 2:567–68. Humphrey later confessed to his biographer that his role in the Communist Control Act was not "one of the things I'm proudest of." Solberg, *Hubert Humphrey*, 159.

7. Joseph L. Rauh to Josephine Goman, November 17, 1960, Rauh Papers.

8. Joseph L. Rauh to Robert M. Stein, October 31, 1955; Stein to Rauh, November 3, 1955, both Rauh Papers.

9. Joseph L. Rauh to Dan Cohen, October 28, 1977, Rauh Papers.

10. Democratic National Convention, *Proceedings*, 1956, 322–23, 325. See also Joseph L. Rauh to Walter Reuther, July 10, 1956, Rauh Papers.

11. Katie Louchheim, ed., *The Making of the New Deal: The Insiders Speak* (New York, 1983), 163–65; Laura Kalman, *Abe Fortas: A Biography* (New Haven, 1990), 201, 203–6, 168.

12. Solberg, *Hubert Humphrey*, 156–57.

13. James Rowe to Hubert Humphrey, January 28, 1959, Rauh Papers.

14. Joseph L. Rauh Jr. to Hubert Humphrey, January 29, 1959, Rauh Papers.

15. Joseph L. Rauh Jr. to Hubert Humphrey, September 30, 1959, Rauh Papers.

16. Joseph L Rauh Jr., "Notes for Robert R. Nathan," n.p., n.d., but probably September 1959, Rauh Papers.

17. Jimmy Wechsler to Arthur Schlesinger Jr., May 25, 1959; and Wechsler to Schlesinger, June 3, 1959, both Rauh Papers.

18. Joseph L. Rauh Jr. to Josephine Gomon, November 17, 1960, Rauh Papers.

19. Joseph L. Rauh Jr. to Jimmy Wechsler, June 11, 1958, Rauh Papers.

20. Joseph L. Rauh Jr., interview, August 20, 1985.

21. Arthur Schlesinger Jr. to John Kennedy, May 11, 1959, Rauh Papers.

22. Rauh, oral history, Kennedy Library, 38.

23. Solberg, *Hubert Humphrey*, 207; Arthur M. Schlesinger Jr., *Robert Kennedy and His Times* (Boston, 1978), 197.

24. Rauh, oral history, Kennedy Library, 40–41.

25. Solberg, *Hubert Humphrey*, 209–12.

26. Rauh, oral history, Kennedy Library, 67–72; Solberg, *Hubert Humphrey,* 212.

27. Joseph L. Rauh Jr. to Edward D. Hollander, May 13, 1960, Rauh Papers.

28. Hubert Humphrey to Joseph L. Rauh Jr., May 30, 1960, Rauh Papers.

29. Joseph L. Rauh, interview, August 20, 1985; Rauh, oral history, Kennedy Library, 74. Rauh was unsuccessful in preventing publication of the story in the *Post.* On the other hand, Kennedy lied to Rauh. He suffered from Addison's and took injections of desoxycorticosterone acetate pellets (DOCA) and later oral cortisone at a high daily maintenance of 25 mg, which stimulated his sexual appetites, caused added weight, and created facial puffiness. See Herbert S. Parmet, *Jack: The Struggles of John F. Kennedy* (New York, 1980), 191–92.

30. Rauh was not alone. In his journal, Arthur M. Schlesinger Jr. recorded, "I believe him [JFK] to be a devious and, if necessary, a ruthless man. I rather think . . . that Ken [Galbraith] and I were in a sense had by him; that he sought our support when he considered it useful before the convention to have liberal Democratic names behind him, but that . . . he will drop us without a second thought." Schlesinger, *Journals,* 78–79.

31. *Newsweek,* July 25, 1960, 21; *New York Times,* July 15, 1960, 1; Joseph L. Rauh Jr., interview, August 20, 1985; Rauh, oral history, Kennedy Library, 93; photo in possession of Rauh family.

32. Leonard Woodcock, oral history, 1970, John F. Kennedy Library, 13.

33. Robert Nathan, oral history, 1967, John F. Kennedy Library, 28.

34. Ibid; Joseph L. Rauh Jr., interview, August 20, 1985.

35. Joseph L. Rauh Jr. to Abe Chayes, July 15, 1960, Rauh Papers.

36. Joseph L. Rauh Jr. to Ronnie Dugger, August 3, 1960, Rauh Papers.

37. Joseph L. Rauh Jr., interview, November 4, 1985.

38. Joseph L. Rauh Jr. to Ronnie Dugger, August 10, 1960, Rauh Papers.

39. Arthur M. Schlesinger Jr. to John Kennedy, August 30, 1960, Rauh Papers.

Chapter Twelve

1. Philip L. Graham to Joseph L. Rauh Jr., December 19, 1960, Rauh Papers; Rauh, Memorandum, "The Effort to Obtain a New Senate Rule XXII at the Opening of the New Congress," December 1960, Rauh Papers.

2. Rauh to John F. Kennedy, December 7, 1962, John F. Kennedy Library.

3. Senate Committee on Rules and Administration, *Senate Cloture Rule* (Washington, D.C., 1979), 21–22.

4. Joseph L. Rauh Jr., oral history, December 23, 1965, John F. Kennedy Library, 101–2.

5. Rauh to John F. Kennedy, December 7, 1962, Rauh Papers.

6. *Griffin v. State,* 171 A.2d 717 (1961).

7. Rauh, Memorandum for *Griffin v. Maryland* File, May 29, 1963, Rauh Papers. William T. Coleman, a former Frankfurter law clerk, stressed the same point to Jack Greenberg: "Even if the Negro does not have an affirmative right to be served at a lunch counter . . he does have a constitutional right to prevent the private owner from using the State criminal and police process to carry out the private owner's racial prejudice." Coleman to Greenberg, July 29, 1963, Rauh Papers.

8. Bernard Schwartz, *Super Chief: Earl Warren and His Supreme Court—A Judicial Biography* (New York, 1983), 508–9.

9. Joseph L. Rauh Jr. to Jack Greenberg, September 9, 1963, Rauh Papers.

10. Lee White to John F. Kennedy, December 19, 1963, Kennedy Papers.

11. *Griffin v. Maryland,* 378 U.S. 130 (1964).

12. *Bell v. Maryland,* 378 U.S. 226 (1964); Schwartz, *Super Chief,* 516–25.

13. Washington Field Office to Hoover, Memorandum on Committee of Inquiry into the Administration of Justice in the Freedom Struggle Sponsored by the Congress of Racial Equality, May 23, 1962, Rauh FBI File.

14. Rauh to John F. Kennedy, September 16, 1963, John F. Kennedy Library.

15. Excerpts from address of Joseph L. Rauh Jr. before New York Civil Liberties Union, February 10, 1965, Rauh Papers.

16. Joseph L. Rauh Jr. to Jerome K. Heilbron, September 16, 1963; see also Rauh to Robert Kennedy, July 19, 1963; and Burke Marshall to Rauh, December 2, 1963, all Rauh Papers.

17. Rauh, oral history, Kennedy Library, 112–13.

18. Schlesinger, *Journals,* 191. Baldwin and other black leaders engaged in a similar confrontation with Robert Kennedy shortly after Birmingham. See Schlesinger, *Journals,* 191–93.

19. Joseph L. Rauh Jr., interview, November 4, 1985.

20. Joseph L. Rauh Jr., interview, November 4, 1985; Mann, *The Walls of Jericho,* 355–58.

21. *Washington Star,* October 18, 1963. See also Carl M. Brauer, *John F. Kennedy and the Second Reconstruction* (New York, 1977), 304–5.

22. Quoted in Mann, *Walls of Jericho,* 373–74.

23. Joseph L. Rauh Jr., remarks at Hofstra University Dream and Reality Conference, February 20, 1988, Rauh Papers; Russell Baker in the *New York Times,* August 29, 1963.

24. Joseph L. Rauh Jr., interview, November 4, 1985; E. W. Kenworthy in the *New York Times*, August 29, 1963.

25. Joseph L. Rauh Jr., interview, November 4, 1985; Brauer, *John F. Kennedy and the Second Reconstruction*, 307–8.

26. John F. Kennedy, *Public Papers of the Presidents, 1963*, 849.

Chapter Thirteen

1. *New York Post*, February 7, 1963.

2. Joseph L. Rauh Jr. to Francis Biddle, February 11, 1963, Rauh Papers.

3. Louis E. Martin, oral history, transcript of Hofstra University Dream and Reality Conference, February 20, 1988, 2. Martin, a Johnson confidant, was deputy chairman of the Democratic National Committee in 1960.

4. Charles Whalen and Barbara Whalen, *The Longest Debate: A Legislative History of the 1964 Civil Rights Act* (Cabin John, Md., 1985), 63.

5. James Farmer, oral history, transcript of Hofstra University Dream and Reality Conference, February 20, 1988, 7.

6. Michael Beschloss, *Taking Charge: The Johnson White House Tapes, 1963–1964* (New York, 1997), 107.

7. Joseph L. Rauh Jr. to Joyce Tucker, May 29, 1988; Rauh to Lyndon Johnson, December 9, 1963, both Rauh Papers.

8. Joseph L. Rauh Jr., interview, November 4, 1985.

9. Ibid.

10. Rauh, Hofstra transcript, 24.

11. Mann, *The Walls of Jericho*, 395.

12. Marvin Rosenberg to Joseph L. Rauh Jr., November 3, 1977, Rauh Papers.

13. Ibid.

14. Ibid.

15. Joseph L. Rauh Jr., interview, November 4, 1985.

16. Nicholas deB Katzenbach, oral history, transcript of Hofstra University Dream and Reality Conference, February 20, 1988,13.

17. On Moses, see William H. Chafe, *Never Stop Running: Allard Lowenstein and the Struggle to Save American Liberalism* (New York, 1993), 86–210.

18. Joseph L. Rauh Jr. to Albert Sayer, March 30, 1964, Rauh Papers.

19. Bob Moses to Joseph L. Rauh Jr., May 1, 1964; and Rauh to Moses, May 8, 1964, both Rauh Papers.

20. Joseph L. Rauh Jr., "Memorandum on the Mississippi Freedom Democratic Party,"n.p., n.d., Rauh Papers.

21. Ibid.

22. Ibid.

23. Telephone conversation between Johnson and Connally, July 23, 1964, in Beschloss, *Taking Charge*, 467–69.

24. Rauh, "Memorandum on the Mississippi Freedom Democratic Party."

25. Joseph L. Rauh Jr. to Tom B. Carvey Jr., August 10, 1964; Rauh, "Memorandum on the Mississippi Freedom Democratic Party," both Rauh Papers.

26. Telephone conversation between Johnson and Reuther, August 9, 1964, in Beschloss, *Taking Charge,* 510–11.

27. Telephone conversation between Johnson and Humphrey, August 14, 1964, in Beschloss, *Taking Charge,* 515; Joseph L. Rauh Jr., interview, November 5, 1985.

28. Rauh, "Memorandum on the Mississippi Freedom Democratic Party"; Taylor Branch, *Pillar of Fire: America in the King Years, 1963–65* (New York, 1989), 457–58.

29. Remarks in Rebuttal of Joseph L. Rauh, Jr., before the Credentials Committee of the Democratic National Convention, August 22, 1964, Rauh Papers.

30. Telephone conversation between Johnson and Humphrey, August 14, 1964, in Beschloss, *Taking Charge,* 515.

31. FBI Memorandum, "Re: Communist Party, United States of America—Negro Question—Communist Influence in Racial Matters—Internal Security," August 20, 1964, Rauh FBI File.

32. Reminiscences of Joseph L. Rauh, Lowenstein Oral History Project, June 9, 1988, 9, University of North Carolina Archives.

33. Chafe, *Never Stop Running,* 197–98; Joseph L. Rauh Jr., interview, November 5, 1985; Branch, *Pillar of Fire,* 465.

34. Joseph L. Rauh Jr., interview, November 5, 1985.

35. Reminiscences of Joseph L. Rauh, Lowenstein Oral History Project, 14.

36. Joseph L. Rauh Jr., interview, November 5, 1985; Branch, *Pillar of Fire,* 473–74.

37. Joseph L. Rauh Jr. to Edward F. Gray, September 16, 1964, Rauh Papers.

38. John Lewis, *Walking with the Wind,* 281.

Chapter Fourteen

1. Joseph L. Rauh to Reinhold and Ursula Niebuhr, October 7, 1964, Rauh Papers.

2. Beschloss, *Taking Charge,* 363.

3. Rauh, oral history, Kennedy Library, 80.

4. Joseph L. Rauh Jr. to Philip Potter, March 29, 1966, Rauh Papers.

5. Paul Douglas to John Kenneth Galbraith, June 13, 1967; and Joseph L. Rauh Jr. to Douglas, June 16, 1967, Rauh Papers.

6. Arthur Schlesinger Jr. to Philip Potter, March 23, 1966; and Schlesinger to Humphrey, March 25, 1966, both Rauh Papers.

7. Steve M. Gillon, *Politics and Vision: The ADA and American Liberalism, 1947–1985* (New York, 1987), 181–87.

8. Allard Lowenstein, speech, ca. 1967, Lowenstein Papers, University of North Carolina.

9. Carl A. Auerbach to Rauh, August 12, 1965; Rauh to Auerbach, August 25, 1965, Rauh Papers.

10. On ILGWU financial support for ADA, see James A. Wechsler to Gus Tyler, July 27, 1967, Rauh Papers.

11. Joseph L. Rauh Jr., interview, November 5, 1985.

12. John Roche to Lyndon Johnson, April 5, 1967, Johnson Papers; Joseph L. Rauh Jr., interview, November 5, 1985; Gillon, *Politics and Vision,* 198.

13. Joseph L. Rauh to Al Lowenstein, April 3, 1967, Rauh Papers; and Gillon, *Politics and Vision*, 197–98.

14. Joseph L. Rauh Jr. to Marvin Rosenberg, May 23, 1967; and Rosenberg to Rauh, May 31, 1967, Rauh Papers.

15. Rauh, Lowenstein Oral History Project, 34

16. Marvin Rosenberg to Rauh, August 8, 1967; Eugene Wyman to Rauh, August 9, 1967, both Rauh Papers.

17. Rauh to Wyman, August 14, 1967, Rauh Papers.

18. Joseph L. Rauh Jr., McCarthy Historical Project oral history, June 10, 1969, 87–115.

19. Joseph L. Rauh Jr. to Mrs. Paul G. Myerson, December 15, 1967; and Joseph L. Rauh Jr., excerpts from address before the Yale Law School Forum, September 27, 1967, Rauh Papers.

20. Joseph L. Rauh Jr. to Al Lowenstein, September 26, 1967; Lowenstein to Rauh, October 1, 1967, Rauh Papers. In a conversation with Marilyn Gorlin, vice chairwoman of the Minnesota Democratic-Farmer-Labor Party, Lowenstein expressed the belief that "Rauh's proposal was merely a holding action . . . merely a way to start working." Marilyn Gorlin to Carl Auerbach, September 28, 1967; and Auerbach to Rauh, September 29, 1967, both Rauh Papers.

Chapter Fifteen

1. Albert Eisele, *Almost to the Presidency: A Biography of Two American Politicians* (Blue Earth, Minn., 1977), 265.

2. Ibid., 276.

3. *Washington Post*, February 10, 1968.

4. Joseph L. Rauh Jr. to Robert S. Benjamin, December 21, 1967, Rauh Papers.

5. Rauh, McCarthy oral history, 101–3.

6. Joseph L. Rauh Jr. to Abram Eisenman, December 11, 1967, Rauh Papers.

7. See John Kenneth Galbraith to ADA Board Members, December 14, 1967, ADA Papers.

8. Joseph L. Rauh Jr., interview, November 5, 1985.

9. *Washington Post*, February 11, 1968.

10. Ibid.

11. Joseph L. Rauh Jr., interview, November 5, 1985; *New York Times*, March 14, 1968, and March 17, 1968.

12. Joseph L. Rauh Jr., McCarthy oral history, 193–222.

13. *New York Times*, July 20, 1968; *Washington Post*, May 19, 1968, and May 20, 1968.

14. Stout, *People*, 280; Eisele, *Almost to the Presidency*, 344.

15. Joseph L. Rauh Jr., interview, November 5, 1985.

16. Robert Dallek, *Flawed Giant: Lyndon Johnson and His Times, 1961–1973* (New York, 1998), 574–75; Joseph L. Rauh Jr., interview, November 5, 1985.

17. Rauh, McCarthy oral history, 253–55; Joseph L. Rauh Jr., interview, November 5, 1985; Carl Solberg, *Hubert Humphrey: A Biography* (Norton, 1984), 370.

18. Solberg, *Hubert Humphrey*, 380–84; Dallek, *Flawed Giant*, 575–92.

19. Joseph L. Rauh Jr. to Abram Eisenman, November 22, 1968, Rauh Papers.
20. Solberg, *Hubert Humphrey,* 407

Chapter Sixteen

1. Brit Hume, *Death and the Mines: Rebellion and Murder in the United Mine Workers* (New York, 1971), 70.
2. Catherine Baker, "They Made All the Money, but I Had All the Fun," *Public Citizen* 8 (January–February 1988): 19.
3. Hume, *Death and the Mines,* 16; Trevor Armbrister, *Act of Vengeance: The Yablonski Murders and Their Solution* (New York, 1975), 36.
4. Joseph E. Finley, *The Corrupt Kingdom: The Rise and Fall of the United Mine Workers* (New York, 1972), 159–91.
5. Hume, *Death and the Mines,* 43; Finley, *The Corrupt Kingdom,* 241–42.
6. Armbrister, *Act of Vengeance,* 48.
7. Ibid., 60–61; Chip Yablonski to author, February 3, 2000.
8. Joseph L. Rauh Jr., oral history, July 30, 1969, Lyndon Johnson Library, 29.
9. *Yablonski v. UMW,* 71 L.R.R.M. 3041 (D.D.C. 1969; *Yablonski v. UMW,* 71 L.R.R.M. 2606 (D.D.C. 1969); and *Yablonski v. UMW,* 305 F. Supp. 868 (D.D.C. 1969); *Yablonski v. UMW,* 305 F. Supp. 876 (D.D.C. 1969).
10. Finley, *The Corrupt Kingdom,* 267–68.
11. Joseph L. Rauh Jr. to George P. Shultz, July 9, 1969, and July 18, 1969, Rauh Papers.
12. George P. Shultz to Rauh, July 23, 1969, Rauh Papers.
13. See *Hearings on Investigation of Mine Workers' Election before the Subcommittee on Labor of the Senate Committee on Labor and Public Welfare,* 91st Cong., 2d sess. (1970), n. 3, at 82–92, 101–2.
14. Armbrister, *Act of Vengeance,* 76–77.
15. Clarice Feldman, notes to author.
16. Joseph L. Rauh Jr., interview, August 23, 1986.
17. Cartha DeLoach to Clyde Tolson, January 6, 1970; Alex Rosen to DeLoach, January 7, 1970, both Rauh FBI File.
18. Joseph L. Rauh Jr., interview, August 23, 1986; Cartha DeLoach to Tolson, April 21, 1970; and Hoover to DeLoach, April 21, 1970, both Rauh FBI File.
19. Joseph L. Rauh Jr., interview, August 23, 1986.
20. *Hearings on Investigation of Mine Workers' Election,* 347–48. The special prosecutor, Richard Sprague, had also stated publicly that he believed the conspiracy to murder Yablonski reached high into the UMW leadership. See *Fortune,* January 1971, 78.
21. *New York Times,* May 5, 1970, and May 27, 1970.
22. Joseph L. Rauh Jr., "LMRDA—Enforce It or Repeal It," *Georgia Law Review* 5 (Summer 1971): 643–60.
23. *Hodgson v. United Mine Workers,* 14 Fed. R. Serv. 2d (Callaghan), 1113.
24. *Hodgson v. United Mine Workers,* 1971 U.S. App. LEXIS 10546.
25. *Trbovich v. United Mine Workers,* 404 U.S. 528 (1972); *Hodgson v. United Mine Workers,* 344 F. Supp. 17 (1972). Joseph L. Rauh Jr., interview, August 23, 1986.

26. *Blankenship, et al., v. W. A. (Tony) Boyle, et al.*, 337 F. Supp. 298 (1972).

27. *Yablonski v. UMW*, 448 F.2d 521, 1175 (1971).

28. Joseph L. Rauh Jr. to Congressman Robert F. Drinan, May 15, 1972, Rauh Papers.

29. Jeremiah Collins to W. A. Boyle and John Owens, May 25, 1972, Rauh Papers.

30. Feldman, notes to author.

31. Joseph L. Rauh Jr. to Marquis Childs, July 26, 1972; Arnold Miller to Paul Porter, September 12, 1974; Rauh to Isaac Hunt and Roger Hartley, December 10, 1975; Joseph L. Rauh Jr., interview, August 23, 1986. Williams never sued Rauh, but in a 1975 exchange in *Juris Doctor*, a member of the Williams and Connolly firm, Michael Tigar, attempted to defend the payments to Pass on the grounds that he was entitled to the presumption of innocence and that his family, dependent upon his salary, included a severely and permanently disabled child. "Our law firm is not ashamed of the advice . . notwithstanding the fact that the judge in the case disagreed and ordered a termination of salary payments." Tigar to *Juris Doctor*, February 19, 1975; and Rauh response, March 13, 1975, all Rauh Papers.

32. Chip Yablonski, interview, September 3, 1987.

Chapter Seventeen

1. The UAW led the effort to enjoin the Right-to-Work Foundation from further financing employee suits against the unions. See Memorandum from Rauh, Silard and Lichtman to counsel for plaintiff unions, August 6, 1974, and November 20, 1974, both Rauh Papers.

2. Joseph L. Rauh Jr., interview, August 27, 1986; "Joe Rauh: Attorney for the Dissidents," *Business Week*, February 10, 1975, 94–95.

3. As head of the AFL-CIO's industrial union division, Abel had a powerful ally in President Meany, who had dismissed Yablonski prior to his murder as "just a guy in the kitchen trying to get into the living room," See Clyde Summers, Joseph Rauh, and Herman Benson, *Union Democracy and Landrum-Griffin* (New York, 1986), 10. Also Joseph L. Rauh Jr., interview, August 27–28, 1986.

4. Rauh, "LMRDA—Enforce It or Repeal It," 643, 660.

5. *Trbovich v. United Mine Workers of America*, 404 U.S. 528 (1972).

6. See Jeffrey A. Weinberg, "Trbovich v. United Mine Workers of America: Move over Mr. Secretary—A Union Member May Intervene in Suits under Title IV of the LMRDA," *George Washington Law Review* 41 (March 1973): 580.

7. *Bachowski v. Brennan and United Steel Workers of America*, 502 F.2d 79 (1974).

8. Ibid., 26, 27, 29.

9. *Dunlop v. Bachowski, et al.*, 421 U.S. 560 (1975), 566–77, 572–74.

10. Joseph L. Rauh Jr., interview, August 27, 1986; *Bachowski v. Brennan*, 405 F. Supp. 1227 (1975), at 1234.

11. *Bachowski v. Brennan*, 413 F. Supp. 147 (1976), at 151.

12. In 1977–78, Rauh, Despres, Scheider, and Yablonski prevailed in the court of appeals on the issue of recovering fees in Sadlowski's initial District 31 fight, a decision confirmed by the Supreme Court when it denied *certiorari*. See *Brennan v.*

United Steelworkers of America, 554 F.2d 586 (1977); and *United Steelworkers of America v. Sadlowski,* 435 U.S. 977 (1978), cert. denied.

13. Joseph L. Rauh Jr. to Leslie W. Dunbar, October 14, 1976, Rauh Papers. In addition to Dunbar's contribution from the Field Foundation, Rauh raised $21,000 from the J. M. Kaplan Fund for the Association for Union Democracy's two attorneys, Schneider and Tom Geoghegan.

14. Bruce A. Miller to Joseph L. Rauh Jr., December 27, 1976; and Rauh to Miller, December 29, 1976, both Rauh Papers.

15. Joseph L. Rauh Jr. to Michael H. Gottesman, January 6, 1977, Rauh Papers.

16. Joseph L. Rauh Jr. and Judith Schneider to F. Ray Marshall, June 30, 1977, Rauh Papers.

17. *Sadlowski v. Marshall,* 464 F. Supp. 858 (1979); and *Sadlowski v. Marshall,* 447 U.S. 905 (1980), cert. denied.

18. Quoted in *Business Week,* February 10, 1975, 94.

19. *Washington Post,* January 3, 1977. Joseph L. Rauh Jr., interview, August 27, 1986. Clayman's letter, in addition to praising Abel, blamed Rauh for the defeat of Hubert Humphrey in 1968. "They got decent people to do indecent things," Rauh remarked later.

20. *New York Times,* November 1, 1979.

21. *Sadlowski v. United Steelworkers of America,* 507 F. Supp. 623 (1981).

22. *Sadlowski v. United Steelworkers of America,* 645 F.2d 1114 (1981), at 1121.

23. *United Steelworkers of America v. Sadlowski,* 457 U.S. 102 (1982), at 112–16.

24. Ibid., at 124–25.

25. Joseph L. Rauh Jr., interview, August 27, 1986. On affirmative action and the USWA see *United Steelworkers of America v. Weber,* 443 U.S. 193 (1979). See also Judith Stein, *Running Steel, Running America: Race, Economic Policy, and the Decline of Liberalism* (Chapel Hill, 1998).

26. On Tucker's career, see Henry Weinstein, "A Less Perfect Union," *Mother Jones,* April 1988, 10–15.

27. Ibid.

28. *Brock, et al., v. International Union, United Automobile, Aerospace, and Agricultural Implement Workers of America,* 682 F. Supp. 1415 (1988).

29. Joseph L. Rauh Jr., to Rev. Msgr. George C. Higgns, May 9, 1988, Rauh Papers.

30. Jordan Rossen to Joseph L. Rauh Jr., June 3, 1988; Rauh to Rossen, June 17, 1988, Rauh Papers.

31. Chip Yablonski to Jordan Rossen, June 27, 1988, Rauh Papers.

32. Copy of "New Directions" broadside, n.d., n.p., Rauh Papers.

33. Joseph L. Rauh Jr. to Douglas Fraser, August 2, 1989; Fraser to Rauh, August 9, 1989, Rauh Papers.

34. *Brock v. International Union,* UAW, 889 F.2d 685 (1989).

Chapter Eighteen

1. Kalman, *Abe Fortas,* 322–78; Bruce Allen Murphy, *Fortas: The Rise and Ruin of a Supreme Court Justice* (New York, 1988), 494–577.

2. Quoted in Ed Cray, *Chief Justice: A Biography of Earl Warren* (New York, 1997), 497.

3. *Washington Star*, August 19, 1969.

4. *Simkins v. Moses H. Cone Memorial Hospital*, 323 F.2d 959 (1963). And see *Burton v. Wilmington Parking Authority*, 365 U.S. 715 (1961).

5. *Griffin v. Board of Supervisors*, 322 F.2d 332 (1963). Compare Black's opinion at 377 U.S. 218 (1964), 234.

6. *Darlington Mfg. Co. v. NLRB*, 325 F.2d 682 (1963); 380 U.S. 263, 275 (1965).

7. Joseph L. Rauh Jr., interview, August 16, 1986.

8. *Nomination of Clement F. Haynsworth, Jr.*, Hearings before the Committee on the Judiciary United States Senate, 91st Cong., 1st sess. (September 16–26, 1969), 163.

9. Ibid., 355.

10. Ibid., 434.

11. Ibid., 464–65; Richard M. Nixon, *RN: The Memoirs of Richard Nixon* (New York, 1978), 420.

12. James Wooton reviewed Eaton's reporting in the *New York Times*, August 24, 1969. Eaton subsequently won the Pulitzer Prize for his reporting in the Haynsworth case.

13. *Nomination of Clement F. Haynsworth, Jr.*, 166.

14. *Washington Star*, November 22, 1969. The *New York Times*, which had urged Nixon to withdraw the nomination but did not ask senators to vote against it, concluded finally that it was "better for the court and country" that the judge had been defeated rather than confirmed by a narrow margin.

15. Ibid., 109.

16. *New York Times*, January 20, 1970.

17. Joseph L. Rauh Jr., interview, August 16, 1986.

18. *Nomination of George Harrold Carswell*, Hearings before the Committee on the Judiciary of the United States Senate, 91st Cong., 2d sess., January 27, 28, 29, and February 2–3, 1970, 21–22. The *New York Times* published excerpts from the speech on January 23, 1970, that Carswell repudiated as "obnoxious and abhorrent to my personal philosophy." He noted in passing that he had lost the election "because I was considered too liberal."

19. Richard Harris, *Decision* (New York, 1971), 26, remains the single best account of the Carswell confirmation fight.

20. Joseph L. Rauh to Lawrence E. Walsh, February 16, 1971, Rauh Papers. Responding to Harris's account of the ABA's role in the Carswell fight, which appeared in the *New Yorker*, December 5, 1970, Walsh claimed that his committee, not Rauh, had initiated contact about the golf course documents. Rauh told Walsh "there is no question I went to Mr. Horsky's office with the documents and that I went there for the purpose described by Mr. Harris."

21. *Due v. Tallahassee Theaters, Inc.*, 333 F.2d 630 (1964).

22. See, for instance, *Steele v. Board of Public Instruction of Leon County*, 371 F.2d 395 (1963).

23. *Nomination of G. Harrold Carswell*, 305–6.

24. Joseph L. Rauh Jr., interview, August 16, 1986.

25. See *Roe v. Wade*, 410 U.S. 113 (1973); *Bowers v. Hardwick*, 478 U.S. 186 (1986); *Callins v. Collins*, 510 U.S. 1141 (1994); and Linda Greenhouse, *Becoming Justice Blackmun* (New York, 2005).

26. *Nominations of William H. Rehnquist and Lewis F. Powell, Jr.*, Hearings before the Committee on the Judiciary of the United States Senate, 92nd Cong., 1st sess., November 3, 4, 8, 9, and 10, 1971, 400.

27. Ibid., 305, 307.

28. Ibid., 309.

29. Ibid., 70–71.

30. See the devastating rebuttal to the claims of Rehnquist and Cronson by Richard Kluger, *Simple Justice: The History of Brown v. Board of Education and Black America's Struggle for Equality* (New York, 1976), 606–10; also the *Washington Post*, December 11, 1971.

31. See, for example, *Roe v. Wade*, 410 U.S. 113 (1973); *Cleveland Board of Education v. LeFleur*, 414 U.S. 632 (1974); *Furman v. Georgia*, 408 U.S. 238 (1972); *Regents of the University of California v. Bakke*, 438 U.S. 265 (1978); and *Johnson v. Santa Clara County Transportation Agency*, 107 S. Ct. 1442 (1987).

32. See "Judicial Record of Justice William Rehnquist," Report for the Leadership Conference for Civil Rights, September, 1986, Rauh Papers; *Bob Jones University v. United States*, 461 U.S. 575 (1983).

33. *Frontiero v. Richardson*, 411 U.S. 677 (1973); *Cleveland Board of Education v. LeFleur*, 414 U.S. 632 (1974).

34. *Washington Post*, July 29, 1986.

35. Ibid., 146–47.

36. Elsie Douglas to Edward M. Kennedy, August 8, 1986, copy in Rauh Papers.

37. "Fact Sheet on William H. Rehnquist," copy in Rauh Papers. Rauh pursued without success another investigation of Rehnquist's attitudes about *Brown* when Dan Edelman learned from William Causey, another attorney with whom he had worked, that E. Barrett Prettyman Jr. had in his possession a letter written by Rehnquist in the 1960s in which the latter stated "time has proven that *Brown* was wrongly decided." Prettyman, however, denied the existence of any reference to the *Brown* decision in a Rehnquist letter and claimed that Causey had confused it with another item. Causey later agreed with Prettyman that he had mistaken the content of a *Time* magazine article for the letter, an explanation that did not entirely convince Edelman or Rauh but that had become irrelevant by 1988. See E. Barrett Prettyman Jr. to Joseph L. Rauh Jr., October 5, 1988; Rauh to Prettyman, November 30, 1988; Prettyman to Rauh, December 5, 1988; Peter Edelman to Rauh, December 12, 1988; and William Causey to Rauh, December 13, 1988, all Rauh Papers.

38. *Nomination of Justice William Hobbs Rehnquist*, Hearings before the Committee on the Judiciary of the United States Senate, 99th Cong., 2nd sess., July 29–August 1, 1986, 915–16.

39. *Nomination of Judge Antonin Scalia*, Hearings before the Committee on the Judiciary of the United States Senate, 99th Cong., 2nd sess., August 5–6, 1986, 212.

Chapter Nineteen

1. Herman Benson to Joan K. Davidson, June 1, 1988, copy in Rauh Papers.

2. Robert Bork, "Civil Rights—A Challenge," *New Republic*, August 31, 1963, 22.

3. Robert Bork, "Neutral Principles and Some First Amendment Problems," *Indiana Law Review* 47 (1971): 15–16.

4. Testimony, *The Human Life Bill*, Hearings before the Subcommittee on Separation of Powers of the Senate Committee on the Judiciary, 97th Cong., 1st sess., 1982, 308–10.

5. Bork, "Neutral Principles," 9.

6. Testimony, *The Human Life Bill*, 310.

7. *Nader v. Bork*, 366 F. Supp. 104 (D.D.C. 1973). The Court of Appeals ruled the issue moot in the wake of Nixon's resignation.

8. *Nomination of Robert H. Bork to Be Associate Justice of the Supreme Court of the United States*, Hearings before the Committee on the Judiciary of the United States Senate, 100th Cong., 1st sess., September 15–23, 18–30, 1987, 869–72.

9. Ibid., 987.

10. Joseph L. Rauh Jr., interview, March 19, 1988; Michael Pertshuk and David Cohen, "Bork Project Interviews—Joe Rauh," November 11, 1988, 7–8.

11. *Nomination of Robert Bork*, 4134–46.

12. Joseph L. Rauh Jr., interview, March 19, 1988.

13. *New York Times*, October 30, 1987.

14. *St. Louis Post-Dispatch*, November 3, 1987; *New York Times*, October 30, 1987, and October 31, 1987.

15. *New York Times*, November 6, 1987.

16. Joseph L. Rauh Jr., interview, March 19, 1988; *New York Times*, November 7, 1987, and November 8, 1987.

17. *Spangler v. Pasadena Board of Education*, 611 F.2d 1239 (1979).

18. *Gerdom v. Continental Airlines, Inc.*, 692 F.2d 602 (1982).

19. *AFSCME v. State of Washington*, 770 F.2d 1401 (1985); *Beller v. Middendorf*, 632 F.2d 788 (1980).

20. *Nomination of Anthony M. Kennedy to be Associate Justice of the Supreme Court of the United States*, Hearings before the Committee on the Judiciary of the United States Senate, 100th Cong., 1st sess., December 14–16, 1987, 300.

21. Testimony of Joseph L. Rauh Jr. on behalf of Americans for Democratic Action, Inc. on the nomination of Anthony Kennedy, December 1987; Rauh to author, December 19, 1987, both Rauh Papers.

22. *Nomination of Anthony M. Kennedy*, 379.

23. *Aranda v. Van Sickle*, 600 F.2d 1267 (1979). Kennedy's concurrence also required the plaintiffs to demonstrate "an invidious intent" behind the at-large system, which ignored the long history of discrimination against Hispanics in Los Angeles. Tribe had misread Kennedy, Rauh believed, because he had become too absorbed in litigation defending corporate clients such as Penzoil. Joseph L. Rauh Jr., interview, March 19, 1988.

24. Nomination of Anthony M. Kennedy, 450–51.

25. Joseph L. Rauh Jr., "Reopen the Hearings on Judge Kennedy," *Washington Post*, January 17, 1988.

26. Quoted in *Manchester Union Leader*, August 4, 1990.

27. *Nomination of David H. Souter to be Associate Justice of the United States*

Supreme Court, Hearings before the Committee on the Judiciary of the United States Senate, 100th Cong., 2nd sess., September 13–14, 17–19, 1990, 122.

28. Ibid., 466.

29. *Los Angeles Times,* June 29, 1991.

30. Ibid.

31. Joseph L. Rauh Jr., interview, September 16, 1991; *New York Times,* July 2, 1991.

32. See Karen Tumulty, "Court Path Started in the Ashes," *Los Angeles Times,* July 7, 1991.

33. Neil Haven, "On Thomas' Climb, Ambivalence about Issue of Affirmative Action," *New York Times,* July 14, 1991.

34. *Nomination of Judge Clarence Thomas to be Associate Justice of the Supreme Court of the United States,* Hearings before the Committee on the Judiciary of the United States Senate, 102nd Cong., 1st sess., September 17 and 19, 1991, 834.

35. Joseph L. Rauh Jr., "Nomination and Confirmation of Supreme Court Justices," lecture in honor of Judge Frank Coffin, University of Maine School of Law. Rauh was to have delivered this speech on October 13, 1992.

36. *Los Angeles Times,* October 16, 1991; Timothy M. Phelps and Helen Winternitz, *Capitol Games: Clarence Thomas, Anita Hill, and the Story of a Supreme Court Nomination* (New York, 1992), passim; Toni Morrison, *Race-ing Justice, En-Gendering Power: Essays on Anita Hill, Clarence Thomas, and the Construction of Social Reality* (New York, 1992), passim; Paul Simon, *Advice and Consent: Clarence Thomas, Robert Bork and the Intriguing History of the Supreme Court's Nomination Battles* (Washington, 1992), passim; Ronald Dworkin, "One Year Later, the Debate Goes On," *New York Times Book Review,* October 25, 1992.

37. *Missouri v. Jenkins,* 515 U.S. 70 (1995).

38. *Adarand Constructors, Inc. v. Pena,* 515 U.S. 200 (1995).

39. *Shaw v. Reno,* 509 U.S. 630 (1993).

40. See Thomas's dissent in *Holder v. Hall,* 512 U.S. 874 (1994).

41. *Farmer v. Brennan,* 511 U.S. 825 (1994).

42. See, for example, *United States v. Lopez,* 514 U.S. 549 (1995); *Printz v. United States,* 521 U.S. 898 (1997); and *United States v. Morrison,* 529 U.S. 598 (2000).

43. *Southwestern Pennsylvania Planned Parenthood v. Casey,* 505 U.S. 833 (1992); *Romer v. Evans,* 517 U.S. 620 (1996).

44. *Lawrence v. Texas,* 539 U.S. 558 (2003).

Chapter Twenty

1. See William N. Eskridge Jr., "Overriding Supreme Court Statutory Interpretation Decisions," *Yale Law Journal* 101 (1991): 331–38; Joseph A. Yablonski to author, February 3, 2000.

2. The landmark cases were *Adams v. Richardson,* 356 F. Supp. 92 (D.D.C. 1973) and *Adams v. Richardson,* 156 U.S. App. D.C. 267, 480 F.2d 1159 (1973).

3. Joseph L. Rauh Jr., interview, August 28, 1986. See also Roland Evans Jr. and Robert D. Novak, *Nixon in the White House: The Frustration of Power* (New York, 1971), 175–76.

4. See *Extension of the Voting Rights Act of 1965,* Hearings before the Subcommittee on Constitutional Rights of the Committee on the Judiciary of the United States Senate, 94th Cong., 1st sess., April and May 1975, 44–68; Joseph L. Rauh Jr., interview, August 28, 1986.

5. Joseph L. Rauh Jr., interview, August 28, 1986.

6. Remarks of Joseph L. Rauh Jr. before the Milwaukee Jewish Council dinner, June 26, 1973, copy in Rauh Papers.

7. Ibid.

8. *DeFunis v. Odegaard,* in *Landmark Briefs and Arguments of the Supreme Court of the United States,* 80, 287 (full cite is in note 3 to chap. 1). The Washington Supreme Court had sustained the program, but a bare majority of the United States Supreme Court dismissed the suit on grounds of mootness because DeFunis had entered another law school and was due to graduate. See *DeFuinis v. Odegaard,* 416 U.S. 312 (1974).

9. *Regents of the University of California v. Bakke,* 438 U.S. 265 (1978). Powell's *Bakke* formula lived on to gain another majority 25 years later in the next critical education case, *Grutter v. Bollinger,* 539 U.S. 306 (2003). Speaking for the Court, Justice O' Connor, who idolized Powell, invoked his views to sustain the race-conscious admissions program at the University of Michigan law school.

10. Phillippa Strum, *When the Nazis Came to Skokie* (Lawrence, 1999). Also Joseph L. Rauh Jr., interview, August 28, 1986; *Collin v. Smith,* 447 F. Supp. 767 (N.D. Ill. 1978); affirmed by the Court of Appeals, 478 F.2d 1197 (7th Cir. 1978); cert. denied, 439 U.S. 916 (1978).

11. *Honda v. Clark,* 386 U.S. 484 (1967).

12. *New York Times,* August 2, 1983; Joseph L. Rauh Jr. to Joan Z. Bernstein, May 21, 1982; Testimony of Joseph L. Rauh Jr. before the House Subcommittee on Administrative Law and Government Relations, April 28, 1986, copy in Rauh Papers; Public Law 100-383, August 10, 1988, 102 Stat. 903; Weekly *Compilation of Presidential Documents* 24 (August 10, 1988).

13. Testimony of Joseph L. Rauh Jr. before the House Appropriations Subcommittee on Commerce, Justice and State, April 5, 1989, copy in Rauh Papers.

14. Joseph L. Rauh Jr., interview, August 28, 1986. Charles McClain, ed., *The Mass Internment of Japanese Americans and the Quest for Legal Redress* (New York, 1994), 389–93; Mitchell T. Maki, Harry H. L. Kitano, and S. Megan Berthold, *Achieving the Impossible Dream: How Japanese Americans Obtained Redress* (Urbana, 1999).

15. Quoted in *St. Louis Post-Dispatch,* May 1, 1977.

16. Joseph L. Rauh Jr., interview, August 29, 1986. On Lindsay see Nat Hentoff, *A Political Life: The Education of John V. Lindsay* (New York, 1969); and Woody Klein, *Lindsay's Promise: The Dream That Failed—A Personal Account* (New York, 1970).

17. *New York Times,* July 4, 1972; *Brown v. O'Brien,* 468 F.2d 563 (July 5, 1972).

18. *Brown v. O'Brien,* 468 F.2d 563 (July 5, 1972); Joseph L. Rauh Jr., interview, August 29, 1986.

19. Joseph L. Rauh Jr., interview, August 29, 1986.

20. Chalmers M. Roberts, "The Rauh-Carter Estrangement," *Washington Post,* July 26, 1976; Joseph L. Rauh Jr., interview, August 29, 1986.

21. "Carter's Record," Memorandum, March 21, 1976, Rauh Papers; Joseph L. Rauh Jr., interview, August 29, 1986.

22. Ibid.

23. Joseph L. Rauh Jr., "Memorandum of Conversation with Jimmy Carter," September 29, 1976, Rauh Papers.

24. *Nomination of Griffin Bell,* Hearings before the Committee on the Judiciary of the United States Senate, 95th Cong., 1st sess., January 11–14, 17–19, 1977, 244–49.

25. *ADA World,* March–April, 1979; Joseph L. Rauh Jr., "Who Says Liberalism Is Dead," *Washington Post,* August 19, 1978.

26. Arthur M. Schlesinger Jr. and Joseph L. Rauh Jr. to ADA Board, September 13, 1980, Rauh Papers; *New York Times,* June 22, 1979.

27. Joseph L. Rauh Jr., speech to D.C. Democrats, September 25, 1979; and speech to Montgomery County Democrats, October 29, 1979, both Rauh Papers.

28. *Washington Post,* August 15, 1980.

29. Arthur M. Schlesinger Jr. and Joseph L. Rauh, Memorandum to ADA members, September 22, 1980; ADA Endorsement of Carter, September 22, 1980, Rauh Papers.

30. Joseph L. Rauh Jr. to Leon Schull, October 24, 1980; and Rauh to Patsy Mink, October 3, 1980, both in ADA Papers.

31. Joseph L. Rauh Jr. to John Anderson, June 22, 1981, Rauh Papers.

32. Joseph L. Rauh Jr. to Arthur M. Schlesinger Jr., October 1, 1982, Rauh Papers.

33. Steve M Gillon, *Politics and Vision: The ADA and American Liberalism, 1947–1985* (New York, 1987), 240.

34. Joseph L. Rauh Jr., "Suggested Op-Ed Piece," December 19, 1988; Rauh quoted in *Birmingham Post-Herald,* October 18, 1988.

Chapter Twenty-one

1. *New York Times,* December 20, 1985; Joseph L. Rauh Jr. to author, September 10, 1986; Shelley Broderick to Rauh, January 23, 1989; and Broderick to Olie Rauh, September 18, 1998.

2. Joseph L. Rauh Jr. to Ralph Neas and Benjamin Hooks, March 31, 1991; Testimony of Joseph L. Rauh Jr. before the House Appropriations Subcommittee on Commerce, Justice and State, April 5, 1989; and Statement of the Leadership Conference on Civil Rights Supporting the Americans with Disabilities Act, July 18, 1989, all Rauh Papers.

3. Joseph L. Rauh Jr. to Meg Greenfield, December 19, 1988, Rauh Papers.

4. Evan Gahr, "The Liberals' Elder Statesman," *Insight,* December 16, 1991, 12; *Nation,* July–August, 1991.

5. 682 F. Supp. 77 (D.D.C. 1988).

6. Unless specifically noted, this account of the *Orlikow* case, the CIA brainwashing project, and other abuses of the agency is based on interviews with Joseph L. Rauh Jr., August 30, 1986, and October 8, 1988; Joseph L. Rauh Jr. and James C. Turner, "Anatomy of a Public Interest Case against the CIA," *Hamline Journal of Public Law and Policy* (Fall 1990): 307–3; *Orlikow v. United States,* Plaintiff's Mem-

orandum in Opposition to Defendant's Motion for Summary Judgment; John Marks, *The Search for the "Manchurian Candidate": The CIA and Mind Control* (New York, 1979), passim; and *Final Report of the Select Committee to Study Government Operations with Respect to Intelligence Activities,* S. Rep. No. 94-755, 94th Cong., 2nd sess. (1976).

7. Rauh and Taylor, "Anatomy of a Public Interest Case," 338.

8. Judge Penn remained notorious in the federal courts for his indecision and dilatory behavior on the bench. In April 1999 he was reprimanded by the court of appeals for failing to resolve a racial discrimination lawsuit brought by black ironworkers 23 years earlier. "The district court's interminable delays are inexcusable and have caused a great hardship to the parties," wrote Judge Laurence H. Silberman for the appeals court. See *Washington Post,* April 12, 1999.

9. Joseph L. Rauh Jr., interview, August 30, 1986; Peter Calamai, "CIA v. Tenacity," *Toronto National Post,* May 1, 1988, 17.

10. Joseph L. Rauh Jr. to author, June 9, 1988.

11. Joseph L. Rauh Jr., interview, October 8, 1988.

12. Joseph L. Rauh Jr. to William Webster, July 20, 1988, Rauh Papers.

13. Webster to Rauh, August 10, 1988, Rauh Papers.

14. Webster to Rauh, August 29, 1988, Rauh Papers.

15. Joseph L. Rauh Jr., interview, October 8, 1988; author's notes.

16. *New York Times,* November 19, 1992.

SELECTED BIBLIOGRAPHY

Interviews: Taped by Author

Thomas Freiberg, with author, December 18, 1985, Los Angeles
David Ginsburg, with author, August 25, 1986, Washington, D.C.
Katharine Graham, with author, September 10, 1987, Washington, D.C.
Chalmers Johnson, with author, August 10, 1986, Washington, D.C.
Max Kampelman, with author, September 14, 1989, Washington, D.C.
Elliott Lichtman, with author, August 16, 1985, Washington, D.C.
Arthur Miller, with author, September 4, 1987, New York City
Daniel Pollitt, with author, August 16, 1985, Washington, D.C.
Carl Rauh, with author, August 20, 1986, Washington, D.C.
Joseph L. Rauh Jr., with author, August 9, 1985, through September 25, 1991,
    Washington, D.C., and Los Angeles
Louise Rauh, with author, September 4, 1986, Cincinnati, Ohio
Maggie Rauh, with author, September 27, 1992, Washington, D.C.
Michael Rauh, with author, August 19, 1986, Washington, D.C.
Olie Rauh, with author, August 17, 1985, Washington, D.C.
Marvin Rosenberg, with author, August 26, 1986, New York City
Arthur M. Schlesinger Jr., with author, August 1, 1987, New York City
Joseph "Chip" Yablonski, with author, September 3, 1987, Washington, D.C.

Oral Histories

Columbia University Oral History Office
    James Lawrence Fly Project
Franklin D. Roosevelt Library
    Joseph L. Rauh Jr.
Harry S Truman Library
    Joseph L. Rauh Jr.
    Wilson Wyatt
Hofstra University
    Dream and Reality Conference: The Modern Black Struggle for Freedom
    and Equality, February 1988

311

James Farmer
Nicholas deB Katzenbach
Louis Martin
Joseph L. Rauh Jr.
John F. Kennedy Library
    Robert Nathan
    Joseph L. Rauh Jr.
    Leonard Woodcock
University of Minnesota
    Eugene McCarthy Oral History Project
        Joseph L. Rauh Jr.
University of North Carolina
    Allard Lowenstein Oral History Project
        Joseph L. Rauh Jr.
University of Southern Mississippi
    Civil Rights Documentation Project
        Joseph L. Rauh Jr.

Manuscripts

Amherst College
    John J. McCloy Papers
College at Old Westbury, State University of New York
    Clarence Mitchell Jr. Papers
Federal Bureau of Investigation
    Joseph L. Rauh Jr. File
Harvard Law School Library
    Archibald Cox Papers
    Felix Frankfurter Papers
    Thomas Reed Powell Papers
John F. Kennedy Library
    Presidential Papers of John F. Kennedy
    Samuel H. Beer Papers
Library of Congress Manuscripts Division
    William J. Brennan Papers
    Benjamin V. Cohen Papers
    Thomas G. Corcoran Papers
    Felix Frankfurter Papers
    NAACP Washington Bureau Papers
    A. Philip Randolph Papers
Lyndon B. Johnson Library
    Presidential Papers of Lyndon B. Johnson
Minnesota Historical Society
    Hubert Humphrey Papers
Rauh Family Papers
    Edgar G. Crossman, "My Experiences in World War II"

University of Maryland
    Americans for Democratic Action Papers
Wayne State University
    Walter Reuther Papers

Secondary Sources

Abramson, Rudy. *Spanning the Century: The Life of W. Averell Harriman, 1891–1986.* New York, 1992.
Alperovitz, Gar. *Atomic Diplomacy: Hiroshima and Potsdam.* New York, 1965.
Anderson, Jervis. *A. Philip Randolph: A Biographical Portrait.* New York, 1973.
Armbrister, Trevor. *Act of Vengeance: The Yablonski Murders and Their Solution.* New York, 1975.
Asbell, Bernard. *When FDR Died.* New York, 1961.
Bailyn, Bernard, ed. *Glimpses of the Harvard Past.* Cambridge, Mass., 1986.
Baker, Liva. *Felix Frankfurter.* New York, 1969.
Barnard, John. *Walter Reuther and the Rise of the Auto Workers.* Boston, 1983.
Beschloss, Michael. *Taking Charge: The Johnson White House Tapes, 1963–1964.* New York, 1997.
Botting, Gary N. A. *Fundamental Freedoms and the Jehovah's Witnesses.* Calgary, 1993.
Branch, Taylor. *At Canaan's Edge: America in the King Years, 1965–1968.* New York, 2007.
Branch, Taylor. *Pillar of Fire: America in the King Years, 1963–1965.* New York, 1989.
Brauer, Carl M. *John F. Kennedy and the Second Reconstruction.* New York, 1977.
Campbell, Tracy. *Short of the Glory: The Rise and Fall of Edward F. Prichard, Jr.* Lexington, 1998.
Caro, Robert A. *The Years of Lyndon Johnson: The Path to Power.* New York, 1982.
Caro, Robert A. *The Years of Lyndon Johnson: Means of Ascent.* New York, 1990.
Caro, Robert A. *The Years of Lyndon Johnson: Master of the Senate.* New York, 2002.
Caute, David. *The Great Fear: The Anti-Communist Purge under Truman and Eisenhower.* New York, 1978.
Chafe, William H. *Never Stop Running: Allard Lowenstein and the Struggle to Save American Liberalism.* New York, 1993.
Cray, Ed. *Chief Justice: A Biography of Earl Warren.* New York, 1997.
Dallek, Robert. *Flawed Giant: Lyndon Johnson and His Times.* New York, 1998.
Eisele, Albert. *Almost the Presidency: A Biography of Two American Politicians.* Blue Earth, Minn., 1977.
Finley, Joseph E. *The Corrupt Kingdom: The Rise and Fall of the United Mine Workers.* New York, 1972.
Gillon, Steve. *Politics and Vision: The ADA and American Liberalism, 1947–1985.* New York, 1987.
Gunther, Gerald. *Learned Hand: The Man and the Judge.* New York, 1994.
Halberstam, David. *The Powers That Be.* New York, 1979.
Hamby, Alonzo. *Beyond the New Deal: Harry S. Truman and American Liberalism.* New York, 1973.

Harris, Richard. *Decision.* New York, 1971.

Hellman, Lillian. *Scoundrel Time.* Boston, 1976.

Horton, Dick C. *Ring of Fire: Australian Operations against the Japanese in World War II.* London, 1983.

Hume, Brit. *Death and the Mines: Rebellion and Murder in the United Mine Workers.* New York, 1971.

Irons, Peter. *Justice at War: The Story of the Japanese American Internment Cases.* New York, 1983.

Irons, Peter. *The New Deal Lawyers.* Princeton, 1982.

Kalman, Laura. *Abe Fortas: A Biography.* New Haven, 1990.

Kluger, Richard. *Simple Justice: The History of Brown v. Board of Education and Black America's Struggle for Equality.* New York, 1976.

Lang, Daniel. "The Days of Suspicion." *New Yorker,* May 21, 1949, 37–54.

Lash, Joseph. *Dealers and Dreamers: A New Look at the New Deal.* New York, 1988.

Lash, Joseph, ed. *From the Diaries of Felix Frankfurter.* New York, 1975.

Lasky, Victor. *Jimmy Carter: The Man and the Myth.* New York, 1979.

Leuchtenburg, William A. *In the Shadow of FDR: From Harry Truman to Bill Clinton.* Ithaca, 1991.

Lewis, John, with Michael O'Orso. *Walking with the Wind: A Memoir of the Movement.* New York, 1998.

Lichtenstein, Nelson. *The Most Dangerous Man in Detroit: Walter Reuther and the Fate of American Labor.* New York, 1995.

Louchheim, Katie, ed. *The Making of the New Deal: The Insiders Speak.* New York, 1983.

Manchester, William. *American Caesar: Douglas MacArthur, 1880–1964.* Boston, 1978.

Mann, Robert. *The Walls of Jericho: Lyndon Johnson, Hubert Humphrey, Richard Russell and the Struggle for Civil Rights.* New York, 1996.

Marks, John. *The Search for the "Manchurian Candidate": The CIA and Mind Control.* New York, 1979.

Martin, John Frederick. *Civil Rights and the Crisis of Liberalism: The Democratic Party, 1945–1976.* Boulder, 1979.

Mason, Alpheus T. *Harlan Fiske Stone: Pillar of the Law.* New York, 1956.

May, Gary. *Un-American Activities: The Trials of William Remington.* New York, 1995.

Miller, Arthur. *Timebends: A Life.* New York, 1987.

Murphy, Bruce Allen. *The Brandeis-Frankfurter Connection.* New York, 1982.

Navasky, Victor S. *Naming Names.* New York, 1980.

Nixon, Richard M. *RN: The Memoirs of Richard Nixon.* New York, 1978.

Olson, James, and Randy Roberts. *Where the Domino Fell: America and Vietnam.* 2nd ed. New York, 1996.

Parrish, Michael. *Securities Regulation and the New Deal.* New Haven, 1970.

Perkins, Frances. *The Roosevelt I Knew.* New York, 1946.

Phelps, Timothy, and Helen Winternitz. *Capitol Games: Clarence Thomas, Anita Hill, and the Story of a Supreme Court Nomination.* New York, 1992.

Phillips, Harlan. *Felix Frankfurter Reminisces.* New York, 1960.

Polenberg, Richard. "Franklin Roosevelt and Civil Liberties: The Case of the Dies Committee." *Historian* 30 (1968): 165–78.

Potts, E. Daniel, and Annette Potts. *Yanks Down Under, 1941–45: The American Impact on Australia.* Melbourne, 1985.

Rauh, Joseph L., Jr. "Government by Directive: A Case History." *Harvard Law Review* 61 (1948): 91–92.

Rauh, Joseph L., Jr. "Informers, G-Men, and Free Men." *Progressive* (May 1950): 9–11.

Rauh, Joseph L., Jr. "LMRDA—Enforce It or Repeal It." *Georgia Law Review* 5 (Summer 1971): 643–60.

Rauh, Joseph L., Jr. "NonConfrontation in Security Cases: The Green Decision." *Virginia Law Review* 45 (1959): 1175–87.

Rauh, Joseph L., Jr. "A Personal View of Justice Benjamin N. Cardozo: Recollections of Four Cardozo Law Clerks." *Cardozo Law Review* 1 (Spring 1979): 1–43.

Rauh, Joseph L., Jr., and James C. Turner. "Anatomy of a Public Interest Case against the CIA." *Hamline Journal of Public Law and Policy* (Fall 1990): 307–63.

Ray, William B. *The Ups and Downs of Radio-TV Regulation.* Ames, Iowa, 1990.

Reuther, Victor. *The Brothers Reuther and the Story of the UAW: A Memoir.* Boston, 1976.

Rollyson, Carl. *Lillian Hellman: Her Legend and Her Legacy.* New York, 1988.

Sarna, Jonathan D., and Nancy H. Klein. *The Jews of Cincinnati.* Cincinnati, 1989.

Schlesinger, Arthur M., Jr. *Journals, 1952–2000.* New York, 2007.

Schlesinger, Arthur M., Jr. *A Life in the 20th Century: Innocent Beginnings, 1917–1950.* Boston, 2000.

Schwartz, Bernard. *Super Chief: Earl Warren and His Supreme Court—A Judicial Biography.* New York, 1983.

Sloan, Irving, ed. *The Fair Labor Standards Act of 1938.* Dobbs Ferry, N.Y., 1984.

Solberg, Carl. *Hubert Humphrey: A Biography.* New York, 1984.

Stein, Judith. *Running Steel, Running America: Race, Economic Policy, and the Decline of Liberalism.* Chapel Hill, 1998.

Summers, Clyde, Joseph L. Rauh Jr., and Herman Benson. *Union Democracy and Landrum-Griffin.* New York, 1986.

Sutherland, Arthur. *The Law at Harvard: A History of Ideas and Men, 1817–1967.* Cambridge, Mass., 1967.

Thurber, Timothy. *The Politics of Equality: Hubert Humphrey and the African-American Freedom Struggle.* New York, 1999.

Viorst, Milton. *Fire in the Streets: America in the 1960's.* New York, 1979.

Watson, Denton L. *Lion in the Lobby: Clarence Mitchell Jr.'s Struggle for the Passage of Civil Rights Laws.* Lanham, Md., 2002.

Wechsler, James. *The Age of Suspicion.* New York, 1956.

White, Theodore. *In Search of History.* New York, 1978.

Woodward, C. Vann. *The Battle for Leyte Gulf.* Nashville, 1989.

Zion, Sidney. *The Autobiography of Roy Cohn.* New York, 1988.

INDEX

Rauh, Joseph L., Jr. (continued)
Act (FLSA) and, 44–47, 49–52; Federal Bureau of Investigation (FBI) and, 70–71, 83, 170; Federal Communications Commission and, 52–55; filibuster and, 135, 148; Frankfurter and, 24–27, 47–49, 68; Freedom Riders and, 152–53; Glen Echo protest and, 150–51; Harvard College and, 13–16; Harvard Law School and, 22–26, Haynsworth nomination and, 227–28; Hellman, Lillian, and, 107–13; Hoover, J. Edgar, and, 69–71, 80–83, 107, 153, 205; Humphrey and 86, 88–89, 136, 138, 186, 192–94, 259–60; Japanese-American redress legislation and, 257–58; Japanese-American relocation and, 64–66; Johnson, Lyndon, and, 144–45, 159, 160–61, 175; Kennedy, Anthony, nomination and, 244–45; Kennedy, Edward (Ted), and, 263–64; Kennedy, John F., and, 126–27, 139–41, 143–45, 149; Kennedy, Robert F., and, 140–41, 156, 126–27; Kohler strike and, 125–29; Kutcher, James, and, 90, 94–95; Landrum-Griffin Act (LMRDA) and, 107, 113–17, 126–27, 196, 198, 201–2, 204–8; Lend Lease Administration and, 56, 58, 60–64, 67–71; Lowenstein and, 179, 181–84; March on Washington (1963) and, 157; McCarthy, Eugene, and, 185–92; McGovern, George, and, 258–61; Medal of Freedom and, 276; Miller, Arthur, and, 113–17, 119–20; Mississippi Freedom Democratic Party (MFDP) and, 165–74; Peters, John, and, 104; Randolph, A. Philip, and, 63–64, 130–32; Rehnquist nominations and, 233–35, 236–38; Remington, William, and, 95–104; Reuther, Walter, and, 117–18, 121–26, 128–29, 166, 172; Sacco-Vanzetti case and, 19; Sadlowski, Ed, and, 213–20; on Skokie march, 257; Souter, David,

and, 246–47; surgery and recovery of, 239; Taylor, Charles Allen, and, 105–6; Thomas, Clarence, nomination debate and, 250; Truman, Harry, and, 82, 87, 92; Tucker, Jerry, and, 220–23; United Automobile Workers and, 2, 81, 124–25, 221; Vietnam War and, 178–83; Voting Rights renewal and, 255; wartime service and, 71–77; Watkins, John, and, 107, 117–19; Williams and Connolly and, 208–9; Yablonski UMW fight and, 199–210; Young, Andrew, and, 11–12, 262
Rauh, Louise, 18–19, 247
Rauh, Michael, 35, 38, 40, 47, 71
Rauh, Olie (Westheimer), 48, 70, 181, 263
Rayburn, Sam, 134
Reagan, Ronald: Bork nomination and, 239; Ginsburg nomination and, 242; Kennedy nomination and, 243
Reardon, Paul, 23
Reeves, Frank, 159
Rehnquist, William H.: called by Rauh "laundered McCarthyite," 234; career of, 233–34; condemned by Rauh, 237; confirmed as associate justice, 235; record on Burger Court, 236; segregation memo by, 234; on Southern racial conflict, 237; voter intimidation and, 237
Remington, William, 106; Bentley, Elizabeth, and, 96, 98–99; loyalty board and, 90, 97–99; perjury trials and, 100–102; prison murder of, 104; Rauh's assessment of, 98
Reuther, Roy, 122
Reuther, Victor, 121, 180, 222
Reuther, Walter, 3, 61, 155; ADA and, 85, 123; anticommunism and, 122; CIO and, 122; civil rights legislation and, 145; conversion of auto plants and, 61; education of, 121; Fifth Amendment and, 117–18, 124; Mississippi Freedom Democratic Party and, 166–67, 172; racial issues in UAW and, 129; on Rauh-LBJ rela-